OXFORD CONSTITUTIONAL THEORY

Series Editors:

Martin Loughlin, John P McCormick, and Neil Walker

The Structure of Pluralism

OXFORD CONSTITUTIONAL THEORY

Series Editors:

Martin Loughlin, John P McCormick, and Neil Walker

Oxford Constitutional Theory has rapidly established itself as the primary point of reference for theoretical reflections on the growing interest in constitutions and constitutional law in domestic, regional and global contexts. The majority of the works published in the series are monographs that advance new understandings of their subject. But the series aims to provide a forum for further innovation in the field by also including well-conceived edited collections that bring a variety of perspectives and disciplinary approaches to bear on specific themes in constitutional thought and by publishing English translations of leading monographs in constitutional theory that have originally been written in languages other than English.

ALSO AVAILABLE IN THE SERIES

The Twilight of Constitutionalism?
Edited by Petra Dobner and Martin Loughlin

Beyond Constitutionalism
The Pluralist Structure of Postnational Law
Nico Krisch

The Constitutional State
NW Barber

Sovereignty's Promise
The State as Fiduciary
Evan Fox-Decent

Constitutional Fragments
Societal Constitutionalism and Globalization
Gunther Teubner

Constitutional Referendums
The Theory and Practice of Republican Deliberation
Stephen Tierney

Constituting Economic and Social Rights
Katharine G Young

The Global Model of Constitutional Rights
Kai Möller

The Three Branches
A Comparative Model of Separation of Powers
Christoph Möllers

After Public Law
Edited by Cormac Mac Amhlaigh, Claudio Michelon, and Neil Walker

The Cosmopolitan State
H Patrick Glenn

Fault Lines of Globalization
Legal Order and the Politics of A-Legality
Hans Lindahl

Constitutional Courts and Deliberation Democracy
Conrado Mendes

The Structure of Pluralism
On the Authority of Associations
Víctor M Muñiz-Fraticelli

The Structure of Pluralism

On the Authority of Associations

Víctor M Muñiz-Fraticelli

OXFORD
UNIVERSITY PRESS

OXFORD
UNIVERSITY PRESS

Great Clarendon Street, Oxford, OX2 6DP,
United Kingdom

Oxford University Press is a department of the University of Oxford. It furthers the University's objective of excellence in research, scholarship, and education by publishing worldwide. Oxford is a registered trade mark of Oxford University Press in the UK and in certain other countries

First Edition published in 2014

Published in the United States of America by Oxford University Press
198 Madison Avenue, New York, NY 10016, United States of America

British Library Cataloguing in Publication Data
Data available

Library of Congress Control Number: 2013953297

ISBN 978–0–19–967388–9

Jacket illustration: Coloquio alado 1983, by Augusto Marín (1921-2011), acrylic over canvas, 68" x 140" Private Collection. Courtesy of Lissy Marín.

A Michelle

Your skepticism comes, I venture, from a further doubt as to the worth of life; my pluralism comes from a certainty—you have yet to meet my wife—of its richness.

—Harold J Laski to Oliver Wendell Holmes

Acknowledgements

This book bears witness to a long and circuitous intellectual conversion. I began my graduate study in political theory very much a monist on matters of value, authority, and law. I believed that all genuine moral dilemmas must be capable of resolution, given enough information and reflection; that sovereignty must reside in a single ultimate authority and when it seemed to be partial or divided this was simply due to a misunderstanding of the structure of the political system; and I thought that surely any conflict between legal norms, whether of one or multiple systems, could be disposed of by systematic application of the appropriate canons and priority rules procedurally acceptable to all. I now hold more or less the opposite view on each of these matters. On the way to Damascus, I also embraced a hard positivist line on the criteria of legal validity and a soft realist line on corporate personality. The resulting account of the authority of associations may not be entirely consistent, and I cannot (alas) dismiss the tensions between the articles of my new creed by invoking the mystery of pluralism. Hopefully I have many years to spend trying to resolve the many problems inherent in an argument anchored on foundational plurality, incommensurability, and tragic loss. But I should begin by pointing the finger at the proselytes who (sometimes unwittingly) led me to give up the certainties of my old faith, and accept the necessity of ambiguity, conflict, and compromise.

My first debt is to the members of my doctoral committee at the University of Chicago. It was Jacob Levy who introduced me to the tradition of British pluralism, in a seminar on 'Freedom, State, and Society', and later guided the dissertation that was the seed of the present book. Our discussions of John Neville Figgis gave theoretical grounding to my inarticulate musings on institutional academic freedom and on urban autonomy, and drove me to change the prospective topic of my research. For six years at Chicago, and now six more at McGill, Jacob has been the very model of a teacher, a colleague, a mentor, and a friend. My greatest intellectual obligation is to him.

In a different seminar, around the same time, Charles Larmore converted me from a meta-ethical monist to a value pluralist, although I stubbornly refused to accept his scepticism about the connection between liberalism and pluralism. Martha Nussbaum graciously accepted to join the committee at a late stage and gave me valuable feedback on the methodology of research. I also benefited greatly from her course on Feminist Philosophy and from the Law-Philosophy Seminar.

I owe a special debt of gratitude to Iris Marion Young, who chaired my committee from the first stages of the proposal until her death in 2006. Her critical encouragement throughout my graduate studies created a perpetual debt that a lifetime of scholarship cannot repay. Many of the questions that she posed at the start of this project remain unanswered, and I am sure that I will turn to them again, many times over, and perhaps never to her satisfaction.

Many of the ideas developed here were first tried out at the Political Theory Workshop at the University of Chicago. I am grateful to all of its participants and especially to my friends Andrew Dilts, Mara Marin, Emily Nacol, Neil Roberts, and Deva Woodly and Professors Nathan Tarcov and Patchen Markell. While he was visiting Chicago, Richard Garnett also attended and commented on a practice job talk where I presented what would eventually become Chapter 8; I am happy that our paths have continued to cross since then.

I have received invaluable intellectual, professional, and inspirational support from my colleagues at the Department of Political Science and the Faculty of Law at McGill University, especially following the launch of the Research Group on Constitutional Studies (RGCS) in 2009. Arash Abizadeh, Mark Antaki, Hoi Kong, Jacob Levy, Catherine Lu, Will Roberts, Christa Scholtz, Hasana Sharp, Natalie Stoljar, Christina Tarnopolski, Daniel Weinstock, and Yves Winter have commented on drafts of articles, suggested improvements to various arguments, or brought authors and articles to my attention. Evan Fox-Decent deserves a special mention for, among much else, introducing me to the *Oxford Constitutional Theory* series and constantly questioning my devotion to Joseph Raz.

Beyond the RGCS, Shauna van Praagh stoked my interest in religious law since my first visit to McGill and René Provost offered me the opportunity to present it to an international audience and launch it in a new direction. And most importantly, Roderick Macdonald, whose office neighbours mine and whose door is always open—I have learned more about pluralism from him than from all the works of Figgis, Cole, and Laski, and much besides on the duties of scholarship, the virtues of pedagogy, and the pleasures of collegiality.

Many other colleagues at McGill have asked questions or offered suggestions that drove this project forward, among them Kirsten Anker, Angela Campbell, Richard Janda, David Lametti, Desmond Maderson, Stephen Smith, and Lionel Smith. My first and current chairs in Political Science, Richard Schultz and Hudson Meadwell, and my first and current Deans in

Law, Nicholas Kasirer and Daniel Jutras, gave me the institutional support I needed to manage the plural commitments of a joint appointment. Two great administrative assistants, first Julie Fontaine and now Libby Parker, ensured that I always met all my academic obligations more or less on time. I have also been fortunate to have a solid succession of research assistants over the years whose work and conversation made this labour much more pleasant and productive: Simon Ayotte, Lawrence David, Molly Krishtalka, Tara Mrejen, John-Andrew Petrakis, Katie Saulnier, Larissa Smith, Talia Smith, and Nancy Termini.

Montreal is a vibrant academic town, especially for political theorists and philosophers, and I thank my colleagues at the Groupe de Recherche Interuniversitaire en Philosophie Politique (GRIPP) and the Montreal Political Theory Workshop, who commented formally and informally on my work especially Ryoa Chung, Peter Dietsch, and Pablo Gilabert. These institutional collaborations have also allowed us to host doctoral and post-doctoral fellows who engaged me in long and fruitful conversations about law and authority and personality. They are now embarked on their own academic careers, so it pleases me to thank, congratulate, and wish luck to Adina Preda, Daniel Silvermint, Robert Sparling, Nina Valiquette Moreau, and Timothy Waligore.

I also presented several chapters (or arguments that wound their way into chapters) at the Political Science Graduate Student Conference at Marquette University, a conference on *Pluralism, Politics, and God* organized by Daniel Cere, the 2008 Young Scholars Conference at the McGill Faculty of Law, the McGill-Tel Aviv Human Rights Conference in Jerusalem, a Workshop on judicial review and democracy at McGill University organized by Natalie Stoljar, and various annual meetings of the New England Political Science Association, the Law and Society Association, the Association for Political Theory, the Canadian Political Science Association, and the Western Political Science Association. The participants at every one of these events offered insightful questions, not all of which I have been able to answer, much less satisfactorily.

Of special note were extensive, thoughtful, and very useful comments I received at critical points in the project from Melissa Williams and Lucas Swaine. Other colleagues commented extensively by correspondence on isolated drafts and chapters, and I especially appreciated the critical commentary by Roderick Macdonald, Jocelyn Maclure, and Ralf Michaels.

The book benefited from significant funding at various crucial stages. While writing the dissertation, I was supported by a Trustees Fellowship from the University of Chicago and a Dissertation Teaching and Research Fellowship from its Department of Political Science, a Junior Fellowship from the Olin Center for Inquiry into the Theory and Practice of Democracy, and a Humane Studies Fellowship from the Institute for Humane Studies. Most of the book, however, was written at McGill University with support from an Établissement des nouveaux chercheurs-professeurs grant from the Fonds de recherche du Québec—Societé et culture and Supplementary Research Support from the McGill University Faculty of Law.

The actual process of turning the manuscript into a finished book passed through the editors of the *Oxford Constitutional Theory* series, Martin Loughlin, John P. McCormick, and Neil Walker, whom I thank for their early confidence and steadfast encouragement. I must also thank Natasha Flemming and Clare Kennedy for their tremendous patience throughout.

My mother and father, Migdalia Fraticelli Torres and Luis Muñiz Argüelles, supported me both as parents and scholars. They are models of both, and I am proud to have followed them first into the legal and academic professions, and later into parenthood. My siblings, Mariana Cristina and Eduardo Luis Guillermo, who have suffered through too many spontaneous lectures on matters juridical and philosophical at the family dinner table, and yet harbour hope for me.

And to my wife Michelle Cubano Guzmán, who 13 years ago trusted me enough to come up north with me...and then up north a little further. I would renounce my pluralism if she were the only sovereign. To my two children, Ignacio José and María Cecilia, I owe apologies for my unexplained absences during their tenderest years, the many dinners missed, the many beds untucked. Perhaps someday they will read this and stare at me with bafflement and smile.

Chapter 8 is a slightly modified version of 'The problem of pluralist authority', published in *Political Studies* (Wiley, 2013) (doi: 10.1111/1467-9248.12065). Chapter 2 draws from a chapter entitled 'The distinctiveness of religious liberty' in the book *Mapping the Boundaries of Belonging: Law Between Religious Revival and Post-Multiculturalism*, edited by René Provost and forthcoming from Oxford University Press.

Contents

Introduction

> L'imagination ne saurait inventer tant de diverses contrariétés qu'il y en a naturellement dans le cœur de chaque personne.
>
> —François de La Rochefoucauld

Many associations in liberal democracies claim to possess—and attempt to exercise—a measure of legitimate authority over their members, and assert that this authority does not derive from the magnanimity of a liberal and tolerant state but is grounded, rather, on the common practices and aspirations of those individuals who choose to take part in a common endeavour. This endeavour, moreover, they often defend as one motivated by values different from (and sometimes incompatible with or hostile to) those that purport to justify liberal and democratic institutions. Some of these associations may covertly or overtly want to supplant the values and institutions of liberal democracy with their own, but most would simply like their authority and autonomy recognized, acknowledged, and respected within the broader society. Beyond a demand for toleration, theirs is an appeal to *political pluralism*: to the coexistence of several sources of (putatively) legitimate authority within a territory, or more accurately, over a part of its population, among which the authority of the state is but one among many such sources.

Political pluralism is a coherent philosophical tradition that makes distinctive and radical claims about the sources of political authority and about the structure of the relationship between associations and the state. The coherence of these claims is well-grounded in both historical ideas of sovereignty and in contemporary philosophical accounts of authority. The pluralist account recommends an approach to legal structures that can accommodate the relations between associations and the state in ways that correspond to the self-understanding of members of various organized groups and to the demands of a stable social order. It is nonetheless aware that there is an irreducible conflict between associations that claim independent authority over their members, and the state, which can admit no challenge to its jurisdictional supremacy.

This book is a response to recent developments in political and legal philosophy and the (re-)emergence of conflicts over state and associational authority. Over the last two decades, there has been a considerable revival of interest in the work of the early British pluralists, and an attempt to rehabilitate their ideas about the autonomy of associations as a more accurate account of social phenomena and for its contribution to the maintenance of a free and diverse society. Most participants in this revival have approached pluralism as a chapter in the history of ideas, or have mined pluralist theses for their support of democratic governance or their implication to current policy debates, and on both fronts they have made important contributions. But too little attention has been paid to explaining the actual content of pluralist propositions and to resolving their ambiguities and moments of incoherence through a rigorous and systematic reconstruction of pluralist arguments.

Despite this resurgence, many of the problems that plagued the original pluralist literature remain unaddressed. First, the central contention of the British pluralists regarding the inherent authority of associations has been cited, even approvingly, by contemporary theorists, but their arguments have not been carefully reconstructed: the central pluralist concepts have not been subjected to rigorous conceptual analysis, and insufficient work has been done to point out what is distinctive about the pluralist critique, what sets it apart from ordinary liberal defences of freedom of association. Second, although one of the central theses of political pluralism is that groups have a source of legitimate authority independent of the state, the grounds of that authority are unclear. The British pluralists often grounded such authority on medieval accounts of natural law or on the simple sociological fact that groups exist and people have an allegiance to them. Third, the idea of sovereignty is invoked as a concept by both pluralists and their opponents—pluralists deny it to the state and claim it for associations, while their opponents do the reverse—yet there has been no convincing attempt to provide a definition of the concept which reconciles the pluralist idea of multiplicity with the common understanding of sovereignty as final and absolute. Scholarly interest in pluralism has coincided with significant economic, religious, educational, and political developments that could be fruitfully addressed by the pluralist paradigm: the assertion of constitutional rights of free expression by corporations in the United States, the various crises in the Roman Catholic Church and the Anglican Communion, the recent attempts by liberal governments on both sides of the Atlantic to control both the content of and entry into institutions of religious instruction, the broader questioning of the independence of academic institutions, and the proliferating conflicts of authority between federal and sub-federal orders in liberal democracies. The time is right for a thorough reassessment of the political pluralist tradition.

My purpose in this book is analytical and conceptual rather than historical or prescriptive. I aim to elucidate the arguments of the leading figures in the political pluralist tradition and their present-day sympathizers, explain how pluralist arguments cause us to re-examine our ideas of authority and sovereignty, and examine concrete legal and political institutions that can structure interaction and intercourse both among associations and between them and the state. I do so through an interdisciplinary approach which, though grounded in analytical political and legal theory, draws extensively from current debates on meta-ethics, moral psychology, legal sociology, and comparative legal doctrine. In order to build a rigorous pluralist theory, I undertake a reconstruction of the arguments of both early twentieth-century and present-day political pluralists, a regrounding of the pluralist critique of sovereignty in the analytical framework of contemporary legal positivism, and a projection of a pluralist polity onto legal and institutional structures which at once acknowledges the possibility of radical conflict between associations, individuals, and the state, yet makes the terms of this conflict intelligible and negotiable. As such, this project stands, on the one hand, against the prevalent position in political theory that upholds the primacy of the state as an incontestable arbiter of disputes in society and, on the other, against various agonistic positions which deem the plurality of cross-cutting loyalties and allegiances of modern society to be impervious to a stable and structured constitutional and legal compromise.

Yet, despite my purpose, I acknowledge that legal and political pluralism have broader theoretical implications both for our understanding of modern liberal democracy and for our moral deliberation on the limits of state action and the obligations of citizenship. As to the first, the associations that I most often refer to in the book are churches, universities, professional and trade groups, and cities. These associations are the ones that have in the past and continue to make the boldest claims of autonomy, and that have the best developed institutions through which to exercise authority over their members. But it should not escape anyone that they are also holdovers of the 'ancient constitution', remnants of medieval constitutionalism.[1] It was the Roman Catholic Church that first asserted corporate independence from secular authority, and despite its eventual reconciliation with the liberal and

[1] Two associations that are nearly absent from the book, but which could also be brought under the pluralist paradigm, are the family and the business corporation. There are good reasons to include both, but ultimately they present problems that I think are unique to each and are too complex for the quick attention that I could give them here. It is difficult to see the family as *an* association, rather than a series of associations similarly constituted; in this way it is even different from a series of churches, since families do not usually claim the same kind of authority over their members or intend to convert members of other families. Business corporations are also different though mainly in the instrumental use to which their members put them, which contrasts with the inherent value that members of other associations attribute to their groups. It is not clear, too, that businesses would like the kind of meta-jurisdictional authority that some groups claim since it may make them less reliable as vehicles for investment. In any case, those are subjects of a different study.

democratic state, it still makes the same claims. Academics, likewise, jealously guard their collegial institutions and resent as illegitimate (and not just ill advised) state and corporate incursion into the university, although perhaps with less zeal than that displayed by the masters and students of the University of Paris in the great strike of 1229 CE. Modern constitutionalism was born of these twelfth century struggles too, not only of the settlement of the Wars of Religion four to six centuries later. If my account of political pluralism is convincing it should also suggest a re-examination of the genealogy of liberal democracy and a reconsideration of the exclusive focus on the Enlightenment as the fount of all that is modern.

As to the normative implications, they are suggested in chapter 8, but should be developed further. If political pluralism is true, then some of the central claims of republicanism must be false, or at least be subject to perpetual contestation. Rousseau was right to note that any sufficiently strong loyalty to any group but the political community would prevent the state's monopolistic exercise of sovereignty. That this is so is a salutary effect of pluralism. If the state acknowledges the authority of associations and accepts that one of its functions is to facilitate the associative ties of its citizens—ties which it neither defines nor controls—then direct regulation of the conduct and policy of groups should give way to policies that set incentives or encourage alternative sources of public goods. Conversely, associations that acknowledge the state as facilitator of their normative structure should accept certain normative conditions for reciprocal attenuation of conflict.[2]

The book is divided into three parts. The first lays out the idea of a pluralist argument and explains its central theses. For associational pluralism, these are the claim that the authority of formally constituted associations is foundationally independent of any other authority, even that of the state, that its basis is incommensurable with that of the state, and that these two factors always harbor the possibility of a tragic conflict between the claims to authority of various associations. I then use this conceptual framework to distinguish pluralism from other arguments that have accorded a significant role to groups of various kinds: multiculturalism (in chapter 2), subsidiarity (in chapter 3), and associative democracy (in chapter 4). I find that none of these paradigms takes associations seriously as foundationally autonomous.

[2] The best development of such conditions that I have encountered is Dwight Newman's account of 'community conditions' in *Community and Collective Rights* (Hart, 2011). These involve a Service Principle—'a normative requirement that collectivities serve their member's interests' (107)—and a Mutuality Principle—the principle that 'a collectivity's claims to rights must be respectful of equivalently weighty interests of non-members' (131).

In the second part, I examine the idea of the authority of associations and its relation to the authority of the state. I begin (in chapter 5) by tracing the conception of sovereignty to its medieval and early modern antecedents, and explain why the medieval constitutionalist conception, which makes legal norms constitutive of sovereign authority, is preferable to the early modern voluntarist conception. With the idea of legal authority in mind, I turn to a reconstruction of pluralist authority from the analytical framework of contemporary legal positivism. I first refute (in chapter 6) the criticism that legal pluralists, especially legal anthropologists, have lodged against positivism as antithetical to a pluralist understanding of law and then justify (in chapter 7) the intelligibility of associational authority on a positivist foundation. I finish this part (in chapter 8) by offering an account of the authority of the state under conditions of pluralism.

The last part is concerned with the idea of group personality, which was a central tenet of the British pluralist movement but has fallen out of favour. I first explain (in chapter 9) the arguments that pluralists like John Neville Figgis advanced in defence of the idea that associations possessed a personality analogous to that of individual human beings. Through the latest philosophical research on group agency I then defend (in chapter 10) the intelligibility of a robust conception of group moral personality that entitles groups to claim legal personality as a matter of right, not of convenience or state concession. I conclude this third part by illustrating (in chapter 11) how the institutions of private property can help in the exercise and development of the personality of groups.

I conclude on an uncertain note. Pluralism does not recommend specific institutions, although it can pass judgment on their adequacy to capture the inner life of associations. It remains true, however, that no set of legal institutions can capture this completely and retain its legitimacy from the perspective of the state. Some unresolved tension remains always and can be a source of freedom or of conflict depending on the willingness of political and legal actors to recognize the limits of their claims to authority.

PART ONE
THE DISTINCTIVENESS OF PLURALISM

The State should watch over these societies of citizens banded together in accordance with their rights, but it should not thrust itself into their peculiar concerns and their organization, for things move and live by the spirit inspiring them, and may be killed by the rough grasp of a hand from without.

—Leo XIII

1

The Structure of Pluralist Arguments

This is a book about philosophical, political, and legal arguments, about their form and structure, and about the institutional contexts that give them concrete meaning. It is a book about the intelligibility of certain normative theses and traditions of thought which have repeatedly emerged at different times in Western political history, although their sway on the minds and hearts of citizens, theorists, and statesmen have waxed and waned with changing historical circumstance. These theses and traditions are broadly labelled *pluralist*, because they postulate a plurality of normative phenomena within one or another domain of practical reason. Within each of these domains, pluralist arguments generally conclude that the normative universe is irreducibly complex, and rife with moments in which discerning what is the right decision is not only difficult but tragically impossible, and some kind of irreparable loss is unavoidable.

The implications of normative plurality in all domains have been hotly debated—and often rejected—at the conceptual, institutional, and practical level. Detractors have claimed that plurality in the realm of value is but thinly veiled relativism, even nihilism;[1] in the realm of politics it is incoherent as an interpretation of sovereignty, dangerous as an invitation to civil strife, and an intractable obstacle to the institution of liberal democracy;[2] in the realm of law, even sympathetic writers worry 'that it is inimical to the rule of law'[3] and that it stretches the definition of legality so far that it 'thereby lose[s] any distinctive meaning.'[4]

[1] Leo Strauss, 'Relativism' in TL Pangle (ed.), *The Rebirth of Classical Political Rationalism* (University of Chicago Press, 1989) 13–26; Jeffrey Friedman, 'Pluralism or Relativism?' (1997) 11(4) *Critical Review* 469, 469–80.

[2] Jean Bodin, *On Sovereignty: Four Chapters from The Six Books of the Commonwealth* (first published 1576, Julian H Franklin (ed. and tr.)) (Cambridge University Press, 1992); Thomas Hobbes, *Leviathan* (first published 1651, E Curley (ed.)) (Hackett, 1994) 115–16; Stephen Holmes, *Passions and Constraint* (University of Chicago Press, 1995), especially chapters 2 and 3. I have used the Franklin translation of Bodin whenever possible, as it is the most accessible English translation. For passages of the *Six Books of the Commonwealth* not included in that edition, I cite C Frémont, M-D Couzinet and H Rochais (eds), *Les Six Livres de la République* (Librairie Arthème Fayard, 1986).

[3] Gordon R Woodman, 'Legal Pluralism and the Search for Justice' (1998) 40(2) *J African Law* 152, 160.

[4] Brian Z Tamanaha, 'The Folly of the "Social Scientific" Concept of Legal Pluralism' (1993) 20(2) *Journal of Law and Society* 192, 193. Tamanaha's later 'non-essentialist' version of legal pluralism—developed in

Against the sceptics, my objective in this chapter is to lay out a plausible account of the structure of pluralist arguments, particularly as they apply to (at least some) associations. While I begin this account with pluralism in the domain of meta-ethics—what is usually called value pluralism—my interest lies rather at the intersection of the domains of politics and law. My reasons are both historical and conceptual. Historically, the representatives of the British tradition of scholarship now referred to as 'political pluralism', of whom I will shortly say more, were most concerned with the claims to autonomy of certain kinds of association—churches, universities, trade unions, cities, and other federal and sub-federal units—who were especially jealous of their independence, which they often traced, directly or through some intervening institution such as the guild, to medieval antecedents. The avowed medievalism of the British pluralists was not nostalgic or antiquarian (or at least not purely so), but demonstrated a serious preoccupation with long-lasting disputes over the constitutive sources of political authority. Conceptually, I find that despite important differences in the ways in which these associations institute and exercise authority, they nonetheless share a significant level of organizational formality not only with each other but also with the state. They are, in a way, state-like enough to allow for interesting comparisons which are not applicable to less formalized groups such as cultures or classes. The associations which concerned the British pluralists and which concern me here are both political and legal authorities, and are sources of ostensibly autonomous claims of legitimacy which take the form of rules and institutions which are familiar to the state. This also has the advantage of inviting interesting contemporary debates about the nature of law into discussions of power and authority, and vice versa.

Because this is a book about the form and structure of arguments, I do not claim to persuade the reader of the correctness or attractiveness of the pluralist position, but only of its coherence and plausibility. I am convinced that some form of political and legal pluralism is true, that it is a natural consequence of our clearest accounts of authority and legality, that it reflects ordinary practices of loyalty and commitment better than other conceptions which prioritize membership in the state, and that it both explains the claims of many associations to an integral sphere of autonomy and justifies the political and juridical structures which make this autonomy effective. But the argument that follows is not an exercise in philosophical justification. It is an

articles leading to *A General Jurisprudence of Law and Society* (Oxford University Press, 2001)—has itself been criticized as being irreparably vague (see Kenneth Einar Himma, 'Do Philosophy and Sociology Mix? A Non-Essentialist Socio-Legal Positivist Analysis of the Concept of Law' (2004) 24(4) *Oxford Journal of Legal Studies* 717).

attempt to clarify an argument and to show its institutional implications so that its merit may be appraised in the best possible light.

1.1 PLURALISM AS IDEAL

There is an ideal structure to pluralist arguments advanced in the several domains of practical reason, and this structure not only makes pluralist arguments similar to each other, but also makes them distinct from other kinds of normative arguments made in meta-ethics, politics, and law.[5] The structure of pluralist arguments is composed of three theses or claims that are reproduced in each domain. The first posits that there is a plurality of sources for whatever is central to the domain (the claim of *plurality*), while the second proposes that these sources are in some way incommensurable (the claim of *incommensurability*), that is, that they are incapable of being categorically ranked. The third claim or thesis holds that there is always a possibility of conflict between any two elements, even if only in principle, such that no solution may be found that does not involve a genuine loss which is not completely compensated by a gain on the other side (the claim of *tragic conflict or tragic loss*).

For ease of reference, I will call this the *parallel structure thesis* (PST). I believe that it reflects well certain structural features of pluralist arguments, and that it provides much needed analytic clarity to some recent revivals of political pluralism in philosophy and political theory. Identifying this structure has two benefits. First, if pluralist arguments are alike across the domains of practical reason, then it may be possible to apply the insights of pluralism in one sphere to the others; this is what I seek to do in this chapter. Second, this common structure distinguishes pluralist arguments from other ostensibly similar arguments in a variety of spheres, and highlights how pluralist arguments are different from arguments about value (or, more properly, about reasons for action), authority, or legality that also refer to plurality, diversity, or conflict.[6] This is especially evident in the domain of political theory, where it explains how political pluralism is distinct from multiculturalism and, despite superficial resemblance, is incompatible with arguments for subsidiarity, corporatism, and associative democracy; I leave these distinctions, however, to chapters 2–4.

[5] I refer to meta-ethics, politics, and law as 'domains' for the lack of a better term. I am not treating them as academic disciplines, but as sites where practical reason is exercised. The choice of these three domains, and not others, is prompted by Joseph Raz's identification of them in *Practical Reason and Norms* (Oxford University Press, 1990) 11.

[6] I have in mind an exercise similar to Charles Larmore's distinction between value pluralism and Rawlsian reasonable disagreement in chapter 7 of *Morals of Modernity* (Cambridge University Press, 1996).

The truth of the PST is not at all obvious, however, because it runs against important historical and theoretical objections. Historically, there is no such thing as a single pluralist line of thought that runs across all domains of practical reason. Meta-ethical pluralists, political pluralists, and legal pluralists have each made claims about normative elements in their respective domains from independent premises, and having little or no documented contact with each other's work. The name pluralism here appears to be a coincidence, and an attempt to make something of this coincidence commits a nominalist fallacy.

Theoretically, there seem to be many examples of political theorists who have quite comfortably held pluralist views in one domain and monistic views in another (whether monism is defined narrowly as the denial of the claim of plurality, or more broadly as the denial of any of the three pluralist claims). On some readings, Benjamin Constant was a political pluralist but a meta-ethical monist;[7] Thomas Hobbes was the opposite on both counts, and indeed was a political monist because of his meta-ethical pluralism.[8] Perhaps, one could argue, pluralist arguments have the same structure because pluralism in one domain implies pluralism in another; but there is, in fact, no such implication, although there might be a strong relationship between pluralism in various domains because of more contingent factors. I will not go into those possibilities in this book. It is enough to say that the practical relationship between meta-ethical, political, and legal pluralism is complicated, and that it neither supports nor undermines the purely formal argument advanced here.

There is a further problem with the argument that requires clarification. It can be convincingly argued that few, if any, actually existing pluralists categorically sustain all three theses about any of the domains of practical reason mentioned here. And this would be right. To take only one prominent example, Michael Walzer holds in *Spheres of Justice* that there is a plurality of incommensurable distributive principles that may apply to important social goods. However, for Walzer, there is little likelihood that the interaction of these principles will result in genuine tragic loss, if only because the determination of which principle applies in each distributive 'sphere' is effectively posited by the political community; any apparent conflict is the result of a

[7] Contrast Benjamin Constant's 'Mélanges de Littérature et de Politique' (at 623) in which he claims to 'have defended the same principle for forty years, liberty in everything, in religion, in philosophy, in literature, in industry, in politics: and by liberty, I understand the triumph of individuality, whether over that authority which would govern through despotism, as over the masses who claim the right of submitting the minority to the majority' (translation mine) with his admittedly instrumental defence of hereditary aristocracy and other groups claiming allegiance to something other than the state apparatus in 'Principes de Politique' (at 344–48 and 531–37). Benjamin Constant in Marcel Gauchet (ed.), *Écrits Politiques* (Éditions Gallimard, 1997).

[8] Hobbes, note 2, ch XI. I thank Desmond Manderson for reminding me of this.

mistake about the true social meaning of the good in question, or at best an invitation to settle that meaning once-and-for-all.[9] So are we left with a general account of pluralism that no one holds, emerging from traditions that have no historical or logical connection to each other? What could possibly be the use of such an argument? It strikes me that pluralism operates here as what Max Weber called an 'ideal type'. Ideal types reflect 'a rational consistency which is rarely found in reality'.[10] Moreover, Weber notes that:

> They enable us to see if, in particular traits or in their total character, the phenomena approximate one of our constructions: to determine the degree of approximation of the historical phenomenon to the theoretically constructed type. To this extent, the construction is merely a technical aid which facilitates a more lucid arrangement and terminology.[11]

Such a construction is especially useful in the current 'revival' (however modest) of normative political pluralism. The original self-identified pluralists (Maitland, Figgis, Laski, Cole, and Follett) were not especially clear about the presuppositions and logical derivations of their accounts of sovereignty, and their successors have been more interested in the application of pluralist intuitions to questions of policy or to contemporary debates about religious liberty or multiculturalism, than the examination of the idea of pluralism itself. The applied method is important but does not exclude more conceptual work.

1.2 META-ETHICAL PLURALISM: THE MODEL OF THE ARGUMENT

There is no single pluralist tradition. Rather, there are different traditions of thought in different domains that have laid claim to the label or had it thrust upon them, and there is no historical relationship between them, nor a relationship of implication from one to another. Pluralism in the domain of meta-ethics, or value pluralism, is most commonly associated with the work of Isaiah Berlin. As Berlin defines it, value pluralism is 'the conception that there are many different ends that men may seek and still be fully rational,

[9] Michael Walzer, *Spheres of Justice* (Basic Books, 1983) 28ff.

[10] Max Weber, 'Religious Rejections of the World and their Directions' in HH Gerth and C Wright Mills (eds), *From Max Weber: Essays in Sociology* (Oxford University Press, 1946) 323.

[11] Weber, note 10, 324. The editors' introduction clarifies the concept further: 'The much discussed "ideal type," a key term in Weber's methodological discussion, refers to the construction of certain elements of reality into a logically precise conception.' The conception must still be a possible object of apprehension and not an incoherent or meaningless argumentative construct (as Lucas Swaine pointed out to me); I beg the reader to assume, for the moment, that this holds for political pluralism, and reconsider at the end of the book whether I have succeeded in presenting a possible ideal type.

fully men, capable of understanding each other and sympathizing and deriving light from each other.'[12] These values—or, more properly, these reasons for action—[13] refer to normative facts that are real and objective, i.e. they can be recognized, even by those who do not share them, as ends pursued for their own sake. Pluralism, in denying that there is any single pervasive source of reasons for action in comparison to which all others may be considered, is committed, by definition, to the idea of incommensurability. If there were such a source, the plurality of ends would collapse into a multiplicity of manifestations of a single dominant value; such a position cannot be called pluralist in the meta-ethical sense Berlin intends.

Pluralism, in this sense, is not a theory on the truth or falsity of any particular source of reasons for action, but rather 'a thesis about the nature of value' itself; it is a species of realism in that it holds, quite explicitly, that there are distinctly moral facts in the world.[14] 'There is a world of objective values', Berlin writes.[15] However, the objectivity of these values—or sources of reasons for action—does not clearly rest on their being 'true' in an absolute, sempiternal, ahistorical sense. Sources of value emerge at some points in history and ground reasons that were unintelligible before, that did not exist. Their validity as reasons for action seems to depend, first, on whether they are held as ultimate by *some* persons, and second, on whether they are intelligible to *all* persons as conceivably ultimate sources of reasons for action. This criterion is ambiguous, and seems to treat with extreme laxity the question of the *truth* of value (and the corresponding judgment that a person may be *wrong* to value something), but I have found in Berlin no recourse to further criteria.[16] Objective and ultimate values, in the end, may be discernible not by philosophy, but by history and the social sciences.[17]

[12] Isaiah Berlin, 'The Pursuit of the Ideal' in H Hardy and R Hausheer (eds), *The Proper Study of Mankind* (Farrar, Strauss, Giroux, 1997) 9.

[13] As I am considering pluralism in the domains of practical reason, it seems to me that 'reasons for action' is a better term than 'value' as a referent. Where I retain the term value in the discussion it is only to maintain some consistency with Isaiah Berlin's own usage. But it is clear to me that, even for Berlin, the important question is not what is good in the abstract, but what one is to do in response to this. I thank Arash Abizadeh for suggesting this clarification.

[14] This is John Gray's conclusion in *Isaiah Berlin* (Princeton University Press, 1996) 62–63.

[15] Berlin, 'The Pursuit of the Ideal', note 12, 9.

[16] Indeed, the last paragraphs of 'Two Concepts of Liberty' seem to disavow an appeal to truth—if truth is in any way akin to sempiternal validity—as measure of value objectivity (see Berlin, 'Two Concepts of Liberty' in *The Proper Study of Mankind*, note 12, 242).

[17] Berlin, 'Introduction' in H Hardy (ed.), *Liberty* (Oxford University Press, 2002) 45. Gray goes further, arguing that Berlin is committed to *internal realism*. 'On this realist view', he writes, 'the elements in the world of value, though they are historical creations [...] are nevertheless independent subject-matters, in respect of which our beliefs may be true or false.' See also Gray, note 14, 72. My preference is for a thoroughgoing constructivism about value and reasons for action, but the choice of meta-ethics has no bearing on the point being made here.

Berlin's characterization of meta-ethical pluralism, however, goes beyond merely pointing out the plurality of sources of reasons for action. Berlin also holds a very strong conception of conflict between these reasons: in his view, values are under constant peril of clashing, contradicting each other, and thus presenting the moral agent with hard and possibly tragic choices. The tragedy resides in the sacrifice and loss entailed by a choice that inevitably precludes the realization of some other, equally objective, yet incompatible reason. Yet choices must be made nonetheless, and to deny this is to misunderstand the nature of value. In Berlin's own words:

> The world that we encounter in ordinary experience is one in which we are faced with choices between ends equally ultimate, and claims equally absolute, the realization of some of which must inevitably involve the sacrifice of others. Indeed, it is because this is their situation that men place such immense value upon the freedom to choose; for if they had assurance that in some perfect state, realizable by men on earth, no ends pursued by them would ever be in conflict, the necessity and agony of choice would disappear, and with it the central importance of the freedom to choose.[18]

Pluralists, then, hold that there are many valuable ideals, pursuits, and aspirations for which human beings yearn. They understand that these ideals are equally real—they are actually experienced, not instigated by illusion or self-deceit—and objective—even those who do not yearn for them can understand that they are worthy of value.[19] Furthermore, pluralists claim that a comprehensive ranking among the sources of reasons for action is impossible even in principle, since these sources are radically distinct—they cannot be reduced to each other or understood on each other's terms—and there is no one source which holds absolute priority over all others. For George Crowder:

> [T]hese objective goods are also irreducibly multiple because 'incommensurable'—they cannot be comprehended under the same measure. There is no super-value to which all other goods contribute more or less. Rather, the basic human goods (which may include liberty, equality, justice, loyalty, knowledge,

[18] Berlin, 'Two Concepts of Liberty', note 12, 239.

[19] There is a difference between:

(1) stating, with the pluralist, that '[t]here is a world of objective values' (Berlin, note 16) which exist and can be recognized by all moral beings, even when they are not shared by all, and that these values are multiple and cannot be ranked in terms of each other;

(2) claiming, with the relativist, that the existence of a value is dependent on perspective, emotion, or cultural context, such that value exists only for those who share it. Pluralism, as opposed to relativism, does not deny the objectivity of value across communities and cultures: 'there are certain things that are good for human beings whatever they happen to believe' (George Crowder, 'From Value Pluralism to Liberalism' (1998) 1(3) *Critical Studies in International Sociology & Political Philosophy* 2, 3).

The pluralist does not deny the objective existence of values, only their susceptibility to be ranked in terms of each other, which is why value pluralism is considered a version of moral realism.

> and so on) are independent sources of value and of ethical argument. This means that there can be no absolute or final ranking of the basic goods: in some cases liberty, say, will come before equality, in other cases the opposite.[20]

Reasons for action, therefore, will inevitably conflict, and this conflict is not a sign of their imperfection, but rather proof of each source's conceptual independence, the fact that none is derivable or reducible to the other. This independence places human beings in the position of making choices, often hard and sometimes tragic, between ideals which cannot be simultaneously realized.

A good painting is 'good' in a different way from a good soldier; they do not each contribute to the overall goodness of the world, or possess a common quality that is manifested differently in different circumstances; rather the painting possesses aesthetic value, and makes the world more 'artful' while the soldier possesses military value and contributes to the effectiveness of his unit. We may see moral value in his dedication to his comrades, instrumental value in his steadiness when pulling the trigger, and even aesthetic value in his posture and movement, and all these may contribute to being a 'good soldier', but they refer to qualities that can each be had independently of each other, and be assessed very differently in different contexts.

Now, the interesting claim that value pluralists make is not that any human practice (or product thereof) may be differently valued depending on one's context or frame of reference. The interesting claim is that there are certain sources of reasons that are *ultimate* in that they are the object of human aspiration for their own sake, and not the instrument towards a further goal.[21] Thus, happiness, beauty, and justice are all objects of human aspiration, but they do not all stem from a common aspiration towards 'goodness' unless 'goodness' signifies the same thing as 'value' or 'desirability'. Ultimate sources of reasons are ultimate in that they are the object of aspiration *in the last instance*, not as a means to some further good; the distinction between meta-ethical monism and meta-ethical pluralism is that monists think that there must be one single thing that we all ultimately desire, while pluralists hold that there are many.

Even if there is more than one source of X in the world, we may avoid conflict or loss if it is possible to rank the instances of X in an order of preference or priority. Pluralism usually denies this by making a second claim, the claim of *incommensurability*: the instances of X, be they values, legitimate authorities, or legal systems, cannot be judged by a common measure. In the case of value, the claim of incommensurability denies that there is a common ranking—utility, say—against which all values may stand. A certain number of units of beauty—if there are such things—does not amount to an

[20] Crowder, note 19, 3.

[21] Berlin, 'Two Concepts of Liberty', note 12, 197.

equivalent number of units of justice. A gain in one value may, in some circumstances, be preferred to a gain in another, but this is, on some accounts, a preference that cannot be rationalized; on others, a purely contextual decision that cannot be generalized and indicates nothing about the general or universal relative merits of beauty and justice.

In evaluating the structure of pluralist arguments we can be agnostic about whether incommensurability implies incomparability, and whether the choice among incommensurables can be rational. Joseph Raz, Ruth Chang, and others have made significant contributions to the debate on what incommensurability entails, and I do not think it necessary to revisit the debate here.[22] A relatively weak theory of incommensurability would suffice—say, one that denied that any a priori ranking of incommensurables was possible while allowing rational contextualized choice in particular situations.[23] Even this modest incommensurability would hold out the possibility that, in some cases, the order or ranking of certain values might be reversed, or that a decision procedure might not in all cases be conclusive about which ought to be preferred.

The importance of incommensurability, aside from illuminating the structure of our moral universe, is that it opens the door to genuinely tragic conflict. The simplest understanding of this claim—the claim of *tragic loss*—is that there is, at least sometimes, no way of resolving the conflict among incommensurable values that does not involve suppressing or giving up on one of those values. In some cases, the decision, and the ensuing loss, may be more dramatic, as when Bernard Williams explains that 'an agent can justifiably think that whatever he does will be wrong: there are conflicting moral requirements and neither one of them succeeds in overriding or outweighing the other.'[24]

1.3 POLITICAL PLURALISM: CONFLICT OVER SOVEREIGNTY

In political science, political pluralism usually brings to mind the theory, closely tied to the name of Robert Dahl, which describes the democratic process as the product of the interaction of competing interest groups.[25]

[22] Joseph Raz, *The Morality of Freedom* (Oxford University Press, 1998); Ruth Chang, *Incommensurability, Incomparability, and Practical Reason* (Harvard University Press, 1998); Charles E Larmore, *Patterns of Moral Complexity* (Cambridge University Press, 1987).

[23] This seems to be Berlin's view.

[24] Bernard Williams, *Moral Luck* (Cambridge University Press, 1981) 74.

[25] Robert A Dahl, *Dilemmas of Pluralist Democracy: Autonomy vs. Control* (Yale University Press, 1983); Robert A Dahl, *Polyarchy: Participation and Opposition* (Yale University Press, 1972); Robert A Dahl, *Who Governs? Democracy and Power in an American City* (Yale University Press, 1961). For the relationship between Dahl and the British pluralist tradition, see Avigail I Eisenberg, *Reconstructing Political Pluralism* (State University

But there is another sense of political pluralism—that of the so-called British pluralists—which concerns not the strategies of groups within the sovereign democratic state, but the constitution and legitimation of the state itself: the very personality of groups, the definition of sovereignty, and the justification and limitation of liberal democracy.[26]

It is to this tradition of normative political pluralism that I refer below, a tradition championed by a motley group of intellectuals writing at the turn of the twentieth century, and recently enjoying a modest but overdue revival.[27] The British pluralists decried what they perceived to be the prevailing, but false conception of sovereignty that dominated modern Western political theory: the idea that the state was the unlimited and unitary source of legitimate authority in any given society, that it was owed allegiance above all other associations, and indeed that those authorities could legitimately exist only as long as the sovereign tolerated them. This conception—which they dubbed *monism*—influenced not only monarchists, but also French radical republicans and English parliamentarians into the twentieth century.[28] Against monism, the pluralists assert that, in any society, there are multiple sources of legitimate political authority personated in various groups and associations, of which the state is but one; none of these has inherent precedence over the others.[29] Groups—e.g. churches, unions, universities—exercise sovereignty in their own right, and it is only this dispersion of authority that secures freedom against the state.[30] The pluralists, however, never formed a coherent school; their arguments were sometimes shoddy

of New York Press, 1995) 96. Dahl's work, to be fair, has always had a normative component, made most explicit in recent writings (e.g. Robert A Dahl, *Democracy and Its Critics* (Yale University Press, 1989)). Still, it is 'very different from the model of a pluralist state envisaged by the British pluralists.' David Nicholls, *The Pluralist State: The Political Ideas of JN Figgis and His Contemporaries* (2nd edn) (St. Martin's Press, 1994) xviii-xix.

[26] FW Maitland in D Runciman and M Ryan (eds), *State, Trust and Corporation* (Cambridge University Press, 2003); John N Figgis, *Churches in the Modern State* (first published 1913) (Thoemmes Press, 1997); Harold J Laski, *Studies in Law and Politics* (first published 1932) (Archon Books, 1969), and *Studies in the Problem of Sovereignty* (first published 1917) (Fertig, 1968); Mary Parker Follett, *The New State* (Longmans, 1918); Ernest Barker, 'The Discredited State' (1915) 2 *Political Quarterly* 101.

[27] For the original British pluralists, see note 26. For the recent pluralist revival, see Eisenberg, note 25; WA Galston, *Liberal Pluralism* (Cambridge University Press, 2002) and *The Practice of Liberal Pluralism* (Cambridge University Press, 2005); PQ Hirst, *Associative Democracy: New Forms of Economic and Social Governance* (University of Massachusetts Press, 1994) and *From Statism to Pluralism: Democracy, Civil Society and Global Politics* (University College London Press, 1997); C Laborde, *Pluralist Thought and the State in Britain and France, 1900-25.* (Macmillan, 2000); D Nicholls, *Three Varieties of Pluralism* (Macmillan, 1974) and *The Pluralist State: The Political Ideas of JN Figgis and His Contemporaries* (2nd edn) (St. Martin's, 1994).

[28] See Figgis, note 26, 56 (on French 3rd Republic minister Emile Combes), and Bernard Baylin, *The Ideological Origins of the American Revolution* (Harvard University Press, 1992) 198–229 (on parliamentary sovereignty).

[29] See generally, Paul Q Hirst (ed.), *The Pluralist Theory of the State* (Routledge, 1993).

[30] David Nicholls, note 27.

and imprecise about the meaning of particular concepts, or presented in formats (such as pamphlets or sermons) that did not lend themselves to careful theoretical scrutiny. Their contemporary advocates have not remedied these deficiencies and pluralism remains, for some, an attractive but poorly defined philosophy of government.

The pluralist critique of the state enjoyed some prominence until the advent of the Second World War, but was also forcefully criticized by legal and political theorists.[31] Much of the criticism was deserved, since the pluralists were often hasty and unclear in their arguments, and incurred their share of contradictions. Cole, for instance, subordinated the authority of associations to a corporatist functionalism: he argued that each association possesses a *function* which emanates from the satisfaction of common wants and the execution of common purposes, and the coherence of society depends on all associations fulfilling their function in a way that is 'complementary and necessary for social well-being.'[32] He therefore dismissed as 'perversions of function' much of the conflict, contradiction, and redundancy that are part and parcel of relations between associations and the state. Laski (an important target of Schmitt's attacks) inveighed not only against state sovereignty, but against authority in general, even the authority of other groups,[33] to the point that some scholars have concluded that he was essentially a philosophical anarchist (a judgment with which he sometimes concurred).[34] Figgis is the most consistent and coherent of the lot, yet he also is ambiguous about the role of the state in adjudicating disputes between groups and between groups and individuals.[35]

The pluralist resurgence has not been the dominant tendency in recent political theory; that is, the distinction of the proponents of deliberative democracy, who see the common interests of citizens of a political society as making special claims to their allegiance, and understand non-state associations, at best, as conducive to a richer political life[36] and, at worst, as hostile to the liberal-democratic project.[37] The prevalent position in political theory makes the claims of legitimacy of the liberal-democratic state continuous with the decidedly anti-pluralist arguments of Jean Bodin and Thomas Hobbes.[38] Indeed, 'between the two philosophically polar approaches to

[31] Carl Schmitt, *The Concept of the Political* (first published 1932) (University of Chicago Press, 2007); Francis W Coker, 'The Technique of the Pluralist State' (1921) 15(2) American Political Science Review 186; see also Paul Q Hirst, 'Carl Schmitt's Decisionism' and Carl Schmitt, 'Ethic of State and Pluralistic State' both in Chantal Mouffe (ed.), *The Challenge of Carl Schmitt* (Verso, 1999).

[32] GDH Cole in Hirst, note 29, 62.

[33] Harold J Laski in Hirst, note 29, 180.

[34] Eisenberg, note 25, 75–83.

[35] Figgis, note 26, 90.

[36] Joshua Cohen and Joel Rogers, 'Secondary Associations and Democratic Governance' (1992) 20(4) *Policy and Society* 393.

[37] Brian Barry, *Culture and Equality* (Harvard University Press, 2001).

[38] See also Holmes, note 2, especially chapters 3 and 4.

association and state in the history of English political thought, the radical scepticism of associational life on the part of Thomas Hobbes and the radical scepticism of the state associated with the early 20th century pluralists, there is no real contest in terms of influence.'[39]

Yet, the central contentions of pluralists—that (some) associations have a claim to legitimate authority over their members that is not derived from the fiat of the state, and that the social and legal institutions of society should reflect this plurality of sovereignties—retained interest. The lack of rigour in their arguments was seen to mask important insights about the relations of authority in modern societies. Interest in pluralist writings would, in fact, experience a resurgence in the latter part of the twentieth century, which continues today. The pluralist tradition was again explored in theoretical scholarship,[40] and explicitly embraced by some,[41] or at least positively referenced by scholars working on the status of groups and their relationship to state authority.[42]

For the PST to hold, the claims of plurality, incommensurability, and tragic loss must be echoed in the arguments of political and legal pluralism. In the case of political pluralism, there must be (at least the possibility of) multiple sources of legitimate authority that are equally ultimate, in that one is not authorized by the other and neither is authorized by a putative third. One such pluralism presumably holds in the international state system, characterized by anarchy, in at least a strict sense: there is no legally recognized common authority to which all other state systems are subordinated. The occasional hegemon may attempt to act as such a power in a practical, *de facto*, manner, but it rarely goes unchallenged in theory or in practice. And even hegemons do not usually make the claim that they are the *source* of authority in every state, or that (historical origins aside) every other state retains its sovereignty only by the fiat of the dominant power.[43] The anarchical nature of the international state system gives some evidence for

[39] JT Levy, 'From Liberal Constitutionalism to Pluralism' in Mark Bevir (ed.), *Modern Pluralism: Anglo-American Debates Since 1800* (Cambridge University Press, 2012) 21.

[40] David Runciman, *Pluralism and the Personality of the State* (Cambridge University Press, 1997); Eisenberg, note 25.

[41] William A Galston, *Liberal Pluralism* (Cambridge University Press, 2002) and *The Practice of Liberal Pluralism* (Cambridge University Press, 2005). Paul Q Hirst, *The Pluralist Theory of the State, Associative Democracy: New Forms of Economic and Social Governance* (University of Massachusetts Press, 1994), and *From Statism to Pluralism: Democracy, Civil Society and Global Politics* (University College London Press, 1997).

[42] See for example Nancy L Rosenblum, *Membership and Morals: The Personal Uses of Pluralism in America* (Princeton University Press, 1998). Many other scholars made claims similar to the pluralists' regarding the authority of groups, even if their theoretical grounding was not in that tradition (Richard W Garnett, 'The Freedom of the Church' (2007) 4 *Journal of Catholic Social Thought* 59; Chandran Kukathas, *The Liberal Archipelago: A Theory of Diversity and Freedom* (Oxford University Press, 2003); L Swaine, *The Liberal Conscience* (Columbia University Press, 2006)).

[43] The Soviet satellite states may have been an exception, insofar as the Soviet Union considered itself the embodiment of a universal proletarian revolution.

some form of political pluralism, one that endorses a claim of plurality. Most political pluralists, however, and especially the British pluralists (Maitland, Figgis, Laski, etc.) did not have the international state system in mind when they argued for multiple sources of sovereignty, but rather the multitude of associations and other formalized groups that exist within a state.[44]

The historical record shows that many of these groups predate the creation of most modern states, and cannot therefore be creatures of government in the sense of being causally created by government. What the quintessential monist writers—Jean Bodin and Thomas Hobbes—attempt, to varying degrees, is to displace the historical argument with a legal one, to supersede the historical record through the articulation of a concept of sovereignty that necessarily excludes a plurality of incommensurable (or equal) claims to authority. So Bodin considers every private corporate body—from guilds to towns to universities—as constituted by 'a right of legitimate community under the sovereign power [where] the word legitimate conveys the authority of the sovereign, without whose permission there is no college.'[45] He does not mean that these corporate bodies have their historical origin in the sovereign's will;[46] rather, he claims that their legitimacy can only follow from sovereign ratification. Though he thought they originally evolved prior to the establishment of the state, he believed that, once the state was in being, corporations had to be sanctioned by it.[47] The corporate bodies are organized through the voluntary association of their members, who come together to pursue a common interest. Yet it is the interest of the state—which is twofold: fellowship and administration—that motivates sovereign sanction and actually constitutes the group as a self-governing entity.[48]

[44] See note 27.

[45] Bodin, *Les Six Livres de la République, Livre Troisième*, note 2, 178–79. (Preston King, translates *droit de communauté legitime* as *lawful community*, which seems to me an unnecessary departure from the original. Preston King, *The Ideology of Order: A Comparative Analysis of Jean Bodin and Thomas Hobbes* (George, Allen & Unwin, 1974) 98. But it is not the actual group of people that is of interest to Bodin, rather their right to be organized and have their actions recognized by the sovereign authority.)

[46] Bodin sketches a history of the origin of corporate bodies in *République*: 'And the origin of the corps and colleges was the family, as there were many branches that had shot from the main stem, [and thus] it became necessary to build houses, then hamlets and villages, and to become so neighborly that it seemed all were but one family.' A familiar account of the state of nature follows: with a growing population, dispute and strife broke out, and this drove villages to raise walls and to appoint princes to defend them. Guilds and colleges may have arisen spontaneously before the state, but they gained legal sanction because they served the sovereign to facilitate the maintenance of order in incipient republics through the organization of trades and professions. Bodin, *Les Six Livres de la République, Livre Troisième*, note 2, 174–78. See also Jose-Manuel Bernardo Ares, 'Les corps politiques dans la "République" de Jean Bodin' in *Jean Bodin: Actes de Colloque Interdisciplinaire d'Angers, 24–27 Mai 1984* (Presses de l'Université d'Angers, 1985) 35.

[47] King, note 45, 96.

[48] Bodin, *Les Six Livres de la République, Livre Troisième*, note 2, 178. 'Fellowship' and 'administration' are Preston King's terms, which he equates with Bodin's 'la religion' and 'la police', respectively (see note 45, 107).

Hobbes is more dramatic. Contrary to Bodin, he takes no unit of social organization as pre-existent: in the beginning, only individuals exist.[49] Hobbes' theory of corporate structure in fact makes no distinctions between the nature of public or private bodies, families or the state. All of these are but different kinds of 'systems'.[50] The sovereign is a system like all others, but the extreme latitude that subjects give to the Leviathan precludes them from undertaking any further act of autonomous association. Once civil government is instituted, all systems, other than the Commonwealth, must be made dependent on the sovereign's will; otherwise, they would threaten it. The distinction between political and private systems, then, pertains only to the attribution of initiative in their origin, and the interests the group is to serve: both need to be permitted by law, although political systems must also have an express grant, letter or writ authorizing them to act on the sovereign's behalf. As Preston King succinctly put it, in *Leviathan* and other writings:

> Hobbes makes three basic points. The first is that there are subordinate organisations within the state. The second is that these organisations may pursue some limited common interest restricted to their members, or a broader interest in which the entire society shares. The third is that corporations can only legitimately exist if they are expressly sanctioned or tacitly tolerated by the sovereign power.[51]

When the British pluralists question the tidy order of the Bodinian and Hobbesian systems, they counter the monist arguments with three claims of their own: the first is that (at least some of) the non-state associations that exist in society are not—and ought not be—subordinate to the state; they have, at times, been deemed superior or parallel to the state (as the early Church), they have been carved out of the state by a separate authority (as free cities and universities were), or are in open conflict with the government (as the early trade unions). The pluralists did not assert this as a descriptive claim, but as a moral assertion about the legitimacy of these associations. The second claim is that the interests of these groups are sometimes—but by no means always—'limited' in scope or ambition; the saving of the soul, the pursuit of knowledge, or the overturning of labour market are not modest aims, although they might not be shared by other citizens. However, these

[49] This represents a paradigmatic shift in the understanding of social organization. 'For Bodin, the family was the irreducible unit of social organization; for Hobbes, it was merely the smallest (and even then with no absolutely fixed character). For Bodin, individuals were born into families; for Hobbes, they were merely born, being related to other individuals on the basis of force and consent. [...] For Bodin, the authority of the state was derived from families, as represented by the father; for Hobbes, it was derived from individuals, as represented by themselves.' (King, note 45, 184).

[50] Hobbes' definition of a system is extremely general: it consists of 'any numbers of men joyned in one Interest, or one Businesse' (Hobbes, note 2, 155).

[51] King, note 45, 222.

limits, where they exist, are self-imposed by associations themselves, and their legitimacy or permissibility does not need to be confirmed by the state. The third claim is that the legal reality of associations does not depend on state fiat or toleration, but on the same social factors that underlie the very origins of the political community; thus the monist's leap from the descriptive account of state authority to the normative claim of its supremacy is unwarranted.

These three claims fit the three elements of the PST quite well. The first is a claim about incommensurability (through the denial of political subordination). Harold Laski made more explicit the link between the sociological description of associational life and the prescriptive endorsement of plural sources of sovereignty. Flipping John Austin's canonical formulation[52] on its head, Laski argued that, if habitual obedience is the measure of sovereignty, then the state cannot be the only sovereign around. The state is but one of many groups competing for the habitual obedience of men and women, and churches, trade unions, families even, hold the loyalty of individuals to at least the same degree as the state.[53] They are, in a real and important way, self-governing, in that they pursue collective goals with unity of purpose, and do not habitually subordinate their values and their ends to those of another authority. The third is a claim of foundational plurality. As Figgis puts it:

> [C]orporate personality, this unity of life and action, is a thing which grows up naturally and inevitably in bodies of men united for a permanent end, and that it cannot in the long run be denied merely by the process of saying that it is not there. In other words this personality is inherent in the nature of the society as such, and is not a mere name to be granted or denied at the pleasure of the sovereign authority.[54]

That leaves the second claim, the claim that the interests of groups were sometimes—but by no means always—'limited' in scope or ambition, open to interpretation. It is here that the idea of tragic conflict enters the political pluralist paradigm. It raises the possibility that all claims, in this case, of ostensibly legitimate collective authority, might not be simultaneously realized without genuine loss. Of course, the denial of foundational plurality or of incommensurability also rules out the possibility of tragic loss: if non-state authority is judged subordinate to state authority, or if it is stipulated that it does not even exist without the express consent of the state, no

[52] John Austin styled the sovereign as a single but determinate individual or body of individuals to whom habitual obedience is rendered by the bulk of society; and who does not, in turn, render such obedience to anyone else, in HLA Hart (ed.), *The Province of Jurisprudence Determined* (first published 1832) (Hackett, 1998) 195.

[53] Laski, note 26, chapter 1 *passim*.

[54] Figgis, note 26, 64.

such loss is possible; the superior authority will trump the inferior, or the privilege of legal existence will be withdrawn.

But tragic loss may also be denied by organicist or functionalist accounts that all too optimistically presume that properly constituted associations will naturally fit into a harmonious social system. For all his ostensible pluralism, GDH Cole's functionalism takes this direction. He proposes that each association has a 'function' which emanated from the satisfaction of common wants and the execution of common purposes. As the function of the state is to represent persons in their common condition—to concern itself 'with things which concern all sorts and conditions of men, and concern them, broadly speaking, in the same way, that is, in relation to their identity and not to their points of difference'—it cannot claim jurisdictional superiority over other associations, which may be the final arbiters on matters peculiar to a discrete group.[55] But the coherence of society depends on all associations fulfilling their function in a way that is 'complementary and necessary for social well-being'; conflict, contradiction and redundancy are perversions of function.[56] Cole's account of function is at once descriptive and normative, but it ultimately has the effect of denying that conflict between groups, or between groups and the state, can result in one association simply losing out. Redundant or conflictive functions are brushed aside as anti-social, legitimacy is predicated on guild-socialist harmony.

A more accurate account of what is at stake when there is a conflict between legitimate authorities derives from the pluralist response to the second Hobbesian point, mentioned earlier. The interests of associations are not always limited in scope or ambition. Figgis, perhaps the truest of the British pluralists, admits as much:

> Of course such societies may come into collision with the State; so may individuals. Always there is a possibility of civil war. But you will not escape the possibility by ignoring the facts.... Harmony must ever be a matter of balance and adjustment, and this at any moment might be upset, owing to the fact that man is a spiritual being and not a mere automaton.[57]

Even if we put aside the theological terms in which Figgis presents the pluralist position, the ineluctability of latent conflict between the jurisdiction of associations and that of the state parallels the potential conflict between goods or values of the meta-ethical model. One important distinction is that, in Berlinean value pluralism, the boundaries of goods are set and given, and conflict between them arises because of the incompatibility of their simultaneous pursuit. The ends or values of associations are not given; the authority of associations is itself the capacity to set, pursue, and alter its collective

[55] GDH Cole in Hirst, note 29, 77 [56] GDH Cole in Hirst, note 29, 60–67. [57] Figgis, note 26, 92.

ends, although in the self-understanding of groups some ends may have a foundational or constitutive place in the group's justification for existence. Yet even these are mutable, as they hold pride of place because of the shared understanding of its members, which is itself mutable. It is a formal pluralism of authorities, not a substantive pluralism of authoritative decisions, which characterizes the potential tragedy of political pluralism. The conflict is ultimately meta-jurisdictional, as it concerns not only the capacity of associations (among them the state) to act within a certain given sphere, but also to define the boundaries of that sphere.[58]

The political pluralist position, thus stated, does not imply that all associations are always right in pressing simultaneous claims of sovereignty; there may, in some cases, be good reasons for disregarding some sovereign claims or refusing compromise with an especially intransigent authority. But the fact that, from an Archimedean position, a sovereign authority is deplorable does not mean that it is not meta-jurisdictionally authoritative. States routinely make claims that are incompatible precisely because they both lay claim to a normative space simultaneously, without conceding primacy to the other. In such a case they can negotiate or one or the other may lose, but there is no way of affirming a solution that concedes the supremacy of both. Churches who claim exemption from certain procedural exigencies of state law, or scholars or universities who resist having their curricula set by the legislature may be made to yield to the demands of the state jurisdiction through penal or financial pressure. Sometimes good may come of their capitulation to the state, but that is beside the point. The point is that their capitulation is not a clarification of where the rightful authority lies. It is a defeat, one that cannot be squared with the sovereign claims of both competing parties. The language of defeat is tinged with tragedy in the instant case, even if in the long run the losers come to accept the loss. That is all that the PST requires.

1.4 LEGAL PLURALISM: CONFLICTS OF LEGALITY

In legal theory, pluralist arguments centre on the multiplicity of legal authorities, and the tendency of state courts to stifle competing juridical claims.[59] This development parallels the tradition of political pluralism and casts an

[58] The term is used by Allen Buchanan to distinguish between '(1) jurisdictional authority (the right to make, adjudicate, and enforce legal rules within a domain), (2) meta-jurisdictional authority (the right to create or alter jurisdictions, including geographical jurisdictions), and (3) the property rights of individuals and groups within jurisdictions.' Allen Buchanan, 'The Making and Unmaking of Boundaries: What Liberalism Has to Say' in Allen Buchanan and Margaret Moore (eds), *States, Nations, and Borders: The Ethics of Making Boundaries* (Cambridge University Press, 2003) 231, 233.

[59] Robert Cover, 'Nomos and Narrative' (1983) 97 *Harvard Law Review* 4.

important light on the pluralist claims about the authority of associations, since many of the groups that are the object of political pluralist theories are themselves governed by sophisticated systems of norms, which suggests that political pluralism and legal pluralism may collapse into each other (but more on this later).

Legal pluralism also endorses the claim of plurality in a fairly straightforward way. In nearly every social setting there are always a number of legal orders which bear down on individuals and groups. These may follow a hierarchical order of similar types of law—international, national, regional, and local—or may overlap without, in all cases, trumping each other—such as provincial and national legal orders in 'strong' federations. Many other, more unfamiliar but not uncommon, arrangements exist, since 'in many societies there are more exotic forms of law, like customary law, indigenous law, religious law, or law connected to distinct ethnic or cultural groups within a society.'[60]

The observation that there is a plurality of legal systems is not reducible to political pluralism. Not all legal orders need to claim sovereignty, although most claim some form of legitimate authority; yet this authority may be theoretical, not practical (to use Raz's dichotomy).[61] Associations may also be organized around principles of personal charisma or shared commitment, as opposed to formal rules; they may thus exist within a legal system without being themselves legal systems, which would make them subjects of political, not legal pluralism.[62] Legal orders may also be transnational or international to varying degrees, and thus escape easy identification with the mostly domestic associations that primarily concern political pluralists. This is especially true of unofficial law, such as customary law, and of law that is organized in ways alien to those of the modern state, such as indigenous or 'chthonic' law.[63] As Brian Tamanaha notes: 'Legal pluralism exists whenever social actors identify more than one source of "law" within a social arena.'[64] Nonetheless, it is generally true that political and legal pluralism are often closely aligned, since many (perhaps all) political claims, when institutionalized and made public, take something resembling a legal form.

Robert Cover is most closely identified with the view that legal orders may, and often do have, independent origins—that they are foundationally plural—and that their rules of legality cannot be understood on the terms of

[60] Brian Z Tamanaha, 'Understanding Legal Pluralism' (2007) 29 *Sydney Law Review* 375.

[61] Raz, note 22, 35.

[62] For the distinction between principles of shared commitment and legal principles, see Lon L. Fuller, 'Two Principles of Human Association' in *Principles of Social Order* (Hart Publishing, 2002) 67ff.

[63] H Patrick Glenn, *Legal Traditions of the World* (4th edn) (Oxford University Press, 2010) chapter 3.

[64] Tamanaha, note 60, 396.

another normative order—that they are incommensurable. This is especially true of insular communities which, while perhaps not being constituted as a corporate person (as Figgis would have associations be) or asserting exclusive authority over their members, nonetheless create a normative world that stands apart from the normative world of the state. Indeed, for Cover: 'Insular communities often have their own, competing, unambiguous rules of recognition. They frequently inhabit a *nomos* in which their distinct *Grundnorm* is supreme from their own perspective.'[65]

Cover also understands that, whatever the merits of the state's actions in any given case, much of the operation of judicial system is *jurispathic*, that is, it routinely suppresses, mutilates, and kills competing sources of legal creation, competing *jurisgenerative* impulses. In Cover's view, the jurispathic nature of courts is a normative problem, something to be avoided. He closes his seminal 'Nomos and Narrative' with the call to 'stop circumscribing the *nomos*; we ought to invite new worlds.'[66] But this claim need not be normative; it may be simply descriptive.

> A clash between or among coexisting official legal systems within a given social arena can also take place, as indicated earlier, and plays out in a variety of ways.... Clashes can be resolved through political compromises arranged by their respective institutional authorities. In some situations the competing official legal authorities will ignore one another, or explicitly refuse to honor their determinations (as when states refuse to honor rulings of the World Court). One official system may acknowledge the contrary official legal system and accept its findings (begrudgingly or enthusiastically). Sometimes they will face off in a direct clash which continues unresolved. Sometimes the more powerful official legal system simply imposes its will on the other through superior raw economic or military or political power.[67]

In either case, something is genuinely lost, either because a normative order is extinguished, or because the rules of legality of a legal order are dismissed or cast aside in terms entirely alien to that order.

Cover's views on the *nomos* as the site of legality are rich but also controversial. Yet there are many other scholars whose avowal of legal pluralism does not depend on Coverian legal ontology. Harold Berman makes legal pluralism a cornerstone of his jurisprudence, as I will discuss in chapter 2. For him '[p]erhaps the most distinctive characteristic of the Western legal tradition is the coexistence and competition within the same community of diverse jurisdictions and diverse legal systems.'[68] Perry Dane, whose writings bear on church–state relations but also on disputes between tribal and federal sovereignty, does not make direct reference to the pluralist tradition,

[65] Cover, note 59, 43. [66] Cover, note 59, 68. [67] Tamanaha, note 60, 405.

[68] Harold Berman, *Law and Revolution* (Harvard University Press, 1983).

but his argument about the intractable conflict between multiple sovereignties parallels pluralist claims.[69] Recently, Dane and other scholars of what has been called the 'New Religious Institutionalism' make direct reference to British or Calvinist pluralists in support of their arguments in favour of ecclesiastical autonomy, even extending them explicitly (in Paul Horwitz's case) to institutions beyond the church, like the universities and the press.[70] And students of the European Union, like Nick Barber, have abstracted the general structure of legal pluralism from the jurisdictional conflicts in the EU.

> [A] legal order can contain multiple rules of recognition that lead to the order containing multiple, unranked, legal sources. These rules of recognition are inconsistent, and there is the possibility that they will, in turn, identify inconsistent rules addressed to individuals. In addition, pluralist orders lack a legal mechanism able to resolve the inconsistency; there is no higher constitutional body that can resolve this dispute through adjudication or legislation. Consequently, pluralist legal orders contain a risk, which need not be realized, of constitutional crisis; of officials being compelled to choose between their loyalties to different public institutions.[71]

The themes of incommensurability and inconsistency, leading perhaps to tragic choices or irresoluble conflicts of loyalty on grounds of legal validity alone, demonstrates the parallel of legal pluralism to meta-ethical and political pluralism.

1.5 PLURALISM ACROSS THE DOMAINS OF PRACTICAL REASON

I have argued that all non-trivial pluralist arguments make three claims about the normative category that is their object, which I refer to as 'X' (whether it is value, sovereignty, or legality). As stated, these three claims are the claim

[69] Perry Dane, '"Omalous" Autonomy', 2004 Brigham Young University Law Review 1715, 'The Varieties of Religious Autonomy', in Gerhard Robbers (ed.), *Church Autonomy: A Comparative Survey* (Peter Lang Publishers, 2001); Perry Dane 'The Maps of Sovereignty: A Meditation', 12 *Cardozo Law Review* 959 (1991) and, note: Perry Dane 'Religious Exemptions Under the Free Exercise Clause: A Model of Competing Authorities', 90 *Yale Law Journal* 350 (1980).

[70] P Horwitz, *The Agnostic Age: Law, Religion, and the Constitution* (OUP, 2011) and *First Amendment Institutions* (Harvard University Press, 2013); R Garnett, 'Religious freedom, church autonomy, and constitutionalism' 57 *Drake Law Review* 901 (2009) and '"The Freedom of the Church": (Towards) an Exposition, Translation, and Defense', Journal of Contemporary Legal Issues, forthcoming (2013). For a criticism of the pluralist position, see R Schragger and M Schwartzman, 'Against Religious Institutionalism' 99 *Virginia Law Review* 917 (2013) and for a response, see P Horwitz, 'Defending (Religious) Institutionalism' 99 *Virginia Law Review* 1049 (2013).

[71] Nick Barber, *The Constitutional State* (Oxford University Press, 2011) 145–46.

of plurality, the claim of incommensurability, and the claim of tragic loss. The three claims are extrapolated from the paradigmatic case of pluralism, and also the best discussed in the philosophical literature: meta-ethical pluralism or pluralism of values. Using the structure of the argument for value pluralism as a model, the structure of normative pluralism in politics and law is found to make equivalent claims about sovereignty and legal orders, respectively.

Pluralism across the domains of practical reason is analogous or parallel in the form of its arguments, but is, in each domain, substantively independent. That is, pluralist arguments follow the same structure whether they refer to a plurality of value, of legitimate political authority, or of the sources of legality, but a defence of pluralism in one of these domains does not entail acceptance of pluralism in another. This is most evident in the relationship between meta-ethical (value) pluralism and political or legal pluralism. One can value individual freedom above all other goods, and think it best protected by a system of countervailing powers and independent associations, as in the case of Constant. Or, one can find in the absence of an ultimate scale of values the justification for absolute and undivided political authority, as in the case of Hobbes.

The relationship between political and legal pluralism is much more muddled, as is the relationship between politics and law, but I think that substantive independence of each domain still holds. Drawing on Weber's tripartite classification of the ways of justifying legitimate domination,[72] we can imagine a charismatic antinomian who contests the authority of the state without thereby presuming to proclaim or institute an alternative set of rules against state law; political pluralism would result, but not legal pluralism, although the claims of law to universal efficacy over a given population may fall short in this case. From the opposite standpoint, we can interpret certain legal institutions as pluralistic in the domain of law, but not of politics. The system of law in early modern Britain, in which the courts of common law coexisted and competed with the courts of chancery and prerogative courts, was a system of legal pluralism, but not political pluralism, as the monarch stood at the apex of both hierarchies.[73]

Whether either political pluralism without legal pluralism or its converse are stable situations is open to question. Lon Fuller suggests that associations founded on shared commitments come to rely more on legalistic principles the more the benefits of membership grow and the cost of exclusion

[72] Max Weber, 'Politics as a Vocation' in HH Gerth and C Wright Mills (eds), *From Max Weber: Essays in Sociology* (Oxford University Press, 1946) 78–79.

[73] Harold Berman, *Law and Revolution, II: The Impact of the Protestant Reformations on the Western Legal Tradition* (Belknap Press, 2003) 307–13.

becomes palpable to the associates.[74] Robert Cover fears that the moment of legal creation—jurisgenesis—that characterizes an emerging *nomos* quickly ossifies into an imperial order in which the legal order is alienated from those who created it.[75] In the cases that occupy political pluralists, the ones most likely to present problems of competing sovereign jurisdiction, political sovereignty is often indistinguishable from legal authority; one is constituted by the other.[76] I will assume this hybrid pluralism as my object of inquiry: an association that makes a claim to sovereignty—as ultimate arbitral authority—which takes the form of a distinct and separate legal order.

[74] Fuller, note 62, 92.

[75] Cover, note 59.

[76] It is no coincidence that most of the associations in question can be traced back to a medieval order in which the dominant theory of sovereignty presumes that political authority is legally constituted. I will have more to say about this in later chapters, especially chapter 5.

2

The Inadequacy of Multiculturalism

In February of 2008, Rowan Williams, the Archbishop of Canterbury, delivered a lecture at the Royal Courts of Justice on the topic of the accommodation of religious law in the secular state, with special attention to the use of sharia by Muslim groups in Britain.[1] Williams' lecture 'set off an international firestorm'—in the words of one commentator[2] —and provoked an overwhelmingly negative reaction from the press and the political establishment, including a denunciation by future Prime Minister David Cameron.[3] Almost invariably, the Archbishop's detractors argued that the recognition of Islamic law by the British judicial system, which Williams considered unavoidable,[4] was an example of multiculturalism gone too far.

The curious thing is that neither in his lecture nor in the question period that followed it does Williams ever mention multiculturalism, whether to endorse it or condemn it.[5] The challenge he sees himself confronting is 'the presence of communities that, while no less "law-abiding" than the rest of the population, relate to something other than the British legal system alone.'[6] It is legal, not cultural plurality that presents a problem and, as he concludes, an opportunity for rethinking the foundations of the political order. As expected of his office, Williams is most concerned with communities of faith, but even then he does not elide the distinction between religious authority and cultural practice but instead emphasizes it: 'it is crucial',—he

[1] Rowan Williams, 'Civil and Religious Law in England: A Religious Perspective', *Ecclesiastical Law Journal* 10(3): 262–82 (2008).

[2] John Witte, 'The Archbishop and marital pluralism' *Ecclesiastical Law Journal* 10(3): 344–47.

[3] <http://www.guardian.co.uk/politics/2008/feb/26/conservatives.race> accessed 12 June 2013. Cameron would again denounce multiculturalism, also with direct reference to British Muslim groups, in his first speech as Prime Minister three years later <http://www.bbc.co.uk/news/uk-politics-12371994> accessed 12 June 2013.

[4] Williams, note 1, 274.

[5] The exception was his approving citation of Ayelet Shachar's book *Multicultural Jurisdictions* (Cambridge University Press, 2001), which is, of course, about multiculturalism, and to which I will return later.

[6] Williams, note 1, 262.

repeats throughout the lecture—'to distinguish between cultural and strictly religious dimensions.'[7] And the religious dimension he has in mind is not the subjective experience of faith, but rather the 'recognized authority acting for a religious group', that is, the religious association.[8]

This, I would argue, is a different concern from that of multiculturalism. It proceeds from different assumptions about the nature of the difference confronted by modern liberal-democracies, it has a different political aim and a different understanding of what counts as successfully overcoming the problem of difference, and it recommends different institutional solutions (or at least a different way to justify these institutions). That is not to say that there is no overlap between multiculturalism and associational pluralism (there is), or that the two are not compatible (they often are), but rather that they are different arguments concerned with different social phenomena. What Williams advocates is an associational pluralism that has great historical and philosophical affinity with the tradition developed by the early British pluralists, especially his fellow Anglican prelate John Neville Figgis. Williams' concern, as was Figgis', is the preservation of a certain ambit of authority for corporate communities which, while not denying the authority of the state, nonetheless refuse to ground their own legitimacy on the state's acquiescence or permission, and insist on their own standing as arbiters of their own normative sphere.

It is easy to trace the source of Williams' attention to religious authorities through the British pluralist tradition, despite some approving references to the literature on multiculturalism. Some three years prior to his observations on sharia, the Archbishop delivered the David Nicholls Memorial Lecture where he endorsed a pluralist theory of the state derived from Nicholls' interpretation of Figgis' thought.[9] The state, on this account, is 'a particular cluster of smaller political communities negotiating with each other under the umbrella of a system of arbitration recognized by all.' The nature of the associations enumerated in the 2005 lecture is decidedly ambiguous and includes 'trade unions, ethnic and cultural groups, co-operative societies, professional guilds (universities, the [British Medical Association], the Bar Association) and, of course, churches and faith groups.'[10] The Archbishop describes them as 'first-level' associations, that is, self-regulated organizations

[7] Williams, note 1, 267. [8] Williams, note 1, 267.

[9] Rowan Williams, 'Law, Power and Peace: Christian Perspectives on Sovereignty' (David Nicholls Memorial Lecture, The University Church of St. Mary the Virgin, Oxford, 29 September 2005). The lecture is available at <http://www.dnmt.org.uk/dnmt/images/docs/dnmlecture_2005.pdf> accessed 12 June 2013. The late David Nicholls authored the only full-length study of Figgis' political philosophy and, in my view, the most penetrating analysis and defence of political pluralism in the literature: *The Pluralist State* (2nd edn) (St. Martin's Press, 1994). Nicholls, like Figgis and Williams, was also an Anglican priest in the tradition of the Oxford Movement.

[10] Williams, note 9.

that claim an inherent 'right to exist and to take corporate action' not derived from the licence of the state.[11]

This is in fact Figgis' position, made only a bit more current. Figgis holds that what Williams refers to as a first-level group is a corporate body bound by the interest of its members, which 'inevitably acts with that unity and sense of direction which we attribute to personality.'[12] Figgis understands that an association is constituted and held together by the common purposes of its members. The purpose of the state is not to interfere in the internal life of groups, but 'to prevent injustice between them and to secure their rights.'[13] Other state purposes include acting as the 'guardian of property and interpreter of contract'[14] —that is, to guard against an association imposing its will upon groups and individuals who do not share its ends—through the erection and enforcement of generally applicable legal institutions (primarily the institutions of private law), and by deference to the corporate will of the association in all other internal matters. The pluralist state takes the form of a *communitas communitatum*—a community of communities—of which individuals are members through the autonomous associations to which they belong.[15]

As articulated by Williams, the state is a largely administrative structure for resolving boundary disputes between these first-level organizations. The state itself has no substantive goals, at least none that 'are potentially in competition with those of its constituent communities.'[16] Its role is to create the institutional conditions 'needed for any one of these groups to do what it seeks to do.' Because these institutional conditions are the concern of all first-level groups, and because the conflicts between groups are adjudicated in state administrative fora, the pluralist order allows and even encourages 'negotiation and limited but significant interaction' among groups. Williams explicitly contrasts this system with multiculturalism, which (perhaps simplistically) he takes to task for preserving the separate integrity of groups without attending to their interaction and 'active partnership' with the state and other groups. The contrast he draws is elusive and not fully worked out, especially in light of his later endorsement, in the 2008 sharia lecture, of at

[11] Williams, note 9.

[12] JN Figgis, *Churches in the Modern State* (Thoemmes Press, 1997) 59.

[13] Figgis, note 12, 90.

[14] 'What we have to secure is our corporate existence, our real life functioning inside a State, itself made up of complex elements and tolerating all religions. The tolerant State is the true State. The uniform State of the past was founded on a lie.... But the State has yet to learn that she must tolerate not merely individual liberty but the religious society, must know that its life is real and must develop, and cannot (not must not) be stopped.' JN Figgis, 'The Church and the Secular Theory of the State' in Nicholls, note 9, 158–59.

[15] Other British pluralists developed political theories that are in many ways objectionable.

[16] Williams, note 9.

least one multiculturalist alternative. But the earlier text makes clear that his later defence of religious jurisdictions is indebted to the pluralist tradition and not to the multicultural literature.

Yet, I bring up Rowan Williams' invocation of pluralism not for its own sake—my interest is in the political tradition of those he invokes, more than on his own argument—but to illustrate the points of convergence and divergence between associational pluralism and multiculturalism. The two paradigms are not incompatible, and while there are certainly points on which they overlap across various sociological and policy dimensions, they remain very different approaches to the question of incommensurable difference in liberal societies.

2.1 THE MULTICULTURAL PARADIGM

What is the multicultural approach to difference? Given the extent and complexity of the literature, I will draw in broad strokes. Multiculturalism refers, on the one hand, to a wide variety of policies adopted mainly (though not exclusively) by some post-industrial liberal-democratic states in the last decades of the twentieth century. The motivations behind the adoption of these policies was twofold: it was, first, a consequence of the institution of more open immigration policies that permitted entry to immigrant populations from a wider variety of geographical (and thus cultural) areas, and a concomitant abandonment of the traditional strategy of encouraging rapid and thorough assimilation of immigrants into the receiving culture.[17] It was also an extension of the gradual restructuring of the relations between central states and national minorities, which recognized greater prerogatives to the latter and held back on monocultural models of nation-building.[18] Canada was the first country to officially adopt multiculturalism—by name—as a national policy in 1971, and eventually to elevate it to constitutional status a decade later,[19] which is unsurprising since it was a society marked both by an ever more open attitude towards migration, and by enduring linguistic and cultural cleavages not only between Canadians of British heritage and Québécois but also

[17] Keith Banting and Will Kymlicka, 'Canadian Multiculturalism: Global Anxieties and Local Debates' [2010] 23(1) *British Journal of Canadian Studies* 43, 49.

[18] Hugh Donald Forbes, 'Trudeau as the First Theorist of Canadian Multiculturalism' in Stephen Tierney (ed.), *Multiculturalism and the Canadian Constitution* (University of British Columbia Press, 2007) 27–42.

[19] The Canadian Charter of Rights and Liberties, adopted as part of the Constitution Act of 1982, reads in section 27, 'This Charter shall be interpreted in a manner consistent with the preservation and enhancement of the multicultural heritage of Canadians.' This section represents the constitutional entrenchment of a policy that had been developing for eleven years. See Michael Dewing, *Canadian Multiculturalism* (Ottawa: Parliamentary Information and Research Service, 2009) Available at: <http://www.parl.gc.ca/Content/LOP/ResearchPublications/2009-20-e.pdf> accessed 10 October 2013.

between both of these groups and the various aboriginal peoples who, in this same period, had begun to be recognized as a national minority.

On the other hand, multiculturalism is also 'a body of thought in political philosophy about the proper way to respond to cultural and religious diversity', marked by a rejection of strategies of 'mere toleration' and by 'recognition and positive accommodation of group differences... through "group-differentiated rights."'[20] The political and philosophical dimensions of multiculturalism are closely related, and have informed each other over the years, even enjoying a parallel wax and wane of popularity. While something recognizable as multiculturalism is an inherent part of any imperial enterprise, and can thus be projected over thousands of years of human civilization and conquest,[21] multiculturalism as explicit policy only comes into being in the 1970s and 1980s, and only becomes a major theme of self-conscious political theory in the last decade of the twentieth century.[22] Here, I will limit myself to the philosophical literature on multiculturalism, and forgo an analysis of historical antecedents or empirical policy comparisons. The history that I take as subject is the history of ideas, because of what it clarifies about the distinctiveness of pluralism.

The emergence and growth of the multicultural literature is both practical and theoretical. Practically, as just mentioned, it is spurred by reflection on the pursuit of policies of cultural accommodation by several post-industrial liberal-democratic countries who were important recipients of immigration, or harboured persistent national minorities. Theoretically, it is an attempt to come to grips with the publication and subsequent reaction to John Rawls' *A Theory of Justice*, the touchstone of twentieth-century liberal political philosophy.[23] This theoretical development, Will Kymlicka explains, passed through several stages.[24] The first stage was the liberal-communitarian

[20] Sarah Song, 'Multiculturalism' in EN Zalta (ed.), *The Stanford Encyclopedia of Philosophy* (Winter 2010 Edition) available online: <http://plato.stanford.edu/archives/win2010/entries/multiculturalism/> accessed 12 June 2013.

[21] Susanne Hoeber Rudolph makes the provocative distinction that '[a] nation-state is a restricted territory in which there is a presumption or at least an aspiration of congruence between the state and a nation or people. By contrast, an empire is an extended territory comprising a group of states or peoples under the control or at least the suzerainty of a dominant power.' 'Presidential Address: State Formation in Asia—Prolegomenon to a Comparative Study' [1987] 46:4 *The Journal of Asian Studies* 731, 736.

The imperial label intuitively fits what Will Kymlicka calls 'multination states' more than it does 'polyethnic states' (Will Kymlicka, *Multicultural Citizenship* (Oxford University Press, 1995) 11–26); but the dynamics of governing difference may be more similar than intuition intimates.

[22] Will Kymlicka, *Liberalism, Community, and Culture* (Oxford University Press, 1989); Charles Taylor et al., *Multiculturalism: Examining the Politics of Recognition* (Princeton University Press, 1994). There were antecedents, of course, especially in the cultural pluralism of H Kallen, *Cultural Pluralism and the American Idea* (University of Pennsylvania Press, 1956).

[23] John Rawls, *A Theory of Justice* (Belknap Press, 1971).

[24] Will Kymlicka, 'The New Debate over Minority Rights' in Ronald Beiner and Wayne Norman (eds), *Canadian Political Philosophy* (Oxford University Press, 2001) 159–76.

debate, in which theorists like Michael Sandel and Charles Taylor objected to what they perceived to be an impoverished conception of the person in Rawls' work, and took issue especially with the lack of attention to the constitutive commitments that individuals draw from their cultural, religious, and other ethical communities.[25] The definitive response from the Rawlsian camp was Kymlicka's *Liberalism, Community, and Culture*—definitive because it was later endorsed by Rawls as representing his position in the so-called liberal-communitarian debate.[26]

This stage was followed by the development of an account of minority rights within a liberal framework. Here, Kymlicka's *Multicultural Citizenship*[27] articulated a terminology and conceptual framework that still defines debates on multicultural accommodation. Kymlicka understands the problem of multiculturalism in distinctly liberal terms: '[a] liberal democracy's most basic commitment is to the freedom and equality of its individual citizens.'[28] Drawing on the different strains of the liberal tradition, he articulates 'a distinctively liberal approach to minority rights'[29] that takes an individual's societal culture—one 'which provides its members with meaningful ways of life across a full range of human activities, including social, educational, religious, recreational, and economic life'[30]—to provide an interpretive context that gives meaning to the different choices with which a person is confronted in a diverse liberal society. The exercise of freedom presupposes such a context, which is why minority cultures need protection. The loss of their context of choice would prove traumatic to their members because of its high cost and the offence to members' self-identity, thus disabling them from exercising their freedom meaningfully and from cultivating the virtues of citizenship.

[25] Michael Sandel, *Liberalism and the Limits of Justice* (Cambridge University Press, 1982); Charles Taylor, *Philosophy and the Human Sciences* (Cambridge University Press, 1985).

[26] John Rawls, *Political Liberalism* (Columbia University Press, 1993) 27, n. 29.

[27] Kymlicka, note 21.

[28] Kymlicka, note 21, 34.

[29] Kymlicka, note 21, 75. Not all multiculturalism is *liberal* multiculturalism. Jocelyn Maclure distinguishes a *communitarian* multiculturalism that sees society as 'a mosaic of cultural communities that relate with one another through institutions and representatives' from a *civic* multiculturalism that shows 'equal respect to citizens [by] recognizing and accommodating their cultural differences, insofar as it does not impact adversely on the rights and freedoms of others.' The difference, for Maclure, is that communitarian multiculturalism encourages isolation of communities and ignores the pursuit of the common good, while civic multiculturalism 'starts from the hypothesis that cross-cultural interaction and deliberation guided by the norm of respect for reasonable cultural diversity is the most promising route to the creation of new forms of belonging and solidarity in multicultural societies'(J Maclure, 'Multiculturalism and Political Morality' in D Ivison (ed.), *The Ashgate Research Companion to Multiculturalism* (Ashgate, 2010) 39–55, 40). Now, the pluralist position I defend differs from communitarian multiculturalism by rejecting that cultures, as opposed to formal associations, have the right kind of structure to be self-governing and, even if they did, they should not be able to completely exclude the competing claims of the state. But conversely, if they were self-governing associations, the state (liberal or not) would have no absolute primacy over them.

[30] Kymlicka, note 21, 76.

Against a backdrop of ostensible ethnic and cultural neutrality, multiculturalists defend exceptions from burdensome general requirements and assistance for disadvantaged minorities as a means towards more general inclusion. But this ostensible neutrality was quickly seen to be illusory, not least by Kymlicka who admits that 'the state cannot help but give at least partial establishment to a culture when it decides which language is to be used in public schooling, or in the provision of state services.'[31] Joseph Carens starkly declares that '[t]he idea of cultural neutrality is an illusion.'[32]

The third stage of multiculturalism, however, not only does away with the presumption that the state can be ethnically and culturally neutral, but also recognizes that in the process of nation-building it is an active promoter and creator of culture. Kymlicka calls this the '"nation-building" model' of the state; a state that inevitably promotes a single societal culture (and, more rarely, a limited number of cultures) even if only to facilitate common goals such as standardized education, social solidarity, and other markers of citizenship.[33] The question at this stage is not only whether minorities will have substantively equal access to liberal political institutions, but whether they will have to accept a public culture that is seen as a necessary condition for accessing those institutions. Minorities then face a choice to integrate into the public culture (the alternative that most immigrants choose), to create alternative—though liberal—political institutions of their own in which their own distinct public culture is assumed (the strategy of some large territorially bound national minorities), or to permanently separate from the broader society (the road taken only by some small religious sects like the Amish or Hutterites).

The communitarian critique of liberalism, which set the first stage of multiculturalism, shares with pluralism the suspicion that individuals can have deep constitutive attachments beyond that conferred by equal legal status. Yet the political turn of communitarianism is clearly incompatible with pluralism. '[T]he idea of a substantive common good which the state must be concerned to promote', argues David Nicholls, elevates one conception of culture, politics, and the good life, and—more importantly—privileges one political agent (the state) with the task of identifying and advancing this conception over others and above other groups and associations.[34] This leaves first-level associations in the same place they were under the dominant liberal theory.[35]

[31] Kymlicka, note 21, 111.

[32] Joseph Carens, *Culture, Citizenship, and Community* (Oxford University Press, 2000) 53.

[33] Kymlicka, note 24, 165. [34] Nicholls, note 9, 101.

[35] It is not Taylor or Sandel—those named by Nicholls—who best exemplify monistic communitarianism in opposition to associational pluralism but, ironically, Michael Walzer.

The distinction between pluralism and multiculturalism is most evident when contrasted at the second stage of multicultural theory, as I discuss in section 2.2. At that stage multiculturalism is, first and foremost, a subsidiary strategy adopted by liberal-democratic societies in order to further the primary or dominant strategy of individual autonomy, and more specifically the autonomy of the individual as a citizen of the liberal-democratic nation-state. Multicultural policies can be constructive or remedial. They are constructive when the cultural context preserved by multicultural policies forms the basis for a deeper identification with a liberal and egalitarian public culture, made all the richer because it is sustained through an overlapping consensus of reasonable views, many of which are culturally rooted. Multicultural policies are also remedial when addressing and attempting to ameliorate historical or structural injustices that undermine the self-respect of members of disadvantaged cultural communities and thus prevents them from standing as equals in a common condition of citizenship.

But the distinction holds even at the third stage, albeit in modified form. Even then, multiculturalism privileges cultural cleavages as being the most salient and the most normatively important sources of identification in modern societies. In deepening its critique of the nation state, it still recognizes that the purpose of cultural accommodation is integration into a liberal-democratic polity, whether the majoritarian one or one created by the national minority, and offers as an only alternative the complete separation from the world. Where it approximates pluralism is in the recognition of collectivities—such as ethnic or cultural minorities engaged in nation-building projects—as morally relevant entities. These groups must ultimately be internally constrained by liberal principles (they may choose the language of delivery of public services, for instance, but must not deny public services on grounds of race or gender); that is, the content of political culture is constrained. However, third-stage multiculturalism recognizes the importance of differentiating between the collective agent that administers that political culture—in this case the national (or sub-national) state as a corporate political association.

This *rapprochement* to pluralism is nonetheless deceptive, because multiculturalism, even at the third stage, only considers difference between ethnic or cultural groups; it either ignores other first-level associations or, when it does consider them, it distorts their nature and their claims by assimilating them under the category of cultures.

2.2 WHAT PLURALISM IS NOT ABOUT

How does the multicultural approach to societal difference contrast with the pluralist one? The first and most obvious divergence between the two paradigms is that pluralism is not especially concerned with cultural difference.

It is concerned with the authority of associations, with the corporate agency and self-direction of groups, and with the legal orders that they generate, sustain, and enforce.

The focus on associations as opposed to societal cultures also yields a more fragmented, more *plural*, assessment of the differences that permeate modern societies. Rowan Williams recognizes that 'our social identities are not constituted by one exclusive set of relations or modes of belonging';[36] Laski wrote that '[w]hether we will or no, we are bundles of hyphens';[37] while Figgis wrote that '[w]hat we actually see in the world is not on the one hand the State, and on the other a mass of unrelated individuals; but a vast complex of gathered unions.'[38] And Nicholls explains that 'British political pluralism... evolved in a situation where people normally belonged to a number of different groups and where group membership was "cross-cutting".'[39]

As a matter of fact, the historical moment in which pluralism was the norm in the West—both in legal and political practice and theory—was a time in which cultural cleavages did not yet define political allegiance. Harold Berman makes pluralism central to the development of the Western legal tradition.

> Perhaps the most distinctive characteristic of the Western legal tradition is the coexistence and competition within the same community of diverse jurisdictions and diverse legal systems. It is this plurality of jurisdictions and legal systems that makes the supremacy of law both necessary and possible.[40]

The central case of pluralism, which initiated the differentiation of jurisdiction that would characterize the medieval order, was the Roman Church's declaration of 'its freedom from secular control, its exclusive jurisdiction in some matters, and its concurrent jurisdiction in other matters';[41] the differentiation of other legal and political orders soon followed: the guild, the town (more of an association of citizens than a local subordinate administrative unit), and eventually the incipient state.[42] Whatever the sources for the conflict between Pope and Emperor—and, for that matter, between guild and town, scholar and monk, lord and merchant—it was not a cultural dispute. It would likewise require an impossible stretch of the concept of culture to cover the American Roman Catholic Church's dogged claim to be exempt from the government mandate to provide contraception in the employment

[36] Williams, note 1, 265.

[37] Harold Laski, *The Foundations of Sovereignty and Other Essays* (Harcourt, Brace and Co., 1921) 170.

[38] Figgis, note 12.

[39] Nicholls, note 9, 92.

[40] Harold Berman, *Law and Revolution* (Harvard University Press, 1983) 10.

[41] Berman, note 40.

[42] These orders are reflected in the kinds of first-level associations that Williams lists: ethnic groups, yes (although understood as associations like the Ancient Order of Hibernians, not as societal cultures), but also unions, guilds, universities and, of course, religious bodies.

health plans of church-run hospitals; the jealous guardianship by the legal profession since the thirteenth century of the power to discipline their members; or the obstinate insistence of university professors to be sole arbiters of the conference of academic rank and title. Jurisdictional disputes indeed often arise even in the complete absence of cultural difference.[43]

The exclusive attention to culture leads some prominent theorists of multiculturalism astray when they try to reduce jurisdictional disputes between incommensurable legal authorities to questions of accommodation of cultural values. As Sarah Song observes, '[m]ost of [Will] Kymlicka's examples [of poly-ethnic rights][44] involve religious practices.'[45] The cases she alludes to are 'exemption from Sunday closing or animal slaughtering legislation . . . from motorcycle helmet laws and from the official dress-codes of police forces . . . the right to wear the yarmulke during military service . . . [and] exemption from school dress-codes so they can wear the chador.'[46] The elision between cultural norms and norms dictated by a formal (and in this case religious) authority is not trivial. Cultural difference is entirely absent from the early British pluralist literature. When Rowan Williams acknowledges it, it is to distinguish it from religious prescription:

> [A]ny recognition of the need for such sensitivity must also have a recognised means of deciding the relative seriousness of conscience-related claims, a way of distinguishing purely cultural habits from seriously rooted matters of faith and discipline, and a way of distinguishing uninformed prejudice from religious prescription.[47]

A cultural practice widely recognized and embraced by an ethno-cultural group may well coincide with a religious prescription mandated by an identifiable authority in the formally organized religious group, but they are analytically different. For one, the formally organized religious group is more likely to have explicit rules of membership, clearer lines of hierarchy, and procedures that enable the group to act in its own name as a corporate person, as when acquiring, holding, and disposing of property and when entering into contracts with third parties. Some cultural groups may be meaningfully said to possess a territory, own a certain class of artefact, or determine rules of

[43] Relatedly, associational pluralism does not depend on value pluralism either. Two jurisdictions may exist in which authorities and subjects hold to identical world views, with concomitant hierarchies of value. The identity in value systems may provide good reasons for the authorities of one community to take advice from their neighbours, but it cannot make the decisions of one set of authorities binding on the other.

[44] These Kymlicka defines as 'group-specific measures . . . intended to help ethnic groups and religious minorities express their cultural particularity and pride without it hampering their success in the economic and political institutions of the dominant society.' See note 21, 31.

[45] Sarah Song, *Justice, Gender, and the Politics of Multiculturalism* (Cambridge University Press, 2007) 65.

[46] Kymlicka, note 21, 31.

[47] Williams, note 1, 267.

membership.[48] The recognition of these capacities may even be owed to the members of the group as a matter of justice, either as constructive or remedial policies or as conducive to an alternative nation-building project. But in those cases, the cultural group (or a part thereof) has transformed into a formally constituted association. It is no longer the culture that possesses land, issues directives, and admits members but rather the authority within the association, although that authority may (rightly or wrongly) claim to be acting in the name of the culture as a means of shoring up its legitimacy.

There are other grounds, just as important, for distinguishing between pluralism and multiculturalism. These derive, in part, from the place (or lack thereof) that culture plays in each paradigm. Given the pervasiveness of societal cultures (on Kymlicka's account) it is natural to think that they exercise a king of monopoly on an individual's cultural membership such that, although one may be 'between' cultures it is difficult to fully participate in more than one. Pluralism, by contrast, is suspicious of such pervasive allegiance and presumes—even requires—multiple and cross-cutting group membership.[49]

2.3 PLURALISM, MULTICULTURALISM, AND JUSTICE

There is also a sense in which pluralism is not motivated directly by demands of justice, especially to justice as an internal or endogenous limit on the liberal state. By endogenous limits I mean any restriction of state authority—whether one that constrains it from enacting certain policies or directives or one that mandates that it confer some benefit or accommodation (and therefore likewise interferes with its discretion)—which is required by the same reasons that confer legitimacy to the state. The most dramatic example of an endogenous limit is Thomas Hobbes' justification of the state on the basis of the two laws of nature: 'That every man, ought to endeavour Peace, as far as he has hope of obtaining it' and 'that a man be willing, when others are so too, as far-forth, as for peace, and defence of himself he shall think it necessary, to lay down this right to all things; and be contented with so much liberty against other men, as he would allow other men against himself.'[50] At the institution of a Leviathan it is accorded all the powers necessary to

[48] These are some of the standard cultural right-claims. Jacob Levy, *The Multiculturalism of Fear* (Oxford University Press, 2000) 127.

[49] So, for instance, Nancy Rosenblum is very ecumenical about the kinds of associations that should be tolerated in a liberal society, but expresses great concern about 'greedy' institutions 'which immerse members in the organization and take up every moment of their lives'. Nancy Rosenblum, *Membership and Morals: The Personal Uses of Pluralism in America* (Princeton University Press, 1998) 98.

[50] Thomas Hobbes, *Leviathan* (Hackett, 1994) 80.

preserve the security and peace commanded by the second law, and the immense scope of its discretion is justified by its equally immense task. But while the Leviathan can demand obedience in almost all aspects of life, it cannot demand it if it attempts to kill or is incapable of defending a subject.[51] Those limits to its authority follow from the very grounds of its claim to legitimacy.

Pluralism, by contrast, proffers exogenous limits to state authority. The limit that first-level associations pose is one of absence of reason: because these associations are not creatures of the state and do not emerge through its fiat, because their claims to authority are incommensurable with state claims as they neither represent a delegated authority nor are they necessarily justified by the reasons that ostensibly justify state legitimacy, there may be no common reasons that the state could invoke when acting towards them; that is, no reasons that would resonate within the normative universe of these associations.

> The Church—like all other 'first-level' communities though for dramatically different reasons from other groups—does not exist by licence of the state. And that fact gives both reinforcement and limit to the state—reinforcement to the state as a system of lawful brokerage and stable provision, not threatened by theocratic claims, limit to the state as an atomistic sovereign system answerable to nothing outside itself.[52]

Associations may share a common ideal of justice with the state, but do not thereby (or necessarily) agree on who is the subject of justice. More likely, they will have some ideals of justice that overlap with those of the state and others that do not. But their claims to authority are couched on principles internal to each association, and are not necessarily derived from a universal standard of justice.

I do not want to overstate the distinction. Contra Williams, cultural practices that are not traceable to an institutional mandate or 'law' can be accommodated through multicultural policy and justified on grounds of justice; my point is simply that the problem that pluralism attempts to understand and solve is, first, not a cultural problem and, second, not directly a problem of justice but of authority. There may be an overlap between multicultural policies and political pluralism, and the interaction between the two paradigms can go both ways. In cases where a sizeable minority group is settled in a geographically bound community, a measure of self-government may be the only way to guarantee that the context of choice of the group is preserved. Even absent the geographical boundedness, multicultural policies may recommend something like a separate personal jurisdiction that appropriates

[51] Thomas Hobbes, *Leviathan* (Hackett, 1994) 218–19.

[52] Williams, note 9.

some of the markers of sovereignty, as is the case when a religious or cultural community is allowed to apply its own personal law in separate tribunals.

One especially robust theory of this kind is Lucas Swaine's defence of quasi-sovereignty for theocratic communities. Swaine defines a theocracy in this context as 'a mode of governance prioritizing a religious conception of the good that is strict and comprehensive in its range of teachings', a group with its own set of values, practices, and ideals.[53] He is motivated primarily by a desire for principles that can be affirmed by theocrats and liberals alike, and which afford a common ground for liberal institutions to govern theocratic communities. But these principles acknowledge that '[m]embers of a theocratic community need to be able to have their own religious leaders, make their own institutions and regulations, and develop their own *nomos*, that is, their own normative universe, if they are truly to pursue their religious conceptions of the good.'[54] The combination of 'communitarian, nonliberal, strict, and comprehensive' theocratic conception of the good demands formal institutions of self-governance, rather than individual exemptions, and distinguishes theocracies from cultural groups. Swaine proposes a semi-sovereign status for such a community provided that it 'be virtually homogenous in its religious affiliations', possess a distinct territory 'free from and clear of neighboring districts and communities', and 'provide a basic plan for its social institutions.'[55] It must also continue to respect certain basic human rights. This would entitle such a community to become 'the ultimate recognized political authority within the territory that it occupies.'[56]

Now, there is a great deal of affinity between the institutions that Swaine recommends and those that political pluralism would accept. But the difference is more telling. For one, Swaine's theocracies are 'retiring' organizations, self-excluded from the world, while most of the associations that political pluralists concern themselves with are very much engaged with the world. This contrast pits a quasi-sovereign landscape of nested identities and loyalties, which afford little in the way of contestation, with a pluralist landscape of cross-cutting and competing allegiances that limit and check each other because no one allegiance can ever lay exclusive claim to the obedience of a subject. This dynamic is central to Laski's and Figgis' arguments about the space for freedom opened by political pluralism—not only freedom to pursue one's good, but also freedom from domination by any one sovereign.[57] Even if Swaine's quasi-sovereignty is

[53] Lucas Swaine, *The Liberalism of Conscience* (Columbia University Press, 2006) 7–8.

[54] Lucas Swaine, *The Liberalism of Conscience* (Columbia University Press, 2006) 86.

[55] Lucas Swaine, *The Liberalism of Conscience* (Columbia University Press, 2006) 94–95.

[56] Lucas Swaine, *The Liberalism of Conscience* (Columbia University Press, 2006) 91.

[57] David Nicholls, *Three Varieties of Pluralism* (Macmillan, 1974) 5.

appropriate to theocrats, it will not do for most mainstream churches, universities, and the like.

Pluralists might, in a specific case, recommend arrangements like those that multiculturalists or quasi-sovereigntists propose, but they might also acknowledge that the state and the non-state group might come to accept pluralist institutions on different grounds. There is a measure of justificational asymmetry here, because members of the group may understand the application of their personal law to be a direct response to a higher (or at least a different) authority than the state's, while the liberal state may consider it a concession to a subordinate jurisdiction, or even an eccentric but ultimately unproblematic exercise of choice of law under ordinary arbitration rules.[58] That is, the group may perceive as something like political pluralism what the state perceives as multiculturalism. Alternatively, there may be no asymmetry at play if neither the members of the group nor the state understands the population in question to constitute an 'association' in a formal sense, but rather an aggregate of individuals with similar concerns. Such a case is still clearly within the purview of multiculturalism, but is wholly outside the concern of associational pluralists.

But in none of these cases (even Swaine's) is the group the proper object of attention, but rather the individual, as is evident in Kymlicka's distinction between group rights and group-differentiated rights.[59] Group-differentiated rights are those that are ascribed to individuals by virtue of their membership in a particular group or possession of a kind of status; they are, however, individual rights even if the criteria for them to obtain refers to the group. Group rights, by contrast, are held by the group directly, as a 'person' in its own right (such as the right of a corporation to own property in its own name, separately from its members). Kymlicka, like many multiculturalists, endorses the former, but is quite suspicious of the latter, especially as it necessarily entails the exercise by the group of authority independent of liberal justification or oversight, and thus might result in illiberal restrictions or 'internal constraints' on the group's members. Whether Kymlicka's antipathy towards group rights proper is a necessary component of multiculturalism is a different issue. At least one commentator has argued that, as applied to religious freedom, Kymlicka's 'high-liberalism' shapes and dominates his multiculturalist thesis.

> Following from his commitment to liberal individualism and his comprehensive view of liberal multiculturalism, Kymlicka's conception of religious freedom is also highly individualistic. He places such an emphasis upon personal autonomy that he not only overlooks many of the collective dimensions of

[58] Marion Boyd, 'Dispute Resolution in Family Law: Protecting Choice, Promoting Inclusion (2004)' <http://www.attorneygeneral.jus.gov.on.ca/english/about/pubs/boyd/> accessed 12 June 2013.

[59] Kymlicka, note 21, 40–43.

> religiosity but goes so far as to view collective liberty as diametrically opposed to liberalism itself.[60]

This assessment is confirmed by Kymlicka's approving acknowledgement that multiculturalism offers little support for the corporate strain of religious freedom and the institutional accommodations demanded in its name: 'the real issue [. . .] is the pre-modern legal doctrine of *libertas ecclesiae*, which gives religious organizations broad exemptions from equality rights, not the post-modern Multiculturalism Act, which firmly endorses the norms and principles of equality.'[61] Suffice it to say that multiculturalism and political pluralism have different objects in sight: for the former it is the individual, for the latter the formally organized group, and it is possible to advocate for multicultural policies without any concession to the sovereignty of an association.

In terms of the three claims that comprise the ideal type of political pluralist argument, multiculturalism is largely silent or indifferent. Consider the conditions that occasion multicultural policies to be proposed. They may, but need not (and usually do not) arise from the simultaneous presence of multiple authorities each claiming a final say over some aspect of conduct of some portion of the population; thus foundational plurality need not be at issue. Even when the conditions of cultural pluralism emerge from or take the institutional form of associations that claim some measure of sovereign authority, as in the case of some multi-ethnic states, multiculturalism largely attends only to the relationship of members of those associations to the central state, not to the claims that the several ethnic jurisdictions may have over their members. In some cases, it may be unavoidable to address the authority of sub-units. Doing so is most prominent in the case of minorities within minorities, or in cases of egregious restrictions on exit and opportunity on members of the groups. This may lead to tensions between multiculturalism and pluralism, but nothing in pluralism per se argues that autonomous associations are bound by certain minimal standards of decency, even if they are not liberal standards. But it does make those claims conditional on jurisdictional boundaries, such that an injustice in one association does not by itself justify interference by the state or any other group. The claim of incommensurability is therefore not at play. Finally, while many multiculturalists know that even the most latitudinarian policy will fail to accommodate all cultural difference, whatever loss may result in terms of genuinely valuable cultural practice is a loss of an entirely different order from that contemplated by

[60] Chris Durante, 'Religious Liberty in a Multicultural Society' [2012] 54(3) *Journal of Church and State* 323, 329.

[61] Will Kymlicka, 'Disentangling the Debate' in *Uneasy Partners: Multiculturalism and Rights in Canada* (Wilfrid Laurier University Press, 2007) 147.

political pluralism. It may be a loss of value, but it is not a loss or curtailment of authority.

2.4 POLITICAL PLURALISM AND JURISDICTIONAL COMPETITION

I began this discussion as a gloss on Rowan Williams' application to religious authorities of a version of political pluralism traceable to the work of John Neville Figgis. I argued that the strain of political pluralism from which Williams has drawn is distinct from, and in some ways in tension with, the accommodation of religious authorities in the multicultural literature. But what, then, of the Archbishop's previously mentioned endorsement of Ayelet Shachar's idea of 'transformative accommodation', laid out in her *Multicultural Jurisdictions*?[62] Is this a paradigm that can bridge the conceptual distance between religious community and formal association, or at least provide a model compatible with associational pluralism?

Ayelet Shachar approaches the conflict between the norms enacted by the state and those that emerge from cultural and religious groups as an opportunity for mutual development. Like the political pluralists, she accepts that normative conflict is an inherent part of interaction among members of various communities in a diverse society. Shachar refers to these groups, interchangeably, as '*nomoi* communities' and 'identity groups', following Robert Cover's *nomos* to refer to a community of meaning that 'generate[s] sets of group-sanctioned norms of behavior that differ from those encoded in state law.'[63] It is important to note here that the idea of an identity group is closer to the multicultural concept of community—like a religious group—than to the idea of a formally constituted association—like a church—although in Shachar's examples it is clear that she applies it to groups with relatively formalized structures of authority in matters like membership, norm-creation, and member discipline. I will therefore put to the side the ontology of the *nomoi* to focus on their relationship to state law.

Shachar's assumptions leading to the concept of transformative accommodation are remarkably similar to those of pluralists such as John Neville Figgis and Harold Laski:

> First, group members living within a larger political community represent the intersection of multiple identity-creating affiliations. Second, in many real-life circumstances both the group and the state have normatively and legally justifiable interests in shaping the rules that govern behavior. Third, the group and the state are both viable and mutable social entities which are constantly affecting

[62] Shachar, note 5. [63] Shachar, note 5, 2.

each other through their ongoing interactions. Fourth, it is in the self-professed interest of the group and the state to vie for the support of their constituents.[64]

All four assumptions, or very similar ones, are also the foundation of political pluralism. Laski, at the height of his pluralism, held individuals to be 'bundles of hyphens' marked by competing loyalties and subject to multiple claims of allegiance and authority.[65] The coexistence of presumptively justifiable interests and claims on the part of the state and of other social groups is the principal claim of figures like Figgis. While some political pluralists (even Figgis) sometimes seem to deny that the state has any independent reasons for governing behaviour (a position that mirrors the monist insistence on state supremacy only in its extremity) a sensible pluralism acknowledges that the state is an association capable of making claims to legitimate authority, and only insists on recognition of the same capacity in other groups. Moreover, the viability and mutability of social groups is essential to the pluralist position. The former may seem more obvious than the latter, and indeed it is a necessary feature of an association that it retains continuity through time, but it is not a necessary feature that it change or adapt the norms by which it conducts its deliberations and governs its membership. All groups are in principle mutable—capable of change—or else it would be pointless to insist that the state not interfere with their development, as Figgis consistently maintained. Even if a group is steadfastly orthodox, it is its potential mutability that grounds its apprehension about state intervention in its structure and affairs.

From these assumptions, Shachar develops three core principles that guide her concept of transformative accommodation.[66] The first defines the site of contestation over the interests of the state and other groups: it is not to be a broad social arena like 'education' or 'family relations' but rather the smaller components or 'sub-matters' into which these arenas can be disaggregated; thus, a social arena like 'family relations' can be disaggregated into sub-matters like the contracting of marriage, its dissolution, divisions over property and child custody disputes, inheritance, etc. The second principle denies any social group a monopoly over any sub-matter: 'neither the group nor the state can ever acquire exclusive control over a contested social arena that affects individuals both as group members and as citizens';[67] this is

[64] Shachar, note 5, 118.

[65] Harold J. Laski, 'The Personality of Associations' in Paul Q. Hirst (ed.), *The Pluralist Theory of the State* (Routledge, 1993)165–183, 181.

[66] The relationship between the three core principles and the four assumptions is not one of implication. Rather, it is guided by Shachar's motivation in developing the model of transformative accommodation, namely, the protection of the most vulnerable members of religious and cultural communities, those most likely to be dominated by authorities within these communities. This is an important goal which often goes unremarked in the political pluralist tradition, but it is a problem for any theory that takes seriously the role of groups in political society.

[67] Shachar, note 5, 121.

ensured by the allocation to different authorities of jurisdiction over specific sub-matters, or the institution of parallel jurisdictions within a sub-matter, so no one authority controls an entire social arena. Given that, under the model of transformative accommodation, group members would face different alternatives when seeking normative guidance or settling disputes, Shachar insists on a third principle: that group members have 'clear options which allow them to choose between the jurisdiction of the state and the *nomoi* group' on an issue-by-issue basis.[68]

One common trope of all pluralist theories, which is shared by Shachar's model of transformative accommodation, is the antipathy towards monopolies of authority. This antipathy can manifest itself in several different institutional forms. For Shachar, the site at which monopolies of authority should be opposed is very local, the 'sub-matter' arena in which complex areas of human interaction may be divided. For pluralists, the site of contestation is precisely the issue at stake. Jurisdictional boundaries cannot be abstractly defined, but involve the attribution of meaning to a social practice, which is an exercise of meta-jurisdictional authority. That is why the focus falls on which of the contesting authorities gets to define the social arena, not on the subject matter over which they contest. Controversies over the applicability of employment or health regulations to religious institutions are paradigmatic: whether the sub-matter of hiring practices in a school or of employment health benefits in a hospital falls under the social arena of education or health, or under the alternative social arena of religious ministry and charitable works, is precisely the issue. One authority defines it in one way, the other in another; both have sound reasons for their judgment because the activities obviously overlap, but defining or construing the activity in one way will give more weight to some policy considerations and perhaps trump others. Thus, to settle the question of meaning is to settle the controversy over which power will regulate the practice. The problem is not exclusive to religious or cultural bodies. Consider the recent controversies over affirmative action in North American universities. Is the decision to admit a student to a university a contract for services, subject to general laws against discrimination, or is it an academic decision pertaining to the measure of diversity the university deems optimal for the student experience it wants to encourage? Unarguably, it is both, and determining which context is dominant dictates whether the sub-matter falls within the more general jurisdiction of the academy or the state. It is difficult to split the difference, although courts have attempted to do so by allowing the consideration of race or ethnicity as part of a holistic judgment of a candidate's merit, while disallowing

[68] Shachar, note 5, 122.

racial quotas or a 'points' system that gives a quantifiable advantage to those of a certain demographic.[69] But it is unclear how a monopoly over the sub-matter is to be avoided without dramatically altering the meaning of the practice: either a student is admitted, or not; either the university is the final arbiter in admission decisions—absent fraud, perhaps—or else it is the state courts.

There are two ways of structuring how a cultural or religious group may exercise authority over a given domain, assuming that we allow such exercise at all: either the group is granted exclusive or primary authority over the domain as a matter of policy, as is the case, for instance, with the consecration of marriage in the state of Israel, where there is no civil marriage (except when admitted through norms of private international law) but only religious marriages governed by each recognized religious group; this is a question of institutional design where the onus of settling conflicts of authority falls on the legislator or policy maker. Or else parallel authorities are set up—the most common of which are arbitration panels—and individuals invited, encouraged, or assisted in choosing the jurisdiction in which they would like their case to be settled. Both setups can and often do coexist, even in the same institution, so for example, a religious tribunal may have exclusive authority to decide on ministerial appointments (the state ordinarily abstains from decisions of this type, so there is no competing forum) but also sit as an arbitration panel to decide on questions that could also be taken to a private non-religious arbiter or litigated in a state court.

So which solution should be preferred, and when? I doubt that an answer can be given at the level of first principles. Take the demarcation of exclusive or primary jurisdictions to a group or to the state. From the perspective of many groups, it is not possible to evaluate particular controversies from an Archimedean point and determine which authority, the state or the group, is best suited for governing a social domain or a sub-matter within it. The determination of the proper authority is simply too intertwined with determinations of the meaning of the practice in question. There are, to be sure, prominent political pluralists who have proposed similar objective criteria for drawing the boundaries between different social arenas. GDH Cole throughout his guild-socialist years and Harold Laski near the end of his pluralist period both advocated a functionalist interpretation of pluralism that proposed to do exactly that: to prevent any social group from claiming a monopoly over the entire social arena. But they were notoriously functionalist about the drawing of boundaries.

[69] Contrast *Grutter* v. *Bollinger* 539 U.S. 306 (2003) with *Regents of the University of California* v. *Bakke* 438 U.S. 265 (1978).

In their view, each group—even the state—has a defined social function to fulfil, and conflictive or redundant social functions are to be avoided, thus pre-empting actual jurisdictional competition.[70] But of course the problem is precisely how to define what the proper function of each 'sphere' ought to be. Absent a consensus, there remains only a clash of incommensurable authorities attempting to articulate and impose equally incommensurable systems of value over the same social field. The other alternative seems more promising, and more in line with the inclinations of pluralists and transformative accommodationists: to set up parallel authorities and allow or facilitate competition between them for the loyalty of a population. This alternative is attractive on several levels. On one hand, it respects the self-understanding of individuals who identify with and sincerely seek to conform to the associational obligations that they perceive themselves to have, even if those obligations do not conform only (or at all) to liberal or democratic ideals. On the other hand, it ideally depends on the affirmation of loyalty, which is presumptively voluntary, rather than coercion; this is, of course, qualified by very reasonable caveats about the vulnerability of certain classes of persons within a social group, but the competitive context in which these groups assert authority over their members is intended to remedy some of this vulnerability.

But there are reasons to think that the applicability of this model to associational life will falter. Competition on a sub-matter basis, in which individuals may select among different jurisdictions without penalty of losing their membership in one or another community, can flourish only in certain circumstances, namely in the case of cultural groups with no determinate locus of meta-jurisdictional authority, or in the case of formally constituted groups that nonetheless do not attach a very strong demonstration of loyalty as a condition of continuing membership. The first circumstance points to the difference between culture and association which I discussed before. An association may lay claim to a culture, but can never encompass it completely without transforming cultural rules into formal institutional norms, which are something else entirely. This means that the boundaries of culture are contested in ways in which the boundaries of a formally constituted association with fixed rules of membership—and discrete rules for identifying those entrusted with the interpretation of those rules—cannot be.

[70] I discuss the problems with functionalist pluralism in the next chapter and conclude, as have other scholars (Eisenberg, Nicholls) that Cole's version, at least, was in the end incompatible with political pluralism.

Shachar, in some of her later writing, makes this distinction explicit. When discussing the response of the state to 'religious-based claims for recognition, accommodation, and exemption'[71] she observes that:

> [w]hen it comes to clashes of religion and culture, arguments that move beyond requests for accommodation (or specific exemption from general laws) to attempts to advance alternative, extrajudicial moral or adjudicative orders appear to fall beyond the limits of tolerance. This is the dividing line where 'diversity as inclusion' ends and 'non-state law as competition' emerges, the latter often bringing with it the wrath of the state.[72]

The distinction between requests for accommodation of cultural norms and demands for recognition of non-state legal orders maps remarkably well onto the difference between culture and association under the theories of law that dominate contemporary jurisprudence. HLA Hart's discussion of law, for instance, refers to the rules of recognition, adjudication, and change acknowledged by a self-appointed body of legal officials.[73] John Gardner explains that '[i]t is no legal system if there are no institutions that are charged with resolving disputes that arise from the non-observance of the rules, or from the incompleteness or obscurity of the rules.'[74] Joseph Raz, likewise, defines legal norms as authoritative claims made by certain kinds of institutionalized normative systems, specifically those which contain adjudicative officials, by contrast with systems which, though normative, are not institutionalized.[75]

The difference is important when it comes to characterizing defections from adjudicative norms on a case by case basis. Simply put, it is possible to disobey an association, but it is not possible to disobey a culture. One may differ from one's fellows in one's interpretation of a cultural practice or in one's openness to hybridity or adherence to tradition, and one may even be 'unfaithful' to one's own understanding of a cultural practice, but there is no authority that can speak for a culture. Particular persons may claim authority derived from the culture to assume institutional authority—this is typically the case with patriarchal authorities which claim legitimacy from tradition—yet even these do not speak for the culture itself, and it is possible to distinguish between *disobeying* a patriarch and being judged '*unfaithful*' to a cultural tradition. Contrast this with disobedience in an associational context. Religious

[71] Ran Hirschl and Ayelet Shachar, 'The New Wall Of Separation: Permitting Diversity, Restricting Competition' [2009] 30(6) *Cardozo Law Review* 2535, 2536.

[72] Hirschl and Shachar, note 71, 2553.

[73] See HLA Hart, *The Concept of Law* (2nd edn) (Oxford University Press, 1994) 94–99.

[74] John Gardner, *Law as a Leap of Faith* (Oxford University Press, 2012) 257. See also Joseph Raz, *Practical Reason and Norms* (Oxford University Press, 1975) 141.

[75] Raz, note 74.

institutions are obviously the case in point: one can be unfaithful to a religious tradition, to be sure, but one can also flatly disobey the instruction of an ecclesiastical authority. If the authority is recognized by the rules of the institution with representing the religious association as such, then it is the association that assumes an authoritative standpoint vis-à-vis the adherent. In this way, an association is like a state, which is also capable of being disobeyed. Under these circumstances, in which there is a distinction between the cultural or religious tradition and the cultural or religious legal authority, it is possible for an individual to disobey the latter without defecting from the former. There is a contingency that may complicate this neat division. If a particular association has managed to capture the loyalty of the vast majority of members of a cultural or religious group, then disobedience will, for all practical purposes, be tantamount to defection.

This brings us to the second circumstance in which competition among authorities might not result in loss of membership: when the competing authority does not see defection on a sub-matter as disobedience. Interestingly, one of the scenarios where this kind of indifference might play out is when there is simply no possibility of defection from an association. Consider again Harold Berman's description of the transformative aspects of jurisdictional competition under conditions of legal pluralism in twelfth-century Europe:

> The very complexity of a common legal *order* containing diverse legal *systems* contributed to legal sophistication. Which court has jurisdiction? Which law is applicable? How are legal differences to be reconciled? . . . The pluralism of Western law, which has both reflected and reinforced the pluralism of Western political and economic life, has been, or once was, a source of development, or growth legal growth as well as political and economic growth. It also has been, or once was, a source of freedom. A serf might run to the town court for protection against his master. A vassal might run to the king's court for protection against his lord. A cleric might run to the ecclesiastical court for protection against the king.[76]

Before the Protestant Reformation, the jurisdiction of the church was coextensive with Christendom, and while defection was certainly possible—and punished as heresy or schism—the monopoly over religious authority did not require that loyalty be signalled by a choice between ecclesiastical and secular authority in each sub-matter.[77] The secular and ecclesiastical jurisdictions

[76] Berman, note 40, 9.

[77] One recalls here the judgment of Adam Smith, who observed that 'antient and established systems of which the clergy, reposing themselves upon their benefices, had neglected to keep up the fervour of faith and devotion in the great body of the people; and having given themselves up to indolence, were become altogether incapable of making any vigorous exertion in defence even of their own establishment.' Adam Smith, *An Inquiry into the Nature and Causes of the Wealth of Nations*, V.i.g. (Liberty Fund, 1976) 789.

competed for influence and patronage, and except for instances in which the stakes were enormous and the personages prominent—as in the dispute between Pope Gregory VII and the Holy Roman Emperor, which prompted many nobles and bishops to choose sides—defection from authority in a certain case did not amount to loss of membership. But with the pluralization of religious identity, the demand of loyalty has arguably increased. The kind of case-by-case autonomous determination of which norms will be binding on the religious citizen itself reveals a choice about religious identity. The kind of choice between normative authorities that a model like that of transformative accommodation envisions, where every sub-matter dispute is an instance of reflection on the bindingness of a norm, is an integral part of some religious traditions; it is, most clearly, the principled position of Reform Judaism. But for the orthodox—understanding the word in lower case, applicable to any religious tradition—it is a point of principle not to consider authority on a case-by-case basis, in which each sub-matter is an opportunity for choice. What to some is an emancipatory competition between jurisdictions, to others is lassitude, something like what some more conservative Roman Catholics have called 'Cafeteria Catholicism.' In fact, former Pope Benedict XVI made rather transparent suggestions to liberal Catholics to either abide by the entire teaching of the Magisterium—which means submitting to church teaching generally, not by sub-matter—or cease calling themselves Catholics. This policy may be changed by later pontiffs, but it nonetheless calls into question the assumption that religious (or for that matter, cultural) associations always strive for the continued loyalty of all their members; perhaps sometimes that are content to keep a smaller but more loyal core.[78]

An explanation of the intractability of conflict between associations that assert meta-jurisdictional authority is perhaps best explained by Andrei Marmor's institutional expansion on Joseph Raz's conception of authority. Marmor argues that 'the legitimacy of practical authorities depends on the nature and legitimacy of the particular social practice or institution that grants the authority the normative powers that it has.'[79] Therefore:

> the legitimacy of practical authorities cannot be detached from all these complex considerations that determine the legitimacy of the practices within which authorities operate. In other words, an authority is legitimate if and

[78] Or perhaps they perceive this as a temporary retreat, since there is some evidence that religious groups that demand stricter compliance from adherents (which currently means more conservative groups) experience greater growth than those that demand less. See generally D M Kelley, *Why Conservative Churches Are Growing: A Study in Sociology of Religion* (Harper Collins, 1972).

[79] Andrei Marmor, 'An Institutional Conception of Authority' [2011] 39(3) *Philosophy and Public Affairs* 238, 239.

> only if the particular practice or institution in which the authority operates is a practice that there are good reasons to have, all things considered.[80]

Raz acknowledges that there may be conflicts among authorities, in which case 'the question whether a given authority's power extends to exclude the authority of another is to be judged the way we judge the legitimacy of power on any matter, namely whether we would conform better to reason by trying to follow its directives than if we do not.'[81] But there is something circular about assertions of meta-jurisdictional authority, and it is a circularity that is not obviously vicious, but not easily escaped. It is participation in a practice that offers us reasons for action, and it is these reasons that help us identify the authorities by whose judgment we must abide. But authorities are often instrumental in defining the meaning and the boundaries of a practice, and participation in a practice is often defined precisely by submission to a given authority. To put it in crude and oversimplified terms, to be a Roman Catholic involves, at a constitutive level, submission to the Magisterium, the teaching function of the Church carried out by the Pope and the bishops. To deny this authority is not to be a bad Catholic; it is to be a Protestant. Likewise, to deny the binding authority of halakha (and of the battei din who interpret it) and assert the primacy of the individual conscience on matters of Jewish law is not to be a bad Orthodox Jew, but to be a Reform Jew. To submit questions of academic merit to political judgment not exclusive to professional peers, be it the criteria of a lone bureaucrat or the vote of the entire *demos*, is not to make a bad academic decision—for all we know the decision may be better on its merits than one made by one's academic peers—but to make a decision that is no longer academic. The determination of the authority that will decide on the merits of a controversy is prior to, or at least separate from, the judgment of the merits themselves.

We are brought back to the pluralist insight that there exists in all societies a foundational plurality of sources of authority which are incommensurable and present always the possibility of tragic loss. Such tragedy cannot be avoided through a movement towards the particular, towards specific areas of social interaction, because the meaning and boundaries of those areas are themselves constituted by the authorities that contest the loyalty of subjects. In the case of cultural membership, or of religious membership considered independently of membership in particular religious associations, the conflict between authorities is less clear, and allows for some negotiation because there is no final source that can define boundaries and meaning. So multiculturalism appears as an attractive theory to manage incommensurability and

[80] Marmor, note 79, 252.

[81] Joseph Raz, *Between Authority and Interpretation* (Oxford University Press, 2010) 143.

tragic loss only because it takes as its subject a different unit of analysis—the culture, the religion—and not the formally constituted association. But in the cases of interest to associational pluralists, the conflict between authorities, while it may be postponed in practice, cannot be avoided in principle and will inevitably surface, at least at the margin, just in those existential moments when the identity of a practice, and of the authorities that manage it, is at stake.

3

The Incompatibility of Subsidiarity

Even in the absence of cultural claims, and well outside the context of liberal accommodation, several other political paradigms recognize the existence of a variety of groups and associations that occupy the space between the individual and the state, groups that exist of their own right and may have different aims and purposes. These paradigms admit that some groups—like a guild—may be set up to regulate a profession and others—like a church—to provide spiritual or other guidance, and in either case they may not always agree on where to draw the boundaries between their various competencies. Unsurprisingly, some of these paradigms may be confused with associational pluralism, and judgment passed on the merits or demerits of pluralism by association with them, in the same way that an invocation of pluralism may elicit a reaction favourable or hostile to multiculturalism and thus miss the conceptual and normative mark.

In this chapter and the next I will deal with three paradigms that I find closely related in both spirit and policy, and which are sometimes implicitly, sometimes explicitly equated with associational pluralism. They are the principles of subsidiarity, the model of corporatism, and the theory of associational democracy. These three paradigms display the greatest superficial similarity to associational pluralism and indeed some invoke the early British pluralists in their intellectual lineage. Yet, all three are ultimately not merely different from (as in the case of multiculturalism), but incompatible with, associational pluralism. This is because none of these paradigms accepts the incommensurability of claims to authority or the inevitability of conflict. All three ultimately negate the foundational plurality, incommensurability of authority, and inevitability of conflict between associations. All three prevent associations from pursuing their own purposes and guiding the relationship between their members. Ultimately, all three effectively conscript associations and render them mere organs of the state.

3.1. BEFORE SUBSIDIARITY

Subsidiarity, corporatism, and associational pluralism are not abstract political arguments but active intellectual traditions, and no less so than pluralism. It is important to study their history in order to perceive their normative assumptions. But to have a point of reference, it is useful to give a barebones definition of each, even if the details of these definitions are contested at the margins. I take subsidiarity to be a principle of governance that allocates authority to the unit or level of governance closest to the individual, and which is able to effectively implement the desired aim of the political or social order. Corporatism is a model of economic and political organization in which state policy is both created and implemented through functionally differentiated groups that hold a representational monopoly over a discrete sector or interest. Associative democracy proposes to harness the organizational efficiencies of functionally- and territorially-differentiated associations in the formulation, coordination, and enforcement of policy in furtherance of democratically defined public purposes.

Some authors trace the origins of subsidiarity in some form to the earliest developments of Western political thought, finding equivalent political concepts as far back as the work of Aristotle.[1] Aristotle's discussion of the genealogy of the *polis*, for example, is heralded as a precursor of the modern notion that 'higher' or more complex levels of organization come into being to supplement the inadequacies of 'lower' or more basic modes. Aristotle begins *Politics* by considering the natural development of the city from 'a conjunction of persons who cannot exist without one another' and must associate in order to meet the needs of daily life. Among those are the household formed by the procreative couple and its attendant slaves;[2] the village, formed for the pooling of resources and the common defence; in addition to the city—the *polis*—which 'while coming into being for the sake of living... exists for the sake of living well.'[3]

There are two problems with the equivalence between subsidiarity and Aristotelian political teleology. The first is methodological and, I expect, controversial, but I don't intend to dwell on it. It has to do with the parallel that we may draw between the historical circumstances of Ancient Greece and those of twenty-first (or twentieth or even nineteenth) century European society. I have no interest in opening a debate over the relevance of the Greek *polis* to contemporary institutional arrangements. While there

[1] Chantal Millon-Delsol, *L'état Subsidiaire* (Presses Universitaires de France, 1992) 15–27. Paolo G Carozza, 'Subsidiarity as a Structural Principle of International Human Rights Law' (2003) 97 AJIL 40.

[2] Aristotle, *Politics* (C Lord tr.) (University of Chicago Press, 1984) 1252a25–1252b15.

[3] Aristotle, note 2, 1252b30.

are important lessons that we moderns may learn from the Ancients about the practice of democracy, the sources of authority, and the constancy of human nature, I find the institutional relevance of those lessons less and less intelligible as we move past the threshold of the twelfth century. The origins of the Western legal—and I would argue, political—tradition lie in the twelfth century, rather than in the early Middle Ages, Rome (whose relevance was interpreted for us, in part, by twelfth-century jurists), or Ancient Greece.[4] The lessons we may draw from more distant sources are too abstract for something as concrete as a principle of governance for a multi-level polity.

Yet, at the abstract level, the Aristotelian progression from family to *polis* highlights a deeper problem. There is in Aristotle an inverse relationship, as it were, between the chronological progression of levels of social ordering and the teleological primacy of those levels. In Aristotle, the *polis* may come last in time but it is first in moral and political importance. To be sure, Aristotle remarks that: 'The city is thus prior by nature to the household and to each of us. For the whole must of necessity be prior to the part.'[5] The insufficiency of lower levels of social ordering to meet certain demands of human flourishing naturally compels individuals to combine into more complex institutions that can meet those demands. Yet once the *polis* is achieved, these lower levels retain value only in being instrumental to the *polis*' preservation. The lower levels are in fact subsidiary to the higher, not the other way around, the task and power of each component serves the whole.[6] On that account, the Aristotelian *polis*, despite superficial similarities, is the opposite of subsidiarity and is closer to organicist or corporatist conceptions of the polity.[7] But on another account, which I will explain below, it merely points out the limitations of subsidiarity in securing genuine deference for forms of social organization within the nation state, whether regions or cities or other non-territorial forms of association.

Modern advocates of subsidiarity might find Althusius to be the intellectual fount of that tradition and (depending on one's favoured interpretation) of federalism, corporatism, associational democracy, and (for that matter) of political pluralism. Althusius' standing in the canon was neglected for centuries and was rebuilt on a series of 'recoverings' of his work from obscurity, first by Otto Gierke—through whom Althusius, translated by FW Maitland and later by Ernst Barker, inspired the British pluralist movement—and more

[4] On this point see, generally, HJ Berman, *Law and Revolution* (Harvard University Press, 1983).

[5] Aristotle, note 2, 1252a20.

[6] Aristotle, note 2, 1253a25.

[7] Part of the reason for this may be the structural limitations to political theorizing imposed by what, by our standards, was a world of relatively small city-states as opposed to nations of several million citizens. But, if that is the case, we are back to the question of relevance.

recently by Carl Friedrich.[8] From these recoverings was built his reputation as a defender of particular groups against centralizing encroachment. But much of this fame is the product of romance, and a close reading of his magnum opus yields precious little material on which to mount a defence of genuinely autonomous associations.

Althusius was a jurist and a politician, and ably integrated both roles into his theoretical and practical labours. He served for many years as a professor in the Herborn Academy, the premier Calvinist educational institution of his day, where he was known for defending university autonomy.[9] At Herborn, he also wrote and published the work that would make him famous, the *Politica Methodice Digesta*. The intellectual reputation he gained from the work secured him the position of syndic—a trustee or civil administrator—of the city of Emden, where he would eventually also be elected elder of the church.[10] As syndic, he guided the city through difficult negotiations with the local Count 'to assist Emden in achieving independent statehood.'[11] His political activities thus dovetailed in defence of academic and municipal autonomy quite well with his legal theory.

Althusius is a jurist, and the imprint of the legal scholar is present in the institutional emphasis and covenantal language in which he presents the association (*consociatio*). The general principle, he writes, that animates all social organization is 'symbiotic': individuals need each other 'for the purpose of establishing, cultivating, and conserving social life among them.'[12] Either of the two basic forms of association—the family and the *collegium*—'is a society and symbiosis initiated by a special covenant... among the members for the purpose of bringing together and holding in common a particular interest.'[13] Yet, the particular interest itself is 'communicated among the symbiotes' by the covenant—that is, it is actively and self-consciously shared by the members.[14] Political society is governed by norms not all of which are voluntary, but all of which are publicly acknowledged and sustained through institutionally-mediated practices. Ever larger and more complex social orders are constructed as a series of delegations from the lower to the higher bodies, not as a merely natural evolution.

[8] FS Carney, 'Translator's Introduction' in J Althusius, *Politica* (FS Carney (ed. and tr.)) (Liberty Fund, 1995) ix–x.

[9] Alain de Benoist, 'The First Federalist, Johannes Althusius' (2000) 118 *Telos* 25, 27.

[10] Carney, note 8, xii (All references to the *Politica* will be given inline and point to the chapter and section in the Carney translation).

[11] Stephen J Grabill, 'Introduction to "Selections from the Dicaeologicae"' (2006) 9(2) *Journal of Markets & Morality* 399, 404.

[12] Carney, note 8, 17, I§1.

[13] Carney, note 8, 27, II§2.

[14] Carney, note 8, IV§5.

At first glance, Althusius' political scheme is similar to Aristotle's, whose *Politics* he references early on. The family, for instance, is for both the most basic natural association[15]—as it is also for Althusius' foil, Jean Bodin, and for nearly every other political philosopher except, notably, Hobbes.[16] The natural association of the family stands alongside the civil association of the *collegium*, which is on the same plane as the household. In the *collegium*, 'three or more men of the same trade, training, or profession are united for the purpose of holding in common such things they jointly profess as duty, way of life, or craft'.[17] The model is clearly that of the medieval craft-guild and underscores Althusius' debt to the heritage of urban constitutional in the High Middle Ages. Yet, as Black observes, it does not, as the medieval did, consider group solidarity 'as simply given, instinctive, [and] implanted on human nature',[18] but rather a result of 'communication': of the sharing of goods, services, laws, and charity among the colleagues.[19]

As Friedrich observes, this would not be an unusual proposition when applied to 'private' bodies like households and craft-guilds.[20] But Althusius makes the symbiotic principle central to the transition from the private to the public associations: the city, the province, and the state.[21] Here, the distinctiveness of the Althusian political order—what endeared him to early pluralists, corporatists, and subsidiarists alike—comes to the fore. Althusius does not consider the citizens as members of the public *consociatio*; rather '[t]he members of a community are private and diverse associations of families and collegia, not the individual members of private associations.'[22] The same phenomenon is replicated between the city and the province (an association of cities, towns, and rural communes), and between the province and the commonwealth (a union of provinces and free cities). While each association has its own laws and exercises discipline over its members, only the commonwealth is called sovereign. But in an interesting reversal of Austin's formula, it is sovereign not because it habitually obeys no superior and is habitually obeyed by inferiors, but because it is authorized by every other association in the realm and authorizes no further association in turn.

Contrary to the absolutists, the private and public associations owe their existence not to authorization by the state, but by their own communion or special covenant. This, for Althusius, is because 'families, cities, and provinces existed by nature prior to realms, and gave birth to them'.[23] The terms by which the commonwealth is governed—the right of the realm—is the tacit or

[15] Carney, note 8, II§13.

[16] Thomas Hobbes, *Leviathan* (Hackett, 1994) 128.

[17] Carney, note 8, 34, IV§4.

[18] Antony Black, *Guild and State* (Transaction Publishers, 2003) 133.

[19] Carney, note 8, 34–35, IV§8.

[20] Carl Friedrich, Introduction to Althusius' *Politica Methodice Digesta* (Harvard University Press, 1932) lxxxiv.

[21] Carney, note 8, V§6, VI§15.

[22] Carney, note 8, V§10.

[23] Carney, note 8, IX§3.

express agreement to communicate goods, services, laws, and charity among them. But this gives rise to two competing impulses which permeate all of Althusius' intellectual progeny. On the one hand, the component members of a realm have an independent origin; they exhibit what I have called 'foundational plurality' in the first chapter. The right of the realm is the product of a constitutional deliberation among the associations that come to form a commonwealth, which explains why Althusius' theory has been taken as a model for federalism. This puts Althusius in direct conflict with Bodin (against whom he argues throughout the *Politica*), for whom inferior political bodies, although historically prior to the sovereign, owe their continued existence to his acquiescence. In a properly ordered Althusian commonwealth, however, these intermediate bodies are guaranteed at least a certain institutional integrity.

Althusius contradicts Bodin by recognizing that the authority of the prince is, by definition, constituted and thus bound by 'civil law and right'.[24] Sovereignty is not a product of will but of law: 'the king, prince, and optimates, recognize this associated body as their superior, by which they are constituted, removed, exiled, and deprived of authority'[25] and later '[the] supreme magistrate' is called supreme in relation to individuals. But he is not supreme in relation to his subjects collectively, nor to law, to which he is himself subject.[26] This gives some protection to the minor associations, insofar as their sphere of activity may be constitutionally enshrined.

Thomas Hueglin also suggests a possible kinship between Althusius' attribution of sovereignty—'[t]he people, or the associated members of the realm'[27] —and Rousseau's defence of popular sovereignty,[28] but he finds Gierke's enthusiasm for the parallel to be disproportionate and 'certainly overdrawn'.[29] Rousseau, after all, seeks to dissolve all political allegiance except the allegiance of the individual to the state. 'It is therefore essential' he writes, 'if the general will is to be able to express itself, that there should be no partial society within the State, and that each citizen should think only his own thoughts.'[30] And this leaves the government—that is, what Althusius calls the administrative power—as the only permissible intermediate association, '[a]n intermediate body set up between the subjects and the Sovereign, to secure their mutual correspondence, charged with the execution of the laws and the maintenance of liberty, both civil and political.'[31] Althusius'

[24] Carney, note 8, IX§21. [25] Carney, note 8, IX§22. [26] Carney, note 8, XIX§4.

[27] Carney, note 8, IX§16, 70.

[28] Jean-Jacques Rousseau, *The Social Contract* (V Gourevitch (ed.)) (Cambridge University Press, 1997).

[29] Thomas O Hueglin, *Early Modern Concepts for a Late Modern World: Althusius on Community and Federalism* (Wilfrid Laurier University Press, 1999) 17–18.

[30] Rousseau, note 28, Bk 2, chapter 3.

[31] Rousseau, note 28, Bk 3, chapter 1. We are not far here from the radical republicanism of Emile Combes, Prime Minister of the Third French Republic and principal architect of the 1905 anticlerical law

language is superficially similar to Rousseau's, but in the context of the political structure he prescribes, it acquires a different tenor. Rousseau's compact is a union of unmediated individuals, while Althusius' is one of nestled associations. The Althusian people is not an association of individuals, but rather of other associations which are in turn composed of other groups. The individual is not a party to the final compact which established political sovereignty.

There is a sense in which the Althusian apparatus can be read as the application of the principle of subsidiarity to constitutionalism itself (as opposed to principles of governance within a state): the larger or higher levels of political organization are set up in order to regulate exchange among the smaller or lower levels, as this benefits those smaller associations and cannot be accomplished through unilateral action. Føllesdal argues that, in Althusius, '[t]he role of the state is not to regulate a political sphere separate from the social communities but to coordinate and secure their common purposes in a symbiosis.'[32] This may, in extreme circumstances, allow the component parts to rebel or secede if the terms of the commonwealth are violated or the interests of the association are not met.[33]

On the other hand, the entire Althusian architecture is hierarchically structured, even if the construction starts at the bottom and not the top. 'Each association', writes Føllesdal, 'claims autonomy within its own sphere against intervention by other associations';[34] but this applies only to associations on the same level, as none can claim exemption from the right of the realm. The institution of sovereignty operates in a way that denies independent agency to any association except in relation to very local interests. And even then, both their internal laws and the external activities of the private and public groups are determined by their function, which is subordinated to one common conception of human flourishing that admits no deviation. This leads Friedrich, against Gierke, to place Althusius firmly in the absolutist camp. According to Friedrich:

> In the last analysis, all activities of the citizens are permeated by this spirit of cooperation and are directed towards the common good. The government turns out to be nothing more nor less than the effort to integrate all these activities. The non-governmental functions are called private, simply because they serve first a private symbiotic group (not an individual!). What Althusius is setting forth is the theory of a corporative state. This state is characterized by the fact that in the last analysis it devours the entire community, becomes one with it.[35]

of Separation of Church and State: 'There are, there can be no rights except the right of the State, and there are, and there can be no other authority than the authority of the Republic'. See Figgis, *Churches in the Modern State* (Thoemmes Press, 1997) 56.

[32] Andreas Føllesdal, 'Subsidiarity' (1990) 6(2) *Journal of Political Philosophy* 190, 201.

[33] Carney, note 8, at XXXVIII§76.

[34] Føllesdal, note 32, at 201.

[35] Friedrich, note 20, lxxxvi.

Gierke sought to make Althusius the standard bearer of an indigenous Germanic political tradition centred on the autonomy and personality of the *Genossenschaft*, or fellowship.[36] Friedrich sought in Althusius an explanation for the transition from scholasticism to modern political science, one that showed the complexity and ambivalence involved in the consolidation of authority in the hands of the modern nation state.[37] Each of these recoveries has yielded valuable information about the transition from late medieval to early modern political theory, and opened up new possibilities in theorizing sovereignty, community, and society. And each has clarified, or at least enlarged, our understanding of the work of Althusius and the critique of the orthodox conception of sovereignty as a process of consolidation of state power at the top and, at best, top-down authorization of subordinate and anodyne voluntary groups at the bottom of the social structure. But while most scholars agree that Althusius must stand at the beginning of some theoretical genealogy, none agree on which is his legitimate heir.[38]

The question is rather pointless, however, since what is most interesting about these various positions (regardless of their genealogy) is the resemblance they bear to each other. They are characterized by what Henrik Enroth has referred to as an overarching preoccupation with finding 'some supposedly more comprehensive or fundamental sources of shared interest or identity, whether actual or potential, present or future, in order to maintain unity in plurality.'[39] Insofar as political pluralism is indebted to the same aspirations and assumptions about a final reconciliation between competing authorities, it is also constrained, as Enroth observes, in its 'capacity for empirical and normative inquiry into current forms of human belonging and interaction.'[40]

[36] Otto Gierke, *Political Theories of the Middle Age* (FW Maitland (tr.)) (Cambridge University Press, 1900); also PQ Hirst, *The Pluralist Theory of the State* (Routledge, 1993) 17.

[37] Friedrich, note 20, xcix.

[38] Gierke claims him for German fellowships but, at the same time, for the Second German Reich. M Dreyer, 'German Roots of the Theory of Pluralism' (1993) 4(1) *Constitutional Political Economy* 7–39. Figgis takes him to propose a federalistic social order, while Elazar embraces him as a federal republican. JN Figgis, *Political Thought from Gerson to Grotius* (Harper Torchbook, 1960) 234; D Elazar, 'Althusius' Grand Design for a Federal Commonwealth' in Althusius' *Politica* (FS Carney (tr. and ed.)) (Liberty Fund, 1995) xxxv-xlvi. Friedrich criticizes him a corporatist, while Black approves of him on the same account. CJ Friedrich, Introduction to Althusius' *Politica Methodice Digesta* (Harvard University Press, 1932), Antony Black, *Guild and State* (Transaction Publishers, 2003) 141. And Hueglin ingeniously traces the lineage of Althusian thought from Gierke, to Otto Bauer, through Michael Walzer to Iris Marion Young, and also points to the debt that associative democrats owe to the German jurist. Ossewarde, by contrast (and with some historical and theological justification), opposes Althusius both to the defenders of absolute sovereignty *and* to the advocates of subsidiarity, placing him instead in the Calvinist tradition of 'sphere sovereignty'. MRR Ossewarde, 'Three Rival Versions of Political Enquiry: Althusius and the Concept of Sphere Sovereignty' (2007) *The Monist* 90(1) 106.

[39] Henrick Enroth, 'Beyond Unity in Plurality: Rethinking the Pluralist Legacy' (2010) 9(4) *Contemporary Political Theory* 458–76, 459.

[40] Enroth, note 39.

Enroth thinks that we must move altogether beyond the pluralist legacy in order to face up to radical difference. I believe that it is sufficient to expunge from pluralism some organicistic assumptions about the natural harmony of human ends and focus instead on the juridical claims of various institutional authorities. But this change of focus passes through rejection of the principal contemporary claimants of the pluralist legacy.

The three political paradigms I discuss in this chapter have a natural affinity with associational pluralism, but are ultimately incompatible with it. Subsidiarity is concerned both with efficient allocation of socially beneficial functions and with local and (sometimes) democratic control over political and economic decisions. Corporatism aims at robust national unity and common purpose. Associative democracy is concerned with opening spaces of participation to individuals through their various allegiances and social roles, and in resisting concentrations of power. But each of these paradigms stands opposed to genuine associational autonomy, and thus to political pluralism, because each subordinates all associations to a set of priorities and a standard of value determined by an authority external to themselves.

3.2. THE PRINCIPLE OF SUBSIDIARITY

The principle of subsidiarity is more familiar to European than North American audiences, although it has received so much attention in academic circles as to produce an intellectual growth industry. The content of the term is somewhat disputed but, as I stated before, it essentially mandates that authority be allocated to that unit or level of governance closest to the individual which is able to effectively implement the desired aim. Føllesdal calls this the condition of 'comparative efficiency', and notes that: 'The central unit must secure the desired outcomes better than the sub-units, due to differential ability or willingness or both.'[41] The meaning of this condition can be contested along two axes: On the first, authority may be allocated to the 'higher' or central unit only when the 'lower' sub-unit is wholly incapable of meeting the condition of comparative efficiency, or it may be allowed whenever the central unit can do a better job at meeting the condition. On the second, '[t]he principle of subsidiarity can *proscribe* central unit action in the absence of comparative efficiency' or, '[a]lternatively, intervention from the central unit may be *required* when it is comparatively more efficient.'[42] In both axes, the first option preserves the authority of the lower units while the second favours centralization.

[41] Føllesdal, note 32, 193.

[42] Føllesdal, note 32, 195.

Yet, besides these inquiries into the content of the principle of subsidiarity, there is the further question of who gets to decide whether an allocation of authority meets the condition of comparative efficiency. Føllesdal considers the question of 'who decides' as an issue of application and gives three options: the sub-unit, the central unit, or some qualified majority of units or individuals.[43] It is interesting to characterize the question of who decides as an issue of application to be determined against the background of a shared principle of governance and a shared conception of the good to be pursued by that governance. Methodologically, it underscores the degree of unity that a political order must possess before the principle of subsidiarity is invoked, a unity reflected at the level of mutual commitment (common governance) and of substantive values (common purpose). I will return to this point later, because it is at the heart of the distinction between pluralism on the one hand, and subsidiarity, corporatism, or associative democracy on the other.

Subsidiarity, in its modern form, is first articulated in Roman Catholic social thought. Given the insistence with which the Church has guarded its institutional autonomy, and the paradigmatic status of religious groups in the pluralist imagination, it would seem reasonable to presume compatibility, and perhaps mutual support, between subsidiarity and pluralism. Yet, subsidiarity as a principle of governance is fundamentally incompatible with the pluralist thesis. It is also in an internal tension with the political autonomy that the Roman Catholic Church has proclaimed for itself over the centuries.

The Catholic principle of subsidiarity prescribes not only the structure of church governance from the papal to the parish levels, but also the proper role of secular government and the distinction between spiritual and temporal social functions. Originally proposed in Pius XI's 1931 encyclical *Quadragesimo Anno*,[44] it is in many ways continuous with a tradition of Catholic theory going back to Pope Gelasius in the fifth century, through Gregory VII in the eleventh, and Leo XIII in the nineteenth.[45] The debt to Leo is especially great—*Quadragesimo Anno*, after all, was written to commemorate the fortieth anniversary of *Rerum Novarum*, Leo's 1891 letter. But there are important deviations in substance and emphasis between these two encyclicals which have been greatly underestimated.

There was no call for subsidiarity in *Rerum Novarum*, or any specific institutional or functional prescription for social order, but there was a public philosophy conceived as an alternative to both revolutionary socialism and

[43] Føllesdal, note 32, 197.

[44] Pius XI, *Quaddragessimo Anno* (1931). Subsequent references are given parenthetically in the text.

[45] Leo XIII, *Rerum Novarum* (1891). Subsequent references are given parenthetically in the text.

industrial capitalism. The state is instructed 'to realize public well-being and private prosperity' for the benefit of all members of society, with a special emphasis on the need to protect the poor.[46] This is the most cited legacy of the papal letter. Yet, even in its advocacy of workers, the bulk of the argument takes the form of a spirited and radical defence of associational autonomy. The dignity of the poor is preserved, writes Leo, through the formation of 'workingmen's unions'.[47] The Pope had in mind mainly religious labour organizations, but, invoking the authority of Thomas Aquinas, he extended the principle more broadly to protect the institutional integrity of private associations. According to Leo:

> Private societies, then, although they exist within the body politic, and are severally part of the commonwealth, cannot nevertheless be absolutely, and as such, prohibited by public authority. For, to enter into a 'society' of this kind is the natural right of man; and the State has for its office to protect natural rights, not to destroy them; and, if it forbid its citizens to form associations, it contradicts the very principle of its own existence, for both they and it exist in virtue of the like principle, namely, the natural tendency of man to dwell in society.[48]

The internal deliberations of these associations, and the rules that held among their members are also outside of the authority of the state, as they emerge from the joint practice of members. As stated in the letter: 'The State should watch over these societies of citizens banded together in accordance with their rights, but it should not thrust itself into their peculiar concerns and their organization.'[49] In the case of religious associations, moreover, '[i]n their religious aspect they claim rightly to be responsible to the Church alone. The rulers of the State accordingly have no rights over them, nor can they claim any share in their control.'[50] The claim of separate and autonomous authority for private groups, and especially for the Church over the 'religious aspect' of associations, is consistent with Leo's longer treatment of ecclesiastical autonomy in *Immortale Dei* (1885). Despite his overblown condemnation of the non-confessional state (a position since rejected by the Second Vatican Council), he also affirms 'this authority, perfect in itself, and plainly meant to be unfettered…[which] the Church has never ceased to claim for herself and openly to exercise.'[51] He also recommends that, even when the state

[46] 'Still, when there is question of defending the rights of individuals, the poor and badly off have a claim to especial consideration.' *RN* ¶37. This doctrine would eventually take the form of the 'preferential option for the poor' e.g. in Pontifical Council for Justice and Peace, *Compendium of the Social Doctrine of the Church*, available at: <http://www.vatican.va/roman_curia/pontifical_councils/justpeace/documents/rc_pc_justpeace_doc_20060526_compendio-dott-soc_en.html#The universal destination of goods and the preferential option for the poor> 182ff.

[47] Leo XIII, note 45.

[48] Leo XIII, note 45, para 51.

[49] Leo XIII, note 45, para 55.

[50] Leo XIII, note 45, para 53.

[51] *Immortale Dei*, para 12.

does not conform with Catholic doctrine, it is still possible to achieve 'peace and liberty' through agreement between the two authorities,[52] which usually takes the form of a treaty or concordat.

Most authors, including Føllesdal, do not question the continuity of Catholic social teaching from the encyclicals of Leo XIII to those of Pius XI. There is a common doctrine that connects them, but in *Rerum Novarum* and *Immortale Dei* the emphasis is clearly put on the independence of religious institutions and the conflicts that may result from the simultaneous assertion of authority by two different bodies. *Quadragesimo Anno*, by contrast, assumes a clean functional differentiation of social roles and promotes the organic coordination of social functions. The change of emphasis, 40 years later, justifies a principle of governance that, when broadly applied, cannot sustain associational autonomy.

It is interesting to note that subsidiarity emerges as a distinct political doctrine just as political pluralism is losing ground in Britain. Yet, it is animated by the same concerns, namely the relationship between labour and capital and the claims being pressed by trade unions and workers' organizations—claims that had similarly inspired John Figgis and Harold Laski in the wake of the *Taff Vale* decision.[53] But where the political pluralists discern conflict and opposition between the interests of the state and those of other associations—particularly associations that were animated by different principles and purposes than those which justified the liberal democratic state—Pius seeks 'harmonious cooperation of the Industries and Professions.'[54] To do this, he proposes, authority should be devolved insofar as practicable, to local jurisdictions and functional groups, so that decisions are taken at the closest practicable level to the individual. In Pius' words:

> The supreme authority of the State ought, therefore, to let subordinate groups handle matters and concerns of lesser importance, which would otherwise dissipate its efforts greatly. Thereby the State will more freely, powerfully, and effectively do all those things that belong to it alone because it alone can do them: directing, watching, urging, restraining, as occasion requires and necessity demands. Therefore, those in power should be sure that the more perfectly a graduated order is kept among the various associations, in observance of the principle of 'subsidiary function', the stronger social authority and effectiveness will be the happier and more prosperous the condition of the State.[55]

[52] *Immortale Dei*, para 15.

[53] *Taff Vale Railway Co v. Amalgamated Society of Railway Servants* [1901] UKHL 1 held that a labour union (as opposed to its members individually) was liable for the employer's losses in the course of a labour strike. The decision was unpopular with the unions, as it subjected them to tort liability, but pluralists like Laski and Figgis lauded it because it implicitly recognized the legal personality of the union, its status as a corporate group.

[54] Pius XI, note 44, para 81.

[55] Pius XI, note 44, para 80.

It is important to note that Pius, like Leo, understands the 'subordinate groups' to emerge through the collaborative effort of their members, and thus not be creations of the state. Their existence is not questioned, only their relative competence and social functions. But the language in Pius' encyclical is very different as it regards the judge of that competence and function. In the absence of jurisdictional boundaries, it is the state that determines when a group may act and when it may be interfered with. Thus, the turn towards subsidiarity represents a significant concession to the state's authority to interfere in the scope and competence of associational authority. The role of the association in the development of human flourishing is unchanged from the encyclicals of Leo XIII, but Pius allows a greater capacity for the state to determine the proper function of each group and enforce coordination over competition, harmony over disagreement.

Paolo Carozza expresses a majority consensus when he writes that '[i]n his encyclical *Quadragesimo Anno,* Pius reformulated the *Rerum Novarum* principle of intervention-but-not-interference with a decidedly stronger emphasis on the limits of public authority.'[56] I disagree. Leo's explanation of the autonomy of associations, and especially religious associations, has a decidedly jurisdictional bent. It recognizes that an association may have religious and economic aspects, and that these may fall under different—and competing—authorities, and is categorical in denying the right of the state to intervene in the internal affairs of a group. Pius' formulation of subsidiarity, by contrast, is infused in functionalist and organicist language. It is a policy for a thoroughly cohesive society, united behind an uncontroversial and uncontested understanding of the common good and governed by also uncontested arbiters of efficiency and competence. Where these conditions are met—as in a purposive hierarchical organization like the Roman Catholic Church—subsidiarity can guide authorities in the allocation of competencies. But when different authorities compete for the allegiance of subjects and simultaneously assert claims over the same domain, subsidiarity will be at best ineffective, at worst centralizing and suppressive of genuine and legitimate expressions of associational loyalty.

Leo defends private associations in fairly stark jurisdictional terms; Pius turns this into a principle of good governance where the determination of the proper allocation of authority depends on a judgment of who will be most effective. So while it looks like the state serves associations in the latter case, where it only stayed away before, in fact subsidiarity gives the state licence to intervene. Under subsidiary, it is the state that ultimately decides on the merits of the allocation, and there are no strong jurisdictional constraints to keep it from interfering.

[56] See Carozza, note 1, 41.

There are two problems with the turn away from the jurisdictional constraints suggested by Leo XIII and towards the principle of governance proposed by Pius XI, one substantive, the other structural. Substantively, as Føllesdal explains, the Catholic conception of subsidiarity rests 'on contested views of the social order and of human flourishing, along with a correspondingly controversial view of personal autonomy.' He continues:

> These assumptions guide the choice of units of association, determine their legitimate activity and set standards of comparative efficiency. Once these assumptions are called into question, the theory can neither settle issues concerning the domain of sub-units nor identify their legitimate powers, which are among the contested political issues within the EU and elsewhere.[57]

It would be easy to dismiss this critique if the principle of subsidiarity was only a Catholic conundrum; if subsidiarity demands adherence to the Catholic conception of the person, it is inapplicable to any society in which there is significant disagreement with the Magisterium, either within or outside the Church.[58] But the critique applies in whatever context subsidiarity is invoked, whether the principle is justified on religious grounds, or grounds of utilitarian efficiency or of participative democracy. For the principle to serve as a guide of comparative efficiency there must be agreement over desired outcomes across all levels of the social order; absent such agreement, it is not clear what there is to be efficient about. Agreement can be secured by a mere social fact (we come to agree about our collective priorities) or, more likely, it is guided by a mutually accepted authority (the church, or the state, or the party decides what the desired outcome is). If there are multiple arbiters of what a desired social outcome is, subsidiarity cannot be invoked to resolve a dispute. It may be possible to negotiate or bargain over the desired outcome, or to simply impose one on all parties, but the reasons for negotiation or imposition will have nothing to do with comparative efficiency, as they are prior to all judgments of efficiency.

Even if we put aside the substantive problem of the controversial assumptions of Catholic subsidiarity, we still face the question of who decides which unit is most capable of applying a certain policy, or achieving a desired social end, which leads to a structural problem with the principle of subsidiarity. The substantive question of what is the desired outcome of social policy is determined in large part by the question of who gets to decide what that outcome will be. It may seem that this is a question about disagreements about values or ultimate ends, but this is not the case. Two different social units may be in complete agreement over the desired end of policy, and may even agree on the means to implement it, but this does not imply that they agree on which of the two

[57] Føllesdal, note 32, 209.

[58] The Magisterium is the teaching authority of the Church, exercised by the Pope and the bishops: *Catechism of the Catholic Church* (2nd edn) (Libreria Editrice Vaticana, 1993) §§2032–40.

should decide these matters were a future disagreement to arise. Disagreements about ends are not the only foundational disagreements. Disagreements about the role, power, and identity of the agents charged with setting, interpreting, and applying those ends can be just as genuine and just as deep.[59]

As I mentioned at section 3.1, Føllesdal considers this a problem of application. And in a sense, he is correct, but this only highlights the fact that subsidiarity as usually understood—as a criterion for deciding the proper assignment of authority in a given case—is not a principle through which to organize a polity, but rather a principle by which to govern a polity already organized, in which ultimate arbitral authority is settled. In contrasting subsidiarity with federalism, which is a system of entrenched jurisdictional limits, Jacob Levy complains that '[s]ubsidiarity may offer a useful critical language, but it fails as an institutional decision rule.' For Levy:

> Subsidiarity calls for case-by-case, issue-by-issue determination of how local a level of government can make a particular decision; this is exactly the wrong way to approach jurisdictional questions in general and constitutional-level institutional design in particular. It presumes a fantastic level of competence, knowledge, and disinterestedness on the part of the body that *allocates* decision-making authority in each case—itself usually one of the contenders for the authority at stake.[60]

There are several lines of criticism here, and I will leave aside the (correct) assertion that subsidiarity demands certain epistemic and moral virtues on the part of the arbiter, usually the state, that it is unreasonable to presume. Yet even if such competence were available, the problem of authority is not resolved, but only pushed back. The allocation of authority to the comparatively most efficient unit involves a number of substantive judgments for which subsidiarity provides no guide, since the authority to make these judgments must be prior to all decisions about comparative efficiency. Before deciding which unit can best implement a desired outcome, someone must decide what that outcome should be. The unit to decide what that outcome should be cannot be the unit that is comparatively most efficient at correctly deciding outcomes; that would either demand another level of subsidiary arbitration, or make the allocation of authority to decide dependent on the correctness of the decision. And, as Levy points out in another context:

> In general, institutionalized decision rules cannot function if, in order to know who has the authority to decide a particular question, the merits of the

[59] To say that the desired outcome should be decided democratically just begs the question, since the foundational assumptions of democratic politics are no less controversial or unclear: Who constitutes the *polis*? What, if any, are the limits of its power? And does its authority admit of delegation division?

[60] Jacob Levy, 'Federalism, Liberalism, and the Separation of Loyalties' (2007) *American Political Science Review* 101(3) 459, 462.

> question must first be decided. The prior determination of the merits of the question must vest in some agent, and we need rules to determine *that* agent. No procedure can rely, all the way down, on settling the question of who is right in order to decide the question of *who may decide who is right*.[61]

The two problems of subsidiarity relate to its two assumptions: that all groups involved in an institution jointly and publicly accept a determinate conception of the good or a hierarchy of values, and that they jointly and publicly accept a common arbiter or a fixed process for authoritatively adjudicating disputes over the application of this aim. In reality the two problems are one and the same: who decides the ends and means of policy, and where does ultimate authority lie. Subsidiarity can only apply if this question is settled, and subsidiarity itself cannot settle it.

Moreover, if one begins by acknowledging that a plurality of claims to legitimate authority is a social fact—that the question of ultimate authority is not settled—the assumptions entailed by the principle of subsidiarity do not apply, at least in relations among groups. It may hold within those organizations that, like the Catholic Church, already share a common end (or, through the Magisterium, recognize the authority that is to identify this end) and already have a clearly defined structure for authoritatively adjudicating disputes over competency; but between such a group and the state, the disputes are about foundational categories, not about application. Leo XIII considers this when he asserts that religious associations '[i]n their religious aspect . . . claim rightly to be responsible to the Church alone.'[62] Presumably, in their non-religious aspect they may be responsible to the state. But who determines if a certain aspect—an activity or domain—is religious or not? When a Roman Catholic hospital refuses to prescribe contraception or perform abortion procedures, the nature of the hospital is disputed; the church deems it an extension of its ministerial function, while the state views it as a participant in the health care industry. It may well be both, but which rules and exemptions apply to it depends not so much on the merits of the question, but on the authority that determines what the relevant question is.[63]

[61] Jacob Levy, 'Self-Determination, Non-Domination, and Federalism' (2008) 23(3) *Hypatia* 60, 70 (Internal citations omitted). The context was a posthumous debate with Iris Marion Young over the proper foundations of federalism. In her last works, Young advocated grounding federal jurisdiction on a neo-republican principle of non-domination, while Levy defended a principle of non-interference. See Iris Marion Young, *Global Challenges* (Polity, 2007) Part I.

[62] Leo XIII, note 45.

[63] Levy addresses this question, also in the context of Iris Young's position evolving regarding protection of oppressed groups.

> The group veto, as [Young] described it, requires a determination that some particular proposal is properly within the domain of one oppressed group's decision-making authority. It requires that someone be able to decide, authoritatively, that abortion is relevantly a women's issue. But this just is to decide the merits; if abortion is in that sense a women's issue—and not, for example, a

Likewise, when a university committee denies tenure to a candidate, or expels a student for a disciplinary infraction, or imposes membership criteria to recognized student associations, the issue may be framed as one of the freedom of the academic institution, or of the scholarly community more generally, to adhere to academic standards. It may also be framed as a labour dispute, or a controversy over contractual expectations, or a violation of freedom of association, and even in the last case there is a question of whether the relevant level of association is the student club, the university, or the broader political society. Or when a trade association—especially one in a field like law or medicine, in which professional self-governance is well established—decides to set rules for training and admission of candidates to the profession, or attempts to discipline a member, again the question can be one of professional standards and ethical obligations, or it may be one of barriers to entry or consumer protection. Turning slightly away from associations and towards territorial units, restrictions on the language of commerce or stringent criteria over trademarks can be understood as matters of domestic policy pertaining to cultural protection or as underhanded tariffs and barriers to interstate commerce. They can, of course, be both, but their legitimacy or illegitimacy often turns on whether they are within the purview of local, national, or transnational authority.

To categorically decide in favour of the state denies that the group has any real authority, identity, and claim on its members, or at least that the claim of the state is prima facie superior to that of the group. Even groups with a narrow scope and moderate to weak claims to allegiance can plausibly claim that, at some margin, state intervention is illegitimate; this is often the case when the state interferes with academics' curricular decisions, appointments process, or research funding criteria.[64] The power to determine the nature of an activity or domain, that is, to decide whether it falls under the authority of one unit or another—whether that unit is a church, a university, or a local government—goes beyond what subsidiarity as a paradigm can provide. The claims that groups like churches, academic communities, and professional associations make involve not only the capacity to act within the domain permitted by the state, but also the capacity to determine the boundaries of that domain, sometimes at the core, but often at the margins where many jurisdictional disputes are contested.

women's-and-fetuses' issue—then of course it must be legal. Or consider a proposal to regulate how a minority religion may treat women members. Deciding *which* oppressed group, the religion or women, has the right to wield a veto requires deciding the moral substance of the question. What agency will do that? May that determination itself be subject to group vetoes? If so, how does one know which groups, at that level? (Levy, note 61, 70).

[64] I take the categories of wide, mid-range, and narrow scope and strong, moderate, and weak claims of allegiance from Rogers Smith, *Stories of Peoplehood* (Cambridge University Press, 2003) 19–32.

Yet, the very contestation of jurisdictional boundaries indicates that the conflict between different claims to authority is more complicated than a problem of interpretation of where the 'real' boundaries are. The boundaries themselves (not just their interpretation) are contested, and this points to a different kind of authority. Daniel Weinstock, in reference to one such (often overlooked) association—the city—refers to this (following Buchanan) as *meta-jurisdictional* autonomy, which is a second-order power that involves 'not only . . . self-determination over certain defined policy areas, but . . . some say as to what the policy domains over which it has jurisdiction are (and perhaps the domains over which it shares jurisdiction with other political entities).'[65] It is this kind of authority that churches, academic communities, and professional associations often make, yet it is a kind of authority that the principle of subsidiarity cannot account for. It is rather the kind of authority that the pluralist tradition refers to under the rubric of sovereignty, and acknowledges as inextricably plural. Subsidiarity can account for foundational plurality, but it presumes that there is an authority that can commensurate all the competing claims and allot competence accordingly. Now, this may be possible in a discrete association where purposes are shared and authority uncontested. But it is not the case in a society where different groups make competing claims to authority over overlapping fields. This desire to commensurate claims and arbitrate away conflicts is the same conceit that Henrik Enroth criticizes as a fixation with unity in plurality. It is both a mistaken impression of the structure of our social world, and an unjustified attempt to pave over it.

3.3 A WORD ON THE EUROPEAN UNION

The development of the principle of subsidiarity in the European Union (EU) offers a more contemporary view of the different and incompatible structures of pluralism and subsidiarity. There are, to be sure, some important differences between the way that subsidiarity operates among nation states whose sovereignty is assumed as a default position in international law, and the way that it is intended to operate at a domestic level.

One important distinction is that both EU and its component states are territorial authorities, and all operate under the principles, however modified through treaties and constitutional conventions, of territorial state sovereignty. Associations within a national state, however, are not territorial

[65] Daniel Weinstock, 'Self-Determination for (Some) Cities?' in A Gosseries and Y Vanderborght (eds), *Arguing about Justice* (Presses Universitaires de Louvain, 2011) 377–78. The term was introduced by Buchanan in 'The Making and Unmaking of Boundaries: What Liberalism has to Say' in A Buchanan and M Moore (eds), *States Nations, and Borders: The Ethics of Making Boundaries* (Cambridge University Press, 2003) 231–61.

entities, but operate on a principle closer to that of personal jurisdiction over their members. Even if the largest associations operate internally under some territorial principle—the church diocese is the most obvious example—membership in the organization does not compete with the state at the same level. Rather, an individual within the territorial boundaries of a state and, through citizenship or equivalent status, presumably subject to its authority, can be as much under the authority of his association as a fellow member in a different state. Questions of membership and authority overflow boundaries and it is difficult to create mechanisms of representation that apply to the same population. In addition, the association's history may predate that of the state, and neither may be said to originate in the other, either historically or in their respective legitimating narratives. This makes questions about delegation or conferral of authority more difficult. Of course, in many cases, no such delegation or conferral occurs and both the association and the state assert a claim of sovereignty over the same population which results in a condition of deep pluralism.

As I discussed in the previous section, the invocation of subsidiarity under conditions of deep pluralism is either irrelevant to the drawing of jurisdictional boundaries between various authorities, or else is not neutral between their claims but presumes that one of these authorities will be the final arbiter of the desired outcome of social policy and the unit most capable of carrying it out. I am careful to make this simply a judgment about incompatibility between two different principles; it is not a denunciation of subsidiarity itself. In a context in which purposes are shared across an organization and structures of authority are uncontested, it may prove an important corrective to heavy-handed action by the highest-placed officials. But in cases where these criteria are absent, subsidiarity is not a neutral principle, but rather pulls in one of two opposite directions: either to a confederal pluralism or, as is more likely, towards a centralization of decisional power. In this sense, the same central concern that distinguished pluralism and subsidiarity and makes the latter incompatible with the former is evident in the operation of the principle at the EU level.

The assessment of subsidiarity in the EU requires a brief excursus into what may be referred to as the ontology of Europe. The standard account of the EU is that it is a union of sovereign nation-states and that the authority of the EU is delegated by the national states, so that there is no problem of foundational plurality.[66] The relationship between European citizenship and

[66] Although it is possible to claim, as José Ortega y Gasset did in his scattered but prescient essays on Europe and nationalism, that the idea of a European state has some cultural priority to the nation state. A fascinating passage in Ortega y Gasset's collected notes lays out an argument structurally similar to that of the pluralists, although aimed at the identification of a common European authority rather than the recognition of a multiplicity of national states (and thus, on some level, at the reduction, not the

national citizenship is nested, so that a person is a European citizen if, and only if, she is also a citizen of one of the nations under the treaty.[67] But just as authority is grounded on a legitimizing narrative, it can be re-grounded if another narrative displaces or amends it, as in the case of a national state forged out of former kingdoms or a federation formed of formerly independent states. But in some situations the primacy of the whole over the parts is not settled, and questions remain of whether the component units retain meta-jurisdictional authority and only cede its exercise to the centre, or the centre monopolizes meta-jurisdictional authority and claims the power to override the component's decisions.

This is, arguably, the case of the EU. Nick Barber makes a clear and well-documented case for deep disagreement between EU and national courts over the hierarchy of constitutional norms in Europe.

> The Court of Justice of the European Union (ECJ) makes three, interconnected, claims of supremacy. First, that the ECJ is entitled to definitively answer all questions of European Law. Secondly, that the ECJ is entitled to determine what constitutes an issue of European Law. Thirdly, that European Law has supremacy over all conflicting rules of national law. These claims are distinct: making any one of the claims does not entail making the other two. National supreme courts have sometimes proved unwilling to accept these assertions. Most famously, the German courts have refused to cede their role as guardians of the German Constitution.[68]

Neither the ECJ or the national courts consider the system pluralistic. Each would deny foundational plurality (for the former, the Treaty grounds European supremacy, for the latter it does not), incommensurability (each considers itself superior), or tragic loss (each demands loyalty of its own officials). It is the coexistence of competing claims, and the absence of rules in one or another system that could authoritatively settle conflicts of paramountcy, that makes the system pluralistic.

increase, of plurality). The European peoples, Ortega argues, have always coexisted (*convivido*, literally 'lived together') and all coexistence generates a society, 'a system of mores' (*sistema de usos*) which leads to the emergence of a common public opinion or pubic culture (*opinión pública*). This public culture in time generates a coercive public power. The political will and juridical form merely follow. J Ortega y Gasset, *Europa y la Idea de Nación* (Alianza Editorial, 1985) 23.

Ortega's philosophical sociology resembles the most robust arguments for the real personality of groups (especially those of Otto Gierke, precursor to the British pluralists): the proposition that legally constituted groups simply emerge from organic social interaction. As legal and political arguments they are surely too ambitious, but they can explain the force of invoking the idea of Europe as a justification for further integration of the countries in the EU.

[67] 'Every person holding the nationality of a Member State shall be a citizen of the Union. Citizenship of the Union shall be additional to and not replace national citizenship.' *Consolidated version of the Treaty on the Functioning of the European Union*, Art. 20(1) <http://eur-lex.europa.eu/LexUriServ/LexUriServ.do?uri=OJ:C:2010:083:FULL:EN:PDF> accessed 22 June 2013.

[68] Nick Barber, *The Constitutional State* (Oxford University Press, 2011) 164.

Neil MacCormick correctly identifies the problem as a question about the site of meta-jurisdictional authority or, using the term he borrows from German constitutional theory, 'competence-competence'. 'In German theory, the critical issue of sovereignty concerns competence-competence. Whoever has the competence to determine the limits (if any) on their own competence is truly sovereign. All other competences are necessarily subordinate or derivative.'[69] MacCormick offers two possible models to resolve the conflictive account of competence-competence proffered by the ECJ and national courts: The first is a situation of 'radical pluralism' in which there are no norms common to both systems which can resolve meta-jurisdictional conflicts, which leaves these to be settled through political compromise and institutional restraint. The other is 'pluralism under international law'.

> [I]t might be held that in a coordinate way, international law functions as a common ground of validity both of member-state systems and of Community law, neither being therefore a sub-system of the other, but both cohering within a common legal universe governed by the norms of international law.[70]

But, of course, this resolves the pluralistic conflict between the two legal orders by uniting them under a common law. MacCormick himself admits that the solution is ultimately 'monistic' and can only aspire to the pluralist label because it fails to settle the hierarchy between the ECJ and the national courts (by setting a higher authority over both).[71] Yet even this solution is incapable of settling the dispute. Even if both orders accept that principles of international law will determine their competence, they can still disagree over the interpretation of those principles. Which legal norm will settle the question of which interpretation—the ECJ's or the national courts'—is authoritative? MacCormick resolves the issue by sublating national sovereignty under the principle of subsidiarity.[72] But as I will argue in this section, this only pushes the settlement of questions of meta-jurisdictional authority one step back.

Subsidiarity was introduced into the EU's constitutional structure with the 1993 Treaty of Maastricht. The prior treaty structure—especially the Treaty of Rome—makes no mention of subsidiarity, although the 1986 amendments in the Single European Act seem to imply it, although only on the subject of environmental protection.[73] But with the Treaty of Maastricht subsidiarity

[69] Neil MacCormick, *Questioning Sovereignty* (Oxford University Press, 2010) 100.

[70] MacCormick, note 69, 116–17. [71] MacCormick, note 69, 121. [72] MacCormick, note 69, 126.

[73] 'The Community shall take action relating to the environment to the extent to which the objectives referred to in paragraph 1 can be attained better at Community level than at the level of the individual Member States.' Single European Act, Art. 25, amending Treaty of Rome, Art. 130(4). <http://www.proyectos.cchs.csic.es/euroconstitution/library/historic%20documents/SEA/Single%20European%20Act.pdf> accessed 22 June 2013.

becomes a full-fledged constitutional principle of the EU. The division of competencies between the EU and the member states is governed by the principle of conferral, which establishes that the EU only has those powers ceded to it:

> Under the principle of conferral, the Union shall act only within the limits of the competences conferred upon it by the Member States in the Treaties to attain the objectives set out therein. Competences not conferred upon the Union in the Treaties remain with the Member States.[74]

In those areas where there is shared competency between the EU and the member states, action by the EU is governed by principles of subsidiarity and proportionality:

> Under the principle of subsidiarity, in areas which do not fall within its exclusive competence, the Union shall act only if and in so far as the objectives of the proposed action cannot be sufficiently achieved by the Member States, either at central level or at regional and local level, but can rather, by reason of the scale or effects of the proposed action, be better achieved at Union level.
>
> The institutions of the Union shall apply the principle of subsidiarity as laid down in the Protocol on the application of the principles of subsidiarity and proportionality. National Parliaments ensure compliance with the principle of subsidiarity in accordance with the procedure set out in that Protocol.
>
> Under the principle of proportionality, the content and form of Union action shall not exceed what is necessary to achieve the objectives of the Treaties.[75]

The principle of subsidiarity was introduced into the European constitutional structure because of the member states' fears about centralization. Unsurprisingly, it came to pervade European treaties just as the powers of the Community were significantly expanded. Especially important were the principles of direct applicability (that the adoption of a Community norm integrates it into a member state's legal order), of direct effects (that a sufficiently clear Community norm confers rights to private parties which may be claimed against member states, again without requiring the formal incorporation of the norm into the member state's legal order), and of supremacy (mandating member states to give supremacy to European over domestic law in cases where they conflict).[76] These had already been effectively adopted by the European Court of Justice, but were made explicit in Maastricht. With this

[74] *Consolidated version of the Treaty on European Union*, Art. 5(2). <http://eur-lex.europa.eu/LexUriServ/LexUriServ.do?uri=OJ:C:2010:083:0013:0046:en:PDF> accessed 22 June 2013.

[75] *Consolidated version of the Treaty on European Union*, Art. 5(3) and (4). <http://eur-lex.europa.eu/LexUriServ/LexUriServ.do?uri=OJ:C:2010:083:0013:0046:en:PDF> accessed 22 June 2013.

[76] GA Bermann, 'Taking Subsidiarity Seriously' (1994) 94(2) *Columbia Law Review* 331, 349.

shift in the normative balance between member states and the EU there was an understandable call for restraint. Yet from the start subsidiarity has proved difficult to implement. It can serve—and has served—both as a defence of national (or more local) interests, and an instrument for increasing centralization of competencies in Brussels. At best, the principle appears largely symbolic, as even its defenders admit that it 'is not legally enforceable but constitutes a declaration of the contracting parties' vision of Europe.'[77]

At worst, however, subsidiarity positively undermines the autonomy of lower orders. It subordinates their goals to the goals of the higher authority and co-opts them into a common enterprise that may be contrary to their interests and over which they have no ultimate control. Gareth Davies puts this in no uncertain terms.

> Subsidiarity misses the point. Its central flaw is that instead of providing a method to balance between Member State and Community interests, which is what is needed, it assumes the Community goals, privileges their achievement absolutely, and simply asks who should be the one to do the implementing work. Thus subsidiarity may protect the right of Member States to be co-opted by the Community to do its work, but it does not protect their right to do their own work. It gives them a right to employment in Community service, wherever they can show they are up to the task, but it does not give them a voice, let alone a seat on the board.[78]

This is not an empirical assessment, although Davies gives examples to prove his thesis. It is inherent in the very structure of subsidiarity. Subsidiarity is not a meta-jurisdictional principle since it does not pertain to the allocation of competencies or the setting of jurisdictional boundaries (that task, in the EU, would be carried out by the conferral principle). It is a principle that is meant to guide judgment when those boundaries overlap or have not been set. When faced with a concrete problem that requires attention by policymakers and government officials, but which does not obviously fall under an area where one set of officials exercise exclusive competence, two judgments must be made. First, what is the desired goal of policy or intervention and second, which set of officials is best placed to achieve it. In those circumstances, the important question is who gets to exercise the final judgment over the desired goal and the relevant competencies. The question of who decides is prior to the question of what is decided.

But then subsidiarity is either an irrelevant principle, or a centralizing one. Suppose the decision to invoke the aid of the higher or more central

[77] Nick Barber, 'The Limited Modesty of Subsidiarity' (2005) 11(3) *European Law Journal* 308, 312.

[78] Gareth Davies, 'Subsidiarity: The Wrong Idea, In the Wrong Place, At the Wrong Time' (2006) *Common Market Law Review* 43(1) 63, 67–68 (internal citations omitted).

authority falls on the lower or more local one. The only discretion left to the higher authority is whether to concur with the lower one and offer the aid, or to disagree with it and withhold it. The latter decision seems unlikely, since central authorities are rarely reluctant to expand their domain. However, we may think that if intervention is too expensive the central authority may not want to bear the cost. In that case, subsidiarity is again irrelevant, since the decision to intervene does not bear on efficiency (the lower authority may or may not be more efficient at the task) but rather on willingness to pay (since neither authority wants to bear the cost). Possibly, however, the local authority may be able to compel the higher one to help, and to do so at the behest of the lower authority. It is the lower authority that must now be restrained in its appeals for aid since otherwise, with limited resources, the central authority would be unable to field competing or contradictory requests by various local authorities. Subsidiarity collapses into a tragedy of the commons, with the commons being the central authority's treasury, or into a set of incoherent policies.

Only the allocation of judgment over the invocation of subsidiary authority to the local level is likely to guarantee its autonomy, but it does so at too high or uncertain a cost. More likely, the adoption of the principle of subsidiarity assumes a unity of purpose that cannot be taken for granted under conditions of political pluralism. Pluralism takes the question of the legitimacy of the authority to make decisions (including meta-jurisdictional decisions) to be separate from the question of the merits of these decisions. Two authorities may arrive at the same goal, they may share a purpose, and decide to distribute competencies between them in order to pursue it in the most efficient way; but under conditions of pluralism even the first step cannot be guaranteed. Again, Davies makes the point succinctly.

> Subsidiarity's weakness is that it assumes the primacy of the central goal, and allows no mechanism for questioning whether or not it is desirable, in the light of other interests, to fully pursue this . . . [I]t assumes that there will be no conflict between the objectives of the different levels. It takes as its starting point that all levels are united in wishing to achieve certain goals and that none has any other interests or objectives which conflict with these.[79]

Within the church, subsidiarity can usefully turn a vast organization with immense internal variability to the single-minded pursuit of saving souls. Within a nation-state it can do the same thing, with the wrinkle that some minds in the state do not acquiesce to the singularity of purpose. Subsidiarity is then not a principle for adjudicating the most effective use

[79] Davies, note 78, 78.

of powers and competencies, but an ideological tool for co-opting diverse authorities to a single purpose. If this is the goal, then subsidiarity may be the principle to achieve it, and may have a salutary effect on a polity once meta-jurisdictional authority is no longer in dispute and purposes are set by a universally accepted hierarchy. But such a polity will not be pluralistic.

4

Associative Democracy and the Corporatist Temptation

An especially promising development for the political pluralist tradition is the recent emergence of associative democracy as an alternative to individualist market provision of social goods and collectivist state-centred provision. One of the major proponents of associative democracy, Paul Hirst, is also one of the central figures in the British pluralist revival and makes explicit the relation between the *fin de siècle* pluralists and his political project. Other writers on the associationalist line, are less directly indebted to the pluralist tradition, but their attention to the role of non-state associations in the deliberation and distribution of social goods—as in the case of Joshua Cohen and Joel Rogers—or their role in governance of deeply divided societies—as in the case of Veit Bader—makes them important interlocutors of the pluralist tradition. Yet the genealogy of associative democracy is complicated and owes much to subsidiarist and especially corporatist social theories, which do not recognize multiple sources of political authority in society but at best admit only the provision and administration of social goods by a variety of functional and local actors.

In the words of one of its main proponents, '[a]ssociative democracy is a political theory, the core proposition of which is that as many social activities as possible should be devolved to self-governing voluntary associations.'[1] These activities include those that improve policymaking through the articulation of a variety of interests—functional, religious, or what have you—that might otherwise be ignored by broader appeals to common features of the citizenry, and those that improve social governance, whether by the provision of social goods of the kind associated with the welfare state, or simply through the development and sustainment of networks of trust and cooperation which make governance more efficient and less frictive. Associative democracy then stands in opposition to those

[1] Veit Bader, 'Introduction' in Paul Hirst and Veit Bader (eds), *Associative Democracy: The Real Third Way* (Frank Cass, 2001) 1.

systems that presume an undifferentiated citizenry governed by a unitary state under a single conception of the public good—the purer or more militant varieties of civic republicanism—or those that take the opposite route and advocate for the unmediated interaction of individuals in a market. Both of these alternatives fear associations, the former because they give force to factional interests that should not have precedence over civil loyalty, the latter because associations—as much as states—can be instruments of entrenched privilege, predatory rent-seeking, or disguised oppression. Between these alternatives, associative democrats seek a middle ground that would recognize the practical and moral importance of groups in social life and reconcile the interests of group members with the needs of democratic governance. The main impetus of associative democracy is the necessity for decentralization of governance in order to overcome a democratic deficit in modern society.

> It tries to develop alternative forms of the state, private-public and private administration and governance, which promises to tackle the overload, inefficiency and lack of democratic accountability of government by democratic decentralization, by making space for a huge variety of voluntary associations in the provision of all kinds of services and their regulation, control and scrutiny, and, thus, by restricting the state to its essential core functions, making it both thinner and stronger.[2]

Two of the most prominent articulations of associative democracy are that of Joshua Cohen and Joel Rogers,[3] and that of Paul Hirst. Both Hirst and Cohen and Rogers share more than an institutional interest in the inclusion of associations in the structure of social governance; they also share a substantive commitment to an egalitarian democracy of a broadly socialist or social-democratic kind and thus see their associative project as an alternative to or curb of capitalist economic models. This has led sympathetic commentators to hold them up as exemplars of an associationist strand of radical pluralism.[4] To be sure, there are differences between them, some of which can be attributed to the political culture from which these writers emerge. Cohen and Rogers' account betrays the heavy stamp that Tocqueville has

[2] Bader, note 1, 7.

[3] Joshua Cohen and Joel Rogers, 'Secondary Associations and Democratic Governance' (1992) *Politics and Society* 20(4) 393.

[4] Mark Bevir and Toby Reiner, 'The Revival of Radical Pluralism: Associationism and Difference' in Mark Bevir (ed.), *Modern Pluralism: Anglo-American Debates Since 1880* (Cambridge University Press, 2012) 179–213. Cohen and Rogers, it is true, 'assume the context of modern capitalism, where markets are the primary mechanism of resource allocation and private, individual decisions are the central determinant of investment.' Joshua Cohen and Joel Rogers, 'Associations and Democracy' *Social Philosophy and Policy* 10(2): 282–312, 283 (1993). But this assumption is a pragmatic compromise, as their earlier rejection of capitalism suggests. Joshua Cohen and Joel Rogers, *On Democracy* (Penguin Books, 1983).

put on American theorizing on the subject of voluntary associations, while Hirst's is more indebted to the struggles of British labour (as a movement and also of Labour, as a party).[5] But their shared egalitarian and democratic ethos shapes their view towards associations in decisive ways.

4.1 COHEN AND ROGERS ON ASSOCIATIVE DEMOCRACY

For Cohen and Rogers, associations represent a resource to be mobilized in the service of the democratic order.[6] They 'can provide information to policymakers on member preferences, the impact of proposed legislation, or the implementation of existing law', 'can promote a more equitable distribution of advantage by correcting for imbalances in bargaining power that follow from the unequal control of wealth', 'can help citizens develop competence, self-confidence, and a broader set of interests than they would acquire in a more fragmented political society', and 'help to formulate and execute public policies and take on quasi-public functions that supplement or supplant the state's more directly regulatory actions.'[7] Now, these authors do not lay claim to the normative pluralist tradition and only discuss pluralism in the sense of interest group representation. But the compatibility of their argument with the pluralist tradition should not rest on banners or labels, but rather on the relationship between the authority of associations and the authority of the state, which is after all the central controversy of pluralism. And on this account Cohen and Rogers' version of associative democracy is patently incompatible with the pluralist tradition.

Cohen and Rogers deny that the social world is foundationally plural in any meaningful way. Associations are instead 'artefactual'.

> Their incidence, character, and patterns of interaction . . . reflect structural features of the political economy in which they form, from the distribution of wealth and income to the locus of policy-making in different areas. And they reflect variations across the members of that society along such dimensions as income, information, and density of interaction.[8]

Since associations are artefactual, they have no genuine claim to maintain their integrity, Cohen and Rogers conclude. While acknowledging that associations are not 'simply political creations or that they ought to be treated as such' they consider the effect of political constraint on associational structure so pervasive to justify that 'the incidence and structure of groups and the

[5] Bevir and Reiner correctly point out that labour unions, as well as guild-like functional organizations, play a central and distinct role in Hirst's work, while they are grouped with all other voluntary associations in Cohen and Rogers.

[6] Cohen and Rogers, note 3, 395.

[7] Cohen and Rogers, note 3, 424–25.

[8] Cohen and Rogers, note 3, 427.

patterns of group representation can be changed through political choice.'[9] But this conclusion simply does not follow. The fact 'that there is no natural structure of group representation that directly reflects the underlying conditions of social life'[10] does not mean that the structures of governance that have developed in associations should be treated as normatively indifferent. The democratic state is no more natural a system of representation, especially as one moves away from direct democracy (whose 'naturalness' is not above dispute), and is shaped as much by resource constraints, prior domestic and international norms, and simple path dependency as any other organized group. The claims of the state to a certain representational structure—as the claims of other associations to the same—are judged on the basis of their responsiveness to the reasons that apply to those over whom they exercise authority. They are claims to legitimacy which have little to do with 'natural structure'.

What they do have to do with is the integrity of an association and of the practices that give rise to it and that it, in turn, protects. Associations are certainly pervasively shaped and constrained by political and legal rules not of their making, but this does not mean that these norms are binding on the association or its members. They may simply be coercive instruments of state policy that are not otherwise justified. Their justification would not turn on their naturalness, but on the content of the reasons that these rules advanced and on the standing of the state to demand compliance with those reasons in the first place. The problem with Cohen and Rogers' vision of associative democracy is not so much the normative ideal that they espouse, 'the abstract ideal of a democratic society—a society of equals that is governed both by its members and for them'.[11] It is the institutional structure that they believe it entails. On their view, the ideal of a democratic society implies a single ultimate arbiter who ensures that all associations converge on this ideal both in their internal structure and in their outward aims. This is the attitude that Nancy Rosenblum has named the 'logic of congruence', the 'imperative that the internal life and organization of associations mirror liberal democratic principles and practices.'[12] There are consequentialist reasons to worry about such domesticated associations: they are incapable of contesting any abuse by the state, they are not fertile grounds for innovation or nurseries of diversity, they will not hold the interest or loyalty of their members which is, after all, derived from 'the conviction that the group's

[9] Cohen and Rogers, note 3, 428. The argument is reminiscent of Bodin's treatment of corporations, which though they precede the sovereign in time and are therefore not created by the sovereign, nonetheless continue to exist at his pleasure and may be changed or abolished in pursuance of his aims.

[10] Cohen and Rogers, note 3, 411.

[11] Cohen and Rogers, note 3, 417.

[12] Nancy Rosenblum, *Membership and Morals* (Princeton University Press, 1998) 36.

standing is unique'.[13] Ultimately, co-option and conscription of associations would undermine the very attractive features that Cohen and Rogers seek to enlist.[14] But the more basic objection is that they would have been co-opted or subjugated by a power that has no evident authority over them, but simply used the powers of purse and sword to cut a rival authority down to size. The content of the ideal of democratic society is not at issue; what is at issue is the authority of the association called to implement it, both its identity and its scope.

Neither do Cohen and Rogers acknowledge that the authority of associations may be incommensurable with that of the state. From the start of their work, they frame the problem of associations as the danger of the 'mischief of faction', 'the potential of secondary associations to deploy their powers in ways that infirm the conditions of well-ordered democracy'.[15] The solution is 'to curb faction through a deliberate politics of association while netting such group contribution to egalitarian democratic governance'.[16] Associations are therefore seen as either enemies of the democratic state or as partners in its realization, and their legitimacy is won or lost along that axis. But some associations are uninterested either in capturing the state for their own purposes, or in being conscripted into its administrative structure. They may, of course, seek rents (as illegitimately as any other social actor) or cooperate with government, but they will do so for their own reasons. Their grounds for legitimacy may have nothing much to do with democratic governance, but with spiritual salvation, scholarly merit, or professional integrity. It is simply not the case that members of associations hold liberal-democratic values to be paramount and, even if they do favour these values (even above others), it does not follow that they believe that every enterprise in which they join should be immediately or obliquely directed at their furtherance. To construe the relationship between the aims of politics and the aims of associations in this way is to do a disservice to the latter to the point of abandoning any distinctly pluralist position.[17]

Associations are there to be conscripted into the state's projects, and to be reformed when they do not conform. This also eliminates, through active state intervention, any possibility of conflict, both through preventive reform of

[13] Rosenblum, note 12, 345.

[14] Cf. Cohen and Rogers, note 3, 446.

[15] Cohen and Rogers, note 3, 393.

[16] Cohen and Rogers, note 3, 425.

[17] In a comment on Cohen and Rogers' essay, Philippe Schmitter minces no words in revealing their agenda. 'At various points in the essay, especially in the last section on "Reforming a Liberal Polity," Cohen and Rogers are manifestly less concerned with improving the quality of associability in the United States than with accomplishing specific policy objectives. To put it bluntly, they are trying to bring social democracy to America by the back door, when it has been unable to pass through the front—that is, the electoral—door.' Philippe Schmitter, 'The Irony of Modern Democracy and Efforts to Improve Its Practice' (1992) *Politics and Society* 20(4) 507, 510.

associational structures and aims and corrective regulation by a strong central power. In a passage reminiscent of GDH Cole's admonishment against redundancy and conflict between functional associations, Cohen and Rogers make the success of the associative project dependent 'on the precise role those groups are assigned and the surrounding framework of articulate public authority. In particular, it depends on their having a relatively clearly defined scope of discretion and obligation and on their operating with clear standards and mechanisms of accountability to fully public authorities.'[18] This is not simply because these groups will be publicly funded, since all groups that perform some quasi-public duty are subject to regulation, even if they receive no state subsidy or if their motivation for performing this duty—provision of education, health services, and the like—is grounded on non-public reasons such as religious obligation or scholarly vocation. If the worry is that even private groups promote factionalism when they provide similar services to the state, though grounded on a different authority, then associational autonomy has been equated to *lèse majesté*.

4.2 HIRST ON ASSOCIATIVE DEMOCRACY

The inspiration of associative democracy includes a prominent strain of political pluralism, and Paul Hirst has been one of the most consistent voices in rehabilitating the movement. Yet the mode of organization that associative democrats recommend is effectively corporatist and many of the objections to the latter apply to the former. The reason seems to be the prominent influence of GDH Cole's version of pluralism on Hirst, which tends to eclipse the more contestatory pluralism of Figgis and Laski.[19] Like Cole, Hirst is interested in providing an alternative to capitalism, and thus disregards the other, non-economic ends that groups pursue. In his more recent work, Hirst expressly acknowledges that a pluralist political order that does not blind itself to diversity will yield to groups' self-regulation and mutual tolerance and impose few requirements on these groups beyond the possibility of exit for their members. But, paradoxically, he retains Cole's concept of function as a standard of governance.[20]

Contrary to Cohen and Rogers, Hirst does acknowledge the foundational plurality of political authority. He takes issue with Cohen and Rogers' assertion of the artefactuality of associations, as it raises questions about

[18] Cohen and Rogers, note 3, 446.

[19] Hirst originally conceived his project as a modern version of GDH Cole's *Guild Socialism Re-Visited*, although he later diverged from this purpose in part because of 'certain fundamental weaknesses in the basic associational concepts that Cole was using'. Paul Hirst, *Associative Democracy: New Forms of Economic and Social Governance* (University of Massachusetts Press, 1994) 203.

[20] Paul Hirst, *From Statism to Pluralism* (Routledge, 1997) 43–50.

'the competence, neutrality, and legitimacy' of the state when it takes on the task of 'crafting' associations to bring them in line with public policy.[21] On the one hand, the task of determining the competencies of associations and of coordinating their functions to avoid conflict or redundancy is enormously complicated. On the other, and from a principled standpoint, a state that takes such an interventionist role cannot simultaneously maintain its neutrality towards associations and its majoritarian legitimacy; if it veers towards neutrality, it must sometimes favour associations that diverge from, and may even undermine, policies decided by the democratic majority, and if it bends towards majoritarianism it becomes an instrument of the larger portion of the population against the smaller, in the process undermining the support that the state would receive from the association.

The alternative, for Hirst, is a relaxation of the artefactuality thesis or, as he proposes in his longer exposition of associative democracy, the assumption that associations owe at least as much to the voluntary convergence of their members as to the economic and legal constraints in which they develop. In three statements, Hirst makes a positive normative case for foundational plurality of associations:

1. That human beings ought to associate one with another to fulfil common purposes, and that they should be able to do so on the basis of free choice;
2. That, as far as possible, such voluntary associations ought to be allowed to develop freely and that their internal affairs should be a matter for their members to arrange as they please;
3. It therefore follows that the state or public power may only abridge the freedom of an association either in order to preserve the freedom of individuals or to prevent harm to the freedom or interests of other associations.[22]

The normative defence of the associative principle goes beyond the merely descriptive claims of the thesis of foundational plurality, but presupposes it. Hirst does not, however, accept the British pluralist arguments uncritically. He distances himself from four important pluralist theses: that association is a natural and spontaneous human propensity; that associations may demand unconditional loyalty of their members; that the state should be considered as just one more association with no higher moral standing than any other, which entitles members of those associations 'to deny obedience to the state if its demands clash with those of their association';[23] and that associations

[21] Paul Hirst, 'Comments on "Secondary Associations and Democratic Governance"' (1992) *Politics and Society* 20(4) 473, 476.

[22] Hirst, note 19, 44.

[23] Hirst, note 19, 45.

have real corporate personalities which should be allowed to develop without constraint. To the first, Hirst argues that associations develop under distinct historical conditions, as a response to concrete human needs, and not through a spontaneous 'spirit of fellowship'. He further observes that a natural propensity to associate does not itself have ethical consequences. There can be no quarrel with either conclusion.

Hirst's replies to the other pluralist propositions bear in mind the question of incommensurability of group and state authority, and the intractability of conflict between them. His conception of associations as wholly voluntary confuses the self-understanding of associations with the coercive power that they may have to enforce their authoritative directives. It is true that non-state associations are voluntary in the sense that they lack the power to persecute apostates or defectors. But there are many ways in which they constrain entry and exit from the group. Associations may define the boundaries of membership in ways that call into question their voluntariness: either by excluding members who might want to be included in the group, or by refusing to acknowledge complete exit from the associations. Religious cases are the most significant. An Orthodox Jewish synagogue has different criteria than a Reform Jewish synagogue over who qualifies as Jewish, and this difference can have important effects especially on important matters of marriage and childrearing, not to mention ancillary services that the association may provide, like schooling.[24] Likewise, associations may refuse to acknowledge the full effect of exit; under Roman Catholic doctrine, for example, the mark of baptism is indelible, and thus a person once baptized as a Catholic remains one throughout life, even if she makes public expressions of apostasy. An association may treat a former or estranged member differently—more or less harshly—than one who has never been a member of the group. Voluntariness, then, is more nuanced a concept than the mere absence of coercive persecution of those who run afoul of a group.

The question of loyalty is inextricably tied to that of disobedience. An association may demand anything of its members, even unconditional loyalty, but this does not make the demand morally sound in the absence of compelling reasons to abide by it. Hirst would be right to think that such reasons are not likely to exist. But most often an association does not demand unconditional loyalty of its members, but rather asks its members to give more weight to associative obligations than to other reasons for action, or else, more strongly, makes authoritative demands of its members of the

[24] This was the controversy in the recent case *R(E)* v. *Governing Body of JFS* [2009] UKSC 15, where a child was denied admission to a school run by the (Orthodox) United Synagogue because his mother had not converted to Judaism in accordance with Orthodox criteria. The mother had, however, converted under the Masorti (Conservative) Jewish tradition. The Supreme Court of the United Kingdom ruled, incorrectly in my view, that the decision criteria were ethnic, not religious, and thus impermissible.

kind that Joseph Raz has called 'exclusionary reasons'.[25] These are reasons for action that also direct the agent not to consider competing reasons in her deliberation. Some examples of such associative obligations may be religious calls for conscientious objection (which demand that the *believer* not heed the demands of the state of which she is a *citizen*), the understanding of academic inquiry as Weberian scientific vocation (which calls on the *scholar* to evaluate the academic merits of a work by putting aside its possible moral or political effects, which she would be obliged to consider were she evaluating the work as a *citizen*), or the professional obligations of a lawyer (whose code of ethics may demand that, as an *advocate*, she take decisive steps that undermine public purposes with which she may otherwise agree, again, as a *citizen*). In all these cases—the religious ones most prominently—the reasons given by the association displace those of the state.

This does not mean that the state is just another organization. As Hirst notes, even Figgis, by far the most forceful advocate among the British pluralists for the autonomy of associations, thinks it necessary that there exist a common public power to create an institutional legal context in which associations could operate. Some pluralists, including Figgis, deny that the state has any purposes of its own, and only exists to provide that context. Other pluralists, GDH Cole most notably, thought the state represented the general interests common to all members of society, as opposed to the functional or sectarian interests that concerned them in their participation in other associations. The latter view is far too optimistic in thinking that general and particular interests will never conflict; to this the pluralist responds that in cases of conflict it is not at all clear that general interests trump particular ones. And even in the former view, that of Figgis, conflict is not ruled out. Some of the claims that the state makes of citizens are instrumental to their membership in associations. Property law, as I will argue in Chapter 11, is a prominent example, since a system of strong property rights allows an association to pursue its own purposes without having to give account of its goals and activities to non-members. A member of an association may have reasons to obey state-enacted property laws in order to better fulfil her associative obligations. But the state may make claims of its members as citizens which may conflict with the claims that associations make of them. In this later capacity, pluralists argue, the state is an association like any other and its claims are not a priori superior to those of other organized groups. There may be reasons for privileging civic obligations over associative obligations in certain situations, or vice versa, or there may simply be no principled way to choose between them in some cases. The dual character of the state, the role it plays as both institutional guarantor of associational rights and as an

[25] Joseph Raz, *The Authority of Law* (Oxford University Press, 1983) 17.

association that makes claims of its members, means that many of these tensions will play out within the state itself, in its legislative deliberations and its judicial controversies, and that sometimes there will be no satisfactory solution except accommodation and negotiation among different authorities.

Finally, Hirst denies the British pluralist insistence on the real personality of groups. The thesis of group personality has two parts: the first is the idea that the convergent actions, practices, and beliefs of individuals involved in an association are sufficient, without requiring a state grant, to constitute the group as an entity; the second is the claim that this entity is a person in a meaningful sense—it is capable of intention and action, and can change and develop over time—and also in a sense that is irreducible to the separate personalities of its members. Hirst wants to deny the thesis of real group personality as too organic and laden with improbable metaphysical assumptions, but his objection seems more directly aimed at pluralist organicist rhetoric than at the more sober descriptions of associative practice that inform the pluralist thesis. On one hand, Hirst posits that 'the group is not an entity, but a relationship between individuals', and yet, he writes:

> The choice made by individuals to create a certain form of ongoing relationship between them alters the condition of their interaction. They can no longer be treated for purposes of explaining their actions in this context as if they were merely individuals acting severally, for they all have the facts of their own relationship and the new interactions it makes possible to contend with when making decisions.[26]

Hirst does not think that the description he gives of associational activity is enough to account for real group personality because groups are sustained by the choice of the individuals who compose them. But this makes too much of affirmative choice and not enough of socialization and organizational structure. The most enduring groups are often sustained by tacit acquiescence by the vast majority of members, and the active management of a few. The relationship between the organization and the members subject to its authority is determined by structurally defined roles, not conscious choice, and yet the group can present itself as a right and duty bearing unit. Changes in the group's policies may or may not reflect the individual beliefs of members, and the translation of those beliefs into official group policies is usually procedurally constrained. This does not negate that it is possible to trace changes in the group's internal and external policies, organizational structure, even 'corporate culture' over time. All these can be described as constituting a group personality that does not depend on organicist assumptions. And, as I will also argue in Part Three, the claim that groups can be considered persons in a meaningful way is not superfluous to the main

[26] Hirst, note 19, 48.

pluralist argument, but essential to it. It underlies arguments about the rights of groups as such, the authority that they have towards their members, and the limits of the state in regulating them.

It should come as no surprise that the radical element in radical pluralism—whether Hirst's or Cohen and Rogers'—has a tendency to absorb the pluralist element. For them, pluralism is a contingent solution to the collapse of the welfare state and not a structural or ontological constraint on the social world. 'Neoliberalism', with its emphasis on the private provision of social goods, has undermined the capacity of the state to perform the functions necessary to sustain egalitarian democracy, and eroded the loyalty that citizens have on centralized political institutions. Into this void, associations emerge as more efficient producers and distributors of social goods, and as stronger social networks that can mobilize individuals to carry out more ambitious collective projects. The principal concern of radical pluralists is economic inequality and local or workplace democracy. They therefore assume a unity of purpose to all state and associative social activity. They also assume a hierarchy between the representative institutions of the democratic polis and those of the various associations. For Cohen and Rogers, 'final authority continues to rest with the more traditional, encompassing, territorially based systems of representation.'[27] For Hirst, the situation is more nuanced. He is far more sympathetic to the free development of associations, and more attentive to the variety of interests and purposes to which they may commit themselves. He does not presume, for instance—as do Cohen and Rogers—to dictate the terms of internal organization of associations that run entirely through private donations and eschew public funding.[28] But for most groups, his associationalism is more administrative than foundational, and differences between associational provision of public goods is a matter of 'style' not of authoritative (and perhaps deeply divergent) determination of the content, meaning, and importance of a social good. This shows that he has particular kinds of associations in mind, namely those that do not make strong claims of meta-jurisdictional authority and who might prioritize this authority over convergence on liberal-democratic ideals.

Hirst is aware of these problems. He acknowledges, with direct allusion to deep religious difference over educational curricula, that '[a]ssociationalism does raise some acute dilemmas in that the desire to allow the maximum democratic self-governance to associations, and the desire to preserve the rights of individuals, will often come into conflict.'[29] This acknowledgement

[27] Cohen and Rogers, note 3, 447.

[28] Hirst, note 19, 192. Cohen and Rogers, by contrast, argue that '[e]ven where groups do not enjoy subsidies for their performance of quasi-public duties, they should be regulated in the conduct of those duties.' Cohen and Rogers, note 3, 450.

[29] Hirst, note 19, 201.

of possible conflict makes Hirst's version of associative democracy significantly more pluralistic than Cohen and Rogers' for a reason that Hirst himself diagnoses: Cohen and Rogers are self-avowed civic republicans and civil republicanism imposes a thick conception of citizenship that trumps all other loyalties, while pluralism presumes that the state does not *by definition* enjoy a claim to the primary loyalty of citizens. Yet even with Hirst, the worry is that the administrative structures of his 'associational and confederal welfare state' will either marginalize or undermine the autonomy of those associations that most cherish it. This can easily happen if the supra-associational institutions that are called upon to coordinate group activity insist on interfering with the internal governance structures of groups, especially those that as a matter of principle are not liberal or democratic, or that diverge on important substantive values from surrounding majorities. Hirst is perhaps too sanguine in his expectation that minimal restrictions on associational abuse—reminiscent of William Galston's caveat that a pluralist polity will have 'no free exercise for Aztecs' who perform human sacrifice—will not be gradually increased through an emphasis on coordination between associations funded through a central treasury, rather than on autonomy of associations who control both their governance and funding.

> Any association accepting public functions must participate in the structure of consociational and state governance of associations as a condition of tax-based financial support. It must accept being part of a collaborative and consultative system of coordination of an association's activities and cooperation in social governance. Associationalism is a form of social governance in which associations are to perform public functions, and not merely a scheme to direct public revenues to private purposes.[30]

The insistence on recruiting associations as partners in governance, as opposed to acknowledging their distinct and perhaps oppositional nature, makes Hirst's version of associative democracy less convincingly pluralistic and approximates it to Cohen and Rogers' model of associational conscription.

4.3 NEITHER CORPORATISM NOR SYNDICALISM

Modern corporatism shares many of the same ideological roots as the original religious current of subsidiarity,[31] and proposes to be an alternative to socialism and laissez-faire capitalism. Its origins predate those of either alternative, however, and are traceable, unsurprisingly, to the medieval economic

[30] Hirst, note 19, 193.

[31] Carl Landauer, *Corporate State Ideologies* (University of California Press, 1983) chapter 5.

order that inspired federalists and pluralists alike. Indeed, corporatism aims at securing the harmony of functions and interests to which the medieval system of guilds and estates ostensibly aspired. Thus it organizes political and economic representation along the cleavages of estate, occupation, and officially sanctioned common interest.[32]

> Corporatism is a specific socio-political process in which organizations representing monopolistic functional interests engage in political exchange with state agencies over public policy outputs which involves those organizations in a role which combines interest representation and policy implementation through delegated self-enforcement.[33]

It is 'the fusion of representation and intervention in the *relationship* between groups and the state' that is distinctive of corporatist governance.[34] The presence of two poles to this relationship makes corporatism appear pluralistic insofar as it postulates an authority other than the state, but the heavy emphasis on coordination and fixed interest domains undermines the autonomy of groups in the bargaining relationship.[35] The state emerges as the head of the corporatist structure and coordinates production among the different associations, which in turn 'have a role to play in ensuring compliance with interventions bargained between them and the state' and can assume a variety of roles in the implementation of public policy.[36]

Corporatism has usually been identified with the political right and some of its most successful proponents were fascists: Mussolini's Italian Social Republic, Pétain's Vichy regime, Schuschnigg's Austria before the *Anschluss*, Salazar's *Estado Novo* in Portugal.[37] The distinction between corporatism and political pluralism is less interesting in those cases, because fascism involved little more than 'corporate structures serving as camouflage for dictatorships.'[38] But corporatism also found adherents on the left, where it took the form of guild socialism. In Britain it was defended most ardently by GDH Cole who, although often counted among the British political pluralists, is far less consistent a defender of the autonomy of associations than

[32] Peter J Williamson, *Varieties of Corporatism: A Conceptual Discussion* (Cambridge University Press, 1985) chapter 2.

[33] Alan Cawson, *Corporatism and Political Theory* (Basil Blackwell, 1986) 38.

[34] Cawson, note 33, 39.

[35] Cawson and other writers on corporatism thus distinguish pluralism and corporatism along the axes of monopolistic or open-ended number of groups, fixed or overlapping interest domains, and formal or informal role of functional groups in policy formation and implementation. But it is important to note that the kind of pluralism they have in mind is that associated with Robert Dahl, not *fin de siècle* British pluralism. There is a relationship between the two, both through history and 'disposition' but it is too complex to discuss here.

[36] Peter J Williamson, *Corporatism in Perspective: An Introductory Guide to Corporatist Theory* (Sage, 1989) 223.

[37] Landauer, note 31, chapter 7.

[38] Landauer, note 31, 93.

Figgis, and even Laski. This fact has not escaped many prominent contemporary pluralists. Thus David Nicholls, a scholar of Figgis' thought, bluntly states that:

> Cole was a significant guild socialist but... was hardly a pluralist at all. He believed... in functional representation at a central parliament or assembly of some kind.... He also manifestly attached little importance to group personality and to the need for groups to manage their own affairs and live their own lives.[39]

For Cole, each association possesses a 'function' which emanates from the satisfaction of common wants and the execution of common purposes. As the function of the state is to represent persons in their common condition—to concern itself 'with things which concern all sorts and conditions of men, and concern them, broadly speaking, in the same way, that is, in relation to their identity and not to their points of difference'—it cannot claim jurisdictional superiority over other associations, which may be the final arbiters on matters peculiar to a discrete group.[40] But the coherence of society depends on all associations fulfilling their function in a way that is 'complementary and necessary for social well-being'; conflict, contradiction, and redundancy are perversions of function.[41]

Cole's theory has rightly been called corporatist as it presupposes an overarching harmony to social life and grants no space for unorthodoxy or opportunities for withdrawal from the 'coherent' functional system. Clearly many artistic, cultural, commercial, and religious groups cannot be brought under this system without distorting their self-understanding and subjugating them to values, ends, and purposes that are not shared by them. Put another way, the functionalist-corporatist strain present in Cole is not coherent with the historical and normative claims of political pluralism. In the end, it does not recognize any true measure of autonomy to associations. The value of an association is measured only in a small part by the attachment that its members have to it, and in a much larger part by how well it performs those social purposes that are found to be generally useful. Associations may have an independent origin, and thus satisfy the criterion of foundational plurality, but they are subordinated to the functionalist standard and their aims are 'harmonized'—which is to say, dictated and constrained—under threat of sanction from a central coordinating authority.

[39] David Nicholls, *The Pluralist State: The Political Ideals of JN Figgis and His Contemporaries* (2nd edn) (St. Martin's Press, 1994) 3. Cf. Hirst, note 20, 32.

[40] GDH Cole, 'The Social Theory' in Paul Hirst (ed.), *The Pluralist Theory of the State: Selected Writings of G.D.H. Cole, J.N. Figgis, and H.J. Laski* (Routledge, 1993) 77.

[41] Cole, note 40, 60–67.

Cécile Laborde, in one of the most thorough studies of pluralist thought, recognizes that '[f]ew concepts in political science have been more ambiguous than those of pluralism and corporatism.'[42] Yet the categories remain useful for situating the associative democrats in relation to the political pluralists and contrasting their positions on the relationship of the state to associations. On this scale, Cohen and Rogers can best be classified as neo-corporatists rather than pluralists, and their version of associative democracy can be seen to be incompatible with any strong defence of associational autonomy. Hirst, who is more sympathetic to the self-conception and autonomy of associations, straddles the line between corporatists and syndicalists, but also betrays a strong divergence with the pluralist tradition. Beyond these authors, there is a broader argument about the distinctiveness of pluralism as a political tradition: its insistence on foundational plurality, incommensurability, and intractable conflict between the authority of associations and that of the state, which casts doubt over the capacity or permissibility of government superseding the multiple loyalties of individuals in complex societies.

Following Laborde, I borrow Philippe Schmitter's definitions of four models of organizing interest representation: monism, corporatism, syndicalism, and pluralism (see table 4.1 for a comparison of the models).[43] The first, monism, is:

> a system of interest representation in which the constituent units are organized into a fixed number of singular, ideologically selective, noncompetitive, functionally differentiated and hierarchically ordered categories, created, subsidized and licensed by a single party and granted a representational role within that party and 'vis-à-vis' the state in exchange for observing certain controls on their selection of leaders, articulation of demands and mobilization of support.[44]

Schmitter takes the Soviet model as paradigmatic of monistic organization of group interests, a system that treats groups as agencies of the state and affords them no autonomous development. The monist system itself is uninteresting for our purposes except by comparison to the corporatist model.

> Corporatism can be defined as a system of interest representation in which the constituent units are organized into a limited number of singular, compulsory,

[42] Cécile Laborde, *Pluralist Thought and the State in Britain and France, 1900-25* (St. Martin's Press, 2000) 153.

[43] A few clarifications about Table 4.1 are warranted. In Schmitter's classification, rather than a representational monopoly of interests in its domain, the monist model grants 'a representational role within that party and vis-à-vis the state' in exchange for the control defined in this section. Schmitter also does not label the constituent units of the monistic system of representation 'compulsory' but rather 'ideologically selective'. By that he means that membership is limited to those who adhere to the party ideology. But as his model is the Soviet system, we can speculate that those who would not pass the ideological test of membership would be severely disadvantaged in their political, economic, and social endeavours. Similarly, he describes the party, not the state, as the one that licenses these units, but the differences between the two are negligible in such a system. These are minor quibbles that do not impair the table from illustrating the comparison across systems.

[44] Schmitter, note 17, 97.

Table 4.1. Schmitter's models of interest representation

	Fixed number?	Compulsory?	Non-competitive?	Functionally differentiated?	Hierarchically ordered?	State created, licensed, and/or subsidized?	State controlled?	Granted a representative monopoly?
Monism	Yes	Yes	Yes	Yes	Yes	Yes	Yes	Yes
Corporatism	Limited	Yes	Yes	Yes	Yes	Yes	Yes	Yes
Syndicalism	No	No	Yes	No	No	No	No	No
Pluralism	No	No	No	No	No	No	No	No

> noncompetitive, hierarchically ordered and functionally differentiated categories, recognized or licensed (if not created) by the state and granted a deliberate representational monopoly within their respective categories in exchange for observing certain controls on their selection of leaders and articulation of demands and supports.[45]

Despite corporatist insistence on the role that it allows for associations, it is structurally similar to the monist model. There is, to be sure, less emphasis on ideological selectivity, but only because associations in a corporatist state are valued for the performance of their functional role and not for the underlying beliefs that motivate this performance. The parallels to Cohen and Rogers' version of associative democracy are evident: groups are assigned a precise role, they are regulated or created by the public authority, and they are required to have a certain internal decisional structure, and in exchange are invited to inform the public authority of the interests of their members.

An alternative to corporatism is the syndicalist model:

> defined as a system of interest aggregation (more than representation) in which the constituent units are an unlimited number of singular, voluntary, noncompetitive (or better hived-off) categories, not hierarchically ordered or functionally specialized, neither recognized, created nor licensed by state or party, nor controlled in their leadership selection or interest articulation by state or party, not exercising a representational monopoly but resolving their conflicts and 'authoritatively allocating their values' autonomously without the interference of the state.[46]

Syndicalism was attractive for many pluralists, and even Figgis once confessed, somewhat cryptically, to be a syndicalist.[47] It is easy to see the reason for the attraction. Syndicalism, unlike corporatism, conceives of groups as independent of the state, not controlled, ordered, or licensed by it, and not dependent on functional roles. As a historical tradition, syndicalism is rooted in the more radical and anarchistic elements of the labour movement, and aspires to supplant the state monopoly of violence with self-organized worker cooperatives. Its focus, like that of the corporatists, however, is on units of economic organization, specifically workers' cooperatives, and although it embraces disorder and conflict, it aspires to an eventual spontaneous coordination between workers.

It is here that there is a marked contrast between syndicalism and pluralism. By pluralism, Schmitter has in mind the descriptive theory of democracy

[45] Schmitter, note 17, 93–94. [46] Schmitter, note 17, 98.

[47] David Runciman tells of Ernest Barker's recollection of the event. 'Barker, for instance, writing during the 1930s, offered this reminiscence of an encounter he had had with J. N. Figgis over twenty years earlier: "I shall never forget him taking me round the house of the community in which he lived at Mirfield [Figgis was a clergyman], and suddenly exclaiming, 'Barker, I really believe I am a syndicalist!'"' D Runciman, *Pluralism and the Personality of the State* (CUP, 1997) 81.

in which interests-groups compete for access to state resources, not the normative theory of the British pluralists, which emphasizes group autonomy in pursuit of its own ends. But for the present contrast, Schmitter's definition will do, since it illustrates a fundamental difference with corporatist and syndicalist analysis.

> Pluralism can be defined as a system of interest representation in which the constituent units are organized into an unspecified number of multiple, voluntary, competitive, nonhierarchically ordered and self-determined (as to type or scope of interest) categories which are not specially licensed, recognized, subsidized, created or otherwise controlled in leadership selection or interest articulation by the state and which do not exercise a monopoly of representational activity within their respective categories.[48]

Pluralism, as a system of representation of interests, does not make the normative or empirical assumption that groups will abstain from competition and conflict, whether through state regulation as in the corporatist view, or through spontaneous coordination as in the syndicalist view. Pluralism as a normative account of social order, likewise, does not assume that the claims to authority of different associations can be reconciled, and always presumes that, at least at the margins, tragic conflict between authorities is intractable and inevitable. This is a natural corollary of each association's autonomous pursuit of its own ends, and recommends that the state not overreach in its own claims over citizens lest it invite or accentuate conflict.[49]

[48] Schmitter, note 17, 96.

[49] Cf. Laborde, note 42, 157.

PART TWO

THE CONSTITUTIONAL THEORY OF PLURALISM

The ultimate sin of absolutism lies in the promotion of total organization, that of pluralism in the promotion of no organization.

—Preston King

5

Two Conceptions of Sovereignty

In Part One of the book I presented the general structure of pluralist arguments, with special attention to political and legal pluralism, and I distinguished these arguments from similar accounts that defer to or make room for associations and groups within the state. But this is still not enough to show that it is possible to develop a theory of sovereignty that allows organized groups and associations to exist and act autonomously. That is the purpose of this second part.

I first present a definition of *sovereignty* that attempts to reconcile the historical and the analytic aspects of the concept. I then examine the early-modern conception of sovereignty, which has dominated Western political thought, and the medieval alternative it replaced. I point out the advantages and shortcomings of the medieval conception, and suggest how it may be improved to provide a conception of sovereignty that is compatible with associational autonomy in contemporary liberal societies. Such a conception should aim to do two things: In the first place, it should provide an independent source of legitimacy for associations; legitimacy derived from the concurrence of their members, not the tolerance or permission of a superior authority. In the second place, it should allow organized groups to act in pursuance of their collective values and interests without having to justify their actions in terms of the values and interests of any other authority, whether the social whole, the state, the church, or some other entity. These two aspects of the pluralist conception of sovereignty will be explained further in Part Three of this book, which deals with corporate personality and private property. The current chapter provides a theoretical background for that discussion.

5.1 THE IDEA OF SOVEREIGNTY

There are two reasons for framing the question of the autonomy of groups in terms of the idea of sovereignty, instead of the more explicit concept, used elsewhere in this book, of an institutional claim to legitimate meta-jurisdictional authority. The first reason is internal to the political pluralist tradition: one of the pillars of British pluralism is an attack on the conception of sovereignty dominant in Western political thought that understands the sovereign as unitary, absolute, and embodied exclusively in the state.[1] The British pluralists attacked this conception because it had historically been used to infringe on the internal life of associations and make them submit to the interests of the central authority.[2] They were right to do so, since claims to unitary and absolute sovereignty arose in opposition to internal groups. For reasons both historical and internal to the pluralist tradition, then, it is important to address the dominant conception of sovereignty and its alternatives.

Yet, despite the dismal view that pluralists held of the dominant theory of sovereignty, the concept is useful to understand the relation between individuals and groups, and between groups and the special kind of association that is the state. This is the second reason for framing the question of associational autonomy in terms of sovereignty. The authority that a sovereign wields over its individual and collective subjects is difficult to classify using any other concept. Apart from the context of slavery and serfdom, it is inappropriate to understand it as a *property* relation (the sovereign does not own the subject). Outside a hypothetical or metaphorical understanding of the social contract, it is also difficult to fully explain sovereignty as the object of a voluntary *agreement*, and even then the contractual element does not go to all the relevant aspects of the relationship between sovereign and subject. Even the instrument of *agency* or representation—which, through Hobbes, has been linked with state authority—must be distorted to make sense of the characteristics of sovereign power. Similarly, the authority that non-state groups (such as families, churches, unions, or universities) sometimes claim over their members is difficult to explain in terms of property, contract, or agency.

Since my discussion is set in the context of the rights of groups and associations, I will not discuss the concept in relation to foreign policy, although such authority is included in the exercise of sovereignty. My focus is primarily internal, to the relationship between the sovereign state and the various groups that operate within its territorial jurisdiction. I take my definition of sovereignty from Preston King, who describes a sovereign as 'an ultimate arbitral agent—whether a person or a body of persons—entitled to make

[1] The other pillars were 'that liberty is the most important political value, and that it is best preserved by power being dispersed' and 'that groups should be regarded as "persons".' David Nicholls, *Three Varieties of Pluralism* (Macmillan, 1974) 5.

[2] Thus the outrage of John Neville Figgis at French Prime Minister Emile Combes' assertion that '[t]here are, there can be no rights except the right of the State, and there are, and there can be no authority than the authority of the Republic.' See John Figgis, 'The Great Leviathan' in Paul Hirst (ed.), *The Pluralist Theory of the State* (Routledge, 1993) 112, quoting Emile Combes.

decisions and settle disputes within a political hierarchy with some degree of finality... [which] implies independence from external powers and ultimate authority or dominance over internal groups.'[3]

King's analytic definition of sovereignty contrasts with a more historically contingent way of defining sovereignty, characterized by the listing of attributes or 'marks' of sovereignty. Jean Bodin and Thomas Hobbes both give general definitions of sovereignty: for Bodin it is 'the absolute and perpetual power of a commonwealth'[4] ; for Hobbes, the representative of the people who 'may use the strength and means of them all, as he shall think expedient, for their peace and common defense.'[5] But these definitions are given substance by the enumeration of concrete institutional powers. Bodin declares the first and most essential of these 'the power of giving law or issuing commands to all in general and to each in particular.' But he sees fit to mention, as rights comprehended in the first, the power of:

> declaring war or making peace; hearing appeals in last instance from the judgments of any magistrate; instituting and removing the highest officers; imposing taxes and aids on subjects or exempting them; granting pardons and dispensations against the rigor of the law; determining the name, value, and measure of the coinage; requiring subjects and liege vassals to swear that they will be loyal without exception to the person to whom their oath is owed.[6]

Hobbes also enumerates various '*rights* and *faculties* of him, or them, on whom sovereign power is conferred',[7] the principal of which is the capacity to decide what means may be used to preserve peace. From it are derived the right to declare what doctrines may be lawfully taught; to make laws establishing property rights; to judge all controversies between subjects, and impose punishments and rewards; to declare war and grant peace, which includes the power to raise armies; to choose 'all counselors, ministers, magistrates, and officers'; to grant honors and titles to subjects.[8]

It is important to keep in mind both manners of defining sovereignty, the analytical and the historical, because both types of definition shed light on the concept. When we speak of the limitation of a state's sovereignty we may describe it abstractly as the curtailment, devolution, division, or reserve of arbitral authority, or concretely as the removal of one of the traditional

[3] Preston King, *The Ideology of Order: A Comparative Analysis of Jean Bodin and Thomas Hobbes* (2nd edn) (Frank Cass, 1999) xviii. I should note that King is not an advocate of the dominant conception.

[4] Jean Bodin (JH Franklin, ed. and tr.), *On Sovereignty: Four Chapters from The Six Books of the Commonwealth* (Cambridge University Press, 1992) 1. King explains however, that Bodin vacillates between an idea of absoluteness as *highest, unlimited*, or *total* power. See King, note 3, 140 ff.

[5] Thomas Hobbes, *Leviathan* (first published 1651, E Curley, ed.) (Hackett, 1994) 109.

[6] Bodin, note 4, 58–59.

[7] Hobbes, note 5, 110.

[8] Hobbes, note 5, 113–15. Hobbes also judges the power to raise money as essential, although that of coining money may be transferred to others.

marks of sovereignty from the control of the sovereign—usually the state. In either case, the person to whom arbitral authority is ceded (or in whom it is recognized) may be entitled to resolve disputes with some degree of finality either over certain issues, certain people, or certain things: the Church may have authority to appoint priests and bishops, a municipal government may set property taxes for its residents, and a landowner may decide whether to plant her parcel or let it lie fallow. In all these cases, an agent other than the state exercises arbitral authority over a domain traditionally counted among the marks sovereignty; if the non-state agent can oppose the right to exercise this authority to the state, and the state cannot simply revoke the right, a concession of sovereignty has occurred. In observing concrete instances of prerogatives traditionally ascribed to the sovereign being exercised by other hands, we can deduce that a transfer, however small, of sovereign authority.

Yet Bodin and Hobbes do not think that such a transfer is compatible with sovereignty. Both conceive of the marks or attributes of sovereignty as an indivisible whole, no part of which may be delegated to a subject without putting the position of the sovereign in jeopardy. Their insistence on unity can be interpreted through King's analytic definition of sovereignty: each mark of sovereignty is an instance of arbitral authority: authority to declare war and command troops, to judge in a given case, or prescribe a set of norms to guide some aspect of human behaviour. This authority should be perceived as legitimate, and must have the effect of resolving social conflicts effectively. This represents the first two elements of King's definition of sovereignty: entitlement, which implies a right that goes beyond the mere exercise of force, and means that a sovereign acts *de jure* and not only *de facto*; and finality, that is, the lack of a further court of appeal from the sovereign's decisions.

The question is why entitlement should imply independence (which means that the sovereign does not receive the grant of authority from somewhere else, but rather exercises it of its own right), and finality imply dominance (which, as the reverse of independence, denies sovereignty to any other group in the political society). The answer, I believe, is that arbitral authority for Bodin and Hobbes—and for adherents of the dominant conception of sovereignty generally—is an attribute of will, not the consequence of a certain normative structure. The will of the arbitral agent, the sovereign as lawmaker, precedes all rules and exists largely unbound by normative constraints. The point is almost ontological: the sovereign's claim to legitimacy cannot depend on a superior norm, because the sovereign is the source of all norms, and there can be no law before a lawgiver. This point precludes any constitutional constraints on the sovereign, and also denies any independent claim to legitimacy by individuals or groups other than the sovereign. Their claims can either come from the sovereign (in which case they are not independent) or from a norm that binds the sovereign and cannot be changed by it, which would beg the question of the origin of the norm.

Now, I believe that Bodin and Hobbes are wrong in reaching this conclusion, and that their error lies in conceiving of sovereignty as the exercise of an unbounded will. This conception of sovereignty, which I call voluntarism, emerges in the early modern period as a reaction against a conception of sovereignty that made all authority dependent on prior moral, religious, and historical norms. If voluntarism takes the sovereign to be prior to the law, the alternative, which I call constitutionalism, has the opposite conception, making the law prior to—or at least simultaneous with—sovereignty. The distinction is best illustrated by tracing the history of both conceptions.

5.2 EARLY MODERN SOVEREIGNTY

Theorists of royal absolutism more generally rejected the binding authority of custom, law or even the promises and charters of their predecessors.[9] Jean Bodin was the first to elaborate a systematic theory of absolute political authority.[10] As mentioned in section 5.1, Bodin defines sovereignty as 'the absolute and perpetual power of a commonwealth', consisting primarily in the prerogative to pass laws binding every subject in the realm.[11] All other rights and privileges of sovereignty—the waging of war, the hearing of appeals from the decision of any magistrate, the institution and destitution of officers, the capacity to require loyalty oaths from subjects—are included in this prerogative, which is only restricted by the (unenforceable) dictates of natural and divine law.[12]

Bodin argues that an exemption from obligation to one's sovereign—as in the case of a subaltern lord acting as judge of last instance in his fief—itself represents a curtailment of the superior's sovereignty, since it allows the exempted party to give law and pass judgment without the superior's approval. '[T]he first prerogative [...] of a sovereign prince is to give law to all in general and each in particular. But this is not sufficient. We have to add "without the consent of any other, whether greater, equal, or below him".'[13] As a result, Bodin dismisses the possibility of divided sovereignty as absurd.[14]

[9] Some of what follows is a more expansive version of some sections of Víctor M Muñiz-Fraticelli, 'The Problem of a Perpetual Constitution' in A Gosseries and L Meyer (eds), *Theories of Intergenerational Justice* (Oxford University Press, 2009).

[10] King, note 3, 74. Indeed, he precedes James on this by 22 years.

[11] Bodin, note 4, 56.

[12] Bodin, note 4, 13.

[13] Bodin, note 4, 56. Later, Bodin writes that all sovereign rights may be seen as comprehended in this first prerogative.

[14] Bodin, note 4, 27 and 91–92. The dismissal of divided sovereignty also implies that magistrates do not have actual sovereignty over their domain, but only the power of administration.

The authority of the sovereign is dependent on his will alone. It rests neither on the consent of the governed, nor on the custom of the land.[15] Indeed, absolute sovereignty is conceptually opposed to customary authority, and is historically defined in terms of the prince's prerogative to overturn traditional rights and liberties. Custom acquires authority only through its ratification—tacit or explicit—by the prince. As stated by Bodin: 'To put it briefly, custom has no force but by sufferance, and only in so far as it pleases the sovereign prince, who can make it a law by giving it his ratification. Hence the entire force of civil law and custom lies in the power of the sovereign prince.'[16]

As no traditional authority may stand but by the fiat of the absolute sovereign, neither can the privileges of corporate bodies—corporations, guilds, estates, and communities—persist without his leave. Bodin counts four types of corporate bodies: colleges, corporations, estates, and communities. The relationship between the civic bodies is not entirely clear.[17] What is clear, however, is their relationship to the sovereign: Bodin considers every private corporate body—from guilds to towns to universities—as constituted by 'a right of legitimate community under the sovereign power [where] the word legitimate conveys the authority of the sovereign, without whose permission there is no college.'[18] Bodin does not mean that these corporate bodies have their historical origin in the sovereign's will.[19] Influenced by the medieval mindset, he understands the political structure as a hierarchical ordering of different groups.[20] What he claims is that the legitimacy of every group other

[15] Bodin, note 4, 23 and 56–58. [16] Bodin, note 4, 57–58.

[17] Colleges and guilds could be associations, e.g. of clerics or craftsmen; several colleges could join to form a corporation, and several (or even all) of these could constitute an estate or a university. Yet towns and other communities, while also corporate bodies, could have within them guilds and corporations, as well as unattached families. It is certain that some hierarchy prevails, but its structure is not obvious. See e.g. King, note 3, 97, 105. See also Jean Bodin, *Les Six Livres de la République, Livre Troisième* (first published 1576, C Frémont, M-D Couzinet and H Rochais, eds) (Librairie Arthème Fayard, 1986) 173–74.

[18] Bodin, note 17, 178–79. Preston King translates *droit de communauté legitime* as *lawful community*, which seems to me an unnecessary departure from the original. It is not the actual group of people that is of interest to Bodin, but their right to be organized and have their actions recognized by the sovereign authority (see King, note 3, 98).

[19] Bodin sketches a history of the origin of corporate bodies in *République*: 'And the origin of the corps and colleges was the family, as there were many branches that had shot from the main stem, [and thus] it became necessary to build houses, then hamlets and villages, and to become so neighborly that it seemed all were but one family.' A familiar account of the state of nature follows: with a growing population, dispute and strife broke out, and this drove villages to raise walls and to appoint princes to defend them. Guilds and colleges may have arisen spontaneously before the state, but they gained legal sanction because they served the sovereign to facilitate the maintenance of order in incipient republics through the organization of trades and professions (Bodin, note 17, 174–78). See also José Manuel Bernardo Ares, 'Les Corps Politiques dans la «République» de Jean Bodin' in J-M Servet (ed.), *Jean Bodin: Actes de Colloque Interdisciplinaire d'Angers, 24-27 Mai 1984* (Presses de l'Université d'Angers, 1955) 35.

[20] The family, which is the ultimate origin of all corporate bodies, is not included among them, since Bodin considers it a natural community, not a civic or 'artificial' entity. It stands apart because it is the most basic of these, and one that is putatively pre-political (see Bodin, note 17, 173 and King, note 3, 99, 102, 110).

than the sovereign can only follow from sovereign ratification. For Bodin, 'Though he thought they originally evolved prior to the establishment of the state, he believed that, once the state was in being, corporations had to be sanctioned by it.'[21] The corporate bodies are organized through the voluntary association of its members, who come together to pursue a common interest. Yet it is the interest of the state—which is twofold: fellowship and administration—that motivates sovereign sanction and actually constitutes the group as a self-governing entity.[22]

The problem for Bodin, one that he evaded rather than resolved, is that the sovereign, as much as any other body in the realm, is dependent on certain norms for its authority. The sovereign can overturn custom, repeal prior laws or overrule the decrees of inferior nobles, but cannot, however, do without the constitutive laws of the realm. The Salic law, for instance—which governs the manner of succession to the Crown, famously restricting it to the male line—is unassailable:

> As for laws which concern the state of the kingdom and its basic form, since these are annexed and united to the crown like the Salic law, the prince cannot detract from them. And should he do so, his successor can nullify anything that has been done in prejudice of the royal laws on which the sovereign majesty is founded and supported.[23]

Finality, then, is the operative principle behind the Bodinian sovereign. Such sovereignty is defined essentially against subaltern groups, and exercised against their independent claims of authority. The problem, of course, is that these groups claim for themselves the same source of legitimacy as the king, and an equal degree of finality in their deliberations. The exemplary case here is the power of the king to impose taxes, which parliaments everywhere maintained could not be done without their consent. Surprisingly, Bodin agrees, appealing, it seems, to the moral principle that no one, not even the king, can take another's property without his consent.[24] But he immediately admits an exception in cases of necessity. The explanation for Bodin's ambivalence is perhaps the position that he occupies in the history of political thought. He is at once a medievalist, who is intent on describing the political constitution as opposed to justifying it, and a modern, intent on freeing the sovereign will from the boundaries that other wills impose upon it. The way that sovereignty operates in his account, however, places him among the voluntarists. It is not law that limits sovereignty, but law made by another will independent of the royal one. Constitutional limits that enable

[21] King, note 3, 96.

[22] Bodin, note 17, 178. *Fellowship* and *administration* are King's terms, which he equates with Bodin's *la religion* and *la police*, respectively (see King, note 3 above, 107).

[23] Bodin, note 4, 18. [24] Bodin, note 4, 21.

the royal will to operate are not to be disturbed, but those that allow other actors to exercise their arbitral authority with some degree of finality are illegitimate.

Political thought in England followed a similar course, but its proponents did not prove so equivocal. King James, in his quarrels with Parliament and the Common Law courts, sustained that the prerogative of the king was absolutely free, he was bound to the law only through his good will, but not because the law set enforceable bounds on his authority.[25] While the king took an oath at his coronation to maintain the constitution of the realm, which James acknowledged as 'the clearest, ciuill, and fundamentall Law, whereby the Kings office is properly defined this oath was unenforceable, as the king was bound neither by the fundamental law nor by the promises of previous monarchs.[26] As another absolutist, Robert Filmer, reiterated, there were kings before there were laws; the law originated entirely from the king and did not constitute his office or prescribe the proper sphere of his authority.[27]

Thomas Hobbes, in turn, shares with James and Filmer an antipathy to arguments of 'ancient constitutionalism to the limitation of the sovereign power by custom, statute or the even promises of prior sovereigns.[28] It is true that Hobbes' sovereign, like its medieval counterpart, is a corporate person, and is constituted by a contract whereby it acquired the authority to act in the name of its subjects. The concept of fundamental law Hobbes reduces to 'that, by which subjects are bound to uphold whatsoever power is given to the sovereign, whether a monarch, or a sovereign assembly, without which the commonwealth cannot stand; such as is the power of war and peace, of judicature, of election of officers, and of doing whatsoever he shall think necessary for the public good.'[29] Hobbes understands the utility of ruling *through* laws,[30] but allows the sovereign to either change the laws at will or, when necessary, to disregard the law and 'demand, or take any thing by

[25] Thus the title of James' 1598 work: 'The Trew Law of *Free* Monarchies' in JP Sommerville (ed.), *King James VI and I: Political Writings* (Cambridge University Press, 1994) 75.

[26] James, note 25, 65 and 81. In the oath, the king promised 'to maintaine the Religion presently professed within their countrie... to maintaine all the lowable and good Lawes made by their predecessours... to maintaine the whole countrey, and euery state therein, in all their ancient Priuiledges and Liberties, as well against all forreine enemies, as among themselues.'

[27] Robert Filmer, *Patriarcha* (first published 1680, JP Sommerville (ed.)) (Cambridge University Press, 1991) 32ff, 57–58.

[28] Hobbes, note 5, 174 (He writes, for instance, that '[w]hen long use obtaineth the authority of a law, it is not the length of time that maketh the authority, but the will of the sovereign signified by his silence, (for silence is sometimes an argument of consent)').

[29] Hobbes, note 5, 189.

[30] Hobbes, note 5, 231 and 239–40.

pretence of his Power.'[31] The Leviathan is, at every moment, a supra-legal creature—the creator of law, not the reverse.

> For having power to make, and repeal laws, he may when he pleaseth, free himself from that subjection, by repealing those laws that trouble him, and making of new; and consequently he was free before. For he is free, that can be free when he will: nor is it possible for any person to be bound to himself; because he that can bind, can release; and therefore he that is bound to himself only, is not bound.[32]

In Hobbes the will is freed from all legal constraints. Even the contract, which seems to exercise a constitutive function in the establishment of the sovereign, is not a legal act (although it takes its form from the law of agency) in the ordinary sense, but an abdication of authority. The sovereign is all that remains after all have given up their right of nature. The sovereign power is exercised with absolute discretion, extending even to the rules of succession, because it is in no significant way formal, but rather purposive. The sovereign has one overarching directive: the maintenance of peace. Its performance is not to be measured by its conformity to an independent normative standard, but rather to a factual result: as long as there actually is peace, subjects are obligated to obey.

Because the constitution of the sovereign is pre-legal and thus extra-constitutional, the apparent similarity between the sovereign and other corporate bodies dissolves. Hobbes' theory of corporate structure—which, despite its normative shortcomings, deserves broader recognition as a masterpiece of political taxonomy—in fact makes no distinctions between the nature of public or private bodies, families or the state. All of these are but different kinds of 'systems'. Hobbes' definition of a system is extremely general: it consists of 'any numbers of men joined in one interest, or one business'.[33] Systems may be *regular* or *irregular*, depending on whether 'one man, or assembly of men, is constituted representative of the whole number.'[34] Regular systems may be *absolute*—a class with the Commonwealth as its only member—, or *dependent*. Dependent systems, in turn, may be either *political*—as are Bodies Politic, corporations, and persons-in-law—, or *private*—those constituted by subjects among themselves. The sovereign is a corporate body like all others, constituted by the consent of all individuals.

[31] Hobbes, note 5, 153.

[32] Hobbes, note 5, 174. It is, however, true that a sovereign who invokes a standing law—even one passed by a predecessor and left standing—must submit to the courts for judgment; but that sovereign is free to change the law if it sees fit, or to exercise its prerogative to take the desired action without invoking legislation.

[33] Hobbes, note 5, 146.

[34] Hobbes, note 5, 101–105 (Hobbes' theory of representation is laid out in Chapter XVI of *Leviathan*; it depends, predictably, on the consent of the persons represented to allow another to act in their name).

But the extreme latitude that subjects give to the Leviathan precludes them from undertaking any further act of autonomous association. All 'systems', other than the Commonwealth, are dependent on the sovereign's will; otherwise, they would threaten it. The distinction between political and private systems, then, pertains only to the attribution of initiative in their origin, and the interests the group is to serve: both must be authorized by law, although political systems must also have an express grant, letter or writ authorizing them to act on the sovereign's behalf.[35]

5.3 MEDIEVAL SOVEREIGNTY

In 1608, the celebrated jurist Sir Edward Coke passed judgment in *Calvin's* case, which concerned the question of a subject's allegiance to King James VI and I. James I of England, Coke explains, although the same *natural* person as James the VI of Scotland, was not one, but two distinct political *persons*.

> It is true, that the King hath two capacities in him: one a natural body, being descended of the blood royal of the Realm; and that this body is the creation of Almighty God, and is subject to death, infirmity, and such like; the other is a politic, body or capacity, so called, because it is framed by the policy of man... and in this capacity the King is esteemed to be immortal, invisible, not subject to death, infirmity, infancy, nonage, &c.[36]

Two years after *Calvin's* case, Coke again referred to the idea that the office of the sovereign was different from the individual who occupied it, and that the constitutional conditions of that office both authorized and bounded the prerogative of the individual who occupied it. According to Coke:

> Note, the King by his Proclamation, or other waies, cannot change any part of the Common Law, or Statute Law, or the Customs of the Realm... And so it was resolved, that the King hath no Prerogative, but that which the Law of the Land allows him.[37]

The idea that the sovereign does not derive legitimate authority by a sheer act of will, but rather that his powers and prerogatives derive from a legal order that precedes him, is the central element in what is often referred to as the medieval theory of sovereignty. The medieval or 'ancient' constitution

[35] King, note 3, 222 ('Hobbes makes three basic points. The first is that there are subordinate organisations within the state. The second is that these organisations may pursue some limited common interest restricted to their members, or a broader interest in which the entire society shares. The third is that corporations can only legitimately exist if they are expressly sanctioned or tacitly tolerated by the sovereign power').

[36] Edward Coke, *The Selected Writings of Sir Edward Coke* (S Sheppard (ed.)) (Liberty Fund, 2003) 189.

[37] Coke, note 36, 488–89; see also the discussion of Coke's legal philosophy in Harold J Berman, *Law and Revolution, II: The Impact of the Protestant Reformations on the Western Legal Tradition* (Belknap Press, 2003) 238–45.

did not recognize absolute political or legislative authority in the sovereign. Sovereignty was bound, on the one hand, by natural and divine law and, on the other, by longstanding customs and charters. But natural law was notoriously difficult to discern, much less enforce; while it was sometimes invoked by jurists and philosophers, its impact on the actual controversies of the time was less than its influence on the philosophy of later centuries.[38] Longstanding custom and royal charters had a much greater effect on the development of constitutionalism.

The most notable example of the authority of custom is probably the *Lex Salica*. Originally, it was a collection of traditional practices among the early Franks, loosely codified in the fifth century, yet it would continue to be invoked as an irrevocable quasi-constitutional guide to the royal succession at least until the end of the *ancien régime*. The importance of the *Lex Salica* and other such customary principles was that they laid down the conditions by which a monarch gained legitimacy, and thereby 'constituted' the monarchy. Not all customs had such high standing, and many were superseded by royal proclamations and statutes, but others were tolerated by the crown and continued to be invoked as binding law. As secular law developed, moreover, much of local custom was assimilated into royal law, either by incorporation into statutes, or by recognition in special charters.[39]

Charters themselves had more pragmatic origins, as they were usually granted by monarchs to stave off rebellion or to procure military or financial support from their subjects. But, once granted, they could also be invoked as restrictions on the sovereign that he (or his heirs) could not cast off without injustice. *Magna Charta* was signed by King John under an imminent threat of violence from the English barons, and he subsequently attempted to repudiate it, yet it was confirmed by his grandson, Edward, not only in his own name but in that of his heirs and successors.[40] The Great Charter became one of the keystones of the 'rights of Englishmen', as Burke, writing nearly six centuries later, still maintained. To be sure, Burke noted that:

> Our oldest reformation is that of Magna Charta. You will see that Sir Edward Coke, that great oracle of our law, and indeed all the great men who follow him, to Blackstone, are industrious to prove the pedigree of our liberties. They

[38] Antony Black, *Political Thought in Europe, 1250-1450* (Cambridge University Press, 1992) 34–37.

[39] Berman, note 37, 456, 470–73, 480–81. By the seventeenth century this practice had been acknowledged as a legal norm. Thus, as the liberties of the City of London were concerned, Sir Edward Coke would write 'that a man cannot claim by custome or prescription against a Statute, unlesse the custome, or prescription be saved by another Statute' (see Coke, note 36, 798).

[40] In that confirmation it was also made part of the Common Law of England, which enabled Sir Edward Coke, four centuries later, to cite it as legal precedent on more than one occasion. Coke stated, without reservation, that it had been King Edward's intention 'that this great Parliamentary Charter [*Magna Charta*] might live and take effect in all successions of ages forever' (see Coke, note 36, 757).

> endeavor to prove that the ancient charter, the Magna Charta of King John, was connected with another positive charter from Henry I, and that both the one and the other were nothing more than a reaffirmance of the still more ancient standing law of the kingdom.[41]

The logic behind charters extended also to parliaments and assemblies of estates, born too of practical necessity. Their chief function was to procure revenue in extraordinary circumstances, as when a king embarked on a military venture.[42] In exchange for additional taxes, the nobles, clergy and burghers often demanded concessions, which the king was obliged to respect. These concessions could eventually rise to the level of custom, or they could be incorporated into royal charters which could then be invoked against a monarch or his descendants.

From the limitations that custom, charters, and parliaments imposed on medieval monarchies came the concept of the 'rule of law' which lies at the heart of both medieval and modern constitutionalism. In his governing or administrative capacity, a king had no superior, no judge but God to limit his authority; in this sense he was above the law. But in another sense, the law itself was the normative source of his authority: the law determined the conditions under which the king could come to assume his office and defined the form and extent of his power. It was constitutive of kingship, both in the sense of creating the office and of defining (and thus bounding) its authority. In the same way, it governed the privileges and duties of the other orders of the realm, from serfs to the highest nobles. This made the king bound to the natural law, to custom, and to his own oaths and charters, and instructed him to govern in accordance with the laws of the realm and not by arbitrary decrees and proclamations.[43] Authority, privilege, and obligation all depended on each other.

The process of 'constituting' the sovereign had another important effect: it differentiated between the natural and the juridical office of kingship, between the man who occupied the throne and the office of the throne itself. The idea was most famously expressed in the image of the king's 'two bodies': a body natural, which was simply the ordinary, human, mortal person of the king, and the body politic, which was a mystical, artificial, immortal person.[44] Most importantly for a theory of sovereignty, however, is that the mystical body was a *legal* person, a juristic construction. The mere act of descent from a bloodline may entitle a man to become king, but it says

[41] Edmund Burke, *Reflections on the Revolution in France* (first published 1790, JGA Pocock (ed.)) (Hackett, 1987) 28.

[42] Black, note 38, 162ff.

[43] See e.g., Charles H McIlwain, *Constitutionalism, Ancient and Modern* (Cornell University Press, 1947) 74–87; E Ernst Kantorowicz, *The King's Two Bodies: A Study in Mediaeval Political Theology* (Princeton University Press, 1997) 148ff; Black, note 38, 152–55.

[44] Kantorowicz, note 43, 13, quoting Plowden's Law Reports.

nothing about the prerogatives of kingship, about the authority of the office or the relation that it may have to other institutions of the realm. The juristic construction of kingship was inherently limitative, but it was also facilitative: through the legal order the king acquired legitimate authority, but only insofar as that authority was available to be acquired.

5.4 THE LIMITS OF MEDIEVAL CONSTITUTIONALISM

There are several problems with the pluralist, constitutionalist conception of sovereignty that undergirded the late medieval political order. The first is the problem of explaining the origin of the legal order itself, from which the rights of sovereignty proceed. The second is the practical problem of how different competing claims to sovereignty can be adjudicated.

There are several ways of explaining how a legal order comes about. The first is straightforwardly historical, as through the operation of ancient custom, the origin of which is forgotten and therefore beyond question or reproach. The Salic Law, mentioned in section 5.3, gives the example. The grant of royal charters, while lacking the benefit of historical amnesia, shares in the historical character of custom, even if the author or grantor of a charter can be identified. The appeal to custom or ancient origin has a considerable drawback, however. It leads inevitably to infinite regress. A norm, however ancient, must have been initiated by someone, and that initiator could not have recourse to historical authority. A custom, true, does not originate through a deliberate act, but the decision to grant it normative weight does. I am not aware that this was much of a concern to most ancient constitutionalists, however, which is perhaps explained by one of the most significant traits of the medieval conception: the medieval theory of sovereignty was essentially descriptive and static. It referred to an order that was taken as given, and made normative judgments with reference to that order. But the order itself is not called into question. Therefore, the problem of the origin of the normativity of custom does not arise, because custom is the measure of normativity, not the subject of it.

One way of circumventing the problem of historical regress is to lay claim to the tradition of natural law, available to and used by medieval jurists to justify (and criticize) the political order.[45] There are two problems with adopting this approach, which I will only mention here. The first is that both constitutionalists and voluntarists lay claim to the natural law as a justification of their conception of sovereignty. For Bodin, the natural law is a true limitation on the sovereign, but not one that any subject is

[45] Black, note 38, 34ff.

entitled to invoke, because the sovereign is subject only to the laws of God.[46] For Hobbes, the natural law—the mandate to preserve one's life above all else—is the motivation for laying down one's rights and accepting the total power of the sovereign.[47] And King James insists that 'by the Law of Nature the King becomes a naturall Father to all his Lieges at his Coronation.'[48] All three considered that a just monarch who acted in accordance with the natural and divine law would look after the welfare of his subjects. Coke, an opponent of James' absolutism, laid claim to the natural law in a different way, by incorporating it into the common law of England, which was interpreted by judges as himself, sometimes as a bulwark to the prerogative of the monarch.[49] The natural law, in short, is so difficult to discern authoritatively that it underdetermines the grounds of sovereignty and transforms a dispute over the historical origin of a sovereign's claim into a dispute over the normative grounds of sovereignty itself.

The second problem of the medieval conception of sovereignty is precisely that of adjudicating disputes between different authorities. McIlwain notes that 'the fundamental weakness of all medieval constitutionalism lay in its failure to enforce any penalty, except the threat or the exercise of revolutionary force, against a prince who actually trampled under foot those rights of his subjects which undoubtedly lay beyond the scope of his legitimate authority.'[50] Preston King echoes this sentiment when he quips that '[t]he ultimate sin of absolutism lies in the promotion of total organization, that of pluralism in the promotion of no organization.'[51] In part because medieval constitutionalism was descriptive and static, it could not resolve this issue without undermining the entire legal order.

The first problem of medieval constitutionalism—that of origins—may be resolved through a transcendental argument.[52] Such an argument is anachronistic in the medieval context, but my interest here is mainly theoretical, not historical. The justification of the constitutionalist theory of sovereignty—the theory that says that the sovereign is constituted by law, and that law is therefore prior to sovereignty—involves a transcendental assumption. As sovereignty is more than the mere exercise of force, it must be the case that there is a norm that grants legitimate authority to the sovereign. Sovereignty presupposes such a norm. While it is true that the norm must have an origin, the sovereign cannot be the source of it, because there is no sovereign before the norm, only an individual or group of individuals exercising power. If anything, the norm and the sovereign come into

[46] Bodin, note 4, 13. [47] Hobbes, note 5, 79–80. [48] James VI and I, note 25, 65, 76.

[49] Coke, note 36, 195ff. [50] McIlwain, note 43, 93. [51] King, note 3, 19.

[52] I develop this argument in a slightly different context in section 5.2 of 'The Problem of a Perpetual Constitution' Muñiz-Fraticelli, note 9.

being at once, because the norm that entitles the sovereign authority also constitutes it. This argument does not exclude the possibility of a unitary, absolute sovereign, but it does not mandate it. The norm or norms that constitute sovereign authority may provide also for a limited or divided sovereign, whether in the manner of a federation or through strong constitutional guarantees of private property and other legal rights.

It is not necessary, however, to accept the ontological commitments of the transcendental argument to understand sovereignty as an authority constituted by law. In criticizing John Austin's model of law as a habit of obedience, a model that invokes many of the same voluntarist assumptions of Hobbes' conception of sovereignty, HLA Hart observes that:

> where the sovereign is not identifiable independently of the rules, we cannot represent the rules in this way as merely the terms or conditions under which the society habitually obeys the sovereign. The rules are *constitutive* of the sovereign, not merely things which we should have to mention in a description of the habits of obedience to the sovereign.[53]

If we apply this reasoning to the medieval theory of sovereignty, we notice first that it embraces a political ontology unavailable to the voluntarists. Take Berman's description of the function of urban charters. An urban charter effects an ontological transformation of the community, and a change of status in its members—from mere individuals to citizens. Indeed, for Berman, 'Acceptance of the urban charter was rather an avowal of consent to a permanent relationship.' He continues:

> [I]t was an agreement to enter into a status, that is, into a relationship whose terms were fixed by law and could not be altered by the will of the parties. In the case of the founding of a city or town, however, the status that was formed was that of a corporation (universitas), ... a body of people sharing common legal functions and acting as a legal entity. In one sense, therefore, the promulgation and acceptance of the urban charter was not a contract at all but a kind of sacrament; it both symbolized and effectuated the formation of the community and the establishment of the community's law.[54]

We are also faced with the theoretical possibility that sovereignty might be plural, as long as the office that is entitled to rule with finality on some matter is (1) dependent on the legal structure (the constitutional structure) as the source of its authority, and (2) not dominant over all other groups in the political society, by virtue of the limitation of its jurisdiction and the allotment of the unassumed jurisdiction to some other authority. This was arguably the case in medieval Europe, where ecclesiastical matters were subject

[53] HLA Hart, *The Concept of Law* (2nd edn) (Oxford University Press, 1994) 76–77.

[54] Berman, note 37, 393.

to the jurisdiction of the Church while secular matters were entrusted to royal, urban, or other specialized authorities. The very individuals who, by their common charter, were now citizens, were nonetheless also Christians, and that in a different capacity. Some of their affairs (marriages, contracts) would be regulated by an ecclesiastical court while others (crimes, taxes) by a secular one. In a way, like King James, their persons were distinct depending on the jurisdiction to which the matter under consideration belonged.

There is, nonetheless, another problem to be solved even in this arrangement. If there are multiple jurisdictions available to hear a case, it is still necessary to determine under which jurisdiction the case belongs. Would this imply a sovereign authority that would be final over both jurisdictions? No such authority was available to medieval pluralist constitutionalism, and the Investiture controversy was one of the effects of this void. Still, no possibility of associational autonomy remains if all possible controversies in a society must be refereed by the same judge; an organized group must be allowed to make some final and unappealable decisions with regards to its interests, its goods, and its members if it is to retain its autonomy. The difficult choice between an omnicompetent sovereign judge on the one hand, and the lack of any discernible authority on the other drove some political pluralists, like Harold Laski, to eschew the concept of political authority altogether, and submit every act of the state to the internal judgment of every person's conscience.[55]

But this is precisely the 'ultimate sin' of pluralism that King decries. Authority, as Joseph Raz has explained, mediates 'between people and the right reasons which apply to them, so that the authority judges and pronounces what they ought to do according to right reason.'[56] The state certainly claims authority of this sort, but so do many associations: churches claim authority on matters of sexual conduct, universities on tenure decisions, parents on what their children should eat and wear. A complete dismissal of the concept of authority because of its abuse when concentrated in the hands of a single sovereign does away with the authority of every other organized group and reduces pluralism to individualism.[57] What is needed is a way of maintaining the concept of authority, but distinguishing between the varied competences

[55] Harold J Laski, 'Law and the State' in Paul Hirst (ed.), *The Pluralist Theory of the State* (Routledge, 1993) 205–206. See also Laski's *Studies in the Problem of Sovereignty* (Fertig, 1968) chapter 1.

[56] Joseph Raz, 'Authority, Law, and Morality' in *Ethics in the Public Domain: Essays in the Morality of Law and Politics* (Oxford University Press, 2001) 214. There are complications in Raz's legal theory for a pluralist account of associational autonomy, but I think that his conception of authority is generally compatible with my views on the status of associations in a well-developed legal system. I intend to develop this point further.

[57] Not surprisingly, Laski is often identified as an individualist pluralist. See e.g. Henry M Magid, *English Political Pluralism: The Problem of Freedom and Organization* (Columbia University Press, 1941) 47ff.

of different arbiters whose decisions are legitimate and final within their scope or jurisdiction.

Here we may again turn to Hart, and his famous distinction between primary and secondary rules. Primary rules, Hart argues, are those that impose obligations directly, like traffic rules, criminal statutes, or the sentence of a court. Secondary rules, by contrast, 'specify the ways in which the primary rules may be conclusively ascertained, introduced, eliminated, varied, and the fact of their violation ascertained.'[58] There is no reason (as Hart himself admits) for the secondary rules of a society to specify that all controversies are ultimately appealable to the same court, that the same legislative body may pronounce law in all matters, and that other bodies are either excluded from attaining legitimate final authority, or only allowed such authority by leave of the sovereign, which is to say, not at all.

Federalism, which is a species of pluralism, proceeds along these lines. Certain matters are relegated to the federal jurisdiction and others to the state or provincial jurisdiction. The rules for determining which jurisdiction is entitled to make final determination on any given case are not entirely uncontested, but at their core, are generally understood. The application of the federal structure to groups has examples in the medieval context, but also in the present. The decisions of ecclesiastical authorities over the selection of clergy and hierarchy, for instance, are generally unassailed by the secular courts. While civil marriage is regulated by the civil law, the same marriage may have a different status in religious court.

Such division of sovereign power is not available to a voluntarist account. It requires a constitutional understanding of sovereignty, one that recognizes the legal order to be prior to the sovereign structures constituted by it. In the voluntarist account, the sovereign authority merely tolerates the group's prerogative by abstaining from intervention in its affairs. But it could intervene if it deems it necessary. A pluralist model, however, denies that the abstention of the political sovereign should be grounded on its own inhibition. Rather, it prescribes that the political sovereign is authorized to act within its sphere of competence to the exclusion of all other authorities (and therefore is entitled to be the final arbiter in that field) but that outside it, it has no authority and acts *ultra vires*. Reversely, associations properly organized under some suitable constitutive norm do not derive their authority from the state, which renders that authority vulnerable. They are, in an important way, equal to it, and by that virtue just as entitled to be final within their domain. If conflicts over jurisdiction arise, state authority can only be justified to associations if it internalizes their own claims to authority (as I argue in chapter 8).

[58] Hart, note 53, 94.

6

A Positivist Pluralism?

Since its emergence in the 1970s and 80s, the literature on legal pluralism has been largely hostile to the legal positivist tradition, while positivism has passed from dismissing pluralism as a logical impossibility, to acknowledging the existence of non-state legal orders but being largely indifferent towards them. This mutual disregard is founded on a misunderstanding. On the one hand, social-scientific legal pluralism remains fixated on John Austin's articulation of legal positivism, but this articulation has been superseded by the later developments of HLA Hart and, especially, Joseph Raz, and is contradicted by contemporary legal philosophers. On the other hand, the positivist tradition, with some justification, has focused its attention on the state as the paradigmatic source of law. When they have nodded in the direction of non-state legal systems, such as church law, they have often treated them as curiosities or exceptions rather than important exemplars of legal validity. Yet nothing in contemporary positivist theory (with few exceptions) is incompatible with non-state law. Rather, the analytical tools of positivism can provide more solid grounding for the claims to legal validity of non-state normative orders, especially when these orders are dependent on institutionalized social facts of common practice and are distinct from more inchoate normative systems, such as ethical or cultural norms.

In Chapter 5 I reconstructed the idea of sovereignty implied in the Western constitutional tradition. Such an idea of sovereignty rests, in the first place, on a methodological conception of sovereignty that is defined both analytically and institutionally: analytically as supreme arbitral authority within a jurisdiction, and institutionally as historically contingent 'marks' of sovereignty that circumscribe the sovereign's jurisdiction. In second place, the idea of sovereignty rests on a substantive conception of sovereignty as constituted by law: the notion, derived from medieval constitutionalism and echoed in the work of legal theorists like HLA Hart, that law is prior to the sovereign, and not the reverse.[1]

[1] See the discussion in Chapter 5. For an extension of Hart's ideas about constitutive conventions, see Andrei Marmor, *Social Conventions* (Princeton University Press, 2009) chapter 2. For a critique of

Both the methodological and the substantive conceptions find expression in the complex tradition of Western constitutionalism, a tradition that retains many structural elements of the medieval ancient constitution even as it adopts Enlightenment rationalism as a justificatory ideal. Because of its complexity, I argue, the Western constitutional tradition can accommodate political and legal pluralism without abandoning the key conceptual elements of the juristic conception of sovereignty. But there remain certain elements in the Western constitutionalist tradition that stand in the way of a pluralist reconstruction, especially the reliance, by many (though not all) strains of that tradition on 'controversial or incredible metaphysical commitments',[2] specifically on comprehensive moral conceptions that are not shared by many of the associations that claim political and legal authority in a pluralist society.[3] This is not a judgment on the merits of these moral commitments. It is a methodological statement about the subject of a pluralist theory: it is a theory about the existence of multiple sources of political and legal authority, not about the merits of the claims to authority that these sources make. It is thus aligned with contemporary accounts of the nature of law identified with legal positivism, and specifically with the version of positivism championed by Joseph Raz, John Gardner, and Andrei Marmor, among others.[4]

Chapters 7 and 8 will round out the reconstruction of the pluralist conception of sovereignty by grounding it in the theses of contemporary legal positivism. The objective of this section is to make the idea of pluralist authority intelligible in the context of analytic legal and political theory and of the concept of authority prevalent in this theory. I will not address the debate between legal positivists and traditional iusnaturalists, or Dworkinian proponents of a theory of 'law as integrity'. Rather, I will focus on the critique of

conventionalism generally, see Leslie Green, 'Positivism and Conventionalism' 12 *Canadian Journal of Law and Jurisprudence* 50 (1999).

[2] Brian Leiter, 'Why Legal Positivism (Again)?' (9 September 2013) *Australasian Society of Legal Philosophy*, 12. Available at: <http://papers.ssrn.com/sol3/papers.cfm?abstract_id=2323013>.

[3] Robert George's interpretation of natural law is ostensibly neutral with respect to the truths of religion, but his more polemical work reveals a much more central place for theological premises in his argument (which is not reason enough to condemn them, but simply to point out that they are, in fact, controversial). Compare Robert George, *In Defense of Natural Law* (Oxford University Press, 1999) 131ff to *Clash of Orthodoxies* (Intercollegiate Studies Institute, 2001). John Finnis expressly disassociates himself from an account of natural law that is dependent on an affirmative answer to the question of God's existence, but again, whether he succeeds is another question. John Finnis, *Natural Law and Natural Rights* (2nd edn) (Oxford University Press, 2011) 48–49. For criticism of the independence of natural law theories see the essays in *Natural Law, Liberalism, and Morality* (Oxford University Press, 2001), especially the ones by Stephen Macedo and Walter Berns.

[4] Joseph Raz, *Practical Reason and Norms* (Oxford University Press, 1975), *The Morality of Freedom* (Oxford University Press, 1986), *Between Authority and Interpretation* (Oxford University Press, 2010); John Gardner, *Law as a Leap of Faith* (Oxford University Press, 2012); Andrei Marmor, *Positive Law and Objective Values* (Oxford University Press, 2001), *Philosophy of Law* (Princeton University Press, 2011).

legal positivism most germane to my own project, namely the school or tradition of legal pluralism, both in its social-scientific and normative varieties.[5] I argue that legal pluralism has been historically hostile to legal positivism, but without warrant, as positivism provides the best grounding for pluralist theses; the hostility of pluralism to positivism rests on mischaracterization or misunderstanding, and should evaporate once the central theses of positivism, as developed in its most recent literature, are laid out. My position is reinforced by explicit discussion of multiple legal authorities in such positivist authors as Raz, Marmor, and Garner. Any remaining pluralist objections to positivism, as well as positivist objections to pluralism, are not disputes about the nature of law or the necessary requirements of a legal system, but rather normative disputes about the relative authority of legal officials and legal subjects. The consequence of adopting a positivist pluralism is a clearer understanding of what makes the institutional normative claims of certain associations recognizably legal in ways that can be acknowledged by state law, which usually treats legal and non-legal norms differently.[6]

6.1 THE ROOTS OF ANTIPATHY TOWARDS POSITIVISM

Positivist is not a term of praise among legal pluralists. It is not even a neutral term, or a mere description of a conceptual stance about the criteria for legal validity, but a term of opprobrium and a charge of ideological obtuseness, and perhaps of conceptual (or perhaps actual) imperialism. Over the several decades in which legal pluralism has moved from 'its combative infancy'[7] to

[5] Brian Tamanaha distinguishes social scientific and normative legal pluralism—the former originating in the legal anthropology of Sally Falk Moore, John Griffiths, and Sally Engle Merry, among many others, the latter separately defended by Lon Fuller and Robert Cover. Brian Tamanaha, 'Understanding Legal Pluralism' *Sydney Law Review* 30(2008): 375–411. For the social scientific pluralists, see John Griffiths, 'What is Legal Pluralism?' (1996) 24 *Journal of Legal Pluralism* 1; Sally Falk Moore, 'Law and Social Change: The Semi-Autonomous Social Field as an Appropriate Subject of Study' (1973) 7 *Law and Society Review* 719; SE Merry, 'Legal Pluralism' (1988) 22 *Law and Society Review* 869; Franz von Benda Beckham, 'Who's Afraid of Legal Pluralism?' (2002) 47 *Journal of Legal Pluralism* 37. For normative pluralists, see Harold Berman, *Law and Revolution* (Harvard University Press, 1983); Robert Cover, 'Nomos and Narrative' (1983) 97 *Harvard Law Review* 4. Some pluralists straddle the line between the normative and the social scientific, e.g. Paul Schiff Berman, *Global Legal Pluralism* (Cambridge University Press, 2012); RA Macdonald, 'Custom Made—For a Non-chirographic Critical Legal Pluralism' (2011) 26 *Canadian Journal of Law and Society* 301–27; Brian Tamanaha, *A General Jurisprudence of Law and Society* (Oxford University Press, 2001). Finally, Lon Fuller is a difficult case to categorize. See Jeremy Waldron, 'Legal Pluralism and the Contrast Between Hart's Jurisprudence and Fuller's' in Peter Cane (ed.), *The Hart-Fuller Debate in the Twenty-First Century* (Hart, 2010) 135–55.

[6] As Roderick Macdonald reminded me, the reverse must also hold true: The criteria that make the law of certain associations recognizably legal to the state must make the law of the state recognizably legal to these associations. This explains Harold Berman's surprising observation in *Law and Revolution* that '[i]t is this plurality of jurisdictions and legal systems that makes the supremacy of law both necessary and possible.' Berman, note 5, 10.

[7] Griffiths, note 5, 1.

'the mainstream of legal discourse'[8] its proponents have consistently identified legal positivism—sometimes by name, sometimes by reference to its principal authors—as one of, if not the main obstacle to the acceptance of the pluralist paradigm. This is partly understandable. Legal pluralism matured at the same time as legal positivism was suffering a multifarious attack on all sides, by critics who 'tried ... to connect positivism to a diverse and jointly inconsistent group of theories, such as legal formalism, legal realism, and originalism' as well as political conservatism and the American ideology of judicial restraint.[9] Legal pluralists borrowed many of these criticisms, even when they were sometimes misguided, contradictory, or counterproductive to the pluralist project.[10]

More specific to the development of the legal pluralist school is the historical intersection of legal positivism and legal monism in the nineteenth century European state and empire. Legal pluralism emerged from the anthropological study of law in nineteenth and early twentieth century colonial societies.[11] The project of formalization and rationalization of norms, and of the submission of all institutionalized coercion to the authority of the state was not isolated to the colonies, but proceeded from and reinforced a process of formalization, rationalization, and consolidation of authority in Europe itself.[12] The move away from the medieval political order was characterized by an assertion of unitary and absolute political authority in the hands of the state, against the plurality of sources of authority in the ancient constitution, and also by an exaltation of the purely positive sources of such

[8] Ralph Michaels, 'Global Legal Pluralism' 2009 (5) *Annual Review of Law and Social Science* 243, 244.

[9] Anthony J Sebok, *Legal Positivism in American Jurisprudence* (Cambridge University Press, 1998) 1 (internal citations omitted). Sebok traces the development of legal positivism and its critics (although he does not include legal pluralism as discussed here) and points out the critics' mistakes. On this point, see also Brian Tamanaha, *Beyond the Formalist-Realist Divide: The Role of Politics in Judging* (Princeton University Press, 2010). But note that over the last decade positivism has recovered from the state in which Sebok found it (see Brian Tamanaha, 'The Contemporary Relevance of Legal Positivism' (2007) 32 *Australian Journal of Legal Philosophy* 1, 1).

[10] See, e.g. William Twinning, 'Normative and Legal Pluralism: A Global Perspective' (2010) 20 *Duke Journal of Comparative & International Law* 473.

[11] Merry, note 5, 869.

[12] Alexis de Tocqueville is an excellent, if paradoxical, witness to the process. In *L'Ancien Régime et la Révolution* he points to the dangers of the consolidation of authority and the gradual abolition or subjugation, but he also defends the colonization and settlement of Algeria. See, e.g. his writings in Jennifer Pitts (ed.), *Writings on Empire and Slavery* (Johns Hopkins Press, 2000); see also Margaret Kohn (2008) 'Empire's Law: Alexis de Tocqueville on Colonialism and the State of Exception' 41 *Canadian Journal of Political Science* 255–78. Similar arguments can be made about John Stuart Mill. See Jennifer Pitts, *A Turn to Empire: the rise of imperial liberalism in Britain and France* (Princeton, 2006); Margaret Kohn and Daniel O'Neill, 'A Tale of Two Indias: Burke and Mill on Empire and Slavery in the West Indies and America' (2006) 34 *Political Theory* 192–228; Duncan Bell, 'John Stuart Mill on Colonies' (2009) 38 *Political Theory* 34–64.

authority, against the morally and religiously grounded apologies of power that marked medieval political philosophy.

It is in the work of John Austin that the parallel developments of legal monism and legal positivism most clearly intersect, and it is the spectre of Austin that has haunted the legal pluralist imagination. Austin famously defined a law as 'a command which... obliges *generally* to acts or forebearances of a *class*';[13] proceeds 'from a *determinate* source, or emanates from a *determinate* author'; is backed by sanction, 'an eventual evil *annexed to a command*'; and is presumed by any duty to obey, where duty is but 'obnoxiousness to evils of the kind'.[14] Commands proceed from a superior to an inferior, and so it is with law, as 'every positive law, or every law simply and strictly so called, is set directly or circuitously by a monarch or sovereign number to a person or persons in a state of subjection to its author.'[15] And there can ordinarily be only one such person, since sovereignty exists only when '[t]he *generality* of the given society [is] in the *habit* of obedience to a *determinate* and *common* superior: whilst that determinate person, or determinate body of persons must *not* be habitually obedient to a determinate person or body.'[16] Austin's positivism allows law to be defined as a purely sociological phenomenon empirically determinable, but the criteria he uses to identify this phenomenon result in a single lawgiver and a single legal system. He is explicit about this:

> It also results from positions which I have tried to establish already, that in every society political and independent, the sovereign is one individual, or one body of individuals: that unless the sovereign be one individual, or one body of individuals, the given independent society is either in a state of nature, or split into two or more independent political societies.[17]

Several scholars have demonstrated quite convincingly that Austin's theory of law, while positivistic in that it makes the validity of a law not depend on its correspondence with a moral principle but rather depend only on its source in the command of the sovereign, is not *as a theory* morally neutral. Austin, following his mentor Jeremy Bentham, thought that the positivity of law was a point in its favour because it made it possible to enact legal reforms not subject to the veto of self-appointed guardians of morality. 'Both [Austin and Bentham] were normative as well as conceptual positivists by virtue of believing that there was a non-descriptive point in separating law from morality, and that point was to facilitate the reform of the law.'[18]

[13] John Austin, *The Province of Jurisprudence Determined* (Hackett, 1998) 24. [14] Austin, note 13, 133–34.

[15] Austin, note 13, 202. [16] Austin, note 13, 195. [17] Austin, note 13, 245–46.

[18] Frederick Schauer, 'Positivism before Hart' (2011) 24 *Canadian Journal of Law and Jurisprudence* 455, 465; see also, more generally Gerald Postema, *Bentham and the Common Law Tradition* (Clarendon Press, 1986).

Legal positivism was, in Austin and Bentham's project, inextricably bound with the reform of state institutions along utilitarian lines. This makes it suspect, in part, because of the checkered role of Bentham's followers in the administration of British colonies. Yet Bentham himself was highly critical of colonialism, unlike his enthusiastic acolytes, and repeatedly demanded the emancipation of Britain's overseas possessions. As Jennifer Pitts has convincingly documented, 'Bentham, for all his aspirations to see legal systems reformed around the world, did not embrace British colonial rule, as many of his self-designated followers did, as a convenient means of imposing his schemes on powerless or incompetent subjects'.[19] But later utilitarians, most notoriously James Mill and his son John Stuart, who had extensive ties to the British colonial apparatus, justified colonial legislation on utilitarian grounds, and thus helped to associate the legal positivists, utilitarians, and colonial apologists and conflate their positions.

Unsurprisingly, the zeal of utilitarian reformers did not correspond with the facts on the ground in the colonies. Colonial authorities, especially British ones in India, were reluctant to assume direct control of subject populations, and governed through a system of indirect rule which ostensibly preserved local religious practice and custom, but in fact provided local elites with an opportunity to craft a 'customary law' to suit their purposes. The pluralism that ensued was not always efficient, was often resented, and perpetuated hierarchical and oppressive divisions that continued into independence.This resulted in a decidedly ambiguous situation. 'From the standpoint of a legal authority trying to consolidate its rule, legal pluralism is a flaw to be rectified. From the standpoint of individuals or groups subject to legal pluralism, it can be a source of uncertainty, but it also creates the possibility of resort to alternative legal regimes.'[20] The contrast between the supposedly rationalist law of former empires, now replicated in newly independent states, and the indigenous legal systems of post-colonial societies, transformed in ways simultaneously heroic and pathological by the colonial experience, was the ground on which the anthropological strain of contemporary legal pluralism developed.

> The idea of legal pluralism was an extension from the analysis of dualism/pluralism in colonial societies where it indicated asymmetrical power (and race) relationships between the white minority and the indigenous majority. Used first for characterising colonial economies, it was extended to cultural and social pluralism ... [21]

[19] Jennifer Pitts, 'Legislator of the World? A Rereading of Bentham on Colonies' (2003) 31(2) *Political Theory* 200, 224.

[20] Tamanaha, 'Understanding Legal Pluralism', note 5, 385.

[21] von Benda Beckham, note 5, 60.

The pluralist attitude toward state law, colonial or otherwise, is generally negative, especially insofar as state law claims a monopoly over the normative landscape. Surveying the literature, Franz von Benda Beckham observes that:

> in many instances the idea of legal pluralism is instrumentalized for moral and political purposes. This is partly done for the purpose of achieving more recognition for legal orders not recognized by the state. In other cases, however, legal pluralism is seen as a symbolic recognition that mutes more radical political and economic claims of oppressed population groups.[22]

The antipathy towards the state monopoly of law leads to a curious ambivalence among legal pluralists. Either the state *monopoly* of the category of law is questioned, and the category is extended to other social institutions, however different in form and structure from state law; or state law is taken as *paradigmatic*, and recognition of the validity of other practices demands other terms or concepts for describing institutional normativity. These strategies are very different, but both coincide in rhetorically identifying the ideology of state legal centralism with legal positivism, especially with the perceived incapacity of legal positivism to admit institutions, other than the state's, to the category of law. The latter view, which finds a home among legal anthropologists and is represented most eloquently in Sally Falk Moore's idea of a 'semi-autonomous social field' does not take direct aim at the positivist concept of law, but argues against its apparent claim of autonomy over all other normative systems.[23] The former view is more openly hostile to legal positivism. It combines a suspicion of the criteria that positivists employ to identify legal systems (whether Austin's habitual obedience or more contemporary positivists' criteria) with a political commitment to democratic creation and enforcement of social norms. These self-described critical legal pluralists—Emmanuel Melissaris, Roderick Macdonald, and others—in effect, reclaim the term legal to elevate the standing of social practices to a position from which they can contest the norms promulgated by legal officials. This second critique is more serious and accurately sets its sights on a central claim of legal positivists from Austin to the present day: that the law is a category that is generated by and primarily directed at legal officials. Critical legal pluralism borrows equally from the anthropological strain of legal pluralism and from the normative critique of legal positivism championed by Lon L Fuller and Robert Cover. But first, I will explain why the anthropological pluralist antipathy against legal positivism is misguided.

[22] von Benda Beckham, note 5, 45, n12.

[23] Moore, note 5.

6.2 THE FALLACIES OF THE CRITIQUE OF LEGAL POSITIVISM

The legal pluralist indictment of positivism commits a fallacy that Stephen Holmes, in a different polemic, has labelled 'antonym substitution'. Holmes observes that:

> [p]olemicists with a bias against liberal thought regularly distort the significance of central liberal ideas by replacing the counterconcepts that originally bestowed political significance on liberal principles with antonyms of their own choosing, which were either ignored or explicitly rejected by the early liberals.[24]

Of course the fallacy is not exclusive to antiliberalism, but can apply to any controversy over the content of a concept. It is especially prevalent in the characterization of legal positivism as a concept or thesis. Legal positivism, which is a thesis about the criteria of legal validity, is transformed, through antonym substitution, into a philosophy of statist centralism and epistemological formalism incompatible with the observable social complexity of normative phenomena. But this is a gross mischaracterization of legal positivism on several levels. On a historical perspective, it takes positions long since rejected or discredited by contemporary positivists as representative of the positivist position: John Austin's legal positivism may have led him to be a legal monist, but contemporary legal positivists are (emphatically) not Austinians. On an analytic level, it makes unwarranted inferences or assumptions about the normative conclusions that should be drawn from ostensibly positivist premises, even when such conclusions are expressly disavowed by positivists themselves: claims about the hierarchical order of norms, or about the centrality of the state, or about the obligatoriness of legal norms on officials are attached to positivism when they have no necessary connection to the positivist claims about legal validity and are often explicitly repudiated by positivists themselves.

In some cases, the fallacy of antonym substitution operates by reflection, by relabelling legal positivism by reference to an undesirable but different thesis; one could call this 'synonym substitution'. For instance, John Griffiths, by reference to Ehrlich's theory of the living law, seamlessly elides 'the legal centralist ideology of [Ehrlich's] day' with legal positivism without pause or comment.[25] Earlier in his paper, he defines legal centralism as 'the ideology

[24] Stephen Holmes, *The Anatomy of Antiliberalism* (Harvard University Press, 1993) 253.

[25] Griffiths, note 5, 23. The reference to Ehrlich as a forerunner of legal pluralism is common, but its accuracy is unclear. For an argument against a pluralist reading of Ehrlich, see David Nelken, 'Ehrlich's Legacies: Back to the Future in the Sociology of Law?' in Marc Hertog (ed.), *Living Law: Reconsidering Eugen Ehrlich* (Hart, 2009) 237–72. I thank Ralf Michaels for pointing me in this direction.

[that] law is and should be the law of the state, uniform for all persons, exclusive of all other law, and administered by a single set of state institutions' and named as legal centralists Jean Bodin, Thomas Hobbes, John Austin, HLA Hart, and Hans Kelsen, the last three clearly legal positivists (Hobbes possibly so, Bodin more doubtfully).[26]

Roderick Macdonald and Jason MacLean, in discussing the statist and monist biases of law school curricula, 'use the expression "unificationist monojurality" by preference to the more common characterization of "analytical positivism."'[27] They give sound reasons for moving away from the label 'positivist' when bringing together theorists like Hart, Raz, Dworkin, and Posner in opposition to those like Tamanaha: those in the former group, they claim, take a single and universal legal order as their analytical subject, while the latter does not. This despite the fact that the former group includes both legal positivists and anti-positivists while the latter, Tamanaha, is a positivist (and a legal formalist, to boot).[28]

These equivalencies could be justified if legal positivism was somehow logically or institutionally connected to the desirability of centralizing all legal authority in the state to the exclusion of other law-making entities (centralism), the certainty that legal deliberation may produce a single correct answer to any legal question (formalism), the claim that the law is autonomous from all other normative orders (autonomism), or the view that 'law is a fundamental category which can be identified and described, or an essentialist notion which can be internally worked on until a pure (de-contextualized) version is produced' (essentialism).[29]

The first three charges are false, not only because legal positivism need not and does not make any of these claims, but also because specific legal positivists have explicitly denied them. The last claim, what Brian Tamanaha has called 'essentialism' is an accurate descriptor of most positivist theories (Tamanaha exempted) but depends on a wrong characterization of law as a

[26] Griffiths, note 5, 3.

[27] Roderick Macdonald and Jason MacLean, 'No Toilets in Park' (2005) 50 *McGill Law Journal* 721, 777.

[28] See, e.g. Brian Tamanaha, *On the Rule of Law* (Cambridge University Press, 2004) and *Law as a Means to an End* (Cambridge University Press, 2006).

[29] Brian Tamanaha, 'The Folly of the "Social-Scientific" Concept of Legal Pluralism' (1993) 20 *Journal of Law and Society* 192, 201. To be sure, Macdonald and other critics of positivism do not always use the term 'legal positivism' to refer to 'a particular jurisprudential theory about the pedigree of legal norms' but more narrowly to 'the widespread belief that it is desirable to reduce all law to written enactments'. (Roderick Macdonald, 'Legal Bilingualism' (1997) 42 *McGill Law Journal* 119, 151). In later writings Macdonald names this belief 'chirographism' and acknowledges that it is neither entailed nor required by positivism. (Roderick Macdonald, 'Custom Made—For a Non-chirographic Critical Legal Pluralism' (2011) 26 *Canadian Journal of Law and Society* 301–27, 309, especially footnote 28). He makes positivism only one of five central tenets of a twentieth-century legal orthodoxy that displaces the legal subject as a constitutive agent of legality. I also take issue with this assessment, but I think Macdonald's current description of legal positivism is accurate and our disagreement is normative, not conceptual.

functional instead of a modal kind. The concept of law need not be exclusive to the state, but it has features that tie it to officialdom and constrain the form of statements and norms that qualify as legal. This may count as essentialism for some, although the label is perhaps distracting. As far as associational pluralism is concerned, the concept of law cannot be so expansive as to deprive it of analytic usefulness, and it must also be able to capture the multiplicity of legal orders that make competing claims on the obedience of a population. But before we get to that point, it is important to dismiss the first three allegations: centralism, formalism, and autonomism.

Centralism

The positivist conception of law is concerned mainly with the norms promulgated by legal officials, even if the pronouncements of those officials are directed at subjects other than themselves. This gives rise to the pluralist objection that legal positivism is inherently centralist. As I mentioned, by reference to Griffiths, legal centralism is 'the ideology [that] law is and should be the law of the state, uniform for all persons, exclusive of all other law, and administered by a single set of state institutions'.[30] Centralism, more than any other criticism of legal positivism, captures the legal pluralist objection to the exclusive focus on state law. But it is not a charge of which any modern positivist is guilty.

The most obvious rebuke to the charge of legal centralism is that centralism is a moral thesis on the desirability of a uniform law for all citizens, not an analytical conception of the criteria of legal validity. It might appear that Hart endorses a weak centralism in his account of a fully developed legal system. Hart distinguishes between social structures composed only of primary rules of obligation and a society that adds to these secondary rules of recognition, change, and adjudication. The difference turns on Hart's famous explanation of primary and secondary rules, and of legal orders as the union of both systems of rules. Primary rules are rules by which 'human beings are required to do or abstain from certain actions, whether they wish to or not.'[31] Secondary rules, by contrast, are rules about rules, rules that 'specify the ways in which the primary rules may be conclusively ascertained, introduced, eliminated, varied, and the fact of their violation conclusively determined.'[32] Hart unfelicitously calls systems without primary rules 'primitive' legal systems, but not much should be read into the term, except perhaps a bias towards the familiar. Leslie Green takes this position while pointing out

[30] Griffiths, note 5, 3.

[31] HLA Hart, *The Concept of Law* (2nd edn) (Oxford University Press, 1994) 81.

[32] Hart, note 31, 94.

that it is anti-positivists who regularly make legality a superior moral condition; Hart, by contrast, does not.

> Although Hart introduces the rule of recognition through a speculative anthropology of how it might emerge in response to certain deficiencies in a customary social order, he is not committed to the view that law is a cultural achievement. … The objection embraces the error it seeks to avoid. … If one thinks that law is a many splendored thing, one will be tempted by a very wide concept of law, for it would seem improper to charge others with missing out. Positivism simply releases the harness. Law is a distinctive form of political order, not a moral achievement, and whether it is necessary or even useful depends entirely on its content and context. Societies without law may be perfectly adapted to their environments, missing nothing.[33]

Hart also momentarily analogizes a system of primary rules alone to one of 'custom', but steps away from the analogy 'because [the term custom] often implies that the customary rules are very old and supported with less social pressure than other rules.'[34] This does not fit the view of many pluralists for whom custom is at worst a colonial construct, and at best simply another form of legality. But the worry of these pluralists is that custom will be rendered inadequate by a teleology of law that makes formal, state law the natural end of all societies.[35] As Green states, Hart lacks such a teleology.

It is telling that the ubiquity of legal artefacts that some legal pluralists find at all levels of society betrays a commitment to the moral superiority of legality as a social condition, while there might not be grounds for this preference. Some other pluralists, Sally Falk Moore among them, accept that distinctions between legal and non-legal normativity and even between state and non-state law may be analytically useful and do not suggest disdain for the non-state or the non-legal.

> For reasons of both analysis and policy, distinctions must be made that identify the provenance of rules and controls. To deny that the state can and should be distinguished from other rule-making entities for many practical purposes is to turn away from the obvious. … To make such distinctions is not necessarily to adopt a 'legal centralist' view.[36]

Legal positivism is only committed in principle to tracing 'the provenance of rules and controls' as a measure of legal validity. If it is able to trace such sources without committing itself a priori to the position that they are only

[33] Leslie Green, 'Legal Positivism', *The Stanford Encyclopedia of Philosophy (Fall 2009 Edition)*, Edward N Zalta (ed.), available at <http://plato.stanford.edu/archives/fall2009/entries/legal-positivism/> accessed 23 June 2013.

[34] Hart, note 31, 91.

[35] Merry, note 5, 875.

[36] Sally Falk Moore, 'Certainties Undone: Fifty Turbulent Years of Legal Anthropology, 1949–1999' (2001) 7 *Journal of the Royal Anthropological Institute* 95, 106–107.

traceable in the case of state norms then there is no centralist objection to a positivist legal pluralism.

There are, however, some legal positivists who do insist on limiting the domain of law to the state, and it is important to explain why they do so, if only briefly, and why their position does not threaten the positivist pluralist position. I will take Jeremy Waldron as representative of this group.[37] Waldron distinguishes between a descriptive understanding of legal positivism—which declares that 'statements about what the law is... may be made without moral or other evaluative judgment. The judgment is simply one of social fact'—[38] and a normative or ethical understanding—which makes the stronger statement 'that the law *ought* to be such that legal decisions can be made without the exercise of moral judgments. Or, if we do not want to state it in the language of obligation: it is the thesis that it would be *a good thing* for the law to be as the descriptive positivist thinks it is.'[39] The argument in favour of a normative or ethical form of positivism is part of Waldron's broader argument in favour of democratic decision-making by legislatures, as opposed to constitutional checks on legislation by the courts, especially those defended by Ronald Dworkin in the name of moralized constitutional principles.[40] There is, therefore, in Waldron's view a connection between positivism and the state insofar as the state is democratic and its decisions those of the sovereign people, but his target is not so much the law of non-state associations, but rather the unchecked reliance on extra-legal norms (those of morality or welfare-maximization, for example) by judges when evaluating (and perhaps overturning) legislative enactments. This connection may be contested—one could argue in favour of a normative positivist conception of law and still consider judges to be best placed to make determinations about the legal coherence of norms in a legal system—but it does not undermine a positivist pluralism, since pluralism is in principle indifferent to democratic or non-democratic forms of lawmaking.[41]

[37] Jeremy Waldron, 'Normative (or Ethical) Positivism' in Jules Coleman (ed.), *Hart's Postscript: Essays on the Postscript to the Concept of Law* (Oxford University Press, 2001) 410–33, *Law and Disagreement* (Oxford University Press, 1999) 164–87. But as Waldron observes, he is far from alone in this position. Evidence of this is Tom Campbell's and Neil MacCormick's essays in Tom Campbell (ed.), *Judicial Power, Democracy, and Legal Positivism* (Ashgate, 2000). For a more extended discussion, see Tom Campbell, *Prescriptive Legal Positivism: Law, Rights and Democracy* (Cavendish, 2004), especially the first part.

[38] Jeremy Waldron, *Law and Disagreement* (Oxford University Press, 2001) 166.

[39] Waldron, note 38, 167.

[40] Ronald Dworkin, *Law's Empire* (Harvard University Press, 1986).

[41] In a recent paper, Waldron insists that 'we need to distinguish between currents in legal positivism that favour legal pluralism (and there are some) and currents in legal positivism that tend to oppose it; we need to understand how the latter currents are permitted to flow through the distinctive channels of the legal theory that Hart set out in his Holmes Lecture and in *The Concept of Law.*' Jeremy Waldron, 'Legal Pluralism and the Contrast Between Hart's Jurisprudence and Fuller's' in Peter Cane (ed.), *The Hart-Fuller Debate in the Twenty-First Century* (Hart, 2010) 135–55, 136.

Formalism

Formalism is an old charge against legal positivism. But the truth of the accusation depends on what formalism is taken to mean. If it means the claim that law has certain formal elements because it is a modal kind—as discussed in the 'Autonomism' section—then the charge is true. But what is usually meant is something different. It is the charge of formalism in the sense meant by the legal realists who reacted against the methods of research and teaching in American universities in the early part of the twentieth century. The charge of formalism in this later sense has been rebuked on many occasions, most notably in Hart's famous article which inaugurated his famous dispute with Lon L Fuller. There, rather than adopt the position that positivism rendered decisions clearer and more predictable, Hart argued that mechanical adjudication failed to acknowledge the ambiguity of laws, but he did not think this ambiguity absolute. Although 'laws are incurably incomplete and we must decide the penumbral cases rationally by reference to social aims' so also 'the hard core of settled meaning is law in some centrally important sense and that even if there are borderlines, there must first be lines.'[42] If this is formalism, it is remarkably weak and does not provide certainty or avoidance of conflicting opinion, but only provides, at best, for bounded disagreement.

Neither do other legal positivists hold that the avoidance of interpretive conflict is an analytic feature of legal systems, although it may be (and probably is) a feature that the proponents and defenders of such systems desire. But desirability as a matter of policy is very different from analytical clarity. Take Raz's understanding of authoritative directives as preemptive, that is, as providing reasons for action and also as ruling out other reasons for action that may conflict with the source of the directive.[43] This is a feature of practical authorities without which, Raz argues (correctly), they would not be practical authorities at all. But it does not indicate that the reasons given by a particular authority ought to be obeyed, or that there are not other preemptive reasons issued by other authorities occupying the same social field which may compete for the subject's allegiance. Famously, Raz does not believe that anything in the analytic structure of law requires the obedience of the subject. He is, for most purposes, a philosophical anarchist, which is an odd thing for the kind of prescriptivist formalist that some pluralists take the typical positivist to be. In more recent writing, Raz has been quite candid about the possibility of conflict among practical authorities and, by extension, among legal systems.

[42] HLA Hart, 'Positivism and the Separation of Law and Morals' (1958) 71 *Harvard Law Review* 593–629, 614.

[43] Raz, *The Morality of Freedom*, note 4, 57–62.

> When several authorities pronounce on the same matter and their directives conflict, we must decide, to the best of our ability, which is more reliable as a guide. Often there are cooperative relations among authorities. The law recognizes the authority of schools and of parents, for example, and lends them legal authority, by directing the relevant people to obey them, or by enforcing their directives through legal procedures. At other times authorities may be hostile to each other, directing their subjects not to obey, and more generally not to cooperate with the working of other authorities. In such cases the question whether a given authority's power extends to exclude the authority of another is to be judged in the way we judge the legitimacy of its power on any matter, namely, whether we would conform better to reason by trying to follow its directives than if we do not.[44]

It is true that for Raz, as for many positivists, law primarily involves claims promulgated and recognized by legal officials.[45] And this is necessarily so because law is authoritative and authority presumes a relation in which one person substitutes their judgment for that of another, or is called to take another's instruction as a valid and legitimate reason for action. Legal pluralism, then, to be meaningful, must refer to a situation in which multiple sets of officials make authoritative claims over the same population, claims that explicitly or implicitly, imply their superiority over their competitors. This has the obvious implication of threatening conflict, either internal to the subject of multiple authorities, or external and manifested by confrontation between the authorities themselves. Raz explicitly acknowledges this.

Of course, Raz's acknowledgement of conflict between authorities operates within certain limits. Overlapping legal systems under conditions of legal pluralism have to have a certain structure to qualify as legal. They must be systems that not only generate norms, but generate norms as authoritative claims. And they must therefore have officials in positions of authority and thus capable of generating these claims. This narrows considerably the range of social systems that qualify as legal under the most expansive pluralist definition. But it also broadens the range of authorities usually considered by legal positivists. It is not that positivists after Austin categorically refuse to acknowledge other authoritative systems. Raz, for instance, makes explicit reference to canon law as a legal system,[46] and Andrei Marmor even takes issue with Raz's assertion of supremacy claimed by legal systems by contrasting it with medieval constitutionalism.[47] It is rather that they have not paid them sufficient attention, although there are few conceptual impediments to consider a conflict between a formally organized association and

[44] Raz, *Between Authority and Interpretation*, note 4, 143.

[45] Raz, *The Morality of Freedom*, note 4, 103.

[46] Raz, *Practical Reason and Norms*, note 4, 152.

[47] Marmor, *Positive Law and Objective Values*, note 4, 39–42.

the state differently from a dispute over applicable law between a domestic and a foreign state.

Andrei Marmor is also explicit in admitting the possibility of conflict, not only among different legal systems, but even within the same system. In response to Hart's account of the rule of recognition underlying the legal validity of a legal system, he suggests that '[i]t is probably an oversimplification to assume that in every legal system there is one master rule of recognition. More plausibly, there are several rules of recognition, and the potential conflicts between them are not necessarily resolved.'[48]

Now, there may be good reasons to adopt some version of formalism in adjudication, such as strong norms of stare decisis, on grounds of judicial accountability or limitation of government, or even on grounds that the law is irredeemably formal once it achieves any level of institutional complexity. But these are reasons to adopt certain interpretive strategies above others because they help to clarify certain norms or reinforce the legitimacy of institutions (which are nonetheless ultimately describable as social sources of norms). And they are reasons to be distinguished from positivism as a theory of legal validity and, for that matter, from pluralism as a theory of the shape of the normative universe.

Autonomism

Another legal pluralist objection to legal positivism is that positivists incorrectly claim that legal systems are autonomous, when in fact they are porous and subject to trespass by other normative systems. Legal pluralists no less than legal positivists have encountered great difficulty when trying to define law. Sally Falk Moore's idea of a semi-autonomous social field attempts to resolve this problem by proposing a category of normativity that is broader than that of law.

> The approach proposed here is that the small field observable to an anthropologist be chosen and studied in terms of its semi-autonomy—the fact that it can generate rules and customs and symbols internally, but that it is also vulnerable to rules and decisions and other forces emanating from the larger world by which it is surrounded. The semi-autonomous social field has rule-making capacities, and the means to induce or coerce compliance; but it is simultaneously set in a larger social matrix which can, and does, affect and invade it, sometimes at the invitation of persons inside it, sometimes at its own instance.[49]

[48] Marmor, *Philosophy of Law*, note 4, 50.

[49] Moore, note 5, 720. In her seminal article, and later ones, Moore denies that the semi-autonomous social field (SASF) is the equivalent of 'law'. The Law is a SASF, but not the only one, and not all SASFs need be law.

The idea of semi-autonomy stands in stark contrast to the apparent closure of positivist systems. John Austin, in the canonical formulation, styled the sovereign as a single but determinate individual or body of individuals to whom habitual obedience is rendered by the bulk of society; and who does not, in turn, render such obedience to anyone else.[50] Once the sovereign is identified, laws are defined as the commands of the sovereign, with some notable exceptions.[51] The main characteristic of the Austinian sovereign is normative autonomy: to benefit from more or less exclusive habitual obedience and fail to render such obedience to another. From an empirical perspective, Austin is clearly wrong in postulating normative autonomy for law. In an echo of the position of the British pluralists, Moore recognizes that:

> [o]bviously, complete autonomy and complete domination are rare, if they exist at all in the world today, and semi-autonomy of various kinds and degrees is an ordinary circumstance.... The law (in the sense of state enforceable law) is only one of a number of factors that affect the decisions people make, the actions they take and the relationships they have.[52]

But it would be incorrect to ascribe Austin's view to legal positivists more generally, as the development of legal positivism in the twentieth century is mainly reacting against Austin's specific arguments while retaining his main insight. In this respect (though not in others) Hart does not stray too far from Austin; he also postulates that a legal system is defined by a rule of recognition, a customary or conventional rule of legal officials that constitutes the ultimate (and only) criterion of validity of a legal system.[53] Kelsen, likewise (and more dramatically) makes legal systems dependent on a Basic Norm (*Grundnorm*), not itself legal or conventional, but required in order to render the legal system intelligibly normative.[54] But later positivists, especially those under the influence of Joseph Raz's version of legal positivism, have not followed suit. From his early work, Raz has claimed that legal systems are open: they contain 'norms the purpose of which is to give binding force within the system to norms which do not belong to it.'[55] Raz identifies the rules of conflict of laws (private international law) as designed to adopt and give force to norms of foreign systems, and the rules of contracts and

[50] John Austin, *The Province of Jurisprudence Determined* (HLA Hart ed., Hackett 1998) 195.

[51] For discussion, see Brian Bix, 'John Austin', *The Stanford Encyclopedia of Philosophy (Spring 2010 Edition)*, Edward N. Zalta (ed.), available at <http://plato.stanford.edu/archives/spr2010/entries/austin-john/> accessed 23 June 2013.

[52] Moore, note 5, 742.

[53] Hart, note 31, 100ff.

[54] As Paulson rightly observes, this made the *Grundnorm* a sort of Kantian transcendental deduction. Stanley Paulson, 'Introduction' to Hans Kelsen, *Introduction to the Problems of Legal Theory* (Oxford University Press, 1992), xxix–xlii.

[55] Joseph Raz, *Practical Reason and Norms* (Oxford University Press, 1975) 152–53.

companies as designed to adopt and give force to norms created by domestic subjects of the state. The latter case may raise some pluralist eyebrows, because the legal validity of non-state law seems conditioned on the state's own positive enactments, but all that is meant by this is that each system—state or otherwise—adjudges the legal validity of the foreign rules. As shown by the parallel invocation of conflicts of laws, the legal validity of state law in a non-state legal system may also depend on the rules of that system.[56]

Now, it may be inappropriate to set Moore's objection to autonomy on a par with Raz's argument about the openness of legal systems.[57] On one hand, Raz's solution to the problem of openness may be insufficient to satisfy a pluralist. As just stated, Raz's openness resembles the norms of settling conflicts of laws, where the laws of one jurisdiction are applicable in another jurisdiction under certain conditions. Some classic examples involve the formal requirements that a contract must meet in order to be valid (whether it must be writen or may be oral, how many persons must witness it, whether it must be registered with the state, etc.) or the substantive obligations that arise from civil marriage (for example, whether the income or property acquired by a spouse once married belongs to that spouse or to the spouses jointly); classically, in the first case, the law of the place where the contract is entered into governs its form, while in the second, the law of the jurisdiction of which the spouses were nationals (or come to reside immediately after the wedding) governs the obligations between them.[58] A dispute may arise in State A that requires the application of the law of State B with regards to the form of a marriage and of State C with regards to the obligations or property relations of the spouses. But it is the law of State A that allows the laws of the other two states to be applied by State A's courts.

The conflicts of law approach has been embraced by prominent legal pluralists like Paul Schiff Berman.[59] Contrary to the anthrolological legal pluralists, Berman is interested in how different legal orders can interact with each other in a way that does not imply subjugation of one to another, but also permits judgments to be reached and decisions about particular cases to be rendered. But Ralf Michaels has cast some doubt on the success of this strategy for legal pluralists generally, concerned as they are with the status of non-state sources of law. State legal systems, he argues, are notoriously reluctant to recognize non-state norms as *legal*, or at least legal on a par with

[56] In Anglo-Americal legal pluralism as it has developed in the legal academy, conflicts of laws is also the paradigm of interaction between legal systems. See e.g. Berman, note 5, chapters 7 and 8.

[57] I thank Ralf Michaels for bringing this question to my attention.

[58] These rules, once set by principles of *ius gentium*, are now often contained in international conventions such as the Convention on the Law Applicable to Matrimonial Property Regimes (1978).

[59] PS Berman, note 5.

laws of other sovereign countries. '[N]on-state normative orders are almost never the applicable law under current choice of law analysis.'[60] The state, when it does not reject them, accommodates them through techniques of incorporation, delegation, or deference. 'Incorporation is the transformation of non-state law into domestic law. Deference is the transformation of non-state law into facts. Delegation is the transformation of non-state law into subordinated state law.'[61]

There is no doubt that these strategies leave each system the ultimate guardian of the gates of legality, which is to say that each system is sovereign. But this is exactly what we should expect from pluralism: mutual and (theoretically) exclusive assertions of meta-jurisdictional authority. That they are multiple and contested is what makes a system pluralistic; that the legal norms that are the object of contestation are formally similar narrows the range of possible normativities, but as long as it leaves the possible range of choices open to several systems, the objection to the positivist criteria is one of degree and not of kind. Which systems ought to be counted as legal, then? This is the most difficult question that a positivist pluralism faces, and one that invites the essentialist objection.

Essentialism

Roderick Macdonald holds that '[a] legal pluralist conception of legal change imagines that each of the persons involved in the functioning of a regime of law has an independent role to play in the interpretation of its artifacts.'[62] Viewed very broadly, it is clear that all participants in a legal system, from the legislator and judge to the practitioner to the citizen as subject of law, has a role to play in the interpretation not only of the content of legal norms but on their legal validity. A rule that is ignored passively (because unknown) or actively (because flouted) by participants in a legal system has little claim on the social sources that identify it as a rule of that system. But to make the matter of legal validity axiomatically democratic or participatory, even if merely as a matter of narrative and meaning, is to disregard the constitutive importance of power—both state and non-state—as a social fact, and thus as an element in a theory that deems legal validity ultimately traceable to social facts alone.[63]

[60] R Michaels, 'The Re-*State*-Ment of Non-State Law: The State, Choice of Law, and the Challenge From Global Legal Pluralism' (2005) 51 *Wayne Law Review* 1209, 1228.

[61] Michaels, note 60 above, 1228.

[62] Roderick Macdonald, 'Unitary Law Re-Form, Pluralistic Law Re-Substance: Illuminating Legal Change' (2007) 67 *Louisiana Law Review* 1113, 1153.

[63] On these grounds, Gad Barzilai has criticized legal pluralism precisely in connection to the pluralist opposition to legal positivism. 'Beyond Relativism: Where is Political Power in Legal Pluralism?' (2008) 9 *Theoretical Inquiries in Law* 395.

In setting up legal positivism as an ideology to be rejected, legal pluralists deny themselves the only theory of law that is compatible with their social scientific aspiration.[64] As Brian Leiter suggests:

> It should count in favor of an account of the nature of law that it complements, and perhaps even wins support from, work in the empirical sciences.... A theory of law that makes explicit the tacit or inchoate concept at play in scientific research is probably to be preferred to its competitors. Positivism is that theory.[65]

The absence of an account about the nature of law has led legal pluralists to render legality so ubiquitous as to deny any analytical value to the concept of law itself. In such a circumstance, some pluralists retreat from their own concepts when faced with the ubiquity of legal artefacts, or at least significantly qualify or attach warnings to them.[66] Others either embrace the ubiquity of legality so than any form of social control is 'legal' or (what is the same) the category of law is unnecessary.[67] Or else 'law' is relativized or transformed into a rhetorical trope. The dismissal of law as a category is not only counterintuitive (because it is meaningfully employed by both legal officials and subjects of law everyday) but also cripples moral and political debate, since it leaves the theorist without means to single out the special iniquity of using legal means to evil ends—an iniquity that has agitated legal positivists since Hart and finds a prominent place in Raz's qualified philosophical anarchism. It also fails to do justice to the development of political pluralism in the West, which took a peculiar form because it was framed in legal terms.[68]

In Chapter 7 I propose a way of understanding the core modal element in law in relation to the historical development of its institutional form, and thus to show how systems that share the core characteristics of legality with the state should be considered presumptively legal by state law. Whether they are so considered depends on the specificity of the criteria of legality which, I argue, should be kept to their formal minimum for the sake of coherence and to avoid historically contingent arbitrariness.

[64] Some legal pluralists have explicitly iusnaturalist commitments (e.g. Melissaris) but these are rare.

[65] Leiter, note 2, 12.

[66] Moore, note 5 and discussion in note 49.

[67] PS Berman, writes that 'the whole debate about law versus non-law is largely irrelevant in a pluralism context because the key questions involve the normative commitments of a community and the interactions among normative orders that give rise to such commitments, not their formal status.' (PS Berman, note 5, 1177).

[68] See HJ Berman, *Law and Revolution*, note 5, 10.

7

Law as Intelligibility

Legal pluralism is, from its origins, an interdisciplinary endeavour and this interaction of disciplines has produced, over time, a great variety of pluralist positions. As discussed in Chapter 6, legal pluralists who emerged from the tradition of legal anthropology have drawn attention to the legality of overlooked and unofficial orders, often suppressed by colonial regimes.[1] They have taken legal pluralism to offer a better description of the multitude of normative orders that subsisted uneasily in colonial societies—imperial state, pre-colonial custom, local authorities that mediated between the two—but also to offer a rebuttal to what they consider the willful ignorance of non-state authority by the dominant tradition of legal positivism.

But there is another, normative, strain to legal pluralism that derives from the jurisprudential and philosophical analysis of law and especially from attention to international law, to religious legal systems, and to legal history. Legal pluralists inspired by Robert Cover's work—which drew with equal measure from what may be best called the distinct phenomenologies of religious traditions and of state violence—have drawn attention to the jurisgenerative capacity of committed communities and the jurispathic consequences of their confrontation with the state.[2] Cover's own description of the emergence and transformation of *nomoi* pushes against the institutional features commonly associated with legal systems, both because he takes normative orders to be dynamic and inchoate at their origin and because he considers their formalization to be an imposition that—sometimes literally and always discursively—cuts off an expression of meaning and denies (forcibly if necessary) an interpretive commitment to a system of norms. As with the anthropological pluralists, Cover rails against positivism because he identifies it with a formalist deference to jurisdiction that stubbornly refuses to seriously consider how legal acts instigated by state officials create or perpetuate interpretive narratives of legality that, in consequence, destroy or

[1] See note 5 of Chapter 6 and the accompanying text.

[2] Robert Cover, 'Nomos and Narrative' (1983) 97 *Harvard Law Review* 4.

undermine the normative commitments that constitute dissenting interpretive communities.[3]

International legal scholars are confronted by a multitude of more or less formalized networks of rules and authorities that possess different pedigrees and are sustained by diverse justifications, some of which appear (and possibly are) inconsistent with each other. The elevation of the dispute over legal pluralism to the international sphere was analytically fruitful, but in some ways it has only restated the classic debates over the status of international law or soft law without clarifying the underlying concepts.[4] Again, the pluralist thesis is pressed against the ideology of law as by definition state-centred or at least (in the case of international law) state-generated law, and this thesis is quickly anathemized as positivist.

On a different stream, legal pluralists who take their bearings from Harold Berman have looked rather to the historical emergence and persistence of a multiplicity of institutions with distinct authoritative hierarchies.[5] Berman himself was suspicious of positivism as a philosophy of law not because he thought it wrong, but rather because he considered it incomplete, an account of one aspect of law that needed to be complemented by historical and moral considerations.[6] Legal pluralists have also looked to Lon L Fuller's work for inspiration because of his treatment of customary law. Not only did Fuller seemingly accord far more respect than HLA Hart to this source of law—Hart is ambivalent about it, hesitating to call systems of customary law fully legal because they lack secondary rules of recognition, adjudication, and change—[7] but he also demonstrated remarkable acceptance of associative normative orders as legal systems (albeit miniature ones).[8]

Now, the antipathy that various kinds of pluralists harbour against positivism is misplaced, as I argued in Chapter 6, because the central theses of contemporary legal positivism sustain, rather than undermine, the methodology

[3] Cover, note 2, 53–60.

[4] Thus, the positivist account of international law in Paul Schiff Berman, *Global Legal Pluralism* (Cambridge University Press, 2012) is put in doubt in Ralf Michaels, 'Global Legal Pluralism' (2009) 5 *Annual Review of Law and Social Science* 243 and 'The Re-*State*-Ment of Non-State Law: The State, Choice of Law, and the Challenge From Global Legal Pluralism' (2005) 51 *Wayne Law Review* 1209.

[5] Harold Berman, *Law and Revolution* (Harvard University Press, 1983).

[6] Harold Berman, 'Towards an Integrative Jurisprudence' (1988) 76 (4) *California Law Review* 779–801. I have some reservations about the broader theoretical schema that Berman seeks to apply to law, and think that one of his most important contributions to legal theory—the reconsideration of historical jurisprudence as relevant to the determination of the content of law and the identification of legal systems—can be explained on positivist grounds.

[7] HLA Hart, *The Concept of Law* (2nd edn) (Oxford University Press, 1994) 44ff.

[8] Lon L Fuller, 'Human Internation and the Law' (1969) 14 *American Journal of Jurisprudence* 1. See also his brief allusion to university rules in *The Morality of Law* (Revides Edition) (Yale University Press, 1964) 125ff.

and conclusions of pluralism. If positivism is understood as the claim that '[i]n any legal system, whether a given norm is legally valid, and hence whether it forms part of the law of that system, depends on its sources, not its merits (where its merits, in the relevant sense, include the merits of its sources)'[9] there is no reason to assume that non-state or supra-state law is excluded from legality. The definition is simply agnostic about the 'stateness' of legal institutions. Nonetheless, contemporary positivists have neglected or brushed aside legal pluralism, and an engagement with this literature can confirm the key positivist thesis precisely by shearing any presumption of the superior merit of state law.

7.1 LAW AS INSTITUTIONALITY

Yet even if legal pluralism is re-described in positivist terms, a problem remains. As many legal pluralists admit, their tradition has failed to provide criteria either for distinguishing legal from non-legal phenomena or for recommending for or against the recognition of a normative system as law. Among them, the term 'law' has been used rather loosely to refer to normative systems at various levels of institutional formality. But legal positivists approaching the concept of law from a more philosophical perspective have emphasized institutionality as a distinctive feature of law. Thus Hart explains law as the conjunction of primary and secondary norms which are accepted by legal officials,[10] Raz refers to law as an institutional system of norms intended to guide conduct and which claims to be supreme, comprehensive, and open to other normative systems,[11] and Shapiro understands '[l]egal systems...[as] institutions of social planning and their fundamental aim is to compensate for deficiencies of alternative forms of planning.'[12] Moreover, the institutional nature of law nearly always marks off legal officials as especially concerned with the identification and application of law, rendering almost superfluous the active participation of the subjects of law in its determination. Their acquiescence is sufficient, provided the relevant officials do the conceptual work.[13]

[9] John Gardner, *Law as a Leap of Faith* (Oxford University Press, 2012) 21.

[10] Hart, note 7.

[11] Joseph Raz, *Practical Reason and Norms* (Oxford University Press, 1999) chapter 4.

[12] Scott Shapiro, *Legality* (Harvard University Press, 2011) 171.

[13] In an important way, Joseph Raz's service conception of authority is an exception to this rule, because it is the interest of the subject that an authority must purport to advance when claiming authority (Jospeh Raz, *The Morality of Freedom* (Oxford University Press, 1986) 42–53); but, of course, this already presupposes a distinction between the institutional role of the authority and that of the subject. Andrei Marmor has elaborated on this point in 'Institutional Conception of Authority' (2010) 39(3) *Philosophy and Public Affairs* 238 and 'The Dilemma of Authority' (2011) 2(1) *Jurisprudence* 121.

The emphasis on the distinction between the criteria of legal validity and other normative criteria when identifying a legal system, the institutional nature of law and its relation to other similar institutional systems, and the differentiation of legal authorities and officials from other kinds of persons in society seems to provide a minimal content to the concept of law. I will not formulate a precise definition of law here, but only suggest that it involves norms whose legal validity is determined by criteria internal to the system, that these norms are inscribed in an institutional context which is distinguishable at the core (although perhaps not always at the margin) from other institutions, and that those officials called in the first instance to identify, interpret, and apply these norms possess a distinct social role which is specified in the institution itself.

Among the various strains of legal pluralism, Harold Berman comes closest to articulating this concept of law. 'The principal characteristics of the Western legal tradition', he writes, are the following:

> 1. A relatively sharp distinction is made between *legal* institutions (including legal processes such as legislation and adjudication as well as the legal rules and concepts that are generated in those processes) and *other* types of institutions. Although law remains strongly influenced by religion, politics, morality, and custom, it is nevertheless distinguishable from them analytically....
>
> 2. Connected with the sharpness of this distinction is the fact that the administration of legal institutions, in the Western legal tradition, is entrusted to a special corps of people, who engage in legal activities on a professional basis as a more or less fulltime occupation.
>
> 3. The legal professionals ... are specially trained in a discrete body of higher learning identified as legal learning, with its own professional literature and its own professional schools or other places of training.
>
> 4. The body of legal learning in which the legal specialists are trained stands in a complex, dialectical relationship to the legal institutions, since on the one hand the learning describes those institutions but on the other hand the legal institutions, which would otherwise be disparate and unorganized, become conceptualized and systematized, and thus transformed, by what is said about them in learned treatises and articles and in the classroom..... The law contains within itself a legal science, a metalaw, by which it can be both analyzed and evaluated.[14]

[14] Berman, note 5, 7–8.

There are other features of the Western legal tradition which emerge during the twelfth century 'Papal Revolution' that is the subject of Berman's book. Of the remaining six features one is especially important for our purposes:

> Perhaps the most distinctive characteristic of the Western legal tradition is the coexistence and competition within the same community of diverse jurisdictions and legal systems. It is this plurality of jurisdictions and legal systems that makes the supremacy of law both necessary and possible.[15]

Berman's depiction of legal pluralism is unique not only because, contrary to the centralizing tendency in Western legal and political theory since Machiavelli, Bodin, and Hobbes, he finds pluralism at the heart of the Western idea of legality. It is also unique in presenting legal pluralism as intricately tied to the supremacy of law. This is a strikingly strange proposition. If we take our bearings from the Hobbesian conception of sovereignty, a plurality of legal systems—particularly the kinds of legal systems that Berman has in mind, viz. the medieval legal order of overlapping and conflictive jurisdictions each of which claimed independent legitimacy for itself—would seem to contradict the axiological premise that all law has its source in the sovereign will, lest the sovereign authority be undermined and intemperate disagreement plunge all again into a state of war. But Berman, of course, does not follow this lead. His main reason is the observation that institutional competition within 'a common legal *order* containing diverse legal *systems* contributed to legal sophistication.'[16]

It is important to note that the institutional competition that Berman writes about is not a simple contest among different powers. Rather, it is a game of jurisdictional one-upmanship in which success is measured through the efficacy of a legal system to serve a putative clientele and guide their conduct (and the conduct of their fellow subjects) more effectively. But this requires that the game be framed in certain ways, namely in terms of mutually intelligible legal institutions. Take a burgher who sought to resolve a dispute before an ecclesiastical court, while one of his rivals would rather it be settled in a town court and another that it be judged under the law merchant. If the dispute is to have a definite legal solution, respected as legally binding by all courts (to prevent a revisiting of the case) two of the courts must be convinced to abstain from entering into the controversy. The reasons given to each must be comprehensible within the interpretive norms of the respective institutions in order for the assumption of jurisdiction by the first to be considered legitimate. Once each of these institutions understands itself as operating within a legal order (a historical achievement of no small significance), it begins to treat legal norms, even the legal norms of another legal

[15] Berman, note 5, 10. [16] Berman, note 5, 10.

system, as different from non-legal norms.[17] It must therefore have a way of differentiating among them.

Put another way, in a world that is replete with powers political, economic, and military, each of which claims an independent source of legitimacy, conflicts among them are settled either through a legal resolution of disputes or through coercion and force. A single, unitary legal system might impose moral constraints upon itself that compel it to govern through law, but this would not be necessary, as it could also govern by direct appeal to shared convictions. If confronted by an alien non-legal authority, what recourse but force could it have to settle disputes? The reasons of the other authority would be unintelligible to it. Those under the alien authority would be 'outlaws' in the strict sense that they had no law to govern them. Under conditions of legal pluralism—that is, of multiple legal systems which see themselves as operating within a legal order—however, any of the actors in the system can recognize the other as a legal system similar to itself. Its subjects are not outlaws, but subject to a different institutional normative system. That system can be relied upon to guide conduct in an intelligible, predictable manner.[18]

At the most abstract level, a legal system could be identified by reference to notions like the conjunction of primary and secondary rules or the claims of supremacy, comprehensiveness, and openness. But these characteristics ordinarily take a more concrete institutional form, namely the presence of legal officials who determine the rules or claims at stake and who are tasked with guarding the boundaries of law. So the differentiation of a legal system from other normative systems in society, the institutional character of the system, and the presence of legal officials who both constitute and are constituted by these institutions, is a reliable guide to recognizing an alien normative system as legal. The features are, of course, somewhat contingent. We can imagine norms of conduct that are widely known, consistently followed, and effectively enforced without institutional differentiation of a corps of enforcers and a mass of subjects (upon my arrival in Montreal I immediately took note of the practice of perfectly regular queuing at bus stops, even in the bitterest winter, and woe to one who tries to cut the line). We can also imagine shared standards of conduct being performed through narrative without distinction between the expectations of behaviour imposed by rules and those imposed by communal identity. But as we explain these practices we find that they look less and less like law to us, even if they inspire our

[17] For a similar statement, see Michaels, 'Global Legal Pluralism', note 4.

[18] There is here the suggestion of a Foucaultian critique: the legal systems recognize each other because they are sure that the other's subjects will be subjected to some disciplinary authority and not left, as it were, 'undisciplined'. Just as there can be no *res nullius* there cannot be *cives nullius*.

acquiescence or inspire our respect. They do not appear institutionally and self-consciously differentiated from other social practices, and lack a class of officials to apply their rules, or at least an institutionally differentiated role which a participant must assume to enforce the norms of the system. The same could be said in reverse: how is a writ of mandamus to be woven into an Aboriginal songline? The law is not superior to other ways of regulating society, but it is different from those.

7.2 A NON-ESSENTIALIST CONCEPT OF LAW?

Among legal pluralists, Brian Tamanaha has best articulated the claim that all attempts at defining the necessary and sufficient features of 'law' have failed because there is no essence to law which may be apprehended through conceptual analysis or sociological analogy. By contrast, his purely conventional 'non-essentialist' legal pluralism proposes that law be defined as whatever people in a social arena conventionally recognize as law through their social practices.

Tamanaha's socio-legal positivist approach to law aimed at a reconfiguration of Hart's concept of law, expanding the narrow (state centric) basis upon which the latter built up his own concept of law. Together, the socio-legal positivist approach to law and the non-essentialist legal pluralism 'provide the conceptualization of law to be used in the general jurisprudence.'[19] Noting the rise in popularity of legal pluralism as a theme in social scientific approaches to law, Tamanaha argues that the multitude of different legal pluralist arguments posited in recent decades are by and large flawed, owing to a continued adherence to essentialist assumptions regarding the nature of law. 'Specifically', he states at the outset, 'the dominant approach to legal pluralism contains two essentialist assumptions: it assumes that law consists of a singular phenomenon which can be defined, and it assumes that law is by nature functional.'[20] The non-essentialist (conventionalist) approach that Tamanaha proposes 'in contrast [. . .] points out that often different kinds and manifestations of law coexist in the same social field.'[21]

From the essentialist features of the dominant understanding of legal pluralism, Tamanaha argues, are derived both analytical and instrumental problems. The analytical problems are twofold, and:

> are quite serious in both of their primary aspects. First, there is no agreed upon definition of law; and, secondly, the definitions of law proffered by legal pluralists suffer from a persistent inability to distinguish what is legal from what is social.[22]

[19] Brian Tamanaha, *A General Jurisprudence of Law and Society* (Oxford University Press, 2001) 134.

[20] Tamanaha, note 19, 171. [21] Tamanaha, note 19, 172. [22] Tamanaha, note 19, 174.

The instrumental problems, which are a function of the analytical problems, are presented as follows:

> Without agreement on fundamental concepts that allow for the careful delineation of social phenomena, there can be no cumulative observation and data gathering. Moreover, current versions of legal pluralism, especially in their conflation of normative systems and legal systems, flatten and join together distinct phenomena, resulting in less refined categories, leading to less information and a reduction in the ability to engage in careful analysis.[23]

Although Tamanaha commends the legal pluralists for their general rejection of the legal centralist ideology, he cites the failure to properly distinguish the legal from the social as a fundamental flaw—and one that may be traced back to the way in which legal pluralists have defined law.

Virtually all attempts to define law, Tamanaha contends, fall into one of two categories: those that see law in terms of 'concrete patterns of behaviour within social groups', or those that see law 'in terms of institutionalized norm enforcement.'[24] He notes elsewhere that:

> All kinds of reasons, from various quarters, have conspired to prevent a consensus from forming in support of any particular definition or concept of law within either category. Not only do both general approaches to the concept of law fail individually; they cannot be combined because the first approach denies the necessity for institutions while the second approach insists upon it. These alternative approaches identify different criteria of existence.[25]

It is for this reason, then, as noted, that the analytical problems besetting legal pluralism have arisen; for the inability to form a consensus regarding the definition of law—which naturally cripples one's ability to distinguish legal from merely social—is a fairly predictable consequence of a dichotomy that forces different scholars, arriving from different points of departure, and with different requirements, to pick one category over the other. The only way out of this impasse, Tamanaha concludes, is to toss the two essentialist assumptions that have constructed the impasse, i.e. law as singular phenomenon that can be defined, and law being by nature functional.

The most important section in this chapter is that in which Tamanaha sketches the outlines of his non-essentialist legal pluralism, which, as was the case with his socio-legal positivism, draws much argumentative force from the shortcomings of essentialist lines of argument. The long-standing attempt to determine what 'law is . . . ' is fundamentally flawed, and 'implicitly presupposes an essentialist view of law because it assumes that law is some particular phenomenon that can be captured in a formulaic description.'[26]

[23] Tamanaha, note 19, 174–75. [24] Tamanaha, note 19, 175. [25] Tamanaha, note 19, 179.

[26] Tamanaha, note 19, 192.

The problem, in Tamanaha's view, is that 'law is a thoroughly cultural construct', which does not allow for easy capture by a single concept, or single definition.[27] The reason theorists have failed to capture the essence of law is thus remarkably simple, in Tamanaha's view: 'it has no essence'.[28] His non-essentialist view of law, then, *requires* law to be seen as essentially empty, insofar as it is devoid of presuppositions regarding any particular content or nature.

> A state of 'legal pluralism', then, exists whenever more than one kind of 'law' is recognized through the social practices of a group in a given social arena, which is a relatively common situation. This approach is different from most approaches to legal pluralism in a fundamental respect [...] In the typical legal pluralist approach [...] law is 'plural' because in a given social arena there are many manifestations of institutionalized norm enforcement (corporations, sports leagues) or many self-regulated semi-autonomous social fields (the garment industry, a university, a family). This kind of plurality involves the coexistence of more than one manifestation of a single basic phenomenon. This is the implication of using a definition with a singular set of necessary criteria. In contrast, I assume that the label 'law' is applied to what are often quite different phenomena—sometimes involving institutions or systems, sometimes not; sometimes connected to concrete patterns of behaviour, sometimes not; sometimes using force, sometimes not. Thus, the plurality I refer to involves different phenomena going by the label 'law', where as legal pluralism as typically conceived involves a multiplicity of one basic phenomenon, 'law' (as defined).[29]

This non-essentialist approach is perhaps surprising, given Tamanaha's earlier insistence on the inability to distinguish legal from social as a significant problem undermining legal pluralist arguments. One of the more interesting features of his approach thus arises in his discussion of how one goes about determining what 'law' is for the purpose of pluralist analysis. Distinguishing between two levels—that belonging to the concepts as developed by the peoples under study, and that belonging to the social scientists or theorists doing the study—Tamanaha states that the general jurisprudence 'will involve the construction of two (at least) qualitatively different sets of categories relative to law: one based on conventionally applied labels; the second based on abstracted features.'[30] Both belong to the second level, in that both are created by theorists/scientists. Both begin with conventionalist identifications of law—but branch out in different directions:

> *The first set of categories consists of conventionally applied labels of law,* i.e. state law, natural law, customary law, indigenous law, international law, transnational law, religious law and any others than might exist.

[27] Tamanaha, note 19, 193.
[28] Tamanaha, note 19, 193.
[29] Tamanaha, note 19, 194.
[30] Tamanaha, note 19, 195.

> [. . .]
> *The second set of categories consists of complexes of shared fundamental features abstracted from phenomena to which the label 'law' has been conventionally attached.*[31]

The end result of this process, Tamanaha argues, will be a set of label-based categories and a set of abstracted feature-based categories, both of which must remain open to new members, given the fact that social actors are always free to establish new labels, and to affix to different social phenomena (with different core features) the label 'law'.

In Tamanaha's view, the advantages of his approach are immediately apparent. Indeed, he begins, 'the problem that completely debilitates current versions of legal pluralism is not even an issue under this conventionalist approach, because it does not resort to a definition that encompasses other kinds of other social phenomena', but instead 'contains a criterion for the identification of law that is parasitic upon how people in a social arena identify law.'[32] What this means for Tamanaha's non-essentialist legal pluralism, then, is (i) a critical distance from subject matter, (ii) a lack of presuppositions regarding anything to which the label 'law' might be affixed, both of which result in (iii) an equalizing approach to all claims about law. The latter of the three in particular facilitates critical examination, 'which is a key reason for, and justification behind, engaging in the project of a general jurisprudence.'[33]

Tamanaha concludes this chapter by anticipating a number of possible critiques of his non-essentialist legal pluralism, noting that:

> [s]everal of the most serious possible points of contention were addressed in the previous chapter, regarding who and how many people must consider a phenomenon to be law for it to qualify, regarding determining which usages of the term 'law' qualify for inclusion in the conventionalist approach, and regarding the difficulties of translation [e.g., the sometimes significant distinctions between 'law', 'droit', 'recht', etc.].[34]

Further, Tamanaha anticipates criticism from legal theorists who believe that law has an inherently moral aspect—to which he notes that, consistent with its grounding in social legal studies, the non-essentialist legal pluralist approach takes an overtly *descriptive* approach to law, and does not preclude legal theorists from remaining committed to a moral view of law. From the social sciences, Tamanaha anticipates two criticisms. The first will come from functionalists, whose view that law is functional 'runs deep'. Regarding these theorists, Tamanaha hopes they 'will see the benefits of coming over to the conventionalist view, which is congenial to many other beliefs about law and legal pluralism they may hold.'[35] The second will come from those

[31] Tamanaha, note 19, 196.
[32] Tamanaha, note 19, 197.
[33] Tamanaha, note 19, 200.
[34] Tamanaha, note 19, 200.
[35] Tamanaha, note 19, 201.

who hold that all societies have law. It is doubtful that the anthropological bent in this last segment of the chapter will be of any great use to the broader aims of this project; yet, it is still worthwhile to consider the final thoughts that Tamanaha offers regarding the criticism coming from this camp of social scientists. The project aimed at establishing that all societies—even 'primitive' societies—have law was a consequence of the mid-nineteenth century evolutionary theory, and self-congratulatory enlightenment in the West. This project, Tamanaha, has since lost all of its political underpinnings (and we detect, here, a similar point vis-à-vis the dissolution of the nation-state). In a final, summarizing passage, Tamanaha writes that:

> [t]he conventionalism argued for here cannot be applied to identify law in primitive societies, then, for precisely the same reasons that forced 'legal' anthropologists to drop claims that they were studying 'law'. Some theorists saw 'law' in terms of patterns of order, and some saw 'law' in terms of institutionalized norm enforcement, and given their starting points there was no way to overcome this divide. Legal pluralists revived all the same old problems when they resorted, once again, to attempts to define law, and did so in essentialist, functionalist terms. The only way to break out of the cycle is to adopt the conventionalist approach to law, and to stop asking the question whether primitive societies had law. The political concerns that prompted legal pluralists to make the claim that they have identified 'legal' phenomena are not furthered by this claim. And the political concerns that initially prompted the question of whether primitive societies had law are no longer present, so there is no reason to ask the question.[36]

Tamanaha's non-essentialist legal pluralism has been criticized for being incoherent and for failing to understand legal positivists' theses about the concept of law embodied in our linguistic practices. Kenneth Himma argues that Tamanaha, in his attempt to discard the essentialist assumptions that seem to underlie the concepts of laws posited by the most important legal theorists, has formulated a concept of law that is, conceptually, far too thin to be of any real use. Once Tamanaha draws his conclusion that law has no essential features, Himma writes, the former 'seems committed to an account of the concept of law that is just too thin to tell us much of anything about the nature of law—as it is determined by our admittedly contingent linguistic practices.'[37] This emphasis on the linguistic features of Tamanaha's argument permeates Himma's own argument. Himma understands the methodological constraint Tamanaha places on his conceptual analysis (i.e. his conventionalism) to orbit around 'conventional *linguistic* practices',

[36] Tamanaha, note 19, 205.

[37] Kenneth Himma, 'Do Philosophy and Sociology Mix? A Non-Essentialist Socio-Legal Positivist Analysis of the Concept of Law' (2004) 24(4) *Oxford Journal of Legal Studies* 717, 738.

ultimately resulting in an adequacy constraint framed as follows: 'the analysis of any particular concept *C* should cohere with conventional practices that govern the core meanings of the concept-term "*C*" (assuming that these practices are consistent).'[38] What is especially important, Himma notes, is the fact that Tamanaha views this adequacy constraint as entirely at odds with the argument that 'law' has any 'essential' characteristics:

> Let *P* be any plausible candidate for an essential feature of law. Since our linguistic practices are contingent, it is possible for our practices to require labelling an entity as 'law' despite the fact that it lacks *P*. But since law is whatever we attach the label 'law' to, it is possible for something to constitute law despite the fact that it lacks *P*. It follows, then, that *P* is not an essential feature of law and hence (since *P* was arbitrary) that there are no essential features of law. The tension arises, then, because the adequacy constraint implies that the content of concepts is contingent, while the view that law has essential features implies that content of the concept is non-contingent.[39]

Himma responds to this point by arguing that Tamanaha has misunderstood the notion of an 'essential' feature of law, and relies upon his own understanding of linguistic contingence. In its most simple form, Himma's argument seems to be that even the notion of an essential characteristic is similarly contingent upon common understanding: 'the claim that such features are essential to law should be construed as conditional upon particular—admittedly contingent—practices of usage', meaning that '[s]hould these conventional practices change, the analysis of what is essential to law would also have to change.'[40]

Tamanaha anticipates such an argument, and Himma cites the passage:

> The problem is not only that social phenomena are difficult to delimit, but that there is a great deal of variation, and furthermore that social practices change. Given this complex and fluid situation, it is difficult to see how any concepts relating to social phenomena, like law, can make claims about necessary or essential elements. Assuming the term 'necessary' means *necessary*, Stephen Perry asked how one can go from identifying an admittedly contingent concept of law—discerning features which are common but not necessarily universal—to insisting that anything which is to qualify as law must have these features.[41]

Himma addresses this anticipatory counter-argument by noting that it effectively misses the point. While social phenomena are such that the concept-terms employed to describe them might change significantly in scope or substance as time passes, this ultimately has little to do with the

[38] Himma, note 37, 732, 733. [39] Himma, note 37, 733. [40] Himma, note 37, 733–34.

[41] Himma, note 37, 735 (referring to Tamanaha, note 19, 150).

practice of identifying (say) X as an essential feature of Y. Himma offers an example:

> Indeed, the term 'bachelor' is a social kind because of the status of being married or unmarried is determined by institutional social practices. Even so, existing usage conventions imply that the property of being unmarried is essential (in the sense of being conceptually necessary) to being a bachelor. Though that might very well change in the future, such a prospect has nothing to do with the current issue: current usage implies that being unmarried is an essential feature of being a bachelor.[42]

Thus, in Himma's view, Tamanaha's critique of legal essentialism—which is *central* to his assertion that 'law is whatever people attach "law" to'—suffers from a problematic distinction between convention-based 'fixed' meanings and convention-based adequacy conditions for an analysis of the concept of law.

The mischaracterization of the basic essentialist argument leads Tamanaha to explain his concept of law without any reference to the features usually associated with the label 'law'. This amounts to an explanation that does not tell us anything that would help distinguish law from those other concepts that could be described in Tamanaha's fashion (X is whatever we attach the label 'X' to)—that is, *any* other concept, in Himma's view. A concept of 'law' should tell us something *about* law—what that might be is not clear (indeed, if we rely upon Tamanaha's account, it never has been), but this, Himma writes, 'is why conceptual analysis have something to do', as 'we simply cannot use "law" to refer to anything if the norms governing its application did not specify certain features of an object that warrant calling it "law." '[43] In particular:

> [a]n analysis of the content of the concept of law should tell us something about the *content* of the conventions that govern the use of the concept-term 'law' and what they presuppose or imply by way of metaphysical commitments. If the preceding analysis is correct, these metaphysical commitments will involve the postulation of certain features that are essential to being an instance of the term 'law'—and such features will include something that is fairly characterized as a conceptual function.[44]

Non-essentialist legal pluralism, while successful at dislodging certain dogmatic attitudes about the necessary elements of the concept of law, does not provide sufficient guidance for distinguishing legal and non-legal phenomena in the cases that matter most: those where a legal system is confronted with an alien norm and must determine whether and how to acknowledge it and apply it. It is at that moment that the identification of this conceptual function is most important.

[42] Himma, note 37, 735.

[43] Himma, note 37, 737.

[44] Himma, note 37, 737.

7.3 INTELLIGIBILITY AS A CRITERION OF LEGALITY

I propose a constructivist interpretation of legal pluralism grounded on the idea of intelligibility as a primary criterion of legality. The formal statement of this account of law is purely conventional: A normative system is a legal system if it is intelligible to other legal systems as a legal system. It is not, however, solipsistic because the convention for identifying a legal system as such is most relevant when one legal system confronts another of dubious status. At this moment, the conceptual content of the conventions that identify the criteria of legality enter with full force. The conceptual content is contingent, but nonetheless provides objective criteria of intelligibility. Whether one calls these 'essential' or not is a rather minor point. What matters is that they provide a way to distinguish legal from non-legal phenomena in a way that is useful for legal theory.

There are several examples of this division of labour between conventionalism and mutual intelligibility, but I will point to one I find especially compelling. Consider the conditions for the recognition of a state in international society. The European state system throughout the nineteenth century did not explicitly recognize any criteria of statehood short of recognition by another state. There were, of course, many well-known theoretical accounts of sovereignty from Bodin's 'absolute and perpetual power of a Commonwealth'[45] to Hobbes' absolute and indivisible representative,[46] to Austin's '*determinate* and common superior' whom '[t]he bulk of the given society are in a *habit* of obedience or submission' and who 'is *not* in a habit of obedience to a determinate human superior.'[47] But these theoretical musings were either too abstract to be of use to diplomats or else were simply disregarded in the practice of *Realpolitik*. In that sense, the criteria of statehood were non-essentialist: any ruler could claim to lead a state with no clear reference to objective standards other than the recognition of his peers; likewise, other states had no duty to recognize a state and had no definite criteria to guide them in granting or withholding recognition.

The criteria for state recognition underwent an apparent dramatic shift with the Inter-American Convention on the Rights and Duties of States, commonly known as the Montevideo Convention. The Convention itself seems to have arisen out of President Franklin Roosevelt's attempt to formulate a 'Good Neighbor Policy' with Spanish-speaking states in the Americas—a policy that aimed at reducing aggression and violence on the part of the

[45] Jean Bodin (JH Franklin, ed. and tr.), *On Sovereignty: Four Chapters from the Six Books of the Commonwealth* (Cambridge University Press, 1992) 1.

[46] Thomas Hobbes (E Curley, ed.), *Leviathan* (Hackett, 1994) 213.

[47] Jean Austin (HLA Hart (ed.)), *The Province of Jurisprudence Determined* (first published 1832) (Hackett, 1998) 203.

United States when dealing with other Central- and South-American states. John Whitbeck has observed that 'this more respectful and egalitarian spirit in state-to-state relations is reflected in the provisions of the convention.'[48] This is perhaps little more than an observation, however, as the text of the Convention reflects no broader social or political objectives as such—that is, the text does not explicitly outline *why* the Convention was drafted, and a reader lacking familiarity with Latin-American history of the twentieth century would not be able to parse these broader political objectives from the text itself. 'The text of the Montevideo Convention', writes Thomas Grant, 'does not explain the origins of the criteria it enunciates.'[49] However, as Grant argues, this lack of contextualization is perhaps due to the fact that the criteria set out in the convention were not at all novel. 'That the framing of the Montevideo Convention has gone largely unexamined', he begins:

> may reflect the fact that this content was a restatement of ideas prevalent at the time of the framing. So apparent were the Montevideo criteria to contemporary observers that few thought to inquire as to their basis or origin. At the crux of the Montevideo criteria lay the concepts of effectiveness, population, and territoriality. In the late 1930s, these may have seemed a long-established feature of international law. They certainly were not new.[50]

This should not lead one to the rushed conclusion that the criteria were unassailable—indeed, the thrust of Grant's thesis is that the criteria ought to be re-examined, in part because of their having been taken for granted in a particular historical-political context—but the fact that the criteria are still cited by many scholars suggests some lasting significance.[51] This is perhaps unsurprising in light of some of the more important principles articulated in the convention. The most cited Article is the first, which sets out the basic criteria for statehood:

> The state as a person of international law should possess the following qualifications: a) a permanent population; b) a defined territory; c) government; and d) capacity to enter into relations with the other states.

If one pulls together the Articles outlining how 'statehood' is formed, a conception of *self-generating* statehood seems to emerge:

> Article 3. The political existence of the state is independent of recognition by the other states. Even before recognition the state has the right to defend

[48] John Whitbeck, 'The State of Palestine Exists' (2011) 18 *Middle East Policy* 62, 62.

[49] Thomas Grant, 'Defining Statehood: The Montevideo Convention and its Discontents' (1999) 37 *Columbia Journal of Transnational Law* 403, 414.

[50] Grant, note 49, 416.

[51] The four criteria of the first article of the convention are referred to as the 'traditional international legal theory' (Sean Murphy, *Principles of International Law* (Thompson, 2006) 32).

> its integrity and independence, to provide for its conservation and prosperity, and consequently to organize itself as it sees fit, to legislate upon its interests, administer its services, and to define the jurisdiction and competence of its courts.
>
> The exercise of these rights has no other limitation than the exercise of the rights of other states according to international law.
>
> [...]
>
> Article 5. The fundamental rights of states are not susceptible of being affected in any manner whatsoever.
>
> Article 6. The recognition of a state merely signifies that the state which recognizes it accepts the personality of the other with all the rights and duties determined by international law. Recognition is unconditional and irrevocable.
>
> [...]
>
> Article 8. No state has the right to intervene in the internal or external affairs of another.
>
> [...]
>
> Article 10. The primary interest of states is the conservation of peace. Differences of any nature which arise between them should be settled by recognized pacific methods.
>
> Article 11. The contracting states definitely establish as the rule of their conduct the precise obligation not to recognize territorial acquisitions or special advantages which have been obtained by force whether this consists in the employment of arms, in threatening diplomatic representations, or in any other effective coercive measure. The territory of a state is inviolable and may not be the object of military occupation nor of other measures of force imposed by another state directly or indirectly or for any motive whatever even temporarily.

The theory that a political body that objectively meets these factual criteria is *ipso facto* a state, with all the rights and prerogatives in international community is the preferred reading of the Convention and conforms the 'declarative theory' of statehood, as opposed to the previously dominant principle which makes statehood dependent on the recognition by other states. In practice, as most scholars observe, the rival 'constitutive theory' of statehood seems dominant, by which the criteria serve at best as a guide to recognition, and 'only when other states decide that such conditions have been met, and acknowledge the legal capacity of the new government, is a new state actually constituted.'[52] And of course, states are free to recognize entities that do not meet these conditions as subjects of international law on a par with states, as they have done with the Sovereign Military Order of Malta.

The key element of the Montevideo criteria, then, seems to be the capacity, most clearly stated in the fourth criterion set out in the first Article, to enter into relations with other states. The interplay between factual criteria

[52] Murphy, note 51, 33.

and recognition suggests that the Montevideo criteria themselves are at their core epistemic: they outline the conditions for conceiving an entity as state-like-enough to be a candidate for recognition. Whether a state should recognize it or not is a political question, but one that can be judged from a standpoint of 'epistemic formalism' as consistent or inconsistent with past practice. The more a state diverges from the paradigmatic features of statehood the less recognizable it is as the sort of thing that 'state' refers to. If non-state entities are shown to be capable of entering into political and legal relations with states, they may become familiar enough to warrant a revision of the criteria. But intelligibility is the measure of essence.

7.4 LAW BEFORE LAW

Legality is a matter of mutual recognition, and the institutional features that facilitate such recognition enter through the criterion of intelligibility. This approach has several advantages. First, it allows for a (somewhat) historically contingent conception of law that nonetheless retains objective institutional criteria for distinguishing legal from non-legal phenomena. Second, it explains why legal systems germane to that of the state (such as canon law) are readily accepted as law, while others (such as cultural practices) are not. The latter may be full-fledged normative systems, but they lack institutional features that recommend the recognition of their norms as *legal* norms to other legal systems.

The institutional criteria for mutual recognition among legal systems are not formal criteria in the sense that they differentiate between legal and non-legal normative systems *sub specie æternitatis*. They are, however, reasons for legal officials in one system to recognize another on the basis of shared characteristics. Put this way, intelligibility is a coherentist criterion of recognition. This has some practical implications both for the recognizer and the one desirous of recognition. Thus, some normative systems which may not have had a conceptual structure similar to that of modern state legal systems, nor the need for one, have self-consciously presented themselves as legal systems in order to have their norms recognized by existing legal systems. Sometimes the appeal to legal form is almost purely rhetorical, to have a practice taken seriously in a way analogous to the use of the word 'business' in Aboriginal English to refer to matters of substantial social or ceremonial weight, adopted because 'business' was (accurately) identified as something especially important to white settlers.[53] But other times, the reference to law is accompanied by institutional reforms intended to mimic the form of the system whose recognition is sought. The drive for mutual intelligibility

[53] I thank Kirsten Anker for bringing this to my attention.

is sometimes also directed by the state when it attempts to accommodate non-state law within a broader legal order. A significant example is the so-called 'Boyd Report' about the status of sharia law in arbitration tribunals privately set up to handle a variety of disputes, including family and custody cases, in the province of Ontario, Canada.[54] Among the reforms necessary to have the judgments of sharia tribunals recognized by courts were requirements of publication of judgments and professional representation of parties, all features that would approximate the sharia tribunals to the kind of institutions recognizable by state courts as 'legal'. Third, it performs the critical role of not only explaining why certain normative systems are in fact recognized as legal systems, but also of identifying good reasons for some systems which have the structural features that render them legally intelligible to be recognized as law. This last feature of the intelligibility thesis is especially important because, as Perry Dane observes, the ever-present conceptual danger of outlawry or anarchy is averted if persons who claim to be subjects to the authority of another normative system are not thereby claiming to be 'outside the law' but rather to be subjects to another law, and therefore governed by norms which may be acknowledged and integrated into other legal systems in more familiar and orderly fashion.[55]

To explain the importance of intelligibility, let us consider the standard positivist description of the application of foreign law in a legal system. Assume two legal systems—Alpha and Beta—each of which is composed of norms (rules, principles, etc.) that are valid under the rules of recognition accepted by legal officials in each system. The norms of system Alpha are accepted by the officials of Alpha as legally valid in Alpha, and the norms of system Beta are accepted by the officials of Beta as legally valid in Beta. Now, the legal officials of Alpha may think that the norms of Beta are legally valid in Beta, but the only reason they can give for that belief is that the legal officials of Beta recognize them as such. The officials of Alpha may think the norms of Beta are good norms, they may think that they govern Beta well, and may even think that they ought to emulate them in their own system.

[54] Marion Boyd, *Dispute Resolution in Family Law: Protecting Choice, Promoting Inclusion* (Ontario Ministry of the Attorney General, December 2004) <http://www.attorneygeneral.jus.gov.on.ca/english/about/pubs/boyd/> accessed 1 July 2013. The provincial government of Ontario ultimately denied recognition to arbitration tribunals that made recourse to sharia law on matters of family and custody disputes, but did so on explicitly political grounds, and implicitly recognized the legal status of sharia by declaring that it would not tolerate deviation from the principle of 'one law for all Ontarians.' Eli Walker, 'Don't Throw out My Baby—Why Dalton McGuinty Was Wrong to Reject Religious Arbitration' (2006) 11 *Appeal: Rev. Current L. & L. Reform* 94.

[55] Perry Dane, '"Omalous" Autonomy' 2004 *Brigham Young University Law Review* 1715; 'The Varieties of Religious Autonomy' in Gerhard Robbers (ed.), *Church Autonomy: A Comparative Survey* (Peter Lang Publishers, 2001); Note: 'Religious Exemptions Under the Free Exercise Clause: A Model of Competing Authorities' 90 *Yale Law Journal* 350 (1980).

This is of absolutely no consequence as to the legal validity of the rules of Beta. Simply put, the opinion of Alpha officials about the norms of Beta does not make any difference in the legal validity of the norms of Beta; if it did, Alpha officials would also be Beta officials.

Nonetheless, officials of Alpha can recognize officials of Beta as legal officials of a (foreign or alien) legal system, and this can make a difference as to their treatment of the norms of Beta. It makes a difference, for instance, in cases in which Alpha officials have to decide on the question 'Is norm X a legally valid norm in Beta?' which can only be answered by asking the question 'Is it valid according to rules of recognition accepted by Beta officials?' This is an altogether different question from asking whether the presumptive rule is a good rule, whether it would be good for Alpha to adopt it, or even if it would be good if it were indeed the rule in Beta. These are genuine questions that are often asked not only by courts but by legal scholars and social scientists, but they are irrelevant to the legal validity of a norm as a norm of Beta. Of course, the question 'Is norm X a legally valid norm in Beta?' can have various degrees of importance. It may only be theoretically important as, for example, the answer to a question in a university examination on the law of Beta. But it may also be practically important if there are other norms in Alpha that grant special consideration to the legal rules of foreign or alien jurisdictions, but do not grant such consideration to non-legal norms as is the case, for example, in much of private international law.

There is a further layer to the problem of the identification of legally valid rules of a foreign or alien legal system. To ask the question 'Is norm X a legally valid norm in Beta?' officials of Alpha have to put themselves in the shoes of officials of Beta, in a sense. That is, they can only be moved by those considerations that would animate Beta officials in determining the validity of the norm. The interpretation of officials of Alpha, however, is always provisional because only officials of Beta have the proper (though self-proclaimed) authority to determine whether a norm is part of their legal system. That is simply what the legal system of Beta is: whatever legal officials in Beta say it is. Legal officials of Alpha have no say in this, insofar as the legal validity of a norm of Beta is concerned. The Alpha officials can ask their Beta brethren for an authoritative answer, or, absent that, they can try to determine such an answer on their own. This may be necessary if, for example, the decision of a case in Alpha depends on the determination of the legal validity of a norm of Beta, but for whatever reason an authoritative answer from Beta officials is not forthcoming. If they choose the latter course, however, their answer is always provisional and does not, by itself, make for an authoritative declaration of legal validity. It is as if Alpha officials have to preface every interpretation of Beta law with the caveat 'We are not sure of whether this is a legally valid norm in Beta, and we are not presuming that our say-so would make it a legally valid norm, but given what we know about the rules of recognition, adjudication, and change in Beta, and the norms flowing from these that have been recognized by Beta officials before, we officials of Alpha have, in good faith, reached the conclusion that this norm is (or is not) legally valid in Beta.' Should officials in Beta later determine the legal validity of the norm in question, it is their interpretation—and only their interpretation—that gives or denies the norm its legal validity as a norm of Beta, even if the interpretation of Alpha officials was a more sophisticated exercise of legal reasoning or even if it rested on superior moral premises or led to more fortuitous consequences. There is no inconsistency in declaring that the Alpha officials' interpretation of a rule of Beta is better in every way that the interpretation that Beta officials have of the same norm, but that the interpretation of Beta officials is the only legally valid one.

This distinction is especially important because it bears on the explanation of the response that Alpha officials may have to a Beta norm. They may have very good reasons for disregarding a norm that is otherwise legally valid. Many norms are unclear, unjust, or downright abhorrent and there may be moral reasons not only to put them aside but to effusively condemn them. Alpha and Beta are different legal systems and neither is subordinate to the other, and the norms that call on Alpha officials to inquire into the legal validity of a Beta norm are, after all, Alpha norms. There may be other norms of Alpha that qualify or limit the applicability of foreign or alien norms in Alpha courts without denying that they are otherwise norms of a legal system, but these qualifying or limiting norms are different from the norms that specify the criteria of legality; they rest on reasons other than criteria of legality and, in effect, declare an offending norm inapplicable *despite being a norm considered legal* by the officials of the other system.

So, in one sense, the identification of the legal validity of norms of a foreign or alien legal system really begins and ends with the identification of the legal officials of that system. If those officials are identifiable, and if they can proffer an answer to a question about the validity of a norm, this is the only interpretation that authoritatively determines legal validity. If they are not able to proffer this interpretation, then the legal interpretation of anyone who is not an official of that system is only provisional.

Once we decide that an association has a legal system, we must acknowledge that it is only the legal officials of that system that can authoritatively identify the norms of that association. And once we decide that we will allow the association to be governed by its own legal norms, we must defer to the interpretation that the association's legal officials give to those norms. We who are not legal officials of the association may disagree with this interpretation, but we cannot substitute our own and pretend that it is legally authoritative. We may choose to ignore the interpretation proffered by legal officials of the association, but we cannot do so on the grounds that ours is a legally better determination. It may be better in some other way, but that is irrelevant to its legal validity. Legal validity is immediately determined by authority, not merit, and cannot be overruled without negating the authority of the official that determined it.[56] What we can do—and what we surely sometimes must do—is to say that we are disregarding the authority of legal officials in the association, that we are not recognizing their authority, and that we are doing so for reasons that have nothing to do with their legal validity but with non-legal considerations. Ralf Michaels explains:

> Treating non-state normative orders as law does not necessarily give them a greater practical importance than incorporation, deference, or delegation. Put another way, contrary to what some argue, legal pluralism does not necessarily imply greater autonomy of non-state communities vis-à-vis the state. The different treatment of law and non-law is a difference of form, not of degree or substance. States may well treat foreign laws as law through conflict of law but still deny them applicability, either because their specific approach to conflict of laws contains a strong preference for the laws of the forum or because that approach uses a far-reaching public policy exception against foreign law. On the other hand, a liberal state may well give generous deference and delegation to non-state normative orders, enabling non-state communities to regulate their own affairs largely without interventions while denying them the status of law.[57]

The question of the treatment of non-state law as law is then not a functional one—what the effect of following a state or non-state norm will be—but rather a modal one—how the norm will be characterized. It is not a question of *what* the norm mandates but *how* it mandates.[58] But the treatment of non-state normative systems as law by the state varies from one case to another. The norms of churches often receive enormous deference in liberal democracies, and there is a growing chorus of scholars who argue that this is because the institutional aspect of the church, rather than the sincerity

[56] One possible counter-example is jury nullification, but I do not think it succeeds as an objection. One can plausibly argue that members of juries are legal officials, at least while occupying their role in a jury. But even then, they are subordinate officials, and the officials self-proclaimed as superior have, over time, stripped juries of the authority to determine the content of law which is now the almost exclusive prerogative of the judge. Instances of jury nullification can also be explained as refusals to apply the law because of superior moral considerations that do not affect its legal validity.

[57] Ralf Michaels, 'The Re-*State*-Ment of Non-State Law: The State, Choice of Law, and the Challenge From Global Legal Pluralism' (2009) 51 *The Wayne Law Review* 1209, 1237.

[58] Modern positivists like John Gardner and Leslie Green explain this as the modality of law (John Gardner, *Law as a Leap of Faith* (Oxford University Press, 2012) 293; Leslie Green, 'The Concept of Law Revisited' (1996) 94 *Michigan Law Review* 1687. Michael Oakeshott had earlier made a similar distinction by saying that the rule of law is adverbial: it does not tell a subject what to do, but rather the manner in which something is to be done (Michael Oakeshott, *On Human Conduct* (Oxford University Press, 1975), 55)).

of belief of its congregants, deserves a special kind of recognition.[59] The characterization of Canon Law as law is questioned less, say, than the characterization of cultural practices as law, and this explains Archbishop Rowan William's insistence on distinguishing religious law from cultural practice when addressing the problem of sharia law in British Courts.[60] Universities, likewise, are often allowed substantial latitude in their deliberation on curricular matters and the process of internal promotion, and reference is usually made to their organizational structures. Informal norms, however, are rarely treated as legal. This suggests that the more a non-state legal system resembles the norms of the state, the more likely its norms are to be accommodated as legal norms. This is also reciprocally true of the admission of state norms into non-state legal systems. Openness is proportional to familiarity, and norms that fit the form of law familiar to one system stand a greater chance of admission.

Let us consider again the question of the relative autonomy or openness of legal systems discussed in Chapter 6. Raz accepts that more than one self-proclaimed legal authority may make simultaneous claims on a putative subject. But his focus is not on the effectiveness of sanctions, but rather on the normative force of the claims advanced by different authorities. What distinguishes authoritative claims from other reasons for action that a subject may have (such as personal preferences, financial pressures, or traditions) is not the force of the claim or the strength of the sanction behind it, but rather their form. Legal claims are authoritative claims given by persons in a particular relation to each other, namely an institutional relation of authority. This means that the legal character of a norm will depend on the characterization of that relationship: where it exists, officials will make pronouncements that are taken as authoritative; where it does not, the commands may be reasons for action but of an altogether different kind. This has nothing to do with their practical effectiveness. As Michaels observes, 'the state's monopoly on law-making does not imply that the state could have unlimited factual power to regulate all transactions. . . . The different treatment of law and non-law is a difference of form, not of degree or substance.'[61] John Gardner, a 'hard' legal positivist, agrees in indicating that the law:

> is not a functional kind. It is a modal kind. There is no social function, nor any combination of social functions, that distinguishes law from any of its near neighbours. Rather, law is distinguished from many of its near neighbours (those that have social functions at all) by how it serves the many social functions that it, in common with those near neighbours, serves or

[59] See note 70 of Chapter 1 and also note 55 of this chapter.

[60] See the discussion of Williams' position in Chapter 2.

[61] Michaels, note 57, 1236–37.

> is capable of serving. Law is not 'whatever resolves disputes' but a special *way* of resolving disputes, and for doing a huge range of other things besides, by the use of rules largely effective across a general population, and officials who apply them and who claim authority and supremacy in doing so.[62]

Raz makes the recognition of the norms of any legal system by another legal system dependent on the latter's own norms. In theory, openness goes both ways. In practice it does too. Religious law provides some of the most telling examples. The classic case is the principle of *dina de-malkhuta dina* in rabbinic law, which states that, on matters not pertaining to religious observance, the law of the state—irrespective of its secular or religious origin—is binding upon Jews.[63] Two things are interesting about this example. The first is that the rabbis claim discretion to distinguish between civil and economic matters (*manoma*) where deference is given to state law and religious matters (*isura*) where no accommodation is permitted. The second is that state law is considered subsidiary to *halacha* (religious law) and grounded on general religious principles of Biblical origin, the Noahide laws that apply to all persons and oblige them to set up institutions for the administration of justice. This is so even when the laws of the state supersede rabbinic law, say, by adjudicating extracontractual liability differently or requiring a different number of witnesses to a contract. Such supersession is allowed by the religious principle, and so, under Raz's own scheme, is still regulated by religious law even when religious law applies it in preference to its own dictates. The rabbinic treatment of secular law also contains formal requirements that the law be prospective and universal, which are similar to the modal conditions recognized by positivists such as Gardner.[64]

If these formal requirements recall Lon L Fuller's 'internal morality of law' it is not by coincidence. Fuller's description of law as possessing normative criteria for it to be law at all has been taken as a critique of legal positivism and a defence of legal pluralism, insofar as non-state legal

[62] Gardner, note 58.

[63] Michael Walzer, Menachem Lorberbaum, and Noam Zohar, *The Jewish Political Tradition, Vol. 1 Authority* (Yale University Press, 2000) 431–34. The phenomenon is not exclusive to the Jewish legal tradition. Ernest Caparros has illustrated, with reference to Québec law, that just as the civil law integrates elements of the canon law of the Roman Catholic Church (and other churches) into its norms—the laws of cementeries or of administration of church property, for example—a process he calls *canonizatio*, so does the canon law of the Church integrate civil law norms into its normative structure, a process he dubs *civilizatio* (Ernest Caparros, 'La "Civilizatio" du Droit Canonique: Une Problématique du Droit Québécois' (1977) 18(4) *Les Cahiers de Droit* 711).

[64] Walzer et al., note 63, 433.

systems conform with the criteria of legality. But HLA Hart did not see Fuller's criteria as contradicting his positivist account of law.[65] A recent monograph on Fuller's legal philosophy, moreover, suggests that there is very little distance between Joseph Raz's positivism, which stresses the authoritative character of law—itself a modal trait—and 'Fuller's focus on law's form and its relationship to a conception of the legal subject as an agent'.[66]

[65] HLA Hart, 'Review of LL Fuller, *The Morality of Law*' (1975) 78 *Harv L Rev* 1281. Although Hart's embrace of Fuller's criteria, as Waldron notes, was equivocal at best. Jeremy Waldron, 'Positivism and Legality: Hart's Equivocal Response to Fuller' (2008) 83(4) *New York University Law Rev* 1135.

[66] Kristen Rundle, *Forms Liberate: Reclaiming the Jurisprudence of Lon L Fuller* (Hart, 2012) 160.

8

Pluralist Authority

The type of polity that political pluralists recommend is, needless to say, highly controversial. Yet philosophers at least as far back as Hobbes have questioned not only the desirability of a pluralist polity or the accuracy of the pluralist description of society, but also, more problematically, the very coherence of the pluralist concept of authority.[1] It is the conceptual coherence of pluralism that concerns me here, that is, not whether all associations are legitimate, but of whether any can ever be legitimate. This conceptual concern is a problem for the pluralist tradition because most of the arguments that political pluralists have used to undermine the claims of the modern state to absolute and indivisible authority leave no room for the exercise of authority by associations themselves. If political pluralism is to make a coherent claim for the authority of associations, it must be able to explain the structure of pluralist authority, and not simply assume that it will be obvious once overstated claims to state sovereignty are cut down to size.[2]

In this chapter I will reconstruct one prominent pluralist critique of state authority—the one proposed by Harold Laski—and explain how it undermines the very basis of the authority of associations. I will then propose an alternative account derived from Joseph Raz's famous 'normal justification' of the authority of law.[3] This alternative pluralist account allows for the

[1] Thomas Hobbes (E Curley (ed.)), *Leviathan* (Hackett, 1994) chapter 18.

[2] As explained in chapter 5, I refer interchangeably to 'sovereignty', which follows British pluralist practice, and 'authority', which I think analytically more precise. This may require justification. Preston King describes a sovereign as 'an ultimate arbitral agent—whether a person or a body of persons—entitled to make decisions and settle disputes within a political hierarchy with some degree of finality...[which] implies independence from external powers and ultimate authority or dominance over internal groups'. Preston King, *The Ideology of Order: A Comparative Analysis of Jean Bodin and Thomas Hobbes* (2nd edn) (Frank Cass, 1999) xviii. Harold Laski similarly defines sovereignty as 'the legal competence to issue orders without a need to refer to a higher authority.' Harold Laski, 'Law and the State' (1929) *Economica* 9 (27): 267–95, 267. Thus, the use of sovereignty by the pluralists approximates that of Joseph Raz in the theory discussed in this chapter.

[3] See: Joseph Raz, *Practical Reason and Norms* (Oxford University Press, 1975); Jospeh Raz, *The Authority of Law* (Oxford University Press, 1979); Jospeh Raz, *Ethics in the Public Domain* (Oxford University Press, 1985); Joseph Raz, *The Morality of Freedom* (Oxford University Press, 1988); Jospeh Raz, *Between Authority and Interpretation* (Oxford University Press, 2009).

recognition of legitimate authority in associations, but it also necessitates the recognition of the authority of the state, both a direct or first-order authority over persons *qua* citizens, and an indirect or second-order authority over persons *qua* members of various groups. Thus, while vindicating the authority of associations, I hope to repudiate the antinomian stance of much of political pluralist theory, and set it on sounder footing.

As I have already mentioned, the renewal of the pluralist thesis about the autonomy of associations seems especially relevant today. Invariably, many cases of conflicting sources of authority come from the experience of churches and other religious institutions: the opposition of Roman Catholic hospitals to provide contraceptive services to their employees on the grounds that it is a violation of the religious freedom of the institution; recent or imminent judicial decisions in Canada and the United Kingdom over religious educational institutions (respectively, the content of secondary school curricula in Loyola High School in Québec, and the religious classification of candidates for admission to the Jews Free School in the UK); the disputes over church property of conservative parishes wishing to leave liberal dioceses in the American Episcopal Church; as well as ecclesiastical opposition to restrictive immigration policy and the subsequent provision of sanctuary on church grounds to immigrants facing deportation. But the theory extends also to other associations, such as universities, which have long affirmed (and long have had trampled) their rights to self-governance. So have the two heirs to the medieval guild: associations of liberal professionals (lawyers chief among them) and trade unions who have long protected their autonomy vis-à-vis both state and private enterprise.

8.1 THE TRADITION OF POLITICAL PLURALISM

A brief recap of the pluralist tradition might illustrate the problem of authority in pluralism. The British pluralists contest the view that the state is the unlimited and unitary source of legitimate authority in any given society, that it is owed allegiance above all other organized groups, and indeed that other associations can legitimately exist only as long as the sovereign tolerates them. This position they label political monism. Against monism, the pluralists contend that, in any society, there are multiple sources of legitimate political authority personated in various groups and associations, of which the state is but one; none of these has inherent precedence over the others.[4] Groups—e.g. churches, unions, universities—exercise a measure of

[4] Laski, note 2, 283.

sovereignty in their own right, and it is only this dispersion of authority that secures freedom against the state.[5]

Among the British pluralists, the most academically inclined was Harold Laski. Laski forcefully contested the state's claim to exclusivity of sovereignty, but his arguments against the state's claims to authority would also serve to undermine the authority of other groups.[6] He was, in essence, more of an anarchist than a pluralist.[7] Yet it is this tension in Laski's thought that makes him an ideal exponent of the antinomian defect of pluralist theory. Laski seems to have reached this conclusion himself and, as a result, his attitude towards pluralism changes considerably later in his life. On one hand, it is Laski who, in his early writings, 'provides[s] a name for what had been a somewhat heterogenous body of thought',[8] and who popularizes such thought in academic circles. But it is also he who later abjures pluralism on philosophical and political grounds on his way to embracing libertarian Marxism and Labour Party politics.[9] The ambivalence he expresses towards the authority of groups leads to his eventual abandonment of some important elements of the pluralist critique: first the idea of group personality and later the idea of the equal stature of the state and other associations.

One reason for Laski's abandonment of pluralism is his rejection of the idea of the 'real personality' of groups, an idea most emphatically advanced by John Neville Figgis[10] and discussed in Chapter 9. A second set of reasons for Laski to abandon pluralism is political. By *The Grammar of Politics*, Laski comes to think of the state as different from other associations on a number of grounds, chief among them that the state is a compulsory territorial association where other groups are voluntary, and that the state alone is able to represent human beings as such, in those common interests that they have as citizens and not as members of any one group. The satisfaction of these common interests is the function of the state, and it is a function that 'involves a pre-eminence over other functions.'[11] Whether the state can fulfil this function, is contingent on historical, social, and economic circumstances and is always subject to the affirmation of citizens *in every particular case*. What changes in Laski's view of associations, then, is not so much the

[5] David Nicholls, *Three Varieties of Pluralism* (Macmillan 1974) 5ff.

[6] Harold Laski, 'The Personality of Associations' in Paul Hirst (ed.), *The Pluralist Theory of the State* (Routledge, 1993) 180.

[7] Avigail Eisenberg, *Reconstructing Political Pluralism* (State University of New York Press, 1995) 75–83.

[8] David Runciman, *Pluralism and the Personality of the State* (Cambridge University Press, 1997) 178.

[9] Runciman, note 8, 188ff; David Schneiderman, 'Harold Laski, Viscount Haldane, and the Law of the Canadian Constitution in the Early Twentieth Century' (1988) 48 *University of Toronto Law Journal* 521.

[10] John Figgis, *Churches in the Modern State* (Longman, Green and Co., 1913).

[11] Harold Laski, *A Grammar of Politics* (5th edn) (George Allen & Unwin, 1967) 70.

principle that human beings are 'community-building animal[s]'—a position sustained throughout his oeuvre[12]—and that they may build quite a large number of them, but that the state is more effective than other associations in carrying out especially important social enterprises.

In one sense the state's power of compulsion is morally irrelevant, as the *de facto* exercise of power does not justify it; but in Laski's view, the effectiveness of the state in carrying out a function that, in his later years, Laski had come to see as pre-eminent, does justify elevating the state above its previous rank. The argument is tied up with the language of function, which Laski borrows from GDH Cole, and which suffers from its own problems. Cole expressly subordinates the authority of associations to his corporatist functionalism. He argues that each association possesses a function which emanates from the satisfaction of common wants and the execution of common purposes, and that the coherence of society depends on all associations fulfilling their function in a way that is 'complementary and necessary for social well-being'; he therefore dismisses as 'perversions of function' much of the conflict, contradiction, and redundancy that are part-and-parcel of relations between associations and the state.[13]

Suffice it to say that Laski recognizes that specifying a function requires the identification of a specifier, and leaving this task up to the agents of the state 'makes them judges in their own cause.'[14] But this does not lead Laski out of the difficulty of setting limits to state discretion.[15] My account does not rest on any such 'thick' functionalism and in fact presumes that a pluralist society is characterized by disagreement over both the content and the arbiters of function, and I am agnostic about even the plausibility of a concept of function, which seems artificially tidy, or of a common good which is more than an overlap of particular allegiances. It does rest on a certain instrumentalism about authority, but this is far from the specification of discrete roles to different social groups.

A further question is how representative is Laski of the early pluralists. In some ways he is not, but only because the school was not especially cohesive. Figgis, for instance, seems much less antinomian than Laski and endorses

[12] Laski, note 11, 67.

[13] GDH Cole, 'Social Theory' in Hirst, note 6, 60–67.

[14] Laski, note 11, 70; Cole, note 13, 80. In this, Laski was more clear-headed than Cole, whose appeal to Rousseau's General Will in orienting social choice towards 'the good of the community as a whole' (GDH Cole 'Conflicting Social Obligations' (1914) 15 *Proceedings of the Aristotelian Society*, New Series, 140–59, 158–59) confirms the view that he was 'hardly a pluralist at all' (David Nicholls, *The Pluralist State: The Political Ideas of JN Figgis and His Contemporaries* (2nd edn) (St. Martin's Press, 1994) 3).

[15] Jens Bartelson observes that 'Laski is characteristically ambivalent about the role of the state, since he wishes to reinterpret this concept along pluralist lines, but he finds it difficult to strip it of all its monist connotations without having to deal with the problem of political order by introducing an equally monist substitute'. Jens Bartelson, *The Critique of the State* (Cambridge University Press, 2001) 106.

something like what I call the 'second-order authority' of the state in his idea of society as *communitas communitatem*. The state has a role in protecting individuals against injustice, whether from each other or from the groups to which they belonged, and it does so mainly through the institutions of private law—'as the guardian of property and interpreter of contract'—but it also should abstain from meddling in the governance of groups, and especially in their development and social reproduction.[16] Yet Figgis is decidedly ambiguous about the role of the state in adjudicating disputes between political authorities, groups, and individuals,[17] so much so that it is doubtful whether he thinks the state has any direct or 'first-order' authority over citizens. Citizens are only members of the state through their membership in other communities, and never to the state directly. This subsidiary structure, which intentionally recalls Johannes Althusius' political theory,[18] misapprehends the claims of the state to direct and independent authority over citizens. So, although Figgis accepts that 'societies may come into collision with the State; so may individuals [and] always there is a possibility of civil war',[19] he must interpret these conflicts as a failure of the state either to set boundaries correctly or to keep its role limited to the provision of institutions of private law. The view that I defend in section 8.4—that the conflict of pluralism is inherent to the state's multiple sources of authority—is not clearly there. So through a criticism of Laski we may also arrive at a broader reconstruction of the pluralist tradition.

Harold Laski makes the most comprehensive case against the modern state's claim of unlimited and exclusive authority. Laski argues that the state's claim to sovereignty is false on moral, pragmatic, and legal grounds. The state makes the *moral* claim that its commands are binding on the subject, not because of the intrinsic merit that they may have, but because they issue from a sovereign authority. The state also makes the *pragmatic* claim that it is—or at least ought to be—the only body that can impose its will on all subjects and associations, as it possesses a monopoly of the legitimate use of physical force. Finally, the state makes the *legal* claim that *only* its will is law because it is the only person or body in society who is habitually obeyed by the bulk of the population, and who does not, in turn, owe habitual obedience to any other body.[20] Laski objects to the truth and to the desirability of all these propositions.

I will take these in reverse order, as Laski's objection to the state's moral claim is the main focus of the following discussion. The question of whether

[16] John Figgis, 'The Church and the Secular Theory of the State' in Nicholls, note 14, 158.

[17] Figgis, note 10, 90.

[18] Johannes Althusius, *Politica* (FS Carney, ed.) (Liberty Fund, 1995).

[19] Figgis, note 10, 92.

[20] John Austin, *The Province of Jurisprudence Determined* (HLA Hart, ed.) (Hackett, 1998) 195.

it is only the rules promulgated by the state that should be properly characterized as 'law' is deeply complicated, and as much the domain of anthropology and sociology as of moral, political, and legal philosophy. The extensive literature on legal pluralism that has emerged over the last half century calls into question the Austinian criteria of habitual obedience and the boundaries drawn to define the 'bulk of the population', and points to a variety of sources of normative order that thrive in even the most modern societies.[21] As a statement of fact, Austinian monism is false, or at least imprecise. Depending on the way that the boundaries are drawn, we observe different objects of obedience, even among the same individuals. For instance: as neither the Catholic Church nor the Italian state habitually regards the other as superior, and as some observing Catholics are also Italians, some Catholic Italians will have two sovereigns…an Austinian impossibility. An apologist for the state's legal claim may argue that the obedience to the Church is the wrong kind of obedience, or that obedience needs to be backed by force, but these answers depend on normative assumptions or extraneous factors. Laski's legal objection seems to be this: the definition of obedience, population, and society—and thus of law—are either so value-laden as to be question-begging, or else provide little guidance to practical conduct.

What Laski calls the pragmatic claim is also valid, but misses the point. Both defenders and detractors of authority agree that the mere ability to impose one's will on another—to whatever extent—is not a sufficient basis for a claim of authority.[22] As Raz explains, not all exercise of power is an appeal to authority. What distinguishes an authority is that it makes a special claim to legitimacy for itself, to the fulfilment of certain moral or rational criteria necessary to demand obedience. The ability to exercise force in defence of an authoritative directive may be one of the criteria relevant to its legitimacy (coordination problems usually require the agent to credibly provide incentives and disincentives, not merely exhortations) but it is not the whole, or even the core, of legitimacy. The pragmatic claim is either irrelevant or, again, question-begging.

The force of Laski's argument thus rests on the moral objection. Laski maintains that the state expects its subjects to obey its commands and its laws because they issue from the state, regardless of their intrinsic merit or conformance to the strictures of morality. This is not to say that the officers of the state do not think its laws and proclamations are moral. Rather, it

[21] As mentioned in chapter 1, there is no evidence that legal pluralism is historically related to political pluralism, except in a common choice of adversaries (see Brian Tamanaha, 'Understanding Legal Pluralism' (2007) 29 *Sydney Law Review* 375). For this reason, I have not discussed legal pluralists such as Robert Cover or (arguably) Lon L Fuller in this chapter, although, as I say elsewhere, their arguments are in many ways similar to those of the political pluralists.

[22] Robert Wolf, *In Defense of Anarchism* (University of California Press, 1998) 9.

means that the obligation to obey depends on the source of the command, not on its content. Laski objects that this claim to moral sovereignty, and its implied duty of obedience, represents a usurpation of the subject's capacity of moral judgment. This usurpation is illegitimate, first, because 'whatever the requirements of legal theory [...] in actual fact no man surrenders his whole being to the state. He has a sense of right and wrong.... The state ... is for him sovereign only where his conscience is not stirred against its performance.'[23]

This usurpation is also illegitimate because no individual ought to support an action that does not conform to morality, even if the state is generally right in other respects, or if the ultimate aim of the state is noble. Laski claims that '[t]he only ground upon which the individual can give or be asked his support for the state is from the conviction that what it is aiming at is, in each particular action, good;' the state must '[command] his conscience.'[24] Laski grounds the legitimacy of authoritative pronouncements on the values towards which the enactments aim, and their efficacy in achieving them.[25] 'The obedience that counts is the obedience of an actively consenting mind; and such a mind is concerned less with the source of law than with what the law proposes to do' and only consents after deliberation on the concrete merits of a given law or policy.[26]

This argument is familiar to contemporary political philosophy. It is the position of philosophical anarchism represented, for one, by Robert Paul Wolff's statement that '[t]he moral condition demands that we acknowledge responsibility and achieve autonomy wherever and whenever possible.'[27] Laski acknowledges that his arguments against state authority come close to advocating anarchism: '[t]his is, of course, a pluralistic theory of law [as] the facts before us are anarchical.'[28] But this conclusion sits uneasily with his pluralism. The reason is that Laski takes the Austinian criterion of sovereignty as his point of departure, even as he criticizes its implications. John Austin styles the sovereign as a single but determinate individual or body of individuals to whom habitual obedience is rendered by the bulk of society; and who does not, in turn, render such obedience to anyone else.[29] Yet if habitual obedience is the measure of sovereignty, then the state cannot be the only sovereign around. The state, Laski contends, is but one of many groups competing for the allegiance of men and women.[30] Churches, trade unions, families even, hold the loyalty of individuals to at least the same degree as the state. They are, in a real and important way, self-governing, in

[23] Harold Laski, *Authority in the Modern State* (Yale University Press, 1919) 43.
[24] Laski, note 23, 46.
[25] Laski, note 2, 274–75.
[26] Laski, note 2, 275.
[27] Wolff, note 22, 17.
[28] Laski, note 2, 294.
[29] Austin, note 20, 195.
[30] Harold Laski, *Studies in the Problem of Sovereignty* (Yale University Press, 1917) 6–20.

that they pursue collective goals with unity of purpose, and do not habitually subordinate their values and their ends to those of another authority. From a normative vantage point, Laski also concludes that competition between these associations and the state, and between the associations themselves, serves to preserve freedom, foster human creativity, and sustain a responsible polity.[31]

But how do associations effectively hold the allegiance of their members? It is not (or not always) by attempting to convince the members of the wisdom, righteousness, or efficacy of every decision, norm, or policy. When a church counsels its adherents not to practice certain modes of contraception, or when a trade union tells its members not to cross a picket line, or when a parent instructs her child not to stay out late on a school-night, they mean these directives to be obeyed even if the subject does not agree with the reasons for the directive. For a group to be self-governing means that it exercises authority over its members. A church must be able to expel heretics, a trade union to negotiate the terms of a contract, a parent to set the rules of a household.

Laski's social and political theory recognizes a plurality of associations, many (and perhaps all) of which exercise authority with regards to their members. But his categorical objection to the moral claims of sovereignty denies the possibility of legitimate authority altogether. It denies associations the capacity to function. Avigail Eisenberg explains the problem well. '[T]he dominance of an extreme form of individualism in Laski's theory undermines the basis for pluralism in it. If the ends to which his theory are directed are individualistic, and if the means are also primarily individualistic (i.e. requiring individual consent, respecting individual rights, and protecting individual liberty), why did Laski need pluralism?'[32]

8.2 AN ACCOUNT OF AUTHORITY

Political pluralism needs a better account of authority if it is to give adequate grounding to the autonomy of associations. A plausible candidate is Joseph Raz's account of authority, which also develops as a response to the paradox of authority presented in Robert Paul Wolff's challenge.[33]

I invoke Raz's theory as a way to resolve the specific problem of grounding the authority of associations. From the outset, there is a possible (and serious) objection: namely, that Raz's approach to the problem of authority is incompatible with Laski's treatment of the subject, especially because

[31] Henry Magid, *English Political Pluralism: The Problem of Freedom of Organization* (Columbia University Press, 1941) 54.

[32] Eisenberg, note 7, 81.

[33] Raz, *Authority of Law*, note 3, 26ff.

Raz reduces authority to the language of instrumental reasons for action, whereas Laski's critique of authority is historical, sociological, and phenomenological and expressly rejects an exclusively rational approach. 'The answer to the problem of obedience' Laski writes:

> is, of course, that all theories which strive to explain it in purely rational terms are beside the mark; for no man is a purely rational animal. The State as it was and as is finds the roots of allegiance in all the complex facts of human nature; and a theory of obedience would have to weigh them differently for each epoch in the history of the State if it were to approximate the truth.[34]

Raz's account of authority is expressly instrumental, that is, it grounds authority on its usefulness in advancing the reasons for action that independently oblige a given subject. Raz is credited, even by critics, with offering the canonical instrumentalist account of authority.[35]

But Laski also couches authority in instrumentalist reasons. This is a constant from his early works, where he argues that 'the state is simply an organization existing for the promotion of an end',[36] to the later, where he reiterates that 'the State is not itself an end, but merely the means to an end, which is realized only in the enrichment of human lives.'[37] Laski does not think, however, that the state's right counsel is sufficient to command obedience. Consent—'the obedience of an actively consenting mind'—is necessary for authority to be legitimate and, while the impetus to obey is complex and socially and historically contingent, it is nonetheless possible to submit it to the examination of reason.[38] In this Raz largely agrees. Raz distinguishes the question of the conditions that could make authority legitimate from the question of whether a subject has an obligation to obey. The question of authority asks whether it is, in principle, ever permissible not to exercise autonomous judgment in every single case. For Raz, it is; for Laski, it is not. But for a given individual to be bound to a given authority, she must possess 'a sense of belonging to the community and identifying with it' which, while not consent, performs the same role in rendering authority legitimate.[39] Raz does not explore the possibility that this feeling may arise with regards to

[34] Laski, note 11, 22.

[35] Thomas Christiano 'Authority' in E.N. Zalta (ed.), *The Stanford Encyclopedia of Philosophy* (Stanford University Press, 2012). Available from: <http://plato.stanford.edu/archives/spr2012/entries/authority/> accessed 2 July 2013. The instrumentalist account contrasts with other explanations of political authority which may seem just as congenial to Laski's pluralism, most notably Ronald Dworkin's recourse to the associative obligations that are generated in genuine political communities (Ronald Dworkin, *Law's Empire* (Harvard University Press, 1986) 195ff; cf. also Stephen Perry, 'Associative Obligations and the Obligation to Obey the Law' in Scott Hershowitz (ed.), *Exploring Law's Empire* (Oxford University Press, 2008) 183–205; and Leslie Green's appeal to consent as a better grounding for political obligation (Leslie Green, *The Authority of the State* (OUP, 1988), 158–87)).

[36] Laski, note 23, 57. [37] Laski, note 11, 88. [38] Laski, note 11, 23.

[39] Raz, *The Morality of Freedom*, note 3, 98.

more than one community, but nothing in his system excludes this possibility, thus opening the way to a genuinely pluralistic conflict of obligations.

Authority, as I mentioned, is not the mere exercise of power. A robber exercises power to force a victim to hand over his money, but does not claim to exercise authority over the victim. This is why Laski's pragmatic objection to the state's claim of sovereignty is inadequate. Anyone with sufficient power—physical or otherwise—may force another to act in a certain way. But only by making a claim to legitimacy does the exercise of power become authoritative. 'What distinguishes authoritative directives' Raz explains, 'is their special peremptory status. One is tempted to say that they are marked by their authoritativeness.'[40] That is why *de facto* authority presupposes *de jure* authority.[41] What matters is that authorities claim the *right* to impose duties on their subjects, to guide their actions, to get them to act in certain ways—and not just the power to do so.

Authorities, moreover, do not claim that their directives are just 'good reasons' to think that certain actions should be done. They claim that their directives are reasons to do these actions. The difference is important. A reason to think that an action should be done is a reason for belief. It remains for the agent to consider this reason, and either accept it or disregard it. Those whom Raz calls theoretical authorities—experts, for instance—expect to be believed, but not to be obeyed. Practical authorities are the ones that concern us: authorities like a state, a church, a trade union, or a parent. Practical authorities expect obedience. They expect their pronouncements to be taken as reasons for action, whether or not the subject agrees with the reasoning behind them in a particular case.[42]

The utterance of a legitimate authority should then be the immediate reason for a subject's compliance. '[T]he fact that an authority requires performance of an action' explains Raz, 'is a reason for its performance which is not to be added to all other relevant reasons when assessing what to do, but should exclude and take the place of some of them.'[43] This Raz calls the pre-emption thesis, a descriptive thesis explaining what authority claims to do.

Now, the pre-emption thesis seems to corroborate the suspicion that authority always entails the illicit usurpation or immoral surrender of judgment. But this suspicion is wrong, Raz insists, when we look at the usual way of accounting for the operation of legitimate authority. To be legitimate in a way that overcomes the paradox of legitimate authority, authority must be a rational and moral response to the problems encountered by

[40] Raz, *Ethics in the Public Domain*, note 3, 212.

[41] Cf. Raz, *The Authority of Law*, note 3, 9; Raz, *The Morality of Law*, note 3, 28.

[42] Raz, *The Morality of Law*, note 3, 35.

[43] Raz, *The Morality of Law*, note 3, 46.

practical reason. It must serve the interest of the subject to conform her conduct to appropriate reasons for action. '[T]he normal way to establish that a person has authority over another person', Raz proposes, 'involves showing that the alleged subject is likely better to comply with reasons which apply to him (other than the alleged authoritative directives) if he accepts the directives of the alleged authority as authoritatively binding and tries to follow them, rather than by trying to follow the reasons which apply to him directly.'[44] The content of those reasons is not the issue. The point is that, whatever one ought to do, one is more likely to do by following an authority than by acting on one's own judgment. This is the *normal justification thesis* (hereafter NJT).

What can we conclude from the application of the NJT to the claims of non-state associations? First, it seems evident that most organized groups in society claim practical authority over their members in conformance with the pre-emption thesis. They claim that their authoritative utterances are reasons for action for their members, that their members should act on these reasons directly, and not merely weigh the authoritative utterance against other reasons for action. The problem is that it is not clear that this pervasive feature of associational life is allowed by a logical extension of Laski's critique of the authority of the state.

At times, especially in his later writings, Laski seems to suggest that the state is a theoretical authority of sorts, that it can assemble commissions of experts to suggest better ways of coordinating collective activity. The state's utterances are at most reasons for belief. This is why Laski advocates for a thoughtful citizenry that can judge the state's proffered reasons. Laski perhaps supports what Raz calls the 'recognitional' conception of authority, which holds that the acceptance of authoritative utterances is to take them as reasons for belief, but not for action.[45] Yet the concession to theoretical authority only reinforces Laski's denial of practical authority, since no state has ever been content with the role of advisor to the populace. All states claim, rightly or wrongly, that the reasons that they proffer are pre-emptive, that they substitute or displace other reasons that citizens could hold, such that the essence of state authority seems to be entwined with pre-emption. But by the same token, Laski's position does nothing to vindicate the authority of associations other than the state, which also claim that their reasons are pre-emptive, at least with regards to their members. Their supposedly authoritative pronouncements become nothing but 'expert' opinions if Laski's supposedly pluralist antinomianism is taken to its logical conclusion.

[44] Raz, *The Morality of Law*, note 3, 53.

[45] Raz, *The Morality of Law*, note 3, 29.

For example, on this interpretation, the Roman Catholic Church's prohibition of certain forms of contraception ceases to be an imperative, and becomes an advisory opinion about the practical implications of doctrine. Some adherents may in fact take the church's dictates as such, but it is not how we ordinarily think of religious canons or commandments, and certainly not how churches and other religious organizations conceive of them. Of course it is essential to the functioning of many organizations (not only churches) that their members accept the dictates of the organization as reasons for action; but to reframe this expectation in terms of theoretical authority is to transform associations into mere aggregations of contingently like-minded individuals. This may, for some, be an attractive depiction of social life, but it is not political pluralism.

At this point, I have not demonstrated that the authority that groups claim for themselves is justifiable, but have at best shown that they do make such a claim. In this, the authority of associations is of a kind with the authority of states and, as a result Laski's objection to the state's authority must also be valid against groups. This makes for a very poor pluralist theory. A separate question is whether the authority of groups could, in theory, be legitimate. How does it fare under the NJT?

The criteria of legitimacy for the authority of an association are the same as those of authority generally: a member of the association, in submitting himself to its authority, would 'better conform to reasons that apply to him anyway…if he intends to be guided by the authority's directives than if he does not.'[46] But what are those reasons? In the case of the authority of state law, it is possible to give a single answer, at least with regards to all subjects of a particular political jurisdiction: the law applies generally and equally to all persons in a political society. But in the case of associations, such a general answer cannot always be given. The reasons that apply to members of one association may not apply to non-members. How does the legitimacy of these claims fare by the standard of the NJT? Consider an example: when the status of a recent convert is contested before a rabbinical court, say because religious status is a condition for receiving some service administered by the religious congregation, there are most likely several legal sources that speak on the matter. For a Jew (at least in the Orthodox tradition), the laws prescribed in these sources are reasons for action, but she is more likely to comply with these laws if she submits to the authority of a rabbinical court and lets the court determine the course of action that better conforms to Jewish law.[47] None of these reasons would apply to a non-Jew. Rabbinical courts

[46] Raz, *Between Authority and Interpretation*, note 3, 135–37.

[47] A similar situation gives rise to the controversy in *R* v *The Governing Body of JFS* [2009] UKSC 15, where the Supreme Court of the United Kingdom rejected the argument that denying preferential admission to a

claim authority over those who come before them, and this authority seems to fulfil the criteria of legitimacy of the NJT.

This argument may apply to other associations as well. A trade union exists to strengthen the bargaining position of its members and secure their rights and exact greater benefits for them in the course of labour negotiations. Presuming that these negotiations take place under conditions that are morally acceptable—e.g. no threats of violence—and that each side in the negotiation intends to make demands that fall within the range of fairness—however defined—then every employee has a reasonable wish to get more, rather than fewer benefits. This is a perfectly acceptable reason for action for the employee. It is also reasonable for the worker to think that, by joining together with others similarly situated, delegating the task of collective bargaining to the union rather than seeking a separate deal, and abiding by compulsory unionization rules to minimize defectors and free-riders, she is more likely to get the benefits she wants. The union claims authority over the worker in accepting a collective bargain, say, or calling a strike, because it is acting for reasons that apply to the worker anyway. The worker accepts this authority as legitimate because she is thus more likely to comply with those reasons. The NJT again obtains. Now, this is not an argument for the rightness or wrongness of the content of the rabbinical judgments or Roman Catholic canon law, nor of the efficacy of compulsory unionization, or of the wisdom of parents. It is a statement about the claims that associations make, which are claims to legitimate authority, the sort of claim that can at least aspire to be right and binding on its subjects.

The claim to legitimate authority, moreover, is essential to the functioning of an association. As Figgis put it, a church cannot exist without the power to excommunicate.[48] This may be an overstatement brought on by Figgis' Anglo-Catholicism, but it is not a gross one; even religious bodies that eschew formal excommunication retain the right to dismiss ministers and demand control over denominational property. Perhaps it is also an exaggeration to say that a trade union cannot exist without compulsory membership and the right to strike, but the union's effectiveness would certainly be limited without them. And a parent certainly cannot raise a child without being able to make some decisions on her behalf, even after the child becomes psychologically capable of deciding some things for herself.[49]

Jewish school to a child whose mother had converted to Judaism in a manner not recognized by the Chief Rabbinate was impermissible ethnic discrimination. As the minority opinion notes, the characterization of Jewish status as religious or ethnic itself involves a conflict of authorities.

[48] Figgis, note 16.

[49] When that moment arrives, however, we must weigh the value of making one's own decisions against the value of making the right ones. Raz recently recognized this as the need to fulfil the 'independence condition' to the question of the morality of authority 'that the matters regarding which the [NJT] is met

8.3 RECONSIDERING THE AUTHORITY OF THE STATE

A final, but important controversy remains: where does this discussion of the authority of groups leave the authority of the state? In a straightforward sense, the same reasoning that applies to associations applies to the state: a citizen is more likely to abide by the reasons that apply to her—contributing her share in common burdens, or coordinating complex activities like automotive traffic or pre-trial discovery—by submitting to the state's authority, than by attempting to abide by her reasons directly. Yet there is another less straightforward way of admitting the legitimate authority of the state in relation to associations. A person may have good reason to submit to the authority of the state when doing so will make it more likely that she will be able to submit to those associations to which she should submit in accordance with the NJT.

I have explained that, under the NJT, it is legitimate to submit to another's authority if doing so will make a person more likely to conform to reasons that apply to her in any case. But this is the same as saying that, in these circumstances, she has a reason (moral or otherwise) to submit to a legitimate authority. This authority may be general, as when the citizen submits to the authority of a just state. But it may also be particular, as when an observant Jew agrees to abide by a rabbinical verdict, a Roman Catholic accepts papal authority, a worker embraces a collective bargain, or a child obeys the orders of his parent.

One may conclude that one or more of these associations does have a valid claim on one's allegiance, but there are myriad reasons that would cause a person to fail to obey them. Internally, she may experience weakness of the will, or insufficient motivation. Externally, the association may not have the means to make its decisions known, or may be subject to undue external influence. It may be in her interest, then, to secure institutional safeguards that would make it more likely that she would indeed be able to abide by the decisions of the association. She might, for instance, want to ensure that it can act in ways that make its authority effective, e.g. by enabling the association's exercise of proper control over its membership, its land, or its money.

It may then be reasonable to accept the laws and policies of the state as legitimate when they enable institutions that allow for the recognition of the identity, or personality, of an association, and for the performance of its actions. Personality and agency are the elements of associational autonomy, and members of associations have reasons to sustain them. The legal

are such that with respect to them it is better to conform to reason than to decide for oneself, unaided by authority.' Raz, *Authority and Interpretation*, note 3, 137.

institutions that the state upholds thus come to have second-order authority over persons, at least as it applies to them *qua* members of associations. This is different from the first-order authority that the state may have over a person *qua* citizen. But it is authority nonetheless and, from the perspective of a committed member of a group, it is legitimate if it indeed secures associational autonomy.[50]

8.4 THE INTRACTABILITY OF CONFLICT

A discussion of pluralist authority is not complete without an acknowledgement of the intractability of conflict, which is directly predicated on the scope of the claims that authorities make for themselves. Here I can only suggest how a pluralist theory of authority reconstructed along Razian lines might approach the problem.

Raz makes several careful distinctions in defining the comprehensiveness of authorities' claims, especially in the case of legal systems.[51] Raz argues that such systems '*claim authority* to regulate all forms of behaviour, that is, that they either contain norms which regulate it or norms conferring powers to enact norms which if enacted would regulate it.'[52] This claim is independent of the authority's means to enforce regulation, and it is present even in the negative, which is to say that legal systems may permit a certain kind of behaviour—through constitutional rights, for instance—but do not thereby fail to regulate this behaviour, as 'an action is regulated by a norm even if it is merely permitted by it.'[53]

Legal systems, Raz continues, also claim to be supreme, to have 'authority to prohibit, permit or impose conditions on the institution and operation of all the normative organizations to which members of its subject community belong.'[54] Raz understands supremacy as entailed by comprehensiveness: if a legal system claims authority to regulate every sphere of behaviour, it cannot simultaneously recognize another authority as independently and non-subordinately regulating any given sphere within the same community.

[50] In principle, these functions could be performed by any legal order, not just the state. Some contemporary theorists have suggested that the functions of the state are being disaggregated to global and transnational institutions (e.g. Andrew Linklater, *The Transformation of Political Community* (Cambridge University Press, 1998) 176–77). I am somewhat sceptical of these arguments and think that the nation state is still central to the generation of legal institutions, but this is a matter of historical contingency.

[51] The importance of the institutional aspect of normative systems that claim authority is clear in Raz's early work, like *Practical Reason and Norms*, see note 3. It fades in later books, but has been convincingly reasserted by Andrei Marmor in 'An Institutional Conception of Authority' (2011) 39(3) *Philosophy and Public Affairs* 238 and 'The Dilemma of Authority' 2 *Jurisprudence* 121 (2011).

[52] Raz, *Practical Reason and Norms*, note 3, 151.

[53] Raz, *Practical Reason and Norms*, note 3, 151.

[54] Raz, *Practical Reason and Norms*, note 3, 151.

The claim of supremacy can be related directly to Raz's argument that the authoritative directives of law are 'protected reasons', reasons for action that at the same time rule out reliance on other reasons for action.[55] A protected reason is both a first-order reason for action and a second-order exclusionary reason to disregard other reasons as authoritative.

In claiming the authority to impose conditions on the institution and operation of other normative systems (to the point of prohibiting them), a legal system is in effect 'protecting' its first-order authoritative reasons, by limiting other sources of authority from intruding upon the comprehensive scope of its legal authority. In this context, the 'normative organizations' regulated should be understood to refer to other autonomous institutionalized systems. The systems are distinguished by possessing institutions 'with power to determine the normative situation of specified individuals, which are required to exercise these powers by applying existing norms, but whose decisions are binding even when wrong.'[56] What is important in the claim of supremacy, then, is not that an individual may disobey or disregard the dictates of the law because she does not believe the order to be justified in the particular case. Rather, the worry is that competing autonomous systems would each claim legitimate authority over an individual. The result would be either an impasse, or a reversion to the standard of judging every case on the basis of individual conscience, which effectively dismantles both state and associational authority. Finally, Raz claims that legal systems are open: they contain 'norms the purpose of which is to give binding force within the system to norms which do not belong to it.'[57] It should nonetheless be emphasized that, just because a legal system is open does not mean that it is pluralistic. Raz identifies the rules of conflict of laws (private international law) as designed to adopt and give force to norms of foreign systems—only *through* the norms of the domestic system—and the rules of contracts and companies as designed to adopt and give force to norms created by domestic subjects of the state—ultimately to be interpreted by state officials. These are compatible with the legal system, as they do not actually question its supremacy or comprehensiveness.

Raz's enumeration of the features that characterize legal systems has been criticized even within the positivist camp.[58] And strictly speaking, these critics are correct: neither supremacy nor comprehensiveness are necessary features of legal systems, or of institutional normative systems more generally. The claims of supremacy and comprehensiveness are bound up with the

[55] Raz, *The Authority of Law*, note 3, 18.

[56] Raz, *Practical Reason and Norms*, note 3, 136.

[57] Raz, *Practical Reason and Norms*, note 3, 152–53.

[58] Andrei Marmor, *Positive Law and Objective Values* (Oxford University Press, 2001) 39–42; Scott Shapiro, *Legality* (Harvard University Press, 2011) 218–19.

emergence of the modern nation state, and are both a product and a justification of the increasing dominance of this form of political organization 'over separatism and medieval political structures.'[59] However, even if we put aside the claim that supremacy and comprehensiveness are necessary features of legal systems, we should not dismiss the model lightly for two reasons: the first is that, regardless of historical contingency, modern nation states do claim supremacy over all other associations in society, and even when they limit the scope of their authority, they do so not because they acknowledge external limits to their authority, but rather because of internal limits such as their own constitutional principles.

The second reason, which pulls perhaps in an opposite direction, is that many of the associations that are the object of pluralist analysis today—churches, universities, cities, etc.—are descended directly from medieval institutions, or at least share important features with those institutions. The jurisdictional conflict that was, in a sense, constitutive of medieval political society can help us characterize certain aspects of current relations between organized groups, especially because many non-state associations did not wholly surrender their claims to institutional autonomy. Roman Catholic canon law, for example, no longer regulates many spheres which were once within its jurisdiction (e.g. the civil accidents of marriage), but rather adopts or defers to the relevant norms of the secular authority. This is not because it deems these domains as having somehow fallen into the inherent secular competence of the state; rather the church has reinterpreted its internal reasons, including its spiritual mission, as indicating deference to state law. But it has not thereby abandoned its claim to be the ultimate judge over its own scope of jurisdiction, or acquiesced to the state's own claims to hierarchical superiority.

Now, political pluralists have often replied to the state claim to supreme authority by denying the claim as false or incoherent. This is misleading on two counts. First, it overstates the claim to supremacy as a logical axiom that once disproven can be dismissed. The claim to supremacy, however, and the accompanying extension of jurisdiction to cover every aspect of human conduct, is a historical process that admits of degrees and an ideological justification that reflects as much an aspiration as a practical political reality; nothing is thus gained by attacking its logic. Second, the claim of supremacy is shared by many associations, if not at the core of their claims to authority, at least at the margin. Take, for instance, a university's assertion of academic freedom against state intromission, whether for the institution directly or by the institution on behalf of its professors, which is an assertion of supremacy over a specific sphere of human conduct and, at the same time, authority to

[59] Marmor, note 58 above, 40.

determine the proper boundaries of that sphere. This authority is ordinarily considered to emerge from the nature of academic practice and community itself and to not require certification from a superior authority. Even those associations that, because of historical or principled reasons, have retreated from claiming supreme authority to regulate all aspects of behaviour, may nonetheless claim supremacy at the margins, and even a modest claim may result in considerable conflict with the authority that the state claims for itself.[60]

All talk of the conflict of jurisdictions is, of course, most applicable to the confrontation between the primary or first-order authority of the state and the corresponding first-order authority of non-state associations. How does the consideration of the intermediate, second-order authority of the state affect our assessment? Here it is useful to see second-order authority as an answer to the problem of pluralist authority, which is to reconcile, (a) the pluralist contention that the existence of multiple associations each of which independently claims legitimate authority over their members imposes an external (or exogenous) limit to the authority of the state, with (b) the dominant contention that the state (and for that matter many other associations) recognizes only internal (or endogenous) limits to its claim of comprehensive authority, limits which it also claims supreme authority to delineate.

Consideration of the second-order authority of the state may help with this reconciliation. If the state derives its second-order authority from its capacity to facilitate a subject's compliance with reasons that apply to her as a member of an association, then the state must take (the existence of) those reasons into account when exercising its authority. Those reasons are mediated by the association—the association is the final arbiter of the ways in which its members would best comply with their associative reasons. For the state to substitute its judgment for that of the association regarding how the latter's members would best comply with the reasons that apply to them as members would be to defeat the second-order reasons for the state's authority, since the basis of this authority is the interest of members in subjecting themselves to the authority of the association directly. Or put in the reverse, a person *qua* member of an association has no reason to respect the state's authority when the state purports to substitute its judgment for that of the association; in such cases, the member is only bound by the association's authority. The pluralist account, then, rather than encouraging submission

[60] There is some similarity here with Rogers Smith's attempt to pluralize (though he does not refer to it as such) the notion of 'political peoplehood' beyond the nation state (Rogers Smith, *Stories of Peoplehood* (Cambridge University Press, 2003) 19ff) which also, because of its reliance on narrative, bears resemblance to Robert Cover's legal pluralism (Robert Cover, 'Nomos and Narrative' (1983) 97 *Harvard Law Review* 4). Not all groups (or states), Smith observes, make claims equally strong or comprehensive, and this may have some bearing on the prevalence and intensity of conflict.

to the state, can serve as a justification for disobedience.[61] The effect of this strategy is to have the state internalize the external limit imposed by the existence of a competing authority. The state need not always defer to the reasons of persons *qua* members of associations over their reasons *qua* citizens; undoubtedly there will be instances when those reasons conflict, and the first-order authority of the state will pull in a different direction than its second-order authority. Political pluralism accepts that such conflicts may arise and that they may have no principled resolution. But they can lead the state to acknowledge the authority of the association not as an exogenous (or external) limit on its authority, but rather as an endogenous (or internal) limit. Any solution 'should be seen as the provisional results of complex acts of creation, not be reified as the basic stuff of social and political reality.'[62] This may facilitate interaction, dialogue, and negotiation over rigid assertion of jurisdictional exclusivity.[63]

To briefly recap, Harold Laski denies the authority of the state for reasons that equally deny the authority of associations, effectively endorsing philosophical anarchism and rendering pluralism superfluous. But it is possible to construct a concept of authority that applies as much to groups as to the state itself by appealing to the capacities that groups have for helping individuals achieve the variety of reasons that they find compelling, and even for helping to constitute those reasons. Yet groups cannot effectively function in the absence of certain institutional conditions, and these the state is especially well placed to provide. The second-order authority that derives from the state's role in giving institutional form to groups is independent of, and does not deny, the first-order authority that the state may have over citizens.

Political pluralism may thus be reconstructed as recommending a hybrid polity in which the state, rather than being dispossessed of all legitimate authority, is endowed with two sources of authority each in tension with the

[61] This is the structure of the argument put forth by some Roman Catholic bishops over the United States government's draft mandate for employers to provide contraceptive coverage in their employees' health plans. The bishops claim that hospitals, orphanages, and other such enterprises are ministerial branches of the religious body, while the state considers them primarily as participants in the labour market who provide employment and services to the general public. It is not clear which authoritative definition is superior, but the state's subsequent exemption of religious employers from the mandate presumptively avoided a conflict that could have invited active resistance. This is not to endorse the result but merely to explain its structure. Under the account of authority I have described, the bishops could call on their congregants to deny the state second-order authority over them if the state undermined their religious mission as they understood it. This would have resulted in a conflict between the state's first- and second-order authority over Roman Catholics which could involve either religious or civil disobedience.

[62] Henrik Enroth 'Beyond Unity in Plurality: Rethinking the Pluralist Legacy' (2010) 9(4) *Contemporary Political Theory* 458, 473.

[63] For a similar strategy in legal pluralism, felicitously dubbed a 'jurisprudence of hybridity', see PS Berman, 'Towards a Jurisprudence of Hybridity' *Utah Law Review* 2010 (1) 11–29, 12.

other. The contribution of political pluralism is to recognize that this tension is a permanent feature of the human condition. Yet it can be better managed and negotiated if we properly construe and acknowledge the authoritative claims of the various organizations, including the state, which hold the allegiance of individuals.

PART THREE
THE PERSONALITY OF ASSOCIATIONS

> I suspect that you and Figgis are working the personality business a little hard, and drawing doubtful conclusions from it.
>
> —Oliver Wendell Holmes to Harold J Laski

9

This Unity of Life and Action

In Part One of the book, I argued that there is an ideal structure to pluralist arguments that are put forth in the several domains of practical reason—meta-ethics, politics, and law—and this structure not only makes pluralist arguments similar to each other, but also makes them distinct from other kinds of normative arguments in these areas. All non-trivial pluralist arguments make three claims about the normative category that is their object (whether it is value, sovereignty, or legality): these three claims are the claim of *foundational plurality*, the claim of *incommensurability*, and the claim of the inevitability of *tragic conflict* or *tragic loss*. The conjunction of these three claims I have called the parallel structure hypothesis.

In the case of political pluralism, the object of plurality is what can be broadly called the 'sovereign' association, that is, the association which makes an institutional claim to legitimate meta-jurisdictional authority. In following the structure of pluralist arguments, pluralism claims that there is more than one such association occupying the same normative space, exercising presumptively legitimate authority over a certain segment of the population; because no one authoritative principle or structure is recognized that can determine the boundaries of the groups, there is always the possibility of tragic conflict, even if only (but not always) at the margins. These claims, of course, respond to a synthetic reconstruction of pluralism as an ideal type and were not always articulated in these precise terms by the British pluralists themselves, but they accurately capture the form and the content of pluralist arguments.

9.1 THE BIRTH OF THE PLURALIST THEORY OF GROUP PERSONALITY

One of the most consistent problems of social and political theory is how to conceive of human collectivities, particularly of those collectivities that have an enduring historical identity, possess a sophisticated institutional structure, and are reflected in the self-conception of their members as ontologically distinct from the aggregate of not only present, but past and future members. This problem was central to the theories of nearly all the British political pluralists and in important ways defined the movement, setting it apart from other political traditions that defended the importance of groups in public life but did not accord such importance to their distinct personality. Some scholars, looking back on the pluralist tradition, have judged that the pluralist case stands or falls on the strength of their account of the real corporate personality of the group and, finding their account unclear or patently incoherent, have dismissed pluralism as a result.[1] And judging by many of the arguments that actual pluralists made in the heyday of the movement, this would seem the right conclusion to reach. The theory of the real corporate personality of the group is central to the pluralist argument and indeed the *fin de siècle* pluralists did a poor job explaining it and muddled it with unnecessary metaphysical and organic imagery. But, as in much of their writing, there is a valuable intuition to be rescued from the pluralists' insistence on real corporate personality.

The realist theory of group personality went through a meteoric rise and equally dramatic fall within the space of little over 30 years. The controversies about the best way to describe the ontological and normative status of groups dates from long before, and is already eloquently discussed by Hobbes in Chapter 22 of *Leviathan*.[2] But at the end of the nineteenth century the discussion took an interesting turn when the foremost English legal historian of his time, Frederick W Maitland, imported to Britain an esoteric scholarly dispute over the character of medieval German associations. Thus began the contemporary debate over the real corporate personality of associations.

The doctrine, and through it much of the British pluralist tradition, can be traced through Maitland to Otto von Gierke's writings on medieval Germanic law. These enter English jurisprudence through Maitland's translation of a portion of Gierke's *Das Deutsche Genossenschaftsrecht* and, especially, through the translator's own elaborate introduction to the work.[3] In his reconstruction of medieval legal history, Gierke had opposed the Germanic legal tradition to the Roman tradition of civil law; the former upheld a robust conception of autonomous groups or 'fellowships' whose rights and privileges—and thereby personhood—were legally recognized, while the latter took these groups to be purely artificial persons or legal fictions whose capacity to be the bearer of rights and privileges—their personality—is derived only from

[1] David Runciman, *Pluralism and the Personality of the State* (Cambridge University Press, 1997).

[2] Thomas Hobbes (Richard Tuck (ed.)), *Leviathan* (Cambridge University Press, 1996) 155ff.

[3] Otto von Gierke (Frederick W Maitland (tr.)), *Political Theories of the Middle Age* (Cambridge University Press, 1900).

a concession of the state.[4] In the context of Germany, which was Gierke's main concern, the Roman tradition was out of place because it did not recognize and could not conceptually grasp the historical experience of medieval fellowships.

As Gierke's interest is in the historical experience of German law, so Maitland's is in the English experience and its application to legal doctrine. Maitland's introduction is a careful work of comparative scholarship, which brings him to discuss the trust—a peculiarly English institution—alongside the more universal business corporation. To an orthodox English lawyer, the trust and the company are entirely different species, different legal categories with discrete histories and bodies of doctrine. But to Maitland they are both juristic accommodations to the social reality of collective endeavours that have need of a recognized institutional form. 'The trust has given us a liberal substitute for a law about personified institutions'[5] especially during the period before the Companies Act of 1862 liberalized the process of forming corporations. What the parallel between the trust and the corporation shows is that, where individuals engage in collective endeavours they create collective interests not reducible to the aggregate of individual interests, and that these properly collective interests require formal legal representation.

Maitland was a scholar of pragmatic disposition, and in elaborating the theory of real personality, he relied on ordinary usage and practice. Associations have personality because they function as persons, and because they are so treated by individuals, the state, and other associations. And this is so because of the shared purpose and fellow-feeling among group members—an observable fact—not because of the formality of concession.

> If the law allows men to form permanently organised groups, those groups will be for common opinion right-and-duty-bearing units; and if the law-giver will not openly treat them as such, he will misrepresent, or, as the French say, he will 'denature' the facts: in other words, he will make a mess and call it law. ... Group-personality is no purely legal phenomenon. The law-giver may say that it does not exist, where, as a matter of moral sentiment, it does exist. ... For the morality of common sense the group is person, is right-and-duty-bearing unit.[6]

The defenders of the fiction or concession theory, according to Maitland, err both on the phenomenological experience of associational life, and on

[4] Ron Harris, 'The Transplantation of the Legal Discourse on Corporate Personality Theories: From German Codification to British Political Pluralism and American Big Business' (2006) 63 *Washington and Lee Law Review* 1421.

[5] Frederick W Maitland (HAL Fisher (ed.)), 'The Unincorporated Body' in *Collected Papers, Vol. III* (Cambridge University Press, 1911) 279.

[6] Frederick W Maitland (HAL Fisher (ed.)), 'Moral Personality and Legal Personality' in *Collected Papers, Vol. III* (Cambridge University Press, 1911) 314–15.

the causal effects of state recognition. A group is felt to be a separate person by its members and it acts as such, to the point of seeking and finding institutional forms to express its collective intention, even if the state does not easily facilitate those forms.

John Neville Figgis was deeply impressed by Maitland's comparative conclusions, and put them to his own use in defending the independence of the Church of England from the authority of Parliament. Maitland self-admittedly remains only at the threshold of philosophizing about the personality of the group;[7] it is only in Figgis' hands that the realist account of group personality becomes a central tenet of the political theory of pluralism. Figgis understands that an association is constituted and held together by the common purposes of its members and 'inevitably acts with that unity and sense of direction which we attribute to personality.'[8] The purpose of the state is not to interfere in the internal life of groups, but 'to prevent injustice between them and to secure their rights',[9] to be a 'guardian of property and interpreter of contract',[10] that is, to guard against an association imposing its will upon groups and individuals who do not share its ends through the erection and enforcement of generally applicable legal institutions, primarily the institutions of private law. Figgis is clear that the state, in performing a social function of minimal coordination of social activity:

> may and must require certain marks, such as proofs of registration, permanence, constitution, before it recognizes the personality of societies, just as it does, though in a less degree, in the case of individuals; and the complex nature of the body may necessitate a more complex procedure.[11]

But these formal requirements track a pre-existing social, or more accurately socio-psychological, reality. This reality must be twofold: first, it depends on the capacity of the group to fulfil the necessary criteria to function as a person, that is, the capacity to develop something like a 'will' separate from that of its members; and second, it must reflect the actual operation of the association, both in terms of the self-conception of the flesh-and-blood individuals who are its members, and in terms of the perception of third parties.

[7] Maitland, note 6, 319.

[8] John Figgis, *Churches in the Modern State* (Longmans, Green and Co., 1913) 59.

[9] Figgis, note 8, 90.

[10] 'What we have to secure is our corporate existence, our real life functioning inside a State, itself made up of complex elements and tolerating all religions. The tolerant State is the true State. The uniform State of the past was founded on a lie.... But the State has yet to learn that she must tolerate not merely individual liberty but the religious society, must know that its life is real and must develop, and cannot (not must not) be stopped.' John Figgis, 'The Church and the Secular Theory of the State' in David Nicholls (ed.), *The Pluralist State: The Political Ideas of JN Figgis and His Contemporaries* (2nd edn) (St. Martin's Press, 1994) 158–59.

[11] John Figgis, quoted in Leicester Webb, 'Corporate personality and political pluralism' in Leicester Webb (ed.), *Legal Personality and Political Pluralism* (Melbourne University Press, 1958) 56.

In brief, the group must be capable of acting as a single person, distinctly from its members, and its identity and actions must be intelligible only insofar as we assume that it is a separate person constituted endogenously by its members' interaction, not by exogenous concession.

Figgis placed great emphasis on the reality and independence of group personality not because he was interested in the capacity of groups to hold property or form contracts (he was interested in this, but not only or primarily in this), but also because he thought them capable of self-directed growth and development. Figgis explained Gierke's medieval Germanic fellowships in organicist language:

> There was, further, the very definite sense that the societies all were organic, that they lived by an inherent spontaneity of life, and that as communal societies they had their own rights and liberty, which did not originate in the grant of the sovereign.[12]

He described the church in the same way:

> Apart from any special or technical points, what we find in this case is that the lawyers refused to consider the body [of the Free Church of Scotland] as a Church, i.e. as a society with a principle of inherent life, but bound it rigidly by the dead hand of its original documents. They construed it as a mechanism, not as an organic life.[13]

And yet there is some dispute about just how organicist and metaphysical was Figgis' realism about group personality, and how much of the language was borrowed idealist Germanism magnified by Figgis' commitment to a certain conciliarist strain in ecclesiastical governance. His more sympathetic readers do not take him to be a substantive organicist or to ground group personality in idealist metaphysics,[14] but his equivocations on the matter negatively coloured the perception of political pluralist theory in the decades that immediately followed.

It is more likely that Figgis' organicist language was less alien to him than to his later critics because of the way that his political concerns flowed from and merged into his religious convictions. The event that incensed Figgis the most, after all, was the resolution of an ecclesiastical dispute by the House of Lords in the famous Free Church case.[15] The theological and political disputes

[12] Figgis, note 8, 76–77. [13] Figgis, note 8, 33.

[14] Paul Hirst, 'J. N. Figgis, Churches and the State' (2002) 71 *The Political Quarterly* 104; David Nicholls, *The Pluralist State* (2nd edn) (St. Martin's Press, 1994) chapter 4. But other writers both sympathetic, e.g. Jacob Levy, 'From Liberal Constitutionalism to Pluralism' in Mark Bevir (ed.), *Modern Pluralism: Anglo-American Debates Since 1800* (Cambridge University Press, 2012) and unsympathetic to pluralism (e.g. David Runciman, *Pluralism and the Personality of the State* (Cambridge University Press, 1997) chapter 6) take Figgis to task for his alleged organicism.

[15] *Bannantyne* v. *Overtoun* [1904] AC 515.

that underlay the controversy are complicated, and both church and Parliament spent many years trying to resolve them. Indeed, the foundations of the case had been brewing for several centuries. Since the arrival of Protestantism to Scotland in the sixteenth century, one of the fundamental divisions among Presbyterians had been the place of the state in supporting and promoting religious institutions. The earliest division had occurred between the established Church—the Scottish Kirk—and those Presbyterians who opposed all establishment and state support—the so-called Voluntaries, which by the mid-nineteenth century had been consolidated, though several schisms and mergers, into the United Presbyterian Church.

But even the established Scottish Kirk, contrary to its counterpart in England, had remained relatively independent of the state.[16] It had not, however, remained free of private patronage; wealthy local landowners routinely imposed their preferred candidates for various ecclesiastical offices, despite the wishes of the congregation. The Kirk had opposed the practice, and had succeeded in abolishing it in the late seventeenth century, but the British Parliament again imposed it by statute in 1792. By the 1830s church opinion had again turned against patronage, and the General Assembly of the Kirk 'declared it "a fundamental law of the church that no pastor shall be intruded on any congregation contrary to the will of the people,"' that is, against the vote of a majority of congregants.[17] The spurned patrons sued, arguing that their patronage was a right of property; the Kirk responded that the matter was entirely ecclesiastical and moreover that, as a corporate body, it was not answerable to any individual. The state court sided with the patrons and, on appeal, so did the British House of Lords. In protest, nearly half the ministers of the Church of Scotland left the Kirk in an event of such magnitude it became known as the Disruption; they forewent their state salaries, property, and positions, and reformed themselves as the Free Church of Scotland. But by their own account their difference with the main body of the Kirk—which was still the established church—was not one of principle, but of application: the Free Church, despite its name, held that 'it was still the duty of the State to legalize and support the true religion.'[18] This ambivalence between establishment and autonomy would sow the seeds of the later conflict.

[16] A fact that incensed King James Stuart to no end, as he protested that the political consequence of presbytery was 'No bishop, no king'. David Hume, *The History of England from the Invasion of Julius Caesar to the Revolution in 1688*, vol. 5 (Liberty Fund, 1983) 12.

[17] Charles Mullett, 'English Presbyterians and the Scottish Disruption: The Legal Phase' (1943) 12(4) *Church History* 255, 256.

[18] SH Mellone, 'The Scottish Church Case and Its Ethical Significance' (1905) 15(3) *International Journal of Ethics* 361, 364. Mellone quotes the dissenters as saying that '[t]hough we quit the Establishment, we go out on the Establishment principle; we quit a vitiated Establishment, but would rejoice in returning to a pure one.'

Over the years, the Free Church moved closer to the United Presbyterian Church in both theology and ecclesiastical polity, in the first case relaxing the doctrine of predestination and in the second realizing that it could sustain itself without state subsidy. By the turn of the century the two dissenting churches voted overwhelmingly to merge into a new body under the name of the United Free Church. Yet a minuscule minority of the Free Church—the Wee Frees—opposed the union, ostensibly on both theological and political grounds, but in actuality mostly on the new church's explicit disavowal of the principle of establishment. Again, the losing faction sued and won on appeal to the House of Lords, and again the victory was pyrrhic. The Lords interpreted the constitution of the Free Church in wholly secular terms, as a trust, but in reading the terms of the trust they unabashedly engaged in interpretation of religious principles, namely the degree to which the United Free Church was continuous with the theological and ecclesiastical tenets of the original ministers who founded the Free Church. They gave the rump the entire holdings of the old Free Church—which today would amount to close to £2 million sterling—although the remnant church was too small to make use of nearly all of it, or to administer the extensive properties, colleges, and missions it had received. It took several years and a Parliamentary commission to sensibly allocate the property.

The disputes in the Scottish Kirk had their effect in England, where some ecclesiastics came to recognize the perils of establishment and to have doubts about its compatibility with the spiritual mission of the Anglican Church. Among them the Tractarians, with whom Figgis sympathized, were most famous in developing the idea of the church as a *societas perfecta* and not a branch of the civil power.[19] The Free Church case, moreover, was not an isolated incident. Half a century before, the Privy Council, in the infamous *Gorham* judgment,[20] had overruled a bishop's refusal to appoint a clergyman whose theological views he judged incompatible with Anglican doctrine. The decision caused several Tractarians to abandon the Church of England and convert to Roman Catholicism. Figgis did not follow this route, but throughout his work expressed doubts about the coherence of establishment and autonomy, and veered markedly in the direction of refusing support from the state and in exchange objecting to Parliamentary meddling in ecclesiastical affairs. There are both spiritual and political elements in his discourse, and these are laid bare in his 1910 article 'Respublica Christiana', reprinted as the first appendix of *Churches in the Modern State*. From a religious perspective, the church is a *congregatio fidelium* and its life proceeds

[19] Charles Mullett, 'English Presbyterians and the Scottish Disruption: The Legal Phase' (1943) 12(4) *Church History* 255, 257–58.

[20] *Gorham* v. *Bishop of Exeter* (1849–50) 163 English Reports 1221.

from that mystical union; from a political perspective, it is 'the body of all the faithful with rights and powers inherent and unconnected with the State.'[21] Ever the historian, Figgis traces the political conception not to a romantic medieval organicism—in fact he opposes it to the medieval conception of society—but rather to the attempt by sixteenth century Reformers to take authority away from clerical officials and hand it to civil officials. The seemingly organicist language in Figgis is mostly inward-looking, it applies to the life of the church, but does not translate well to the encounter between the church and the state.

The best study of Figgis' political philosophy confirms this. David Nicholls, who shared Figgis' religious vocation, is sensitive enough to the connection between religion and politics to dedicate an entire chapter of his study of political pluralism to the question of authority in the church, and to highlight the significance of Figgis' lectures on church governance, *The Fellowship of the Mystery*, to the analysis of his political views. It is enough here to say that Figgis' pluralism goes all the way down, and he resists centralism in the church as much as in the state and encourages the formation of 'permanent and semi-permanent groups within the church [that] have an inherent life which is not derived from the centre.'[22] In such a context, organicist language can echo mystical and allegorical conceptions of the *ecclesia* as a church invisible or the bride of Christ. That is not to say that Figgis' reference to internal life is merely allegorical or mystical. There is a sense, which I refer to in Chapter 10, section 10.5, in which it is of crucial importance to his argument about the self-development of groups and to a broader pluralist argument about the personality (and not merely the agency) of associations. But it is possible to distinguish tone from substance in his appropriations of Gierke, and to read Figgis as less committed to metaphysical collectivism than was sometimes the case with his contemporaries.[23] Nonetheless, there is a sense in Figgis that the self-conception of a church can never be fully apprehended in secular terms, and that the best we can do is offer a formal structure that is intelligible to those outside the *congregatio fidelium*, so that they may interact with the association without having to accept (or inquire into) its principles, and that at the same time allows the inner life of the group to flourish. The personality of associations and the status of a legal person accorded by the state are in some sense incommensurable, and that there is always a hint of

[21] Figgis, note 8, 217.

[22] Nicholls, note 10, 115.

[23] The metaphysical reading prompted Oliver Wendell Holmes to try to persuade Harold Laski to abandon the discussion of the theory of real corporate personality ('OW Holmes to HJ Laski (19 July 1916)' in Mark DeWolf Howe (ed.), *Holmes-Laski Letters* (Harvard University Press, 1953) 5–9), and later Morris Cohen's dismissal of pluralism because of its attachment to the theory (Morris Cohen, 'Communal Ghosts and Other Perils in Social Philosophy' (1919) 16 *The Journal of Philosophy* 673).

tragedy, an irretrievable loss or lack of both theoretical and practical apprehension, in the move from social to legal existence.

9.2 THE DEATH OF REAL PERSONALITY

The theory of real corporate personality of groups had gone out of favour by the late 1930s. Maitland had died in 1906, Figgis in 1919, both quite young. GDH Cole, whose pluralist credentials were quite subordinate to his guild socialism, had never defended the personality of groups with much zeal, and focused instead on the functions of different kinds of social organization. The direction of his functionalism went in precisely the opposite direction as Maitland and Figgis' realism about group personality, as it made the group even more subordinate to an overarching social order. It was left to Harold Laski to carry the torch of pluralism, but he would not prove a steadfast custodian. This was probably due to the divergence in the causes that animated Figgis and Laski. The former was moved by a defence of the autonomy of the ecclesiastical association, which possessed a long tradition of formal institutional cohesion and of corporate opposition to the state, against external interference. As Runciman observes, Figgis' idea of the church was essentially separatist: '[t]he doctrine of group personality would seem to encourage group members to value the integrity of their association above everything else' as a means of preserving their freedom, and but this conception of freedom is especially valuable to members of a sectarian church.[24]

Laski's motivation, by contrast, was to do away with the pathologies of capitalism through the self-organization of workers. It is unclear whether this made labour associations inherently valuable (as they might be to a religious believer) or only instrumentally so. The labour movement's move away from syndicalism, which attempted to replace the bourgeois state with independent workers' cooperatives, and towards industrial unions, which instead engaged in bargaining with industry for better wages and working conditions, mirror's Laski's move from a sympathy towards guild socialism to the chairmanship of the Labour Party. The activity of partisan politics depends on the existence of independent and powerful political associations,[25] but these are best viewed, even by partisans themselves, as purely instrumental in two senses: first, in that they are contingent societies of like-minded

[24] Runciman, note 1, 142–43. Runciman suggests that it is perhaps only valuable to members of a sectarian church. But this is not clearly so. Universities, professional associations, and some federal and sub-federal levels of government can also find this conception of freedom not only attractive, but constitutive of the association.

[25] For a robust defence of this, see Nancy Rosenblum, *On the Side of Angels* (Princeton University Press, 2008).

individuals whose aim is not the preservation of their associative ties, but the obtention of an external good; and second, in that they seek the opposite of autonomy from the state—they intend to govern, that is, to control the state. These motivations do not foster a strong commitment to real personality. Coupled with his political transition from pluralist to Labour partisan, Laski was marked by Morris Cohen's philosophical objections to the strongest statements of real group personality which, Cohen thought, rested on excessively obtuse metaphysics. Cohen warned that:

> to speak, as many do nowadays, of the union or group as having a single mind is a convenient but dangerous metaphor. Apart from its questionable metaphysics, it hides the fact that what we call group action is and must often be the result not of the unanimous agreement of all the members of the groups but only of a more or less limited part thereof.[26]

Cohen did not target Laski alone, but also Figgis and, rather indiscriminately, French pluralists like Léon Duguit who were sceptical of the realist theory; but his rebuke hit Laski very hard, so much so that he abandoned his previous adherence to real group personality and, soon enough, to pluralism altogether.[27] Perhaps this is not surprising, since Laski arguably never had much use for pluralism and wavered instead between socialism and individualistic anarchism. By the publication of *Studies in Law and Politics* in 1932 he had adopted a kind of philosophical anarchism which was only nominally pluralist, and by the next decade had settled into Marxism.

> When Professor Cohen insisted that the corporate person was a 'communal ghost,' he cleared the ground, I think, for a clearer understanding of social organizations, as well as for a deeper insight into the functions of law. A group of human beings is not a person, in the sense in which each member of the group is a person. It is only by metaphor that we say that 'it' acts, that 'it' has this opinion or that, that 'it' has a reputation which can be damaged, or that 'it' concludes agreements or commits torts.[28]

Laski, true to form, raged against the real theory of group personality with the same passion with which he had defended it some years prior. Surely much of the explanation for Laski's reaction was due as much to Cohen's prescriptive reasons for rejecting group personality—that it facilitated the oppression by well-placed hierarchies of the members of their associations—as to the objection to pluralist metaphysics. But there is reason to think that Laski missed the opportunity for a more nuanced defence of the realist theory. Cohen, after all, had gone too far in his criticism, imputing to Figgis,

[26] Cohen, note 23, 678. [27] Nicholls, note 14, 62.

[28] Harold Laski, 'Morris Cohen's Approach to Legal Philosophy' (1947–48) 15 *University of Chicago Law Review* 575, 580.

Maitland, and Gierke patently silly ideas which they did not hold.[29] And the identification of the 'will' of the group always with the will of its leaders or directors oversimplified and misconstrued important legal categories. It is notoriously difficult, for instance, to determine who constitutes the will of a business corporation. Its managers do not own its assets, although they may direct their use. Even then they may be dismissed by the board of directors, who in turn may be voted out by the shareholders; the shareholders themselves may intervene in management directly in exceptional circumstances.[30] Likewise, it makes no sense to say that the corporate will of the bishops of a church is the will of the ecclesiastical body—any more than the president of a country directs the will of the state—without a significant amount of institutional description about the way that authority is represented, restrained, and recognized.

The other critique of the realist theory came from a staunchly anti-theoretical front: a 1926 article by John Dewey that reflected the increasing frustration of legal scholars and social scientists with a debate that was increasingly disjointed from the economic development of the business corporation. Dewey acknowledged that '[t]he definition of a legal subject is thus a legitimate, and quite conceivably a practically important matter. But it is a matter of analysis of facts, not of search for an inhering essence. The facts in question are whatever specific consequences flow from being right-and-duty-bearing units.'[31] Dewey rightly called for empirical evidence of the supposed 'will' of a corporate entity, and for an evaluation of the theories in term of consequences for legal and social practice. He found that:

> There is no clear-cut line, logical or practical, through the different theories which have been advanced and which are still advanced in behalf of the 'real' personality of either 'natural' or associated persons. Each theory has been used to serve the same ends, and each has been used to serve opposing ends.[32]

Rather than call for an end to debate, Dewey invited for the debate to be put aside 'until the concrete facts and relations involved have been faced and stated on their own account.'[33] But his challenge was not taken up, as the debate over corporate personality—which was stirred by a concern for all

[29] For instance, the view that '[t]he state or the church is the permanent reality of which individuals are the phenomenal appearances' (Cohen, note 23, 683).

[30] So, for example, the Canadian Business Corporations Act allows shareholders, by unanimous agreement, to 'restrict, in whole or in part, the powers of the directors to manage, or supervise the management of, the business and affairs of the corporation'. Canada Business Corporations Act (R.S.C., 1985, c. C-44), sec. 146(1).

[31] John Dewey, 'The Historic Background of Corporate Legal Personality' (1926) 35(6) *Yale Law Journal* 655, 661.

[32] Dewey, note 31, 669.

[33] Dewey, note 31, 673.

sorts of association, and only secondarily by business corporations—was displaced by the discussion of corporate governance.[34] And for that debate the doctrine of real personality had less to say than the emergent methods borrowed from economics which yielded a new version of the fiction theory: the idea that a corporate body was nothing but a convenient shorthand for the aggregate of contracts that shareholders had among themselves, and between them and the managers of the company.[35]

The problem with the contract theory is that it renders every association a version of the business enterprise, as a loosely committed group of individuals who have no obligation towards each other except those specified in the acts of incorporation itself. And they do not pretend to have such obligations either. The business corporation has certain peculiarities that make it too specific a model of the broader category of 'corporate persons'. It is peculiar in that it is both a subject and an object of economic activity, both an owner of property in the world (the property of the corporation) and something that is owned (by shareholders, who may themselves be corporate persons in a broad or a narrow sense). Thus, some of the features of the business corporation sit oddly with a broader category of collectives that act with a unity of purpose separate from and not reducible to that of their members.

The separation between ownership and control of the corporation, made famous in the first half of the twentieth century by Adolf Berle and Gardiner Means, reflects the fact that the shareholders, who technically own the corporation through their fractional participation, are nonetheless restricted in their interference in the management of the business.[36] Now, a corporation in which one shareholder owns a majority of the shares will be effectively both owned and controlled by the same person, but the principle of role differentiation is preserved and can be invoked in cases in which minority shareholders think that

[34] Adolf Berle and Gardiner Means, *The Modern Corporation and Private Property* (Transaction Publishers, 1999).

[35] Frank Easterbrook and Daniel Fischel, *The Economic Structure of Corporate Law* (Harvard University Press, 1991).

[36] Berle and Means, note 34. Berle and Means' thesis was that the separation between ownership and control was leading to the entrenchment of a class of professional managers who were insulated by their position and expertise from any responsibility to the shareholders themselves. This thesis was always explicitly political, and had parallels in the perpetual democratic anxiety over the emergence of a professional political class, which was but a moralized expression of the principal-agent problem in economics. The Berle-Means thesis has been criticized especially in light of developments in corporate structure, specifically the emergence of sophisticated institutional investors who—contrary to individual investors who might own but a few shares in some corporation—own vast numbers of shares, are themselves answerable to temperamental investors, and can put management under enormous pressure to produce short-term returns in the forms of dividends or share value. (See Gerald F Davis, 'The Twilight of the Berle and Means Corporation' (2011) 34 *Seattle University Law Review* 1121.) But the political problem is the same: when ownership is diffuse and expertise is concentrated, power is in the hands of management; when ownership is concentrated and shareholders are as knowledgeable as managers, power shifts in the opposite direction.

the principal shareholder's interests as an owner run contrary to the best interests of the entity, which she as a manager should hold paramount. A corporation is also a vehicle for investment and, as such, must give sufficient flexibility to attract capital; thus shares in a corporation are easily transferable (sometimes many times over in a few minutes) and ownership in the corporation is always in potential flux.[37] This poses problems of moral and political accountability that I will not enter into, but they are enough to show the contrast between the business corporation and the groups that are of concern to associational pluralism.

9.3 THE CONTEMPORARY RESURRECTION OF GROUP PERSONALITY

By the late twentieth century, the debate over the correct theory of corporate personality, as it originally played out in the pluralist debate, was of mainly historical interest. Yet in this same period, several factors conspired to resurrect the spirit, if not the body, of the theory of real personality. Most important for legal theory was the rise of large, complex, often multinational business corporations, which fostered interest among business ethicists and scholars of corporate law on the responsibility of such entities towards third parties. This brought back to the fore many questions of collective intention and group agency which shared many features with the old pluralist debate. Peter French's influential and controversial article 'The Corporation as a Moral Person' argued that 'corporations can be full-fledged moral persons and have whatever privileges, rights and duties as are, in the normal course of affairs, accorded to moral persons.'[38] French alluded to the roots of philosophical realism about corporate personality, made his project continuous with the tradition represented by Otto Gierke,[39] but he shifts the debate from vague considerations of a corporate person's 'inner life' to more modest yet robust attributions of intention and agency. His argument, in brief, is that moral personality is the capacity 'to be a party in responsibility relationships' and that intentionality is central to that capacity. If a corporation can form an intention that is not reducible to the intention of the biological agents that comprise it, French argues, then the actions that follow from that intention can be intelligibly redescribed as the actions of the corporate agent and not those of its members. And for this, the only necessary feature is that the

[37] For a general overview, see Robert Clark, *Corporate Law* (Little, Brown, and Co., 1986).

[38] Peter French, 'The Corporation as a Moral Person' (1979) 16(3) *American Philosophical Quarterly* 207, 207.

[39] After contrasting Gierke's realism with the competing fiction and concession theories of corporate personality, French writes that '[w]hat is needed is a Reality Theory that identifies a *de facto* metaphysical person not just a sociological entity.' French, note 38, 210.

group possess an internal decision structure which 'delineates stations and levels within the corporate power structure' and one or more rules of recognition—a term French borrows directly from HLA Hart—that 'a decision on an act has been made or performed for corporate reasons.'[40] While French hints at a thicker conception of corporate personality, one that reflects the members' understanding of the historical extension of the entity, for example, he effectively reduces corporate personality to corporate agency. As a result, he does not need to question whether corporate agents (and not just business corporations) are creatures of law or if their personality is located in a pre-legal or extra-legal existence which the law then acknowledges rather than creates.

In philosophy, meanwhile, a growing literature on joint intention tried to make sense of commonplace assertions about the practices that individuals undertake together. Margaret Gilbert has been the most prominent advocate of the position that individuals engaged in cooperative enterprises can intelligently speak of jointly intending an action in a way that is not reducible to the individual intention of participants.[41] Gilbert recognizes that some actions that people undertake are 'necessarily partnered', that is, that they not only require more than one participant, but also that the participants have a certain belief, attitude, or disposition toward the activity.[42] This attitude need not involve a common goal in the sense of an objective or an external state of affairs that the participants, individually or collectively, desire to achieve; the goal or state of affairs immediately contemplated is the joint activity itself—its 'jointness', if one will—even if the further purpose of the activity is to obtain some further objective. A group of people of which all members have such an attitude constitutes a 'plural subject', one that entitles the members to refer to their joint enterprise in the first-person plural, as 'we'.[43] What is necessary for the participants to constitute a plural subject is for all to express to the others their readiness to undertake the enterprise as a group, for all to make clear that 'they are jointly committed to doing something as a body—in a broad sense of "do."'[44] This joint commitment generates obligations between participants, although Gilbert is clear that these

[40] French, note 38, 212–13.

[41] Other authors have also developed accounts of joint agency, although they differ on how close their accounts approximate a holistic or collectivist ontology that avoids the reduction of joint agency to the tenets of methodological individualism. See, for instance, John Searle, *The Construction of Social Reality* (Free Press, 1995); Michael Bratman, 'Shared Intention' (1993) 104 *Ethics* 97–113 and *Faces of Intention* (Cambridge University Press, 1999); Raimo Tuomela, 'Group Beliefs' (1992) 91 *Synthese* 285–318.

[42] Margaret Gilbert, *On Social Facts* (Princeton University Press, 1992) 156.

[43] Gilbert, note 42, 199ff; Margaret Gilbert, *A Theory of Political Obligation* (Oxford University Press, 2006) 101–102.

[44] Gilbert, note 43, 145.

are associative rather than moral obligations.[45] Central to the joint activity is the condition that 'absent pertinent background understandings [such as an agreement between the parties or a societal convention that regulates the joint activity]...no one party is in a position unilaterally to decide on the details of a joint action.'[46] Gilbert has more recently applied the idea of plural subjects to political philosophy by arguing that political societies are themselves plural subjects composed of individuals jointly committed 'to uphold as a body a particular set of institutions of governance.'[47]

It would be wrong, however, to characterize Gilbert's work as contributing to a theory of real group personality. She is concerned with the existence of subjects who are ontologically distinct from, and irreducible to, the individuals who compose them, but her attention is to the obligations that hold between these individual members, not to the standing of the social group as itself an agent or as a subject of rights and obligations. Her work is a defence for the use of the central case of 'we'—of the first-person plural—which is a mode of self-reference by participants in a joint practice. The plural subject account captures one aspect of the realist theory, but not all or even the most important aspect which is the problem of pluralist authority.

The turn away from organicist metaphors and towards structural features of corporate organization has had an impact beyond philosophy and legal theory. Perhaps the most explicit embrace of the philosophical literature by a social scientist is Alexander Wendt's defence of scholarly treatment of states as unitary intentional actors. In his apology for state personhood, Wendt refers to both the joint agency and the group agency strands, but his argument is solely indebted to the latter.[48] Still, unlike Gierke or Figgis, Wendt advocates only a 'thin' conception of personhood—in line with French's equation of personality with formally organized collective agency; he also distinguishes the empirical fact of the corporate personality of states from the desirability of treating them as such. This kind of agency may be sufficient to model states as individual actors on the international stage, but it may prove insufficient for more normative projects, like the argument that there are normative reasons why some associations should be accorded the

[45] Thus two thieves may have jointly committed to robbing a bank and this created an associative obligation between them, albeit one that they should not have committed to in the first place. Margaret Gilbert, *Sociality and Responsibility* (Rowman and Littlefield, 2000) 105; and *A Theory of Political Obligation*, note 43, 289. In this sense, Gilbert's view of associative obligation is similar to the legal positivist view about legality: that a given norm is a legal norm, that is, that it is part of a legal system, does not mean that it is a desirable norm, only that it meets the system's internal criteria for legal validity.

[46] Margaret Gilbert, *A Theory of Political Obligation: Membership, Commitment, and the Bonds of Society* (Oxford University Press, 2006) 106.

[47] Gilbert, note 46, 288.

[48] Alexander Wendt, 'The State as a Person in International Theory' (2004) 30(2) *Review of International Studies* 289.

status of persons, and that some important consequences for moral and political philosophy follow from this accordance.

But joint intention is not group agency and agency is not personhood. There is still some small but significant distance between the contemporary rediscovery of the plural subject, the collective agent, or the corporate person and the pluralist idea of group as an entity capable of acting, relating, and developing autonomously. Certainly pluralists think that groups are plural subjects, yet they do not focus on the horizontal commitments and obligations that hold between their members (these they rather presuppose) but turn their attention instead to what may be called the vertical authority of the group in relation to their members and in opposition to other authorities that claim the loyalty of the same population. This may require a turn from 'we' to 'you', from a first-personal to a second-personal conception of authority. Pluralists take group agency to be central to the distinction between groups and mobs; despite their misgivings about Hobbes' political conclusions, they seem to accept (although mutedly) the difference between a regular and an irregular system, that is, a group that presents itself as a single actor capable of will, action, and identity as opposed to a mob without a distinct organizational structure. Figgis' historical study of the emergence of the doctrine of group personality, summarized in section 9.1 in relation to the Free Church case, emphasizes the connection between the fragmentation of the unitary medieval order into separate societies—church, state, and other groups—and the formal differentiation between clerical and lay officials and ecclesiastical and secular law. Pluralists also recognize the need for the law to give form to the group and to create the institutional conditions for it to act in ways that its members and third parties could identify with the collective, not the agents severally. But they insist that, at least with regards to those groups that claim a measure of sovereignty over their members, the law only acknowledges that life and action are already there, and it neither creates nor can entirely capture the structures, intentions, and self-understandings that made an association more than the sum of individuals within it. There is nothing mysterious about it except the mystery of ordinary human sociality.

10

The Personality of Associations

The normative question at the heart of the debate over the personality of associations is not, as it might first appear, whether these associations have legal personality as recognized by the legal system of the state. That is the consequence of the argument, not its point of departure. Of course an association, much like a natural person, has the capacity to hold property, enter into contracts, and be liable in tort. If that is all that pragmatists like Dewey demanded of a theory of personality, any theory would do, since both the real theory and the concession and contract theories grant that legal personality is 'real' in terms of its juridical consequences.

What matters in the debate over real personality is whether an association can claim to have its personality recognized as a matter of right, not of privilege or concession, and whether it is the association corporately that makes this claim, rather than the claim being made by members in furtherance of their individual rights. To make this argument work, an association needs to possess certain characteristics that function as criteria for the grant of personality to those entities which uncontroversially have it. That is, an association must have capacities equivalent to those of 'natural' flesh-and-blood individuals which, in the case of natural persons, entitle them to legal personality. Strong methodological individualists might object that the common purpose that motivates associative activity is reducible to individualist 'microfoundations'.[1] An association is, of course, made up of associates who are themselves natural persons, and without whom the association would, to invoke Figgis' phrase, have neither life nor action. But the reconstructed argument for real corporate personality does not deny these microfoundations; what it denies is that associative intention, agency, and identity are reducible to an aggregate of individual interactions or transactions.

Certain associative endeavours possess structural features that resist such reductionism, as I hope to show over the course of the argument. There

[1] For a vigorous (some say too vigorous) defence of methodological individualism, see Jon Elster, *Making Sense of Marx* (Cambridge University Press, 1985) 5ff.

must, for example, be a certain sort of capacity in the association that allows it to form intentions ontologically distinct from those of their members; otherwise a grant of personality to the members severally would capture all relevant reasons for recognizing the group. It requires also that associations be capable of sustaining their identity through time, that members understand the group itself—regardless of its changing membership—as guided by past intentions and bound by past decisions. This also means that intentions can be formed and decisions can be taken in contemplation of future states of affairs in which the identity of the group will remain stable; but the maintenance of this identity may require that certain legal capacities be recognized in order to allow groups to intelligently realize themselves over time as autonomous entities. And finally, associations must be the kinds of entities that can act in the world, to intelligibly obligate themselves, and reciprocally place others under obligations; this goes beyond the formation of intention, and moves into the realm of responsibility. These elements of the argument are best appreciated in contrast to the most extensive objection to the pluralist account of real corporate personality.

10.1 THE ARGUMENT AGAINST REAL PERSONALITY

David Runciman is prominent among the opponents of the idea of the personality of groups for the care he has taken to understand and explain the pluralist tradition. His denial of the intelligibility of group personality is the conclusion of a careful and thorough study, so it is especially important to discuss his rebuttal of an idea so central to pluralist arguments. Runciman takes his cue from Ernest Barker's elaboration of personality from its etymological origin—as a philosophical riff on the dramatic *persona* that originally denoted the mask worn by an actor on the Roman stage, which indicated his character and allowed him to project his voice, and eventually came to denote the actor himself impersonating the character. The ambiguity about the meaning of personality, Runciman explains, reveals deep tensions in the pluralist argument about the capacity of groups to represent themselves on the political and legal stage. On the one hand, personality may refer to the public performance of certain social roles and functions (the part), or it may point to psychological processes and capacities that enable (and perhaps compel) an agent to play a part at all (the actor).[2] If personality is the performance of a role, this immediately drives one to look for the playwright, because even if the part allows for interpretive licence, the general contours are presumably defined by an author. At the very least, it drives one to look for someone to coordinate the parts (a director?) or to state whether a play is

[2] David Runciman, *Pluralism and the Personality of the State* (Cambridge University Press, 1997) 231.

being performed at all (a producer?); the *persona* as part is dependent on who 'creates' it, who gives it that status. If, however, personality is a matter of psychological disposition, there is always a possibility that the actor is 'playing herself' in a drama of her own authorship, but also of her own direction and production.[3]

For Runciman, the pluralist insistence on the real personality of groups is mistaken on either acceptation of personality. The pluralists insist that it is not state concession that defines, authorizes, or creates the parts that group actors can play, but rather that these are developed by groups themselves through an extended practice of self-reflexive interaction between their members and with third-parties; that is, members engage in practices that have, as a publicly acknowledged goal (though perhaps not the only goal), the creation and perpetuation of a corporate agent. But pluralists also insist that (at least some) groups have a capacity equivalent to that of natural persons for self-directed action and development, which should entitle them to be considered as legal persons on the same grounds as those accorded to flesh-and-blood individuals. In the first sense, the group is a part or role that the actors play together, as it were; in the second sense, the group is itself an actor in its own right. The claims are of different kinds: the first is a claim about how personality emerges, and can be read as a descriptive claim about the existence of a social fact;[4] the second is a normative claim, a demand for recognition on grounds of consistency with the criteria of recognition of individual personhood, and of fittingness of the group for the powers and abilities the exercise of which legal personhood allows.

Runciman denies both pluralist arguments. He argues that groups can only be persons in a narrow legal sense if the state creates them as such, either through express case-by-case concession, or by making available a generic mechanism of incorporation that enables a group of people to act *as if* they were a group and for others to treat them as such in legal practice. Adopting the Hobbesian antipathy towards social groups, Runciman insists that, through the concession of legal personality, '[t]he group itself does nothing, which is what makes it a fiction, and depends for everything on the natural persons (its members) who give it a mask and the artificial person (its representative) who wears it.'[5] The most that we can do is to imagine the group leading a life, but not the group itself leading it.[6] To put it differently,

[3] Runciman explains that this is not the same as saying that the actor is improvising, as improvisation still suggests a separation between the actor and the part that she is creating through the improvisational performance. The psychological acceptation of *persona* presumes the identity of the actor and the part. I have doubt that this is ever the case with legal personality, and doubt whether this is ever the case with personality in any other social scope, but only legal personality is the subject of my argument.

[4] On social facts, see Margaret Gilbert, *On Social Facts* (Princeton University Press, 1992) 408–16.

[5] Runciman, note 2, 238.

[6] Runciman, note 2, 243.

we can write a history in which the group is the passive object of inquiry, but not a biography in which the group is the active subject. This Runciman believes is the 'fallacy of the doctrine of real group personality, that it confuses our ability to imagine groups having their own personality with the ability of groups to decide that personality for themselves.'[7] The dramatic metaphor is especially illustrative of Runciman's objection to the theory of real personality and deserves to be quoted at length.

> First, it is only the natural person concerned who can truly know what is represented by the mask of their own natural personality. That mask will be set out over the course of a life-time, and it is only those who can recognize it with certainty. For natural persons, it is life itself that is the drama, and the drama of each life will be different. Many others will receive many glimpses of each life, but none can be sure of what the mask represents unless they have seen it all. Where there is doubt about what is represented by the mask of a fictitious person, certainty can be achieved by referring to the 'letters' or 'laws' by which that personality is authorized. Second, natural personality, in this sense, can only belong to individuals who are capable of perceiving their lives as a kind of dramatic unity. . . . Natural personality requires purposive actions to be related to a sense of personal identity, and it was for this reason that Hobbes did not consider children, madmen or fools to be natural persons. . . . Finally, if groups are to be possessed of masks, or personae, comparable to the masks, or personae, of natural persons, it must be because they too are capable of generating personality out of the actions that they perform. Groups can only be persons as individuals can be persons if they are capable of acting out their own, personal dramas.[8]

All three objections go at the heart of the pluralist defence of real personality. Maitland observes that groups, not only by the disposition of law but by the operation of moral sentiment and the treatment accorded by members and third parties, acquire some sort of personality. His statement that 'the group is [a] person, is [a] right and duty bearing unit' presumes that a group's actions should be attributed to it, not to its representatives or to its members derivatively.[9] Figgis' invective against the decision in the Free Kirk case denies precisely that the purpose or 'role' of a fictitious person (the first acceptation of personality) is exhausted by its 'letters' or 'laws', that is, by its charter. And the implication of this denial is that the group's identity is formed through its evolving collective self-conception, what one author has called the group's *Bildung*,[10] which emerges from, but is distinct from, the individual conception of its members.

[7] Runciman, note 2, 243. [8] Runciman, note 2, 240–41.

[9] Frederick Maitland, 'Moral Personality and Legal Personality' in HAL Fisher (ed.), *Collected Papers, Vol. III* (Cambridge University Press, 1911).

[10] Jacob Levy, 'From Liberal Constitutionalism to Pluralism' in Mark Bevir (ed.), *Modern Pluralism: Anglo-American Debates Since 1800* (Cambridge University Press, 2012).

For the argument that groups possess real group personality to succeed, it must explain how (at least some) groups may be deemed 'capable of acting out their own, personal dramas'. This involves a multitude of claims. It implies that the group is capable of something like authorship, of actions that communicate intention, that the group be able to interact with other actors in ways that are intelligibly the group's own, and that the group be able to reflect on these actions, to understand them as its own, and perhaps to perceive them as a basis for its own development. There is here a resemblance to John Rawls' conception of moral persons as 'self-authenticating sources of valid claims'.[11] Groups, on Runciman's account, cannot self-validate their claims, but require the individuals who represent them to validate the claims for the group. If so, it seems that there is no escape from outlandish metaphysical assumptions of the kind that drove Laski away from pluralism. But I contend that there is a methodical way of proceeding through this argument that does not rely, at any point, on implausible metaphysical or psychological assumptions.

This explanation is, I think, closely related to the argument about the authority of associations, as both turn on the capacity of a group to form, communicate, act and reflect on intentions that are irreducible to those of its members. In the discussion that follows, I draw on Andrei Marmor and Jeremy Waldron's debate about the nature of authority to explain the importance of personality for arguments about the authority of groups. I then discuss Philip Pettit's recent work on group agency to clarify how formally constituted associations can claim personal authority. In Chapter 11 I will draw out some implications of this argument.

10.2 THE IMPORTANCE OF GROUP PERSONALITY

It is not self-evident that group personality is important to a political pluralist argument about the authority of associations. Historically, group personality was one of the main theses of the British pluralist tradition, inspired as it was by Gierke's conception of medieval German fellowships, compounded by Maitland's discussion of the ways in which the common-law trust had been employed to allow groups to act autonomously and without state sanction, and most importantly by Figgis' assertion of a 'unity of life and action' in corporate bodies and especially in the Church.[12] But it is equally true that some contemporary and later pluralists disavowed the idea that groups were persons in any but a metaphorical sense. Laski notoriously abandoned the

[11] John Rawls, *Political Liberalism* (Columbia University Press, 1993) 32.

[12] Otto Gierke (Frederick Maitland (tr.)), *Political Theories of the Middle Age* (Cambridge University Press, 1900); Frederick Maitland (David Runciman and Magnus Ryan (eds)), *State, Trust and Corporation* (Cambridge University Press, 2003); John Figgis, *Churches in the Modern State* (Thoemmes Press, 1997); and David Nicholls, *Three Varieties of Pluralism* (Macmillan, 1974).

idea of group personality after a rebuke from Morris Cohen, after years of epistolary criticism from no less a figure than Oliver Wendell Holmes.[13] More recently, Paul Hirst, who more than any other author is responsible for the pluralist revival, brushes away the idea of real group personality as so much useless metaphysics.[14] The idea of real personality has fared little better in the theory of corporate law. While there are still defenders of the realist theory of corporate personality in legal academia, the economic analysis of the corporation as a nexus of explicit and implicit contracts between individuals seems to have carried the day.[15] Why then give so much importance to the argument that (at least some) groups possess traits that approximate them to individual rational agents to such a degree that they ought to be treated as persons and granted legal recognition as a matter of moral right?

Group personality has important philosophical consequences, especially for the account of the authority of associations and the claims that they may put forth against their members and against the state. The underlying assumption that justifies this is the thesis, implied in the work of Joseph Raz and defended most eloquently by Andrei Marmor, that all authority is personal authority.[16] What this means is that:

> for something to be able to claim legitimate authority, it must be the case that the authority is capable of forming an opinion on how its subjects ought to behave, distinct from the subjects' own reasoning about their reasons for action. In other words, a practical authority, like law, must be basically personal authority in the sense that there cannot be an authority without an author.[17]

The notion of authorship ties Marmor's argument about the personal character of authority to Runciman's objection that groups cannot be persons, in part, because they cannot perform 'purposive actions . . . related to a sense of personal identity'.[18] It is precisely that kind of action that Marmor understands as essential to the capacity to claim authority. Authority is a communicative practice which, at the very least, involves a claim of legitimacy by the authority directed at a subject from whom obedience is expected. As a result, 'only persons who can communicate with others are capable of possessing

[13] 'OW Holmes to HJ Laski (19 July 1916)' in (MD Howe (ed.)), *Holmes-Laski Letters* (Harvard University Press, 1953) 5–6; and 'OW Holmes to HJ Laski (9 August 1930)' 1272–73.

[14] Paul Hirst, *Associative Democracy: New Forms of Economic and Social Governance* (University of Massachusetts Press, 1994), discussed in chapter 4.

[15] Michael Phillips, 'Reappraising the Real Entity Theory of the Corporation' (1994) 21 *Florida State University Law Review* 1061.

[16] Joseph Raz, *The Morality of Freedom* (Oxford University Press, 1986) 56; Andrei Marmor, *Positive Law and Objective Values* (Oxford University Press, 2001) especially chapter 5, and *Interpretation and Legal Theory* (2nd edn) (Hart, 2005) especially chapter 8.

[17] Andrei Marmor, *Positive Law and Objective Values* (Oxford University Press, 2001) 54.

[18] Runciman, note 2, 241.

authority'[19] and this communication must entail a judgment of some kind, a decision about the reasons that apply to the subject of authority.

Jeremy Waldron has voiced the most prominent objections to the argument that all authority is personal. He accuses Marmor of holding on to an antiquated Austinian conception of authority in which law is the product of the mind of a single author, the legislative expert. But this image does not reflect either the empirical reality of modern legislation, not its normative presuppositions. It is simply not the case, Waldron argues, that laws are conceived, written, and enacted by single authors; rather they are put together by deliberative assemblies. And it is those deliberative assemblies, if anyone, not the members severally or even the majority of members, that can be described as the authors of a legislative measure. Yet even here Waldron is cautious, as he prefers to discuss 'the structures and proceedings of legislative assemblies' as the institutional context in which legislation is produced, rather than the intention of the body in the absence of these institutional features. Waldron's argument has thus been considered an institutional—as opposed to personal—account of authority, the difference being that institutions, as opposed to persons, do not possess minds and are not capable of forming intentions. In an institutional context, then, authority must derive from the way in which institutions 'integrate a diversity of purposes, interests, and aims among their members'.[20]

But the choice between personal and institutional authority is a false dichotomy. The simple way to reconcile the two accounts is readily available to Waldron. Several times in his argument he toys with the idea that, if there is an intentional agent behind legislation, 'it is the legislature considered as a body and as distinct from the individual members (or any subset of the individual members) that it comprises.'[21] It would be possible, then, for the group considered as a corporate author constituted by a set of formal decision-making procedures to have authority. But Waldron is unsatisfied with this answer. His contention is that authority in modern (and perhaps in all) legal systems is institutional and systemic, not personal, and that it is the products of legislation—statutes—that have authority because of the institutional context from which they originate, independently of the personality of legislators. Does this point to an irreconcilable difference with the idea that persons, and only persons, can claim authority?

The problem is that the simple way to reconcile the institutional and personal conceptions of authority—to assume that certain formal institutions are persons—misses the importance of the personalist conception.

[19] Marmor, note 17, 96.

[20] Jeremy Waldron, *Law and Disagreement* (Oxford University Press, 1999) 121.

[21] Waldron, note 20, 142.

The confusion comes from a slippage between the capacity to issue authoritative directives and the interpretation of the content of those directives. Personalism about authority is sometimes tied to intentionalism in legal interpretation, 'the thesis that interpreters must rely on the intentions of law-makers when interpreting legal rules.'[22] But I do not think this connection is warranted, and I do not assume it here.[23] Marmor does believe that those called to interpret the laws (or norms more generally) issued by legitimate authorities should adhere to the intention of the law-makers, but he qualifies his statement in many ways and his point is largely normative (what ought judges to do) rather than conceptual (what does authority entail), and confined mostly to statutes that rely for their authority on the expertise of legislators.[24] I prefer the more modest statement of personalism in which he states that '[t]he only assumption of the personal conception of authority is that somebody in an authoritative capacity must have issued the law. This is a conceptual point about the sources of law.'[25] This statement may fall short of the work that Marmor wants personalism to do, but it rightly stresses that the importance of personalism about authority is not related to the content of an authoritative directive, but to the standing of the authority to issue binding directives at all.

This shows in Marmor's most recent work, where he expresses the view that authority is 'essentially institutional' without abandoning his earlier position that authority is also necessarily personal. Authority, Marmor argues, 'is determined by some social or institutional practice'.[26]

> The essential feature of any practical authority is to have *power*, in the normative sense of the term.... The existence of power, however, is an essentially institutional matter... Only rules or conventions of an institution, or a well structured social practice, can confer power. And this is why authorities are essentially institutional in nature, and the obligations to comply with their directives are institutional obligations.[27]

The appeal to institutional power-conferring norms resolves the tension between the personal and institutional accounts of authority by differentiating between the norms that confer authority and the agents on whom

[22] Natalie Stoljar, 'Is Positivism Committed to Intentionalism?' in Tom Campbell and Jeffrey Goldsworthy (eds), *Judicial Power, Democracy and Legal Positivism* (Ashgate, 2000) 169.

[23] For an overview of intentionalism and its alternatives, see Natalie Stoljar, 'Interpretation, Indeterminacy and Authority: Some Recent Controversies in the Philosophy of Law' (2003) 11(4) *The Journal of Political Philosophy* 470.

[24] Andrei Marmor, *Interpretation and Legal Theory* (2nd edn) (Hart, 2005) 132–39.

[25] Marmor, note 17, 107.

[26] Andrei Marmor, 'An Institutional Conception of Authority' (2011) 39(3) *Philosophy and Public Affairs* 238.

[27] Andrei Marmor, 'The Dilemma of Authority' (2011) 2 *Jurisprudence* 121, 129–30.

it is conferred. The norms that confer authority are internal to whatever practice the putative authority and the putative subject are engaging in. Once the putative subject has a reason to engage in the practice, the rules of the practice, which are by definition institutional, specify the criteria by which the authority will be identified. This is not a new turn in Marmor's thinking. It was present at the start of his dispute with Waldron, when he stated that:

> It is not the personal attributes of the author, however, which render him or her an authority. We defer to certain people as authorities not because they have certain personal attributes, but because they act in an authoritative capacity or role. It is their role identity and not their personal identity that matters. Of course, it normally matters who occupies the particular role. We are never indifferent to the personal identity of the authority; it always matters who the legislators are. But the reasons for deferring to an authority are basically role-dependent reasons: we defer to the authority of X, because X is an authority and not because he is X.[28]

Going back to the pluralist perspective, it seems that if a group is to claim authority over one of its members, and this authority is not to be understood simply as the particular authority of a person in power in the group, but rather the expression of the corporate intention of the body, then the group as such must be a person, it must be capable of forming an intention and communicating it to the putative subject of authority. Only then would the normal justification of authority come into play, and the putative subject be asked whether she is more likely to comply with the reasons that apply to her by following the authority's instructions than by acting on those reasons independently.[29]

10.3 SUPERVENIENCE AND GROUP PERSONALITY

Philip Pettit has for two decades been developing an account of groups that avoids individualist reductionism about joint practices, but emphasizes external agency over internal commitment.[30] His theory is therefore more appropriate for discussing the central pluralist concern over group personality, which was especially important for describing and prescribing the

[28] Marmor, note 24, 106.

[29] There are important outstanding issues with Marmor's (and, by extension, Raz's) conception of authority and their connection with personality. One of the most stimulating objections comes from Stephen Darwall's influential account of authority: Stephen Darwall, *The Second Person Standpoint* (Harvard University Press, 2006) and also, 'Law and the Second Person Standpoint' (2007) 40 *Loyla Los Angeles Law Review* 891. I believe that the pluralist insistence on the real personality of groups also makes it compatible with Darwall's account, but that discussion is the focus of a different project.

[30] I thank Will Roberts for helpful discussion about the matters treated in this section.

relationship between groups and the state.[31] Pettit has long been concerned with the problems posed by joint intention, and his concerns have always been intended by their author to generate strong normative implications, most notably as they undergird his arguments in favour of republicanism.[32] In the earlier elaboration of his account, Pettit argues that it suffices to say that an agent exhibits certain 'intentional regularities', that it exhibits certain traits of minimal rationality, and moreover—for the purposes of social and political theory—that these regularities can also be observed in social settings. Such 'social regularities' exist simply when 'a number of individuals... display certain attitudes or perform certain actions, at the same or at different times' and these actions or attitudes are causally connected to the intention of the agents.[33] Social regularities may also have structural properties—like boundary-conditions (norms restricting entry or demanding certain expectation of participants) which enable them to endure over time, whereas other social regularities are ephemeral. The concept is surely too broad (Pettit admits as much) but it can be given content by something like Rawls' two moral powers: people regularly form conceptions of the good and conceptions of justice, and they do so under social circumstances, taking these (and other external circumstances, such as moderate scarcity) into account. The fact that these responses are sufficiently regular makes it possible to call upon people to abide by certain moral principles.

The same argument applies in the case of legal personality. Persons exhibit certain regularities of behaviour, certain responses to the social environment—such as a consciousness of our physical embodiment and vulnerability to harm and want, a desire of stability in the foreseeable future, an expectation of certainty in our dealings with others—that makes the construction of a subject of rights and duties possible. People regularly make decisions, are able to communicate them, and understand what it means to keep promises and hold others to a bargain. Similar regularities are present in the case of 'artificial' persons—those who do not correspond to a flesh-and-blood individual. Pettit observes that 'there are a variety of social entities we distinguish, in particular a variety of social continuants, so there are many potential

[31] Pettit and Christian List distinguish their work from Gilbert's precisely along the axis of group agency. (Christian List and Philip Pettit, *Group Agents* (Oxford University Press, 2011) 216. n18). While Gilbert is concerned about individuals joining to do things together, Pettit and List are concerned with individuals forming a collective or group mind that itself does things. Because Pettit and List's conception of agency is more robust, they accuse Gilbert of over-ascribing agency to plural subjects. This may be a semantic point caused by Gilbert's emphasis on the collective subjectivity of individuals performing joint actions, but it underscores an important distinction: not all joint activity or joint intention is aimed at constituting a corporate agent.

[32] Philip Pettit, *The Common Mind* (Oxford University Press, 1993) 288ff; *A Theory of Freedom* (Oxford University Press, 2001) 152ff.

[33] Philip Pettit, *Common Mind*, note 32, 119ff.

areas in which we can look for examples of structural regularities.' He gives as examples '[g]roups, like the party and the firm, whose essence it is to have a mode of collective behaviour'; '[g]roups that may have only a non-behavioural collective identity like genders, races, and classes'; '[i]nstrumentalities whose essence is tied up with the behaviour of designated officers: for example, museums, libraries, and states'; and '[i]nstrumentalities, like the sub-culture of teenage males, whose essence is independently given: these will include cultures, territories, markets, and the like.'[34] Most of the entities mentioned do not possess a capacity for intentional thought similar to that of individuals, at least of individuals as contemplated in liberal legal orders, but the first stands apart in Pettit's account as the only one 'whose essence it is to have a mode of collective behavior.' It is interesting that states stand so far from parties and firms on his typology, and one wonders where other complicated groups (like large hierarchical churches), or groups which have the character of both a group and an instrumentality (like universities) fit in.[35]

In more recent work Pettit reframes his argument about collective intention in terms that specifically address the agency of groups and point towards the possibility that some of these groups are persons in their own right. He argues that there are collective as well as individual subjects, and that collective subjects are capable of being held responsible and of holding others responsible. The basis of this is his theory of freedom as discursive control.

[34] Philip Pettit, *Common Mind*, note 32, 124–25.

[35] There are some remarkable things about this typology that should not pass without a brief remark. The first is that groups can come in different structural forms and only some will be able to act as agents in any intelligible way. Even the most ardent revolutionaries, on both the fronts of class and nation, postulate a vanguard party to represent the interests of the inchoate social system. The inexorable logic of history—a sort of teleologically-infused structural regularity—may lead us to a new golden age, but it cannot make a speech, declare a war, or coordinate a traffic system. But this observation does not single out groups 'whose essence is to have a mode of collective behavior'; it also includes at least some (though perhaps not all) '[i]nstrumentalities whose essence is tied up with the behaviour of designated officers'. It seems arbitrary to place parties and firms in one category and states in another. But perhaps the distinction that Pettit imagines is not strictly structural but also political. This is suggested by remarks in his later work about the failure of dictatorships to track truth, that is, to 'form true rather than false beliefs about the world' including, presumably, true rather than false beliefs about the preferences of its members acting collectively and about the moral reasons that they may have for acting both jointly and severally (List and Pettit, note 31, 81). By centralizing decision-making, a group becomes progressively less capable of tracking truth, to the point perhaps that it ceases to be a group in any meaningful way because the epistemic role of its members is progressively reduced until it is irrelevant to the decisions of the collective. Thus, in one sort of group, the epistemic role of the members is more active and genuinely contributes to collective rationality while in another it is not the case. But this seems to distinguish one type from the other on the basis of concrete organizational structure: a closely-held corporation would be more like the third type and a small participatory republic more like the first. Or perhaps the difference lies in the relationship of the members to the group and whether they understand their collective behaviour as essential for the group to act. The more the agency of the group is unaffected by lack of participation, the more we shift from the first to the third type. Once we put aside the typology, however, and focus both on structure and self-conception the line between the first and the third kinds of group becomes less relevant.

Discourse, for Pettit, is a mode of reasoning together, of attempting 'to resolve a problem by reference to what all parties regard as inferentially relevant considerations or reasons.'[36] Discursive control is the ability of an agent to discourse, provided she has access to discursive relations.[37] Discursive control is both a sufficient and a necessary condition of agency, and collective subjects are fit to be held responsible insofar and only insofar as they enjoy discursive control. This bears some explanation. When individuals have to form collective views on rationally connected issues, Pettit argues, they have to choose between being sensitive to individual reason (allowing collective irrationality) or enforcing collective rationality (and reducing individual reason). A collectivity pursuing a purpose will have to impose discipline of reason at the collective level. The intentions of the group will possibly be discontinuous with the intentions/judgments of the members. This discontinuity demonstrates that the collective entity is entirely separate from the individuals that comprise it. These collectivities are candidates for freedom because they can enter discourse with others as convertible interlocutors by giving their word and living up to those words. They enjoy freedom in person, self and action and act as free persons insofar as they enjoy discursive control vis-à-vis other persons, individual and institutional and do not systematically elude past commitments, but live up to those commitments. Their actions are free because they are controlled by discursive considerations as free persons.[38]

Is Pettit's work continuous with the realist theory of group personality advocated by the pluralists? Pettit is one of few prominent political philosophers who seriously engages with the pluralist tradition, but his relationship to it is, alas, complicated. He expressly refers to his account of group agency as a 'realist' account, which it is, but his appraisal of the pluralist theory of corporate personality is mercurial. In *The Common Mind* he is sceptical of collectivist and organicist descriptions of group life, and cites Maitland as an example.[39] But in *A Theory of Freedom* he endorses the pluralist tradition, stating that '[t]here is a long tradition of ascribing personality—personhood and selfhood—to collectives, though it has recently fallen out of favour. I believe that the tradition is fundamentally sound and that it is perfectly proper to ascribe personality to integrated groups and groupings.'[40] And yet in *Group*

[36] Philip Pettit, *A Theory of Freedom*, note 32, 67.

[37] Pettit, note 36, 70.

[38] Pettit, note 36, chapter 5. It is also possible for groups to be responsible when the component individuals are not. The foreseeable results of individual actions may not extend to what the group does in consequence to individual actions.

[39] Pettit, *Common Mind*, note 32, 126–27.

[40] Pettit, *A Theory of Freedom*, note 32, 116. Pettit cites David Runciman's *Pluralism and the Personality of the State* (Cambridge University Press, 1997) in this passage to identify the tradition.

Agency he and List distance themselves from pluralism, with explicit reference to the main figures in the tradition, which they call the 'emergentist approach' to groups entities. List and Pettit's objection is that the emergentism of Gierke, Maitland, and the others is that '[i]t offends against methodological individualism in suggesting that group agency requires something above and beyond the emergence of coordinated, psychologically intelligible dispositions in individual members. This is metaphysically incredible.'[41]

Pettit and List's misgivings about the pluralist tradition are explained in a lengthy technical discussion about the supervenience of group rationality on individual rationality. But the discussion is essential for understanding how group personality emerges and how it relates to the structural or constitutional features of associations. For List and Pettit, group rationality supervenes doxastically on the individual rationality of the group's members. What this means is that while the group can be said to have intentions and reach decisions that are not reducible to an aggregate of individual decisions, every change in the beliefs and intentions of the group must be traceable to changes in the beliefs and intentions of individuals who compose it.[42] This is not a causal change, but a structural one and is best illustrated by List and Pettit's own example.

> Think of the relation between the shapes made by dots on a grid and the positions or coordinates of the dots. The positions of the dots do not cause the shapes to be such and such, as there is no lag between the dots assuming those positions and the shapes materializing. Nothing causal needs to happen in order for the positions to give rise to the shapes; suitably positioned, the dots simply constitute the shapes and are not distinct enough to be causes. But although the positions of the dots do not causally determine the shapes, they still determine those shapes.[43]

Supervenience holds even if the identities of the individual members who take part in the underlying structure change; it may even hold if the number of members increase or decrease (to a point) as long as they remain in the same pattern. List and Pettit propose that '[t]he attitudes and actions of a group agent supervene on the contributions of its members.'[44] Through a series of examples reminiscent of Kenneth Arrow's impossibility theorems,

[41] List and Pettit, note 31, 9.

[42] The analogy, from which the concept of supervenience comes, is between the brain and the mind. To avoid reductionism, some philosophers of mind postulate that the mind is distinct from the brain, but every change in mental phenomena implies a change in the physical and chemical structure of the brain. 'Such supervenience might be taken to mean that there cannot be two events alike in all physical respects but differing in some mental respect, or that an object cannot alter in some mental respect without altering in some physical respect.' Donald Davidson, *Essays on Actions and Events* (Oxford University Press, 1980) 214.

[43] List and Pettit, note 31, 65.

[44] List and Pettit, note 31, 66.

they demonstrate that a group cannot achieve collective rationality by a serial consideration of propositions that are put to it. Individual preferences, made in the absence of feedback from the group's prior preferences, will lead to inconsistent outcomes. Rather, the individual's preference on one proposition must be influenced by the group's intention including, most importantly, the decision procedures of the group itself.[45] This may involve, tellingly, the relative position of members within the group, or put a different way, the theoretical or practical authority of some members over others.

List and Pettit consider that what they call the emergentist tradition—that is, the tradition of British pluralism—denies that group rationality is supervenient on individual rationality, and posits instead 'that the force by which a collection of individuals constitutes a group agent is an add-on to the individual contributions of the members; it is something that accompanies those contributions but does not logically derive from them.'[46] But, as I have explained, this is not what the British pluralists themselves held (though Otto Gierke's view on this is debatable). The pluralists' language of organic emergence of group identity was mostly metaphorical, although it did point to a social psychology that afforded the social group a primary role in shaping the individual character. But their account of the emergence of group agency and personality refers consistently to the sustained cooperation of individuals in a common practice, not 'a mysterious, individualistically inaccessible force.'[47] Thus Maitland writes that group personality is a matter of 'common opinion' and 'moral sentiment',[48] and expressly disavows any metaphysical presuppositions. And while it is true that Figgis writes that 'in truth the notion of isolated individuality is the shadow of a dream' and '[i]n the real world the isolated individual does not exist' these are statements about socialization and the development of psychological personality, not metaphysical theses.[49] Elsewhere, Figgis explains that '[s]ociety is inherent in human nature, and that means inevitably the growth of a communal life and social ties.' What this means is that individuals are naturally drawn to form groups, and that once formed the structure of these groups shapes the character and beliefs of their members, and also develops norms and structures of authority that direct their members' intentions and energies in ways previously absent. Figgis' language is organicist, and this has some implications for his theory of socialization and of group development,[50] but the underlying mechanics of his argument are compatible with the modest methodological individualism that List and Pettit want to salvage.

[45] List and Pettit, note 31, 77. [46] List and Pettit, note 31, 74–75. [47] List and Pettit, note 31, 9.
[48] Maitland, note 9, 68. [49] Figgis, note 12, 88. [50] Levy, note 10, 37–38.

The structure of group agents, moreover, lends more credence to the pluralist contention that groups, once formed, can develop an intentionality of their own which does not depend on canvassing members' intellectual states. In a response to List and Pettit, Don Ross has argued that the claim that group doxastic rationality supervenes on individual doxastic rationality is overstated. Doxastic rationality refers to rationality about beliefs, so put a different way, Ross argues that List and Pettit overstate their case when they argue that the beliefs of a group supervene on the beliefs of their members. In contrast, Ross argues that all that is required for group rationality is that group rationality supervene on individual behaviour. Most of the time, members go along with a group's decisions without reflecting much on them, making up their minds about the reasons the group gives, or even contributing to them. There may be good and bad reasons for this indifferent attitude, but whatever the case, the regularity in behaviour can reinforce the rationality of the group by further entrenching its decision procedures. 'Either way group rationality supervenes on individual rationality; it's just that sometimes or usually only some members of a group need have intentions about group rationality because the rest are sheep and blow with the prevailing epistemic winds.'[51] This is not a favourable judgment on group membership, but it is likely more accurate, especially in large groups. In these bodies the constitutional structures, the internal deliberation procedures, acquire more importance to group personality the more entrenched they become, and the group as a whole comes to depend less on the individual epistemic idiosyncracies of its members. As with natural persons, the group can become set in its ways, but it may on occasion be shaken up by new ideas or realizations.

Another important conclusion of the structural account of group rationality, one that further emancipates the group from the individuals that compose it, is the identity-independent nature of supervenience. The more formally constituted a group, the more decisions are made on the basis of internal procedures and constitutional practices rather than spontaneous deliberation, the less the individual personalities of its members matter. Of course, there will—and ought—always be a place for individual differentiation. It is not salutary for a group to function with bureaucratic mindlessness, and both grassroots reform and inspired leadership depend on members of a group reflecting on the association's policies and practices. But for the most part, the rationality of a group depends largely on the roles that are defined by its structure.[52] This has at least one important consequence: it

[51] Don Ross, 'Group Doxastic Rationality Need Not Supervene on Individual Rationality' (2006) 44 *The Southern Journal of Philosophy* 106, 112.

[52] I should add that this role-dependence links the account of supervenience to Marmor's institutional conception of authority.

complicates the causal link between individual and group agency and makes individuals, as long as they are acting in their role-capacity as members of a group (whether in a leadership role or not) somewhat constrained in their influence on the intention of the corporate agent. Again, this has been a consistent thesis of Pettit's work, from his influential article with Frank Jackson, where they conclude that:

> while the program model [of structural explanation] does not undermine individual agent autonomy, neither does it particularly flatter the individual. It suggests that for many of the things that happen in social life—specifically, those that are subject to structural explanation—the particular attitudes and actions of particular individuals which led to those things were not necessary prerequisites. If those people had not done those things, other people would have wittingly or unwittingly stepped into the breach.[53]

Pettit's structuralism serves as a counterargument to Runciman's insistence that groups cannot be persons because they require persons to act for them, and only those later are 'capable of acting out their own, personal dramas'. The individual unreflexibly acting out their role in an institutional structure need is not acting out their drama, but rather the drama of the structure itself. If she reflects on what she is doing, she may be able to integrate her role in the institution with the other roles that she plays in her life, and even with her broader understanding of her life's direction. But only in rare (though important) cases will her role in the institution involve a protagonism that supplants the institution's method of arriving at corporate decisions with her own.

The explanation also accounts for Figgis' statements about the corporate agency of organized groups, the 'unity of life and action' which grows out of an association's 'collective, not individual . . . constitution.'[54] Despite Figgis' recurrence to organic imagery, what he describes is, on the most basic level, a structural pattern that allows collectivities that possess a certain authoritative structure to form intentions and communicate them in a manner intelligible to other individuals and groups, in other words, to possess discursive control. This is the most fundamental condition of agency, and one that underlies the legal conception of corporate personality. A brief diversion into this area is warranted.

[53] Frank Jackson and Philip Pettit, 'Structural Explanation in Social Theory' in (David Charles and Kathleen Lennon (eds)), *Reduction, Explanation, and Realism* (Oxford University Press, 1992) 97–131, 130.

[54] Figgis, note 12, 69.

10.4 TWO KINDS OF LEGAL PERSONALITY

It is a common argument against the full-blown realist theory of corporate personality that the marks of personality that the law confers on a group are either legal fictions or mere conveniences and are too barebones to justify inferring that the group possesses an inherent and autonomous intentional capacity. But is there any difference between the legal personality of the group and that of the natural person, the flesh-and-blood individual?

The question is how far can the analogy between corporate and natural personality be pushed, and the answer must lie in the expectations we have of the natural person in a given institutional setting. The task, then, is to construct something like a political, not metaphysical, concept of corporate personality that is equivalent to the political, not metaphysical, personality of the flesh and blood individual. The idea is, of course, borrowed from John Rawls' discussion of the person in *Political Liberalism*. Like Rawls, I begin with an institutional perspective. Rawls began 'with the idea that society is to be conceived as a fair system of cooperation over time between generations' and proceeds to derive from it a conception of the person *qua* citizen.[55] Pettit begins from a different perspective, but follows the same method. The conditions of discursive control set the criteria of what can be counted as an agent, and thus what can be a claimant of rights in a given institutional setting.

From this perspective, it is perhaps not surprising that the natural person, as she appears in politics and law, is in a large part an 'artificial' or 'fictional' construct. The content of personhood—the bundle of rights and duties that the law refers to—responds to certain social, psychological, and moral considerations. Unsurprisingly, in the following section I argue that the case of the 'artificial' corporate person is formally identical, although the content of personhood may change because some of the social, psychological, and moral considerations that lead to the recognition of certain rights and duties in the natural person may not be present in the corporate case, and vice-versa. Now, this thesis about the artificiality of natural personhood is not especially original. It is endorsed by the British pluralists who 'in their more clear-sighted moments... saw that *all* legal personality (including that of the individual) is "artificial", and that it is created by being recognized in legal practice.'[56] It is, in part, inspired by the Humean intuition that justice is not 'natural' but 'artificial', because it only finds its place in ongoing social

[55] John Rawls, *Political Liberalism* (Columbia University Press, 1993) 18.

[56] David Nicholls, *The Pluralist State: The Political Ideas of JN Figgis and His Contemporaries* (2nd edn) (St. Martin's, 1994) 70–71.

interaction and is therefore, in some relevant sense, a social construction.[57] And it also echoes the Kantian encouragement to exit the state of nature through the institution of law, because only thus can we realize institutionally our full moral capacity as intelligible beings.[58] These institutions transform our actions and identities; where before we possessed our belongings, now we own them, and we could not have done so before the law made us creatures capable of owning things. That we needed to move from a state without law—where we nonetheless had moral duties towards our own person and towards others—to a civil state responds to moral concern considered in light of facts about human psychology and social interaction.[59]

The Kantian paradigm serves as a template for the attribution of 'civil rights' in the original understanding of the term: the capacity to be a source of norms, to become the subject of legal rights and obligations.[60] Now, I do not argue that the rights and obligations that emanate from the law directly (say, the right to vote, or the obligation to refrain from criminal activity) or those that emanate from the legally recognized capacity of persons to be sources of law (say, the obligations imposed by the terms of a contract, or the right to dispose of one's property) are exhaustive of the normative principles that apply to a person. There is good reason to believe that there are some rights that are natural, in the sense that they might be claimed by any rational being against any other even outside of the framework of social institutions. Part of being a person, surely, involves not being the object of wanton cruelty at the hands of another person, and of not having one's serious and immediate needs callously disregarded by those who could effortlessly meet them. It involves also a claim to equal freedom—as Hart put it, 'if there are any moral rights at all, it follows that there is at least one natural right, the equal right of all men to be free'—which is not trivial, and forms one of the most important bases of the justification of a legal order, and many legal norms within that order that contemplate attributes of legal personhood.[61]

[57] David Hume, 'An Enquiry Concerning the Principles of Morals' in LA Selby-Bigge (ed.), *Enquiries Concerning Human Understanding and Concerning the Principles of Morals* (Oxford University Press, 1975) sec. 3.

[58] Immanuel Kant, 'The Metaphysics of Morals' in Mary Gregor (ed.), *Practical Philosophy* (Cambridge University Press, 1996) 407–408 (GS 6:253–54).

[59] Kant refers to the principles of Ulpian—*honeste vive, neminem laede, suum cuique tribue*—as the reasons to institute a civil state. Only in such a state could one have hope of keeping to these canons.

[60] The kind of right involved is the 'droit subjectif' of the civil law tradition, which is roughly (but only roughly) equivalent to 'right' as distinct from 'law' in the common law. It generically encompasses the entire spectrum of Hohfeldian rights, and sets the subject as an immediate *source* of legal rules; the 'droit objectif', by contrast, is the normative structure that recognizes the subject's capacity to be a source of rules, and sets general limits on the content of these rules. Geoffrey Samuel, '"Le Droit Subjectif" and English Law' (1987) 46 *Cambridge Legal Journal* 264.

[61] HLA Hart, 'Are There Any Natural Rights' (1955) 64(2) *The Philosophical Review* 175.

Some things a human being can do without law, in that legal categories are not constitutive preconditions of the action; the law, in these cases, is a force from without that permits, coordinates, or prohibits action. Any human being can cut a path through a field, crash a car, or kill a man. She cannot, in the absence of an applicable legal framework, define a prædial servitude of right of way, be liable for the damage resulting from her negligent driving, or commit second-degree murder. The physical act, and even the psychological motivation behind the act, may be the same in each case, but the legal frame in which the act is set changes its meaning. It does more, even, since it transforms one action into another and alters the claims that others may have against the agent. It is not so much the nature of the act that gives reason to imbue it with legal meaning (although the act itself is not irrelevant to the content of such meaning). Rather, it is the mode in which the act is presented, the claim that is involved in claiming that it has certain intangible transformative consequence.[62] Through the action of cutting through a field with the intention of making of this path a permanent passage from one's land through a neighbour's, an agent may simply be hoping for uninterrupted access in the future, and may even be prepared to use force as an incentive for her neighbour to refrain from restricting that access. But given a suitable normative context, the agent would instead be making a claim of right that is independent of the physical actions involved in clearing a path and laying down gravel. She would be claiming to alter the normative landscape and bind the present owners of the neighbouring property to allow her this right in the future, and preserve the conditions of its exercise (say, by not building a wall over the path), and moreover to transmit these obligations to future owners, who will likewise be obliged to observe it.[63] It does not follow from the 'nature' of a person that she should be able to engage in such complex exercises in the creation of norms and obligations. To be an owner is to control the use to which a thing is put, which any brute with a strong-enough grip can do, but it is also to dispose of it and perhaps destroy it, and to alter it in ways that give other persons—even persons yet unnamed or unborn—certain rights over it. That these rights, and not others, are recognized by law may respond to a myriad of justifications but they are not directly derived from natural conditions.[64]

[62] Several legal theorists have argued, correctly in my view, that law is a modal kind, not a functional kind, because it prescribes a way of doing something rather than an intended consequence or effect. See, for example, Leslie Green, 'The Functions of Law' (1998) 12(2) *Cogito* 117, 121, and 'The Concept of Law Revisited' (1996) 94(6) *Michigan Law Review* 1687, 1711; and John Gardner, *Law as a Leap of Faith* (Oxford University Press, 2012) 293.

[63] The legal details of how this is done are beside the point, although I must observe that not all jurisdictions allow for the creation of prædial servitudes of rights of way in the same manner. But these differences go to specific norms about real property law in each system, not to the concept of a servitude per se.

[64] We can stipulate that, in the natural state, absent a framework of social institutions, it is possible for a (moral) person to incur obligations of her own making; promises may be binding in such a state. But

In the case of the natural person, the powers of legal personality usually follow 'legal capacity' at maturity. They are a kind of office or role that the individual assumes, a kind of legal status which recognizes the capacity to exercise civil rights and at the same time confers them. The office of the legal person is like a mask, a veil, just like the legal corporate personality is a mask or veil of the group. I am a human being, but I am also a citizen, a contractor, an owner (hopefully), a tortfeasor (regrettably), a legal entity endowed with civil rights. A human being conceived as a natural kind cannot own, contract, or bequeath, but a person in law can. The distinction between recognition of capacity and conferral is important because recognition of capacity may grant a right to conferral of rights but such conferral is not automatic.[65] Now, it is true that the office tracks certain functional characteristics, but these functional characteristics may be present without the office following; they give reasons to demand bestowal of the office, but do not constitute it. Cases like the historical disenfranchisement of women and slaves are not the most interesting in this regard because in those cases the capacity to exercise civil rights was itself questioned. The most interesting case is that of civil death, which serves as a kind of *modus tollens* for the idea that individual legal personality is somehow natural. Civil death was a penalty attached to felony conviction (and also, less commonly, to banishment or entry into a religious order) which resulted in the loss of all civil rights, that is, the right to contract, own property, and sue and be sued in court.

> A state of civil death, or *civiliter mortuus* as it was known at early English common law, resulted under certain circumstances in which a person though living, was considered dead.... Civil death... resulted in the loss of the convict's civil rights and he was thereby disqualified from being a witness, prohibited from bringing an action or performing any legal function, and he was in effect regarded as dead by the law.[66]

promises are not *ipso facto* contracts, even when they may ground contractual obligations. See e.g. Charles Fried, *Contract as Promise* (Harvard University Press, 1981).

[65] And it finds a direct analogy in the law of business corporations in international or federal settings (like the federal system in Canada). When a company is chartered in one jurisdiction—putting aside whether the charter recognizes a pre-existing social reality or creates it; the case may be different with business corporations than with churches—it is at once granted the civil rights to contract, sue and be sued, and be liable in court in that jurisdiction, and also the capacity to solicit the recognition of these rights in other jurisdictions. Absent some rule like the US Constitution's full faith and credit clause, the original incorporation only grants rights in the jurisdiction in which the company was incorporated. But once created the company can demand these rights in its own name; it does not need to incorporate in every new market, but can simply register its legal personality in the other jurisdiction. See *Reference in the matter of the Incorporation of Companies in Canada* [1913] SCJ 29, 48 SCR 331 and *Bonanza Creek Gold Mining* v. *The King* [1916] 1 AC 566.

[66] Harry Saunders, 'Civil Death: A New Look at an Ancient Doctrine' (1970) 11 *William and Mary Law Review* 988, 998–99.

Civil death persists in some form through the incapacities that follow bankruptcy and the electoral disenfranchisement of felons. The former can be justified as a temporal precautionary measure because insolvency suggests that the bankrupt has a demonstrated incapacity to manage financial affairs; the latter has been demonstrated time and again to be unjustified and barbarous, both because it does not track capacity to make political decisions and because it is enforced with discriminatory effect and intent.[67] But for our purposes, the importance of civil death is that it demonstrates that capacity to act as an agent in a certain institutional setting, such as the system of private law, represents a moral claim to receive the rights and powers of personhood, but does not create or constitute these rights automatically. It is the fact that natural persons of sufficient maturity and ordinary intellectual capacity meet the criteria set by legal institutions that entitles them to the concession of these rights. But then any other entity that meets the threshold should likewise be entitled to them.

The argument I have laid out seems to invoke the old debate about the nature of rights: whether they are grounded in the capacity of agents for rational choice (the 'will' theory of rights) or in the interests that these agents enjoy. I am very much inclined towards the will theory, especially in relation to corporate personality. This would seem to go counter to the consensus among defenders and detractors of group personality, the first of whom (e.g. Joseph Raz) defend the possibility of group rights because individuals may have an interest in the continued existence of groups,[68] and the latter (e.g. Carl Wellman) reject group rights because they consider groups to be inadequate candidates due to their lacking a suitable will.[69] Let us take each of these in turn. Joseph Raz defends the idea of group rights as a way of protecting an interest in a public good that the group provides to individual members. It is a right ultimately derived from the right of individuals as members of a group, and which they can only have collectively because no single member of that group in that public good is 'sufficient by itself to justify holding another person to be subject to a duty.'

> Rights, even collective rights, can only be there if they serve the interests of individuals. In that sense collective interests are a mere *façon de parler*. They are a way of referring to individual interests which arise out of the individuals' membership in communities.[70]

[67] Alec Ewald, '"Civil Death" The Ideological Paradox of Criminal Disenfranchisement Law in the United States' 2002 (5) *Wisconsin Law Review* 1045; Andrew Dilts, *Punishment and Inclusion: Race, Membership, and the Limits of American Liberalism* (Fordham University Press, forthcoming).

[68] Jospeh Raz, *The Morality of Freedom* (Oxford University Press, 1986) 207–13. The interest theory of rights is also the basis of Dwight Newman's defence of group rights in *Community and Collective Rights* (Hart, 2011) 10–11, 91–92.

[69] Carl Wellman, *Real Rights* (Oxford University Press, 1995) 157–65.

[70] Joseph Raz, *The Morality of Freedom* (Oxford University Press, 1986) 208.

As Adina Preda has recently demonstrated, such a collective conception of rights as shared interests in public goods cannot ground the rights of a group *qua* group.[71] The interest theory of group rights treats groups as collectivities, not corporate entities, that is, as collections of individuals who have some interest in common that can only be realized or only has sufficient moral weight if shared. But such a conception of rights cannot ground group rights proper because group rights are the rights that the group holds as a group, not the rights that its members hold individually by virtue of their membership.[72] Some defenders of group rights, especially multiculturalists and some advocates of non-institutional religious freedom, justify national self-determination or the autonomy of religious groups as derived from the group-differentiated rights of members of a cultural or religious community, but this leads to problems. In particular, it renders potentially incoherent the proposition that the community itself may make claims that conflict with those of its individual members, that the group may have rights against its members, because this would make some group members have rights against themselves.[73]

The will or choice theory of rights is much more promising in this regard. It states, at a minimum, that groups can be right-holders because they are agents, because they are capable of forming intentions and acting for reasons, and that these intentions and actions are independent of those of their members, in the ways described in section 10.3. But defenders of the will theory of rights have had some trouble recognizing in corporate agents the necessary capacity for choice. Carl Wellman disputes Peter French's account of corporate personality as derived from the internal decision procedures of the corporation. These procedures, Wellman complains, describe a distinction between the individual and official capacity of the officers of the corporation. It is the officials, acting as agents of the corporate body, that act.

> Accordingly, attributions of actions to corporations are best interpreted as statements about the actions of individual human beings acting as officials in corporate groups. Such statements do not presuppose or imply that a corporation in and of itself possesses agency; they presuppose a normative distinction between an individual moral agent acting in her official capacity and acting as a private person.[74]

[71] Adina Preda 'Group Rights and Shared Agency' (2012) 9 *Journal of Moral Philosophy* 229, and 'Group Rights and Shared Interests' *Political Studies* (2012) 61(2) Political Studies 250.

[72] Recall the discussion of multiculturalism in Chapter 2, which makes this point in a different way.

[73] Adina Preda, 'Group Rights and Shared Interests', note 71, 10.

[74] Carl Wellman, *Real Rights* (Oxford University Press, 1995) 165.

Preda answers this critique by distinguishing 'between a *capacity for acting*, or agency in a limited sense, and *full-blown* or *autonomous* agency.'[75] Wellman denies the status of rights holders to groups because he believes that the capacity for choice presupposes personhood understood as full-blown agency.[76] But Preda disputes this, and replies that only a more constrained capacity for acting is required to have rights. This capacity is a feature of organized groups (not, however, of unorganized groups).

> In order to make a choice, a group will need a decision-making procedure, that is, a way to amalgamate the choices of its individual members; furthermore, in order to satisfy the 'awareness' requirement this procedure should be a public one, namely one that is known to the group's members. In addition, we should probably stipulate that a decision-making procedure should be a 'coherent' one, namely one that yields a definite result in a given choice situation.[77]

It may be that the opposition between the will and the interest theory of rights does not present as many problems when applied to groups as when applied to individuals, because the very ascription of distinct interests to groups implies that the association has a formal mechanism for determining those interests. The conditions of having an interest that is the group's (as opposed to a shared interest of its members) is the same as the condition for having a distinct will, as it is the will that determines, identifies, or affirms the interest. Anna Moltchanova marshals Pettit's notion of freedom as discursive control to justify the status of groups as right-holders, on a par with other agents that also enjoy discursive control, such as normal adult individuals.[78] But as Preda shows, this still presupposes a corporate and not a collective theory of rights, and the corporate theory is far more compatible with the will theory than with the interest theory of rights, at least as these theories have been traditionally defended.

10.5 FROM GROUP AGENCY TO GROUP PERSONALITY

The pluralist defence of group personality, however, is not limited to an account of intentional group agency. It goes further and puts forth a claim closer to Preda's description of full-blown or autonomous agency for the group, which requires the ability 'to choose one's goals, after careful deliberation and reflection and be able to revise them in the light of moral reasons.'[79]

[75] Preda, 'Group Rights and Shared Agency', note 71, 233.

[76] Wellman, note 74, 162.

[77] Preda, 'Group Rights and Shared Agency', note 71, 247.

[78] Anna Moltchanova, 'Collective Agents and Group Moral Rights' (2009) 17(1) *The Journal of Political Philosophy* 23, 27.

[79] Preda, 'Group Rights and Shared Agency', note 71, 233.

That groups are intentional agents can be granted without granting that they are persons in their own right. But if, as I think Preda has conclusively shown, agency is the necessary and sufficient condition to have rights, do we need to insist on personality? The reason, I think, is that agency entails a capacity to exercise rights that are conferred by a legal authority, but it does not necessarily entail the right to *demand* that those rights be conceded.

Some associations depend on a constitutive authority to give effect to group agency. The paradigmatic case is that of the business corporation. Under the two most dominant theories of the business corporation, a company is either a fiction or an artifice of law.[80] On the first theory—the theory of the corporation as a nexus of implicit and explicit contracts among individuals, the company is treated as a right and duty bearing unit because it is convenient to do so in order to identify it in contracts, property liens, and the like; this is the theory that prevails in the contemporary literature, especially in the law and economics movement. In the alternative theory—the theory that corporations exist by concession or permission of the state—the company is treated as a real entity, not a mere figure of speech, but its existence is conditioned on its chartering by the state, absent which it is only an aggregate of unconnected individuals with no legal obligations to each other; this is the traditional theory espoused by Bodin and Hobbes, who applied it especially to non-business corporate entities like churches and professional organizations.

But in the case of associations other than business corporations, does the capacity for intentional agency depend on state authorization or does it precede the state? In the case of natural persons, it is clear that it precedes the state. Natural persons can form intentions, they can act on those intentions, and they have a conception of themselves that extends through time such that they can understand themselves to be the authors of the actions that they took in the past on the basis of intentions then formed, and can form intentions that guide the actions they undertake with respect to situations in which their future selves may find themselves. But I would argue that at least in the case of some corporate persons, these elements also obtain irrespectively of a grant from the state. The recognition of their legal personality by the state, then, is not constitutive of personality (as it is in the case of most business corporations) but declarative of it.[81]

[80] Michael Phillips, 'Reappraising the Real Entity Theory of the Corporation' (1994) 21 *Florida State University Law Review* 1061.

[81] I do not want to put too much weight on the distinction between business corporations and other kinds of groups. It is simply the case that for most business corporations the corporate form is instrumental to an external end, while in the groups of principal concern to associational pluralism the relationship of members to the association is non-instrumental. It is normal, then, that businesses would not presume that any collective rights or obligations between them or towards third parties exist

Near the end of their treatment of group agents, Pettit and List ask whether corporate agents could be considered persons, and in that capacity not only have responsibilities imputed on them but also have standing to claim that rights be conferred upon them. Their argument depends on a performative conception of personhood, which they distinguish from an intrinsicist conception. The former defines a person according to what it *does*: 'the mark of personhood is the ability to play a certain role, to perform in a certain way',[82] while the latter invokes some conscious state or substance that singles out personhood. The performative conception is satisfied if 'persons, natural or corporate, are distinguished by the fact that they can enter a system of obligations recognized in common with others, and limit their influence on one another to that permitted within the terms of that system.'[83]

But is the performative conception of personhood sufficient to ground the pluralist understanding or associations? Perhaps this is not strictly necessary. Perhaps pluralists like Figgis simply went too far in their evocations of organic life. Figgis, after all, not only thought that groups were performative agents, but also that they shaped and structured individual personality. He proposed that individual personality was dependent on associative membership as a matter of social psychology—'personality is a social fact; no individual could ever come to himself except as a member of a society, and the membership of any society does not leave even the adult individual where he was.'[84] And he steadfastly held that groups had inherent life, that they had a self-understanding that could grow, deepen, and develop with time. Jacob Levy distinguished Figgis' evocative description of personality from Maitland's more sober and lawyerly one.

> There is tremendous distance between saying that groups will be spontaneously socially viewed as persons in the sense of being right-and-duty bearers, and that the law ought to reflect this, and saying that groups are persons in the sense of having inherent life, much less organic life.... Among the attributes of natural persons is that they *grow*, they *develop*. They change over time in ways that are at least partly self-directed. They are capable, to use a word Figgis does not but might have, of *Bildung*.[85]

prior to formal incorporation (except perhaps some rights that arise in the good faith contemplation of imminent incorporation), while it is odd to think that members of an unofficial religious organization can simultaneously think of themselves as a group and dismiss the existence of any special obligation between themselves.

[82] List and Pettit, note 31, 171.

[83] List and Pettit, note 31, 178.

[84] Figgis, note 12, 70–71; Avigail Eisenberg focuses her study of pluralism precisely on the aspects that bear on the psychological development of individuals. Avigail Eisenberg, *Reconstructing Political Pluralism* (SUNY Press, 1995).

[85] Levy, note 10, 37.

The idea of group *Bildung* is intriguing. The concept is most famously associated with Wilhelm von Humboldt, who used it to structure his theory of education as well as his political theory. In its essence, it states that the highest vocation of an individual is his self-development, the fullest realization of his innate capacities. In *The Limits of State Action*, he declares that '[t]he true end of Man, or that which is prescribed by the eternal and immutable dictates of reason, and not suggested by vague and transient desires, is the highest and most harmonious development of his powers to a complete and consistent whole.'[86] There is a political connection between Humboldt's idea of *Bildung* and the pluralist insistence on group autonomy. Because complete self-directed freedom is necessary to achieve such development, Humboldt calls for limiting the functions of the state so as to allow individuals the largest space of self-development.[87] As Raymond Geuss observes '[s]tate action directed at providing for the welfare of its citizens will both prevent the individual citizens from being self-active and will tend to create uniformity of conditions; this will have a deleterious effect on the *Bildung* of the individuals in the state.'[88]

It is no surprise, then, if we assume—following Levy—that Figgis means something like *Bildung* when he writes about the organic development of a group, that Figgis too would privilege the role of the state as 'guardian of property and interpreter of contract.'[89] At stake was the recognition of churches and other associations 'as a social union with an inherent original power of self-development, acting as a person with a mind and will of its own.'[90] Opposed to this idea of self-development was the theory that the church existed only as a creature of the state or of its original acts of incorporation.

> What really concerns us is not so much whether or no a religious body be in the technical sense established, but whether or no it be conceived as possessing any living power of self-development, or whether it is conceived either as a creature of the State, or if allowed a private title is to be held rigidly under the trust-deeds of her foundation, thereby enslaved to the dead. Not indeed that all change should be taken as admissible, but that those changes sanctioned . . . by the constitutional authority of the Church, and declared by them to be in accordance with the spirit of their society, should be accepted as such by the courts, and no further question asked. In other words, is the life of the

[86] Wilhelm von Humboldt, *The Limits of State Action* (Liberty Fund, 1993) 10.

[87] David Sorkin, 'Wilhelm Von Humboldt: The Theory and Practice of Self-Formation (Bildung), 1791–1810' (1983) 44(1) *Journal of the History of Ideas* 55, 59.

[88] Raymond Geuss, 'Kultur, Bilung, Geist' (1996) 35(2) *History and Theory* 151, 159.

[89] John Figgis, 'The Church and the Secular Theory of the State' in David Nicholls (ed.), *The Pluralist State: The Political Ideas of JN Figgis and His Contemporaries* (2nd edn) (St. Martin's, 1994), and also *Churches in the Modern State*, note 12, 104.

[90] Figgis, note 12, 99.

> society to be conceived as in inherent or derived? Does the Church exist by some inward living force, with powers of self-development like a person; or is she a mere aggregate, a fortuitous concourse of ecclesiastical atoms, treated it may be as one for purposes of convenience, but with no real claim to a mind or will of her own, except so far as the civil power sees good to invest her for the nonce with a fiction of unity?[91]

Levy argues that Figgis' insistence on the group's right to *Bildung* is a failure of pluralism, since it 'insists that all churches, all associations, are *really* committed to evolution in religious doctrine and congregationalism or majoritarianism in religious authority.'[92] But surely there are dogmatic churches that do not accept ongoing revelation, and hierarchical churches that distinguish sharply the role of the priesthood and episcopate and that of the laity in interpreting doctrine and making decisions for the group. And there are plenty of other associations, like universities, that function on something like an aristocratic principle of governance in which decisional authority is tied to position in a titled hierarchy.

I think that Levy makes too much of the broader import of Figgis' position on the Free Kirk case. In the Free Kirk case, Figgis' vocations overlap, and his ecclesiology becomes hard to distinguish from his political theory. Figgis does not necessarily recommend a congregational or democratic model applicable to all church decisions—as I mentioned before, his pluralism allows for a multiplicity of associations to flourish in the heart of the religious confession—but he does lean towards conciliarism, and rejects, for that reason, a centralized authority on the lines of the Roman Catholic papacy. Now, the structure of authority in an ecclesiastical polity does not necessarily correspond to rigidness of doctrine, since the majority of a church's followers could be more conservative than its leadership (as has been witnessed several times in mainline Protestant denominations over the past few decades),[93] and it is arguably rigidness of doctrine that is ruled out by the *Bildung* model. But it can also be *Bildung* to come to embrace orthodoxy if in doing so one has reflected on one's reasons for adhering to the tried and true, if one develops a better understanding of one's beliefs and a more comprehensive or coherent justification for the institutions by which one orders one's life. Either this reflexive confirmation of orthodoxy or an equally reflexive reform is only possible if the authority of the association is 'accepted as such by the courts,

[91] Figgis, note 12, 39–40. [92] Levy, note 10, 38.

[93] The recent vote on the ordination of women bishops in the Anglican Church is a sad but pertinent example. The vote in favour of allowing ordination passed the houses of bishops and clergy, but fell short of the two-thirds majority required in the house of the laity. This not only demonstrates that it is not always the ecclesiastical officials that enforce more conservative teaching in religious bodies, but also reinforces the claim that the internal decision procedures of a corporate agent, like the Church of England, can yield a group decision that is not only irreducible to, but also vastly divergent from, the opinion of its individual members.

and no further question asked'. The question of *Bildung* becomes a matter of political jurisdiction, as it would in Humboldt.

Is it the group, however, that develops? Is it not the individuals that compose it? In the most straightforward way, it is obviously the individual members. But we should not dismiss the idea of a group *Bildung* so quickly. I would like to call again on List and Pettit's model of supervenience to suggest a way of describing group membership that approximates a deeper notion of group personality. Recall that List and Pettit have a holistic conception of supervenience, in which group attitudes towards a proposition depend on the individual members' attitude towards a set of propositions. What this means is that when individuals act as members of a group they do not only take account of the decision before them, but also of other decisions that they have collectively made and prospectively may be called to make, and they may give priority to some beliefs and attitudes over others.[94] Notably, they may give great priority to their identity as group members, and perhaps extend that identity over time, to consider themselves as continuing an interpersonal or intergenerational endeavour.[95] In this sense, an individual may identify with the group to the point, in List and Pettit's words, of 'investing' oneself in the group, to 'treat group agents as entities that make the same intimate claims on them as their individual selves do.'[96] This is, of course, not a phenomenon that we expect of every group agent, nor should we. But it is a claim of some associations, especially those that the British pluralists like Figgis were most concerned about. This finally links Figgis' social psychology to his description of groups as self-developing. 'Within any social group, if the members are sufficiently loyal, there may grow up all kinds of ties and arrangements which could not be enforced at law, and yet are practically restrictive.'[97] Groups that are formally constituted in a certain way and that provide their members with the capacity of shaping the development of the group, even if it is only towards a greater self-consciousness of the beliefs, values, and practices that animate the association, can create a feedback mechanism in which individual self-awareness is discursively shared. It is impossible to describe each member as developing their understanding of the body without realizing that they are doing it together, that the group itself is moved 'by some inward living force, with powers of self-development like a person.'[98]

[94] This structure holds even if we move away from group doxastic rationality supervening on individual doxastic rationality and towards Ross' alternative of group doxastic rationality supervening on individual behaviour. How an individual behaves is determined in part by attitudes held previously and patters set before the action at hand.

[95] I defend this conception of political society in 'The Problem of a Perpetual Constitution' in Axel Gosseries and Lukas Meyer (eds), *Theories of Intergenerational Justice* (Oxford University Press, 2009), but it is extensible to associations that share the form of the state.

[96] List and Pettit, note 31, 196.

[97] Figgis, note 12, 104.

[98] Figgis, note 12, 40.

11

Property, Personality, and Public Justification

An association can acquire legal personality though the use of legal instruments—corporate forms—that allow its members to present themselves as a single collective agent, and if it is a certain kind of association it can demand that it be accorded legal personality as a matter of right. The acquisition of collective legal personality effects an ontological transformation in the persons who organize themselves into a group: what was before an aggregate of individuals, each of whom was subject to a different set of obligations, is now a single agent capable of assuming obligations and holding others (including its own members) reciprocally accountable. While some common enterprises could be pursued by several individuals acting in concert, but not constituting a separate agent—say, by several mountain climbers cooperating to reach a summit—in the case of associations, members think of themselves as related to a common body, not only as cooperators. Important reasons for attributing personality to an association are that such an attribution conforms to the self-understanding of its members as participants in a common enterprise, that associations possess the institutional capacity to act with singleness of purpose, and that they can represent themselves to their own members and to others as agents.

But the mere self-perception of individuals as participating in a discrete collective enterprise, while necessary for personality to emerge, is not sufficient. Personality is incomplete if the collective agent cannot act as such, if it is incapable of making its intentions effective; if its existence is limited to the internalized understanding of its members. An association must be able to do things as an agent if it is to have any effective personality. To the ontological reality of personhood must be added a practical reality. This reality is best instantiated in the institutions of private law: property, contract, and tort or extra-contractual obligation; I will focus on private property as a paradigmatic case.

II.1 PROPERTY AND PERSONALITY

The importance of property for the existence and exercise of personality is most famously explained by Hegel in *The Philosophy of Right*, and can ultimately be traced to Kant's argument, in the *Metaphysics of Morals*, for the moral necessity of entering the civil condition.[1] Both philosophers argue that property is intrinsically linked to personality, although their discussion is directed at the development of personality in the individual. I will argue, however, that their arguments equally support the concession of personality to associations, and the necessity of making this personality effective through the institution of property.

Kant distinguishes between two ways in which an external object, a thing, may be possessed. The first—empirical possession—refers to actual physical control of something, consequent on one's ability to protect it from appropriation by others. The second—intelligible possession—consists of a guarantee that what one has rightfully acquired will not be appropriated by others, even if it is not in one's (empirical) possession.[2] In the state of nature, that is, in the absence of a civil constitution that determines the rules for the acquisition, use, and alienation of property, all possession is provisional.[3] Physical possession creates at best a presumption that what is possessed rightfully belongs to the possessor (thus its provisional character, as it is held 'in anticipation of and preparation for the civil condition'), but this presumption ultimately depends on 'the mechanical ability, from which I *reside*, to secure my land against encroachment by others.'[4]

In contrast, intelligible possession is conclusive in two ways: first, it is settled, in that it can be ascertained by a public system of rules regarding acquisition, use, and alienation, viz. a civil constitution; second, it is not dependent on physical control, but to a 'concept of the understanding.'[5] According to Kant:

> [s]o the way to have something external as what is mine consists in a merely rightful connection of the subject's will with that object in accordance with the concept of intelligible possession, independently of any relation to it in space and time.—It is not because I occupy a place on the earth with my body that this place is something external which is mine.... It is mine if I still possess it even though I have left for another place; only then is my external right involved.[6]

[1] Georg WH Hegel (A Wood (ed.) and HB Nisbett (tr.)), *Elements of the Philosophy of Right* (Cambridge University Press, 1991); Immanuel Kant, 'The Metaphysics of Morals' in Mary Gregor (ed.), *Practical Philosophy* (Cambridge University Press, 1996).

[2] Kant, note 1, 408–409 (GS 6:255–56).

[3] Kant, note 1, 410 (GS 6:257).

[4] Kant, note 1, 420 (GS 6:269).

[5] Kant, note 1, 407 (GS 6:253).

[6] Kant, note 1, 407–408 (GS 6:253–54).

The possibility of intelligible possession is for Kant not merely a prudential conclusion. It is doubtlessly true that it is more efficient for property claims to hold *erga homnes* than for a provisional owner to be required to secure a promise from every other person who might take possession of the thing were the owner to relinquish physical control of it.[7] But Kant's concern is with the moral implications of the different kinds of possession. Empirical possession reflects only our nature as physical beings, who are free insofar as we willfully control our bodies; but we know ourselves to also be intelligible beings, capable of conforming our will to rules and reasons. As Robert Pippin explains:

> [s]uch beings must be able to avail themselves of exclusive possession in the accomplishment of their ends, and that possession need not be restricted to the empirical conditions of physical possession or proximity. Given that I am a being that can institute rational relations with others, I ought to be able to secure such nonphysical ownership by such relations with others.[8]

In the case of embodied, 'flesh-and-blood' individuals, the distinction between empirical and intelligible possession pertains to their self-conception as rational, and therefore moral, beings. It is possible for an individual to act as a moral being while she is in the state of nature, although her possibilities of moral action will be limited without a civil constitution. She is required to exit the state of nature and enter a civil state because she would otherwise be denying this evident dimension of her personality.

But in the case of corporate persons the possibility of intelligible possession cuts much closer to the essence of personality. There is nothing in a collective agent to correspond to physical control, which rules out purely empirical possession. But there is nothing in the idea of intelligible possession that would rule out corporate persons from conclusively owning things in their own name. The corporate agent, imbued with legal personality, is in the unusual, but by no means incoherent, position of only being able to possess noumenally, and never only phenomenally. Indeed, when a corporate agent acts in its own name there is always a natural person who must perform the physical movements for the action to take place: sign the contract, write the check, publish the decree, etc.[9] There is little to distinguish the action of the corporate person from that of the natural person other than the name, which is a purely intelligible construct.

[7] This is arguably Hobbes' position.

[8] Robert Pippin, 'Mine and Thine? The Kantian State' in Paul Guyer (ed.), *The Cambridge Companion to Kant and Modern Philosophy* (Cambridge University Press, 2006) 431.

[9] Thus the aphorism, credited to Léon Duguit, 'Je n'ai jamais dîné avec une personne morale' is answered by another, attributed to Prof. Jean-Claude Soyer: 'Mais j'ai l'ai souvent vu payer l'addition.'

The fact that a corporate person cannot act except through representatives who conduct themselves in its name, as opposed to natural persons who act in their own name, has been taken as an objection to the real theory of personality. The distinction is real, but the objection is not conclusive. In the absence of a 'civil constitution' (which defines property rights) natural persons clearly exist as physical individuals and can acquire empirical possession of things. Corporate persons do not exist in the same way, and can be said to have only a sociological existence: individuals who conceive of themselves as members of a group may take empirical possession of things with the intention and expectation that these will be used to advance collective aims. But there is no certainty in this—much like there is no certainty in empirical possession, which makes it provisional—and no assurance to outsiders that the actions of a member are, in fact, those of the association.

While Kant admits that, in the hypothetical moment when a transition is made from the state of nature to the civil state, all empirical possession is to be transformed into intelligible possession without regard for the justice or injustice that led to its initial acquisition (thus seeming to trace a causal connection from physicality to property), this is a purely contingent and prudential strategy; it is simply impractical, if not impossible, to settle old scores when entering the civil state. The essential effect of the transition is that it makes property possible. And in making property possible, it makes discrete corporate owners possible, whereas before groups were mere recipients of their members charity. It is only at this point that the 'unity of will and mind' of the association, arrived at through whatever internal mechanisms guide the group's deliberation, can be exercised directly.

II.2 HEGEL ON ABSTRACT RIGHT

In the first part of the *Philosophy of Right*, devoted to abstract right, Hegel also contends that there is a necessary connection between property and personality. His point of departure is the same as Kant's—the consideration of the person in abstraction from her particular ends or from the concrete conditions of social life—but his analysis of the development of personality and its relation to private property is more sophisticated.[10] Hegel is unsatisfied with the purely formal development of personality that occurs at the level of abstract right, which leads him to develop an account of the emergence of morality, and the concrete institutionalization of both legal and

[10] Paul Franco, *Hegel's Philosophy of Freedom* (Yale University Press, 1999) 194; Karl-Heinz Ilting, 'The Structure of Hegel's "Philosophy of Right"' in ZA Pelczynski (ed.), *Hegel's Political Philosophy: Problems and Perspectives* (Cambridge University Press, 1971) 91–92.

moral personality in the sphere of civil society, and ultimately of ethical life in the form of the state. I will not follow Hegel down the entire length of this path for two reasons: first, my aim is more modest than his, and intends only to lay out the political and legal structures that allow for associations to develop autonomously, while leaving open the divergent ways in which they may develop. Second (though relatedly), my normative assumption—pluralism—denies the necessary or desirable unification of purposes, functions, or identities, which is the 'highest goal' of Hegel's organicism.[11]

Nonetheless, Hegel's discussion of abstract right is useful in explaining the relationship between personality as pure self-consciousness and the concrete juridical institutions, such as property, which render such personality concrete, or effective. Hegel's analysis begins with a consideration of the person as self-conscious will. Knox explains that self-consciousness, in this regard, involves a distinction 'between one's self and those determinate characteristics which differentiate one from other people' and an abstraction of 'the unitary self from these determinate characteristics and ignoring or negating these.'[12] That is, the self understands itself as different from other people and things, but at once conceives of itself as a unity, and not merely that which is not-another.[13]

From this starting point, Hegel makes a move similar to Kant's: 'The person' he writes, 'must give himself an external *sphere of freedom* in order to have being as an Idea.'[14] Against advocates of property as an efficient tool for the satisfaction of needs and wants, Hegel defends the institution on the sole ground that it is the vehicle through which a person can relate to another concretely. This bears some explanation. At this point in Hegel's argument, the idea of personality is merely abstract; it is devoid of content, of intentions, desires, and inclinations. The relation between persons in the sphere of abstract right is strictly juridical. It is the relation between generic legal persons, whose interaction with each other occurs without regard to individual characteristics or dispositions, but only through alienable objects owned, or services rendered.

The importance of property for personality, however, is that it allows for freedom, it allows for the will to give itself direction by acting upon the external world. This world itself has no meaning, no purpose, no end. It is the will acting upon it that imbues it with purpose, that is, that uses objects

[11] Ilting, note 10, 129.

[12] Thomas M Knox, 'Translator's Notes' in Thomas M Knox (tr.), *Hegel's Philosophy of Right* (Clarendon Press, 1952) 320 (Knox's reference is to section 40 of Hegel's *Philosophy of Right*).

[13] Several commentators point to the origin of the Hegelian concept of personality in the struggle for recognition. (Franco, note 10, 196–97; Allen W Wood, *Hegel's Ethical Thought* (Cambridge University Press, 1990) 77–93).

[14] Georg WH Hegel, *Philosophy of Right* (first published 1821) §41.

to pursue the objectives of the person. This externalization of the will is necessary because freedom is a practical concept; it involves action, not merely self-contemplation. Now, at this stage in the development of personality all that Hegel considers is the abstract form, which correspond to the legal institutions of private law that are used by legal agents for concrete ends. To understand the formal aspect of these institutions we do not need to know what those ends are. Legal institutions, in the sphere of abstract right, are what Oakeshott calls 'adverbial' rules,[15] or *lex*: 'rules which prescribe the common responsibilities (and the counterpart "rights" to have these responsibilities fulfilled) of agents and in terms of which they put by their characters as enterprisers and put by all that differentiates them from one another and recognize themselves as formal equals—*cives*.'[16]

There are important points of connection between Hegel's analysis of abstract personality, the merely self-conscious will, and the emergence and exercise of personality in associations. Now, Hegel certainly does not subscribe to an account of corporate personality that favours associational autonomy.[17] But the Hegelian development of individual personality though property can help illustrate the institution's importance to associations. As Margaret Radin explains:

> Hegel's incompletely developed notion that property is held by the unit to which one attributes autonomy has powerful implications for the concept of group development and group rights.... [I]n a given social context certain groups are likely to be constitutive of their members in the sense that the members find self-determination only within the groups. This might have political consequences for claims of the group on certain resources of the external world (i.e. property).[18]

Property is important to groups because it consolidates group agency in response to the need to interact with the external world, and especially with non-group members. The members of an association are distinguished from the aggregate of individuals in a mob because of their consciousness of being engaged in a collective enterprise, one that transcends the added wills

[15] Michael Oakeshott, *On Human Conduct* (Oxford University Press, 1975) 55–56 (I will have more to say about Oakeshott's account later).

[16] Oakeshott, note 15, 128.

[17] In the debate between the Germanic idea of corporation as autonomous 'fellowship' and the Roman idea of the corporation as existing by fiat of the state, Hegel 'follows in the tradition of the latter school which makes the legitimacy of the corporation dependent upon the state and does not recognize any "natural" right to associate' (George Heiman, 'The Sources and Significance of Hegel's Corporate Doctrine' in Pelczynski, note 10, 125).

[18] Margaret J Radin, *Reinterpreting Property* (University of Chicago Press, 1993) 47–48 (Later in the chapter, Radin points to 'some fragmentary evidence [that] suggests that *group* property rights, if connected with group autonomy or association, are given enhanced protection' against the exercise of eminent domain, 66).

of its participants. The two elements of self-consciousness, or at least close analogues, are present at this moment: members of an association taken together, when conceiving themselves as a group, understand the group as distinct not only from non-members, but also from the members severally considered. They are also a discrete unit, and not merely an aggregate of persons sharing some trait or disposition. In the same way, red-headed individuals may share a distinguishable characteristic (and may each even be conscious of that fact) but, save for their confederation in a Red-Headed League, they are not a unit.

Property is also important because it allows groups to develop over time. Waldron makes this point as part of his critique of the Hegelian insistence on private property. It is not clear, he argues, that individuality, the differentiation of the will from its surroundings and its assertion as a unitary self, requires something as strong as the institution of private property; why not '[a] system of common (or collective) property [that] may involve assigning rights over objects to individual wills—*this* person has the right to use the tractor today, *that* person has the right to use the tractor tomorrow, and so on?'[19] The development of personality over time, however, requires an enduring relationship with the objects of the external world. According to Waldron, '[t]his is how an object can embody a will—by registering the effects of willing at one point of time and forcing an individual's willing to become consistent and stable over a period.'[20] Indeed, the process by which property helps constitute the personality of a group continues in the will's move towards self-determination, in the sphere of morality. For Hegel, 'the cultivated [*gebildete*] and inwardly developing human being wills that he should himself be present in everything he does.'[21] In property it finds a more concrete instrument for self-development.[22] The incidents of property, especially the capacity to exclude others from its exercise, may favour the development of responsibility both to third-parties, and to the individual members of the association. It may also reinforce the self-understanding of

[19] Jeremy Waldron, *The Right to Private Property* (Clarendon, 1988) 373. [20] Waldron, note 19.

[21] Hegel, note 14, §107. (The root of the term is the same as that of *Bildung*, and the cultivated is contrasted with the uncivilized. See also Allen Wood's comment on the necessity of *Bildung* for the emergence of the moral self, as evidenced in the *Phenomenology of Spirit* and the *Lectures on the Philosophy of World History* (Allen W Wood, *Hegel's Ethical Thought* (Cambridge University Press, 1990) 25).)

[22] This is consistent with Figgis' insistence that associations, as real persons, develop over time. (See e.g. John N Figgis, *Churches in the Modern State* (Thoemmes, 1997) 39–40; David Nicholls, *The Pluralist State: The Political Ideas of J.N Figgis and His Contemporaries* (2nd edn) (St. Martin's, 1994) 66.) Moreover, Jacob T Levy interprets Figgis in terms also consistent with Hegel's. According to Levy, 'Among the attributes of natural persons is that they *grow*, they *develop*. They change over time in ways that are at least partly self-directed. They are capable, to use a word Figgis does not but might have, of *Bildung*' (Jacob T Levy, 'Liberalism, Pluralism, and Medievalism' ('Principles of Association in British History' conference, Nicholson Center at the University of Chicago, 8 April 2005).)

members of the group by exhibiting the consequences of their agency *qua* association, as opposed to their separable agency *qua* individuals.

This self-understanding, which is analogous to the self-consciousness of the association, is distinguishable from the formal institutions of deliberation that allows an association to arrive at discrete decisions and make its will known to its members and to others. But the self-consciousness of the group and its institutions of decision-making are closely related, and emerge and develop together. It should not be ignored, however, that formal institutions may sometimes also undermine the values of the group. Thus, Robert Cover writes:

> [w]ere there some pure paideic normative order for a fleeting moment, a philosopher would surely emerge to challenge the illusion of its identity with truth.... Differences arise immediately about the meaning of creeds, the content of common worship, the identity of those who are brothers and sisters. But even the imagined instant of unified meaning is like a seed, a legal DNA, a genetic code by which the imagined integration is the template for a thousand real integrations of corpus, discourse, and commitment.[23]

Lon Fuller also distinguishes between two different principles of association: association on the basis of 'shared commitment', which is to say 'for the achievement of shared ends and purposes', and association on the basis of 'legal principle... where an association is held together and enabled to function by formal rules of duty and entitlement.'[24] Fuller recognizes that both principles are operative, to some degree, in all associations, but observes that, over time, the legal principle tends to become dominant, weakening the bonds of shared commitment. This development is tied to the growth and success of the association; as the 'tangible advantages' of membership increase the demand for explicit procedures of governance will increase, and eventually embroil the state legal system in the affairs of the group.[25] What Fuller calls 'creeping legalism' may be the price to pay for the effective deployment of personality.

II.3 PROPERTY AND PUBLIC JUSTIFICATION

As property may facilitate the development of a discrete personality in associations,[26] it also structures the normative relation that they have with non-members and other associations. In effect, property exempts associations

[23] Robert Cover, 'Nomos and Narrative' (1983) 97 *Harvard Law Review* 4, 16. (The 'paideic', for Cover, is a system of normative life characterized by strong, 'culture-specific designs of particularist meaning'.)

[24] Lon L Fuller, 'Two Principles of Human Association' in Kenneth Winston (ed.), *Principles of Social Order* (Hart, 2001) 85.

[25] Fuller, note 24, 90ff.

[26] As noted, the role of property is complemented by other institutions of private law, most notably contractual and extra-contractual obligation.

(just as much as individuals) from some of the burden to publicly justify their actions. Because of this exemption, the institutions of private property enable associations to pursue their own distinct goals, within a legal order that is morally justifiable on independent grounds.

The argument is grounded on the distinction, made by John Rawls over several decades, between the justification of institutions, on one hand, and actions that take place within the framework of these institutions. In an early essay, Rawls attempted to defend utilitarianism by distinguishing between two different levels of justification, one which asked agents to consider the consequences of their actions in each particular case, and another which demanded consideration of the consequences of the practice within which the action occurred. There is, for Rawls, a 'distinction between the justification of the general system of rules . . . and the justification of particular applications of these rules to particular cases by the various officials whose job it is to administer them.'[27] This distinction made certain kinds of principles available at different levels of argument. According to Rawls,

> [i]ndeed, the point of the practice is to abdicate one's title to act in accordance with utilitarian and prudential considerations in order that the future may be tied down and plans coordinated in advance. . . . It is a mistake to think that if the practice is justified on utilitarian grounds then the promisor must have complete liberty to use utilitarian arguments to decide whether or not to keep his promise. The practice forbids this general defense; and it is a purpose of the practice to do this.[28]

Over the years, Rawls abandoned the attempt to justify utilitarianism, but retained the distinction between the two levels of justification. Now, in the early essay, Rawls' language seems to consider the intercession of the rules of a practice to be a sort of interdiction, an 'abdication' of the prerogative to appeal directly to moral principles in order to justify one's actions. But in later works the distinction between the two levels of justification undergoes a re-evaluation, and is revealed as emancipating, not restrictive. In *A Theory of Justice*, Rawls applies the distinction to 'background institutions', with a clear focus on economic justice. The basic structure of society—the arrangement of the major institutions which 'define men's rights and duties and influence their life prospects'[29] —operates through ordinary social mechanisms, not

[27] John Rawls, 'Two Concepts of Rules' in Samuel Freeman (ed.), *Collected Papers* (Harvard University Press, 1999) 27 (As Rawls points out at the start of the essay, he did not originate this distinction, but it is now familiar through his statement and elaboration of it).

[28] Rawls, note 27, 31. [29] Rawls, note 27, 6.

through the deliberate intervention of individuals.[30] He makes this clear in the restatement of his theory:

> [s]ince a public conception of justice needs clear, simple, and intelligible rules, we rely on an institutional division of labor between principles required to preserve background justice and principles that apply directly to particular transactions between individuals and associations. Once this division of labor is set up, individuals and associations are then left free to advance their (permissible) ends within the framework of the basic structure, secure in the knowledge that elsewhere in the social system the regulations necessary to preserve background justice are in force.[31]

Principles of justice apply to the arrangement of background institutions, not to the behaviour of individuals within them. The latter is justified by references to the public rules of the basic structure, and does not need to be further justified in terms of higher principles.[32]

Rawls' realization, in *Political Liberalism*, that the position he had elaborated in *A Theory of Justice* was inadequate to address the plurality of reasonable comprehensive doctrines in a liberal-democratic society, makes the distinction between the two levels of justification more salient. The major institutions of society, including the institutions of private law, may need to be justified by common principles, but particular transactions within the system do not need to be. They may be pursued because of a host of reasons that are not necessarily shared by other individuals or associations. A plurality of conceptions of the good may find shelter in a conception of the right. While the basic structure may be instituted to preserve the conditions of justice, these do not constitute a 'final end' of society, but rather terms of association through which justice is achieved.[33] Within these

[30] Rawls, note 27, 76. Rawls uses an infelicitous image to explain the operation of background institutions—four (or perhaps five) 'branches' of government charged with allocation (to regulate the price system and prevent monopoly), stabilization (to bring about full employment), transfer (to ensure a social minimum), and distribution (to prevent the accumulation of wealth through inheritance and gift taxes); a possibly fifth branch, of exchange (to raise revenue for the provision of public goods) is mentioned a few pages later. The image of government branches had the effect of painting background institutions very much in the foreground of social action, subject to constant corrective measures to maintain the conditions of justice-as-fairness. In *Justice as Fairness: A Restatement* this image is dropped and a mere mention of 'laws regulating bequest and inheritance of property, and other devices such as taxes': John Rawls, *Justice as Fairness: A Restatement* (Harvard University Press, 2001) 51.

[31] Rawls, note 27, 54.

[32] Similar reasoning undergirds the four-stage sequence for making social decisions. See John Rawls, *A Theory of Justice: Revised Edition* (Harvard University Press, 1999) 171–76.

[33] John Rawls, *Political Liberalism* (Columbia University Press, 1993) 41–42. Rawls is ambiguous on the question of whether society has a common end, and how that end should be characterized. On the one hand, he quotes Michael Oakeshott approvingly and seems to align himself with Oakeshott's distinction between civil and enterprise association, ascribing the characteristics of the former to society and the latter to associations. On the other hand, he does expressly refer to citizen's 'common shared end of justice.' I believe the two constructions are not contradictory.

terms, associations may pursue their own ends for their own reasons. In this context, both individuals and associations may espouse reasonable doctrines, yet even when the purposes of an association do not rise to the level of comprehensive doctrine, they may shape and partly constitute the doctrines of their members.

The further distinction that Rawls draws between public and non-public reason is also important. Public reason is the reason of citizens, directed at the good of the public and matters of fundamental justice, and carried out in public view, in an open forum, within the context of 'the ideal and principles expressed by society's conception of political justice.'[34] Non-public reason, by contrast, is the reason of associations. It is, Rawls clarifies, public with respect to their members, but not to the citizens generally.[35] Different ideals and principles may apply in deliberation that occurs within an association than that which occurs in society generally. Necessarily, then, every individual who is both a citizen and a member of an association will be engaged in different spheres of reason at different times. What the citizen owes to a fellow citizen, in terms of reasonableness, is not what she owes to a fellow associate.

What is the institutional conclusion of these distinctions between levels of justification, and between spheres of public and non-public reason? It points, again, to the institution of property, and especially to its capacity to shield an owner from the burden of justification determining the use to which an object is put. Now, it is clear that property rules must be justified through moral principles. Even arguments that seek to derive property rights from natural law ascribe moral value to that law, and arguments that appeal to efficiency elevate the justificatory power of that criterion over, say, that of civic virtue or distributive justice. The justification of property, however, does not attend to all the possible incidents to which owners may put the objects they own. Owners of property, for the most part, are left to use their possessions as they see fit, within the rules that govern the institution.

The distinction between the two levels of rules that Rawls develops reflect the actual operation or the judicial adjudication of property disputes. When controversies over the ownership or use of a certain object arise, moreover, it is usually neither necessary nor advisable to appeal to principles of justice in resolving it. The question of whether a house belongs to Alex or to Brenda does not turn on who needs the house more urgently, or whose behaviour has made them more deserving of the dwelling. It turns on who holds the title, who signed the deed, in brief, who complied with the adverbial rules of acquisition, possession, use, and disposition of the thing. And once the question of title has been settled, the use of the house is at the owner's discretion.

[34] Rawls, note 33, 213.

[35] Rawls, note 33, 220.

Certainly, the owner may be subject to general norms of behaviour which somewhat restrict the use of her property, but these ordinarily only circumscribe marginal behaviour that threatens the interests of third-parties.[36] For the most part:

> [o]wnership... expresses the abstract idea of an object being correlated with the name of some individual, in relation to a rule which says that society will uphold that individual's decision as final when there is any dispute about how the object should be used.[37]

In the context of public versus non-public reason, moreover, property creates a jurisdictional space in which associations may deliberate in light of their own principles and goals, and in accordance with whatever decision procedure they see fit. A hierarchical church may ascribe all administration of houses of worship, alms, and maintenance of clergy to a bishop, while a congregational one makes all decisions through direct democratic deliberation. Neither the structure of their decision-making, nor the principles in light of which the decision is made need to be justified to outsiders. It is sufficient that the use to which the property is put comply with the general rules of the institution for the justificatory burden to be discharged.

Under conditions of reasonable pluralism, private property in the hands of an association allows for the structural differentiation of the public and non-public sphere, which may follow different justificatory, and often incommensurable, logics. Gerald Gaus emphasizes the point: '[a] regime of rights, and in particular of regime of private or "several" property, is a form of social commensuration or, perhaps better understood, a way to avoid the requirement of social commensuration.'[38] After citing Waldron's summary of the institution of ownership, Gaus adds that '[f]rom a moral perspective, a system of private property lessens the burdens of public justification and the demands on devices of social commensuration.'[39] It is precisely the release from the burden of justification that makes property so fundamental to the exercise of autonomy by associations.

To summarize, property allows associations to exercise and develop a discrete legal personality. There are different ways of arriving at this conclusion;

[36] The case of closed residential communities is an exception, but these communities are, for the most part, associations. The restrictions on ownership that they enact are ostensibly in pursuit of associational objectives, and the residents of these communities are simultaneously private owners and members of the association. Restrictive covenants in an otherwise open neighbourhood, however, would not necessarily pass this test.

[37] Waldron, note 19, 47.

[38] Gerald Gaus, 'Public Justification and the Moral Right of Private Property' (Workshop on Capitalism and Morality, University of North Carolina-Chapel Hill, 9-10 April 2004), 26 <http://www.unc.edu/~jabaker/gaus.pdf> accessed 16 September 2012.

[39] Gaus, note 38.

I have explicated a Kantian route that lays emphasis on property as intelligible, as opposed to empirical possession, and a Hegelian account that emphasizes the role that private property plays in the development of individuality. The two routes are complementary. The Kantian strategy begins with the difference between so-called natural and juristic or corporate persons, a difference that has often been used to undermine the claim of the latter to legitimacy; it concludes, however, that it is precisely the intelligibility, as opposed to physicality, of property that puts associations on a par with flesh-and-blood individuals.

The Hegelian strategy traces the development of personality through differentiation from the external world and assertion as a unity, which occurs in associations as much as in individuals, because associations, to have a discrete existence, must differentiate themselves both from the external world and from the several personalities of their own members. Through the ownership of property associations assert their discreteness, and also become capable of self-development; the use of property, however, is not without dangers to (at least some) associations, because it may weaken the social bonds of the group and replace them with legalistic proceduralism.

The concern with the development of personality that is at the heart of Hegel's account incorporates a concern for individuality, for differentiation between the person and the world, which includes not only things but other agents. In the case of associations, this differentiation is manifested in the distinct, non-public, reason that guides deliberation among members. But the exercise of such reason demands a jurisdictional boundary between the public and the associative spheres. Because the institutions of private law, and those of private property in particular, distinguish two levels of justification—justification of the institution itself and justification of actions taken within the institution—they are especially capable of providing the structure in which associations may act autonomously, in pursuance of their particular ends.

CONCLUSION

And I see that richness so largely evolved out of the multiplicity of groups which are trying to think out some way of life, crudely and in ill enough fashion if you like, that where they conflict with the state, the reality, as I see it of the corporate mind, the intrinsic value of their real effort, makes me hesitate to say that they must yield, *e.g.* the Roman Church was right as against Bismarck in the *Kulturkampf* and Rome as against Titus Oates. I want my variety validated in its freedom to make itself felt. I hope I am clear.

—Harold J Laski to Oliver Wendell Holmes

12

The Spectre of Intractability

The kind of associational pluralism that I have described helps to explain the pretensions of various associations to be final arbiters of disputes that arise in a certain sphere, and to define—or at least contest—the boundaries of that sphere. This is what I think that the British pluralists, Figgis especially, meant by sovereignty, and what I have tentatively defined as an institutionalized claim of legitimate meta-jurisdictional authority. In short, associational pluralism renders these claims intelligible, at least more intelligible than rival explanations. The associations that I discuss—churches (and religious institutions more generally), universities, professional associations, and cities—are those that historically concerned the British pluralists, which gives them a certain claim to priority in the discussion. But I think that the theoretical reasons for discussing them go deeper than mere intellectual biography.

There are two reasons for focusing on these 'robust' associations. The first is that they are—now and historically—the associations that make the strongest and more salient institutionalized claims to legitimate meta-jurisdictional authority. The central case of political pluralism has always been the confrontation between spiritual and temporal power, between church and state, between the Roman Catholic Pope and the Holy Roman Emperor. With the French Revolution, the imperial power was replaced first by the sovereign people, then by a succession of emperors and kings, and eventually by the Republic. With the Protestant Reformation, Christendom was fragmented into many churches and denominations, and the ecclesiastical category eventually expanded to non-Christian groups. But the opposition between ecclesiastical and state authority did not diminish. Even those British pluralists whose interest in cutting state sovereignty down to size was motivated by their sympathies to the emerging labour unions and the guild socialist movement—Laski the most prominent among them—devoted many pages to the confrontation between church and state.[1]

[1] Harold Laski, *Studies in the Problem of Sovereignty* (Yale University Press, 1917), *The Foundations of Sovereignty and Other Essays* (Harcourt, Brace and Co., 1921).

Aside from the church, there are few other groups that have consistently resisted the state's claims to a monopoly of sovereignty on the grounds that they, not the state, had the inherent authority to govern their members. One of these has been the universities and, by extension, the universal community of scholars, which have elevated the principle of academic freedom to the level of constitutional norm. Another has been the liberal professions, especially those of medicine and the law, for which professional ethics serves a similar constitutional role.

In a different way, the old *lex mercatoria* that defined relations among tradesmen has also persisted into modern commercial law, and the guilds have given way not only to professional organizations but also to labour unions. But the business corporations do not habitually raise the same type of claims to associational autonomy that churches, universities, and professions do; their contestation now takes the form of individualist freedom of commerce or the language of efficiency. As for labour unions, they have retained the language of solidarity and of contestation against state power, but have also turned their interest away from autonomy and self-help (which was the goal of early syndicalists) and towards the negotiation of more favourable working conditions for their members. Somewhat less emphatically, local governments have often aspired to, and sometimes claimed, an authority that is derived from the distinctive social fact of urban cohabitation and is not reducible to the claims of the central (national or provincial) state. I feel that there are arguments germane to those of associational pluralism in both cases, and I think that a pluralist analysis can clarify some of their sources of contention with government, but they are different enough to be distinguished and generally omitted from the present account.

The second reason for focusing on these associations has to do with the genealogy of our political institutions. One of the surprising patterns to emerge from the list of claimants to pluralist authority is that most of these associations or their immediate predecessors trace their origin to medieval institutions. It is no coincidence that the high-point of medieval pluralism, the renaissance brought on by the rediscovery of the Digest of Justinian and the Gregorian reform of the eleventh and the twelfth centuries, is also the moment in which the Papacy makes its strongest claims to exclusive authority over the personnel and property of the church, now organized as a formally corporate body; in which the students of Bologna and the masters of Paris constitute themselves as educational corporations with authority to regulate admittance, accreditation, and discipline of their members; in which legal advisors and advocates constitute themselves into a profession, giving themselves a code of ethics and demanding criteria for admission to legal practice; and in which cities, grown full of merchants and craftsmen who sought to gain from the dramatic increase in trade ushered by the Crusades, demanded charters of self-rule and gave themselves a law to govern them as citizens. The choice of cases is determined, in part, by this common medieval lineage.[2]

But it is justified through a narrative about the foundations of the modern state—one may perhaps call it a genealogy—that argues that liberal democracy is not only the result of a seamless progression from the nailing of Luther's theses on the Wittenberg church door, through Hobbesian individualism, Lockean self-ownership, Kantian autonomy, and Millian self-realization, and eventually to the Rawlsian synthesis.[3] That story—the story of the modern liberal democratic state as the victory over all things medieval—is in many ways a true story. I want to stress this: the story of the modern state *is* the story of opposition to the entrenched and hierarchical pluralism of the Middle Ages. But it is also—simultaneously, contradictorily, irreconcilably—a story of continuity with some (positively labelled) medieval institutions and incomplete victory against other (negatively labelled) ones. The failure to acknowledge the constitutive tension at the heart of liberalism obscures its own genealogy and distorts its capacity to confront associational pluralism. This would not be a problem if associational pluralism could be subordinated and conscripted to serve the post-Reformation narrative of liberal democracy, or if the character of all organizations could be reshaped to conform with principles of liberal and democratic legitimacy; these false and dangerous hopes Nancy Rosenblum has labelled the *logic of congruence* and the *liberal expectancy*.[4]

But the story, so told, is incomplete and ignores or distorts the pluralist tensions that persist in modern societies. The medieval order was generally displaced, at least as a grand narrative of order and legitimacy, and the dignity of the undifferentiated citizen took its place. But as the institutions of liberal democracy built on medieval precedents and repurposed medieval institutions, they were unable to entirely suppress or alter their previous meanings, and the narratives of autonomy and the claims to independent authority persisted and never settled comfortably in the new order. Some of the inheritance of the middle ages was transformed in a kind of dialectical sublation that developed the system of estates into the separation of powers; the principalities and duchies, palatinates and counties, free cities, and

[2] There are many histories of the medieval ancestry of modern institutions. Joseph Strayer's *On the Medieval Origins of the Modern State* (Princeton University Press, 1970) is a classic, as is by now Harold Berman's *Law and Revolution* (Harvard University Press, 1983).

[3] The most pugnacious statement of this genealogy is probably Stephen Holmes, *Passions and Constraint* (University of Chicago Press, 1995). For a critical assessment of Rawls' own genealogy, see Ronald Beiner, 'John Rawls' Genealogy of Liberalism' in Shaun P Young, *Reflections on Rawls: An Assessment of His Legacy* (Ashgate, 2009) 73–89.

[4] Nancy Rosenblum, *Membership and Morals* (Princeton University Press, 1998).

bishoprics of the ancient constitution into federal states; and the royal charters and privileges of peerage and clergy into modern bills of rights. This the state internalized and came to justify (sometimes tortuously) as manifestations of the will of the people as sovereign, although it was sometimes hard to discern who the people were, especially in federations where one boundary was drawn around the province and another around the national state, and in what fashion they remained sovereign, when the constituent power had been delegated and divided and numerous obstacles been placed to preclude its direct popular exercise.

This story is not new, and has emerged as an influential voice in the theorization of the modern state which tends to disrupt the narrative, running from Hobbes to Rawls, that emphasizes the primacy of citizenship. Harold Berman, as I have already mentioned, argued that '[p]erhaps the most distinctive characteristic of the Western legal tradition is the coexistence and competition within the same community of diverse jurisdictions and diverse legal systems', and went further in claiming that the competition between overlapping legal orders has been decisive to the development of the rule of law.

> Legal pluralism originated in the differentiation of the ecclesiastical polity from secular polities. The church declared its freedom from secular control, its exclusive jurisdiction in some matters, and its concurrent jurisdiction in other matters.... The pluralism of Western law, which has both reflected and reinforced the pluralism of Western political and economic life, has been, or once was, a source of development, or growth legal growth as well as political and economic growth. It also has been, or once was, a source of freedom. A serf might run to the town court for protection against his master. A vassal might run to the king's court for protection against his lord. A cleric might run to the ecclesiastical court for protection against the king.[5]

The distinctiveness of the pluralist legacy identified by Berman is that freedom is guaranteed not only by the liberal principles internal or endogenous to the state, but also by the presence of external authorities that push against state authority. This argument resembles the familiar triad of exit, voice, and loyalty that is often invoked when allowing a sphere of multicultural toleration to cultural or religious communities.[6] But on closer examination, Berman reverses the argument by presenting the state—even the most just and liberal state—as an authority in need of limits, precisely because absent these limits it will have difficulty limiting itself, curbing its advance into all areas of social life, even those that it had little hand in creating and those that have, through independent development, turned to values very different from those of liberal democracy.

[5] Harold Berman, *Law and Revolution* (Harvard University Press, 1983) 9.

[6] Albert O Hirschman, *Exit, Voice, and Loyalty* (Harvard University Press, 1970).

> Underlying the competition of ecclesiastical and royal courts from the twelfth to the sixteenth centuries was the limitation on the jurisdiction of each: neither pope nor king could command the total allegiance of any subject. Becket died for the principle that royal jurisdiction was not unlimited (which the king did not deny) and that it was not for the secular authority alone to decide where its boundaries should be fixed (his assassins did deny that).[7]

Berman admits that 'time was on the side of the expansion of the secular jurisdiction at the expense of the ecclesiastical'[8] and that once the church—and the panoply of plural jurisdictions—became merely voluntary associations (though Berman qualifies that this happened only 'in the secular mind' as many churches' conception of membership is not one of unrestrained entrance and exit) they were effectively absorbed into the legal system of the nation-state. Berman observes that limits to national jurisdiction remain most forcefully in the form of federal jurisdictional constraints, but also in constitutional limits to state authority. The most important thing to note about these limits is that, though they appear as internal limits on state authority, as corollaries of liberalism's insistence on the inviolability of a private sphere, they are hardly ever completely justifiable in terms of liberal democratic principles. There is still 'a residual conflict of jurisdictions and of laws'.

> There are still restrictions upon the power of legislatures and courts to interfere in purely religious affairs and to punish purely moral activities. There are still difficulties in defining the legal boundaries of these affairs and activities. There is still the belief or was, until recently that if the legal boundaries set by the state conflict with a higher law, then there is a right and a duty to violate them.[9]

Berman adds to the pluralist argument by insisting on the *legality* of non-state authority, whether that of the church, the university, the merchant guild, the town, and even the royal court. The articulation of claims to authority through law performs a dual function: it makes the claims of one intelligible to the other and allows certain kinds of reasons to be raised to justify the assertion of jurisdiction or resist encroachments upon it. But it also guarantees that all persons, no matter which jurisdiction they may fall under, are covered by *some* law. The pluralism that Berman describes is anarchic only in a narrow and technical sense, and it depends on the effective and reliable exercise of legal authority at all levels and in all spheres, and the coincidence of tension between these authorities at the margins but mutual confidence that those subjects even to a different law are not outlaws, but always legal subjects.[10]

[7] Berman, note 2, 269. [8] Berman, note 2, 269. [9] Berman, note 2, 269.

[10] There is an obvious parallel to the extreme aversion that international law has for statelessness, which more than being motivated by humanitarian concerns (which perhaps should play a larger role here) is

But some of the medieval inheritance was not internalized because it could not be comprehended in terms of a single popular sovereign will, but rather held back from that will and remained in opposition to it. This is a natural corollary of democratic government, legitimized and shaped by legitimate liberal concerns for the protection of individual dignity. But as such it displays little patience for alternate sources of legitimation and external limits to the exercise of its authority. Tocqueville astutely diagnosed the phenomenon:

> The Americans believe that in each state supreme power should emanate directly from the people, but once this power has been constituted, they can hardly conceive any limits to it. They freely recognize that it has the right to do everything. As for particular privileges granted to towns, families, or individuals, they have forgotten the possibility of such things. It has never come into their heads that one cannot simply apply the same law uniformly to all the parts of one state and all the men living in it.... In all of them the idea of intermediate powers is obscured and obliterated.... the idea of the omnipotence and sole authority of society at large is coming to fill its place.[11]

The applicability of different legal norms to priests, scholars, guildsmen, merchants and burghers, while a natural (if far from uncontested) aspect of medieval constitutionalism, can find little justification in the logic of the modern state. The status of citizen first asserts itself as superior to all other statuses, thus denying the possibility of tragic conflict among claims to authority. It then reduces those statuses to mere voluntary membership, denying incommensurability among them. The foundational plurality of claims is, by then, trivial or non-existent, since individual affirmation is the only and common source of legitimacy among associative obligations. Yet, for many subjects, those statuses persist and the claims of various associations to their loyalty and obedience do not always sit well with claims of state supremacy. That is not to say that crisis of conscience are constant and pervasive. Most of the time, for members of most mainline denominations, there is little conflict between civic and religious obligation; for most university professors, there are even fewer occasions in which academic freedom is directly infringed by government policy; and it is in rare cases that professionals ethics directly contravene government directives. We should see the rarity of these cases as a welcome historical achievement, but it should

due to the fear that a stateless person has no one to answer to and no one responsible for her. Of note, also, is Berman's observation of the removal of disputes from secular to an ecclesiastical court, even in cases outside the ordinary competence of canon law courts, by prior agreement of the parties (who considered ecclesiastical law much better developed than the primitive secular systems of the time) or by petition of the parties on the grounds of 'default of secular justice'. Berman, note 2, 223.

[11] Alexis de Tocqueville (JP Meyer (ed.), George Lawrence (tr.)), *Democracy in America* (HarperCollins, 1969) 669 [internal paragraph breaks omitted].

not blind us to the novelty of this truce and the persistence of important conflicts at the margin.

That the lack of constant conflict is, in part, a product of mutual adjustment and accommodation between the state and other associations which has resulted in the former allowing a wide sphere of non-interference in civil society that protects associations (as in the individual guarantee of freedom of assembly) and the latter moderating its claims (in the case of the church) or collaborating with state and market forces for its own gain and preservation (in the case of universities and professional associations). These adjustments, however, disguise a good measure of self-delusion about the claims to authority that each side is making. The state's retreat from some spheres of social life is not only motivated by the internal premises of liberal democracy, but in many cases is a post-hoc rationalization of resistance by associations themselves.[12] By the same token, associations have substantively amended their positions and come to accept as legitimate arrangements that they previously denounced and only begrudgingly tolerated.[13] This is an inevitable and welcome consequence of pluralism, and is as old as the Concordat of Worms. A society with many cross-cutting, overlapping, and competing allegiances should lead to some adjustment and compromise on all sides. But it does not lead to complete capitulation or permanent subordination of one authority by another. The action, again, is at the margins where there remains what Perry Dane has called a 'specter of intractability' that haunts the confrontation of law and religion.[14] I would take the image further and claim that a spectre of intractability haunts the confrontation between state law and all robust associations. Churches, universities, and professions make claims that are unintelligible except as declarations of meta-jurisdictional authority, and the state accommodates some (though by no means all) of these in ways that are unintelligible except as a tacit acknowledgement of such authority.

The examples of the associations mentioned illustrate how incomplete is the monopolization of meta-jusrisdictional authority by the state, and how plural sources of authority are either presumed in state legislation itself, or asserted—even against the state—by various associations. I have not

[12] The best case is the *Querelle des inventaires*, the popular resistance against the confiscation of church property by the Third French Republic following the 1905 Law of Separation of Church and State. Madeleine Reberioux, *La Rèpublique Radicale?* (Éditions du Seuil, 1975) 83–88.

[13] Again, the religious example is the core case and can be traced from Leo XIII's the condemnation of wide-ranging religious toleration in *Immortale Dei* to the Second Vatican Council's declaration of religious freedom in *Dignitatis Humanae*. The development of Christian Democracy in Europe presents a more ecumenical example.

[14] Perry Dane, 'Constitutional Law and Religion' in Dennis Patterson (ed.), *A Companion to Philosophy of Law and Legal Theory* (Blackwell, 2010) 119–31, 128.

attempted a substantive defence of the claims to authority of the various groups mentioned. I suspect that not all such claims to authority will succeed (though I am probably more sympathetic than most to many of such claims) and those that do succeed may do so on a variety of grounds.[15] But I do think that clarifying the structure of these claims is necessary in order to evaluate them morally, politically, and legally. The pluralist account I offer is a better descriptor than alternatives that do not take account of the multiple sources of authority whose interaction constitutes our social world.

In essence, the pluralist account contends that associations—at least the 'robust associations' I have described—not only make an institutionalized claim to legitimate meta-jurisdictional authority, but are more-or-less constituted by *competing* claims to authority. This description applies as much to the state as to other associations, and is reflected in the two-levels of state authority that I described before. Some associations (say, churches) make a very strong claim to authority, one that is in principle independent of recognition by another. But as soon as these associations begin to interact with non-members, or even to encounter disagreement among their own, they need to rely on mediating legal institutions. Insofar as the state, in exercising its second-order authority, provides common legal forms that associations may use to give effect to their corporate agency, this external authority comes to bear on them too. The disputes between the association's self-understanding and the legal forms that it uses to make that self-understanding effective inevitably give rise to incongruence, but this incongruence is endemic to associative life under conditions of pluralism.

[15] It is not obvious that political pluralism must seek the grounds of the authority of associations, including the state, on a plurality of principles. It may be that the same general principle (say, the agreement of the participants in an association) grounds the authority of more than one group without providing ways to arbitrate between competing claims among the groups. But it may also be the case that some claims to authority are grounded in one way and other claims to authority (made by the same group or by other groups) are grounded in a different way. Some of these sources of authority may be commensurable; others may not be. Jonathan Wolff makes a similar argument about political obligation, which is the correlative of authority: Jonathan Wolff 'Pluralistic Models of Political Obligation' *Philosophica* 56(2): 7–27 (1995).

Bibliography

Althusius J (FS Carney (ed. and tr.)), *Politica* (Liberty Fund, 1995)

Ares JMB, 'Les Corps Politiques dans la "République" de Jean Bodin' in J-M Servet (ed.), *Jean Bodin: Actes de Colloque Interdisciplinaire d'Angers, 24-27 Mai 1984* (Presses de l'Université d'Angers, 1985)

Aristotle (C Lord (tr.)), *Politics* (University of Chicago Press, 1984)

Austin J (HLA Hart (ed.)), *The Province of Jurisprudence Determined* (Hackett, 1998)

Banting K and Kymlicka W, 'Canadian Multiculturalism: Global Anxieties and Local Debates' (2009) 23(1) *British Journal of Canadian Studies* 43

Barber NW, *The Constitutional State* (Oxford University Press, 2011)

Barber NW, 'The Limited Modesty of Subsidiarity' (2005) 11(3) *European Law Journal* 308

Barker E, 'The Discredited State' (1915) 2 *Political Quarterly* 101

Barry B, *Culture and Equality* (Harvard University Press, 2001)

Bartelson J, *The Critique of the State* (Cambridge University Press, 2001)

Barzilai G, 'Beyond Relativism: Where is Political Power in Legal Pluralism?' (2008) 9 *Theoretical Inquiries in Law* 395

Baylin B, *The Ideological Origins of the American Revolution* (Belknap, 1992)

Bell D, 'John Stuart Mill on Colonies' (2009) 38 *Political Theory* 34

Benda Beckham F von, 'Who's Afraid of Legal Pluralism?' (2002) 47 *Journal of Legal Pluralism* 37

Benoist A de, 'The First Federalist, Johannes Althusius' (2000) 118 *Telos* 25

Berle A and Means G, *The Modern Corporation and Private Property* (Transaction Publishers, 1999)

Berlin I (H Hardy (ed.)), *Liberty* (Oxford University Press, 2002)

Berlin I (H Hardy and R Hausheer (eds)), *The Proper Study of Mankind* (Farrar, Strauss, Giroux, 1997)

Berman HJ, 'Towards an Integrative Jurisprudence' (1988) 76 (4) *California Law Review* 779

Berman HJ, *Law and Revolution* (Harvard University Press, 1983)

Berman HJ, *Law and Revolution, II: The Impact of the Protestant Reformations on the Western Legal Tradition* (Belknap, 2003)

Berman PS, 'Towards a Jurisprudence of Hybridity' 2010 (1) *Utah Law Review* 11.

Berman PS, *Global Legal Pluralism* (Cambridge University Press, 2012)

Bermann GA, 'Taking Subsidiarity Seriously' (1994) 94(2) *Columbia Law Review* 331

Bix B, 'John Austin' in E N Zalta (ed.), *The Standard Encyclopedia of Philosophy, Spring 2010 Edition* <http://plato.stanford.edu/archives/spr2010/entries/austin-john/> accessed 21 October 2013

Black A, *Guild and State* (Transaction, 2003)

Black A, *Political Thought in Europe, 1250-1450* (Cambridge University Press, 1992)

Bodin J (C Frémont, M-D Couzinet, and H Rochais (eds)), *Les Six Livres de la République, Livre Troisième* (first published 1576) (Librairie Arthème Fayard, 1986)

Bodin J (JH Franklin (ed. and tr.)), *On Sovereignty: Four Chapters from The Six Books of the Commonwealth* (Cambridge University Press, 1992)

Boyd M, *Dispute Resolution in Family Law: Protecting Choice, Promoting Inclusion* (Ontario Ministry of the Attorney General December 2004) <http://www.attorneygeneral.jus.gov.on.ca/english/about/pubs/boyd/> accessed 1 July 2013

Bratman M, 'Shared Intention' (1993) 104 *Ethics* 97

Bratman M, *Faces of Intention* (Cambridge University Press, 1999)

Buchanan A, 'The Making and Unmaking of Boundaries: What Liberalism Has to Say' in Allen Buchanan and Margaret Moore (eds), *States, Nations, and Borders: The Ethics of Making Boundaries* (Cambridge University Press, 2003)

Burke E (JGA Pocock (ed.)), *Reflections on the Revolution in France* (first published 1790) (Hackett, 1987)

Campbell T (ed.), *Judicial Power, Democracy, and Legal Positivism* (Ashgate, 2000)

Campbell T, *Prescriptive Legal Positivism: Law, Rights and Democracy* (Cavendish, 2004)

Carens J, *Culture, Citizenship, and Community* (Oxford University Press, 2000)

Carozza PG, 'Subsidiarity as a Structural Principle of International Human Rights Law' (2003) 94 *American Journal of International Law* 40

Catechism of the Catholic Church (2nd edn) (Libreria Editrice Vaticana, 1993)

Chang R, *Incommensurability, Incomparability, and Practical Reason* (Harvard University Press, 1998)

Christiano T, (2012) 'Authority' in EN Zalta (ed.), *The Stanford Encyclopedia of Philosophy*. Stanford CA: Stanford University Press. Available from: <http://plato.stanford.edu/archives/spr2012/entries/authority/> accessed 2 July 2013

Clark R, *Corporate Law* (Little, Brown, and Co., 1986)

Cohen J and Rogers J, *On Democracy* (Penguin Books, 1983)

Cohen J and Rogers J, 'Secondary Associations and Democratic Governance' (1992) 20(4) *Politics and Society* 393

Cohen M, 'Communal Ghosts and Other Perils in Social Philosophy' (1919) 16 *The Journal of Philosophy* 673

Coke E (S Sheppard (ed.)), *The Selected Writings of Sir Edward Coke* (Liberty Fund, 2003)

Coker FW, 'The Technique of the Pluralist State' (1921) 15(2) *American Political Science Review* 186

Cole, GDH 'Conflicting Social Obligations' (1914) 15 *Proceedings of the Aristotelian Society*, New Series, 140

Constant B (Marcel Gauchet (ed.)), *Écrits Politiques* (Éditions Gallimard, 1997)

Cover R, 'Nomos and Narrative' (1983) 97 *Harvard Law Review* 4

Crowder G, 'From Value Pluralism to Liberalism' (1998) 1(3) *Critical Studies of International Society and Political Philosophy* 2

Dahl RA, *Democracy and Its Critics* (Yale University Press, 1989)

Dahl RA, *Dilemmas of Pluralist Democracy: Autonomy vs. Control* (Yale University Press, 1983)

Dahl RA, *Polyarchy: Participation and Opposition* (Yale University Press, 1972)

Dahl RA, *Who Governs? Democracy and Power in an American City* (Yale University Press, 1961)

Dane P, 'Constitutional Law and Religion' in Dennis Patterson (ed.), *A Companion to Philosophy of Law and Legal Theory* (Blackwell, 2010) 119

Dane P, ' "Omalous" Autonomy' (2004) *Brigham Young University Law Review* 1715

Dane P, 'The Varieties of Religious Autonomy' in Gerhard Robbers (ed.), *Church Autonomy: A Comparative Survey* (Peter Lang Publishers, 2001)

Dane P, Note: 'Religious Exemptions Under the Free Exercise Clause: A Model of Competing Authorities' (1980) 90 *Yale Law Journal* 350

Dane P, *The Maps of Sovereignty: A Meditation*, 12 *Cardozo Law Review* 959 (1991)

Darwall S, 'Law and the second person standpoint' (2007) 40 *Loyola Los Angeles Law Review* 891

Darwall S, *The Second Person Standpoint* (Harvard University Press, 2006)

Davidson D, *Essays on Actions and Events* (Oxford University Press, 1980)

Davies G, 'Subsidiarity: The Wrong Idea, In the Wrong Place, At the Wrong Time' (2006) 43(1) *Common Market Law Review* 63

Davis GF, 'The Twilight of the Berle and Means Corporation' (2011) 34 *Seattle University Law Review* 1121

Dewey J, 'The Historic Background of Corporate Legal Personality' (1926) 6 *Yale Law Journal* 655

Dreyer M, 'German Roots of the Theory of Pluralism' (1993) 4(I) *Constitutional Political Economy* 7

Durante C, 'Religious Liberty in a Multicultural Society' (2012) 54 (3) *Journal of Church and State* 323

Dworkin R, *Law's Empire* (Harvard University Press, 1986)

Easterbrook F, and Fischel DR, *The Economic Structure of Corporate Law* (Harvard University Press, 1991)

Eisenberg AI, *Reconstructing Political Pluralism* (SUNY Press, 1995)

Elazar D, 'Althusius' Grand Design for a Federal Commonwealth' in Johannes Althusius (FS Carney (tr. and ed.)), *Politica* (Liberty Fund, 1995)

Elster J, *Making Sense of Marx* (Cambridge University Press, 1985)

Engle Merry S, 'Legal Pluralism' (1988) 22 *Law and Society Review* 869

Enroth H, 'Beyond Unity in Plurality: Rethinking the Pluralist Legacy' (2010) 9(4) *Contemporary Political Theory* 458

Falk Moore S, 'Certainties Undone: Fifty Turbulent Years of Legal Anthropology, 1949–1999' (2001) 7 *Journal of the Royal Anthropological Institute* 95

Falk Moore S, 'Law and Social Change: The Semi-Autonomous Social Field as an Appropriate Subject of Study' (1973) 7 *Law and Society Review* 719

Figgis JN, 'The Great Leviathan' in Paul Q Hirst (ed.), *The Pluralist Theory of the State* (Routledge, 1993)

Figgis JN, *Churches in the Modern State* (first published 1913) (Thoemmes, 1997)

Figgis JN, *Political Thought from Gerson to Grotius* (Harper Torchbook, 1960)

Figgis, JN, 'The Church and the Secular Theory of the State' in David Nicholls (ed.), *The Pluralist State The Political Ideas of JN Figgis and His Contemporaries* (2nd edn) (St. Martin's, 1994) 158

Filmer R (JP Sommerville (ed.)), *Patriarcha* (first published 1680) (Cambridge University Press, 1991)

Finnis J, *Natural Law and Natural Rights* (2nd edn) (Oxford University Press, 2011).

Follesdal A, 'Subsidiarity' (1990) 6(2) *Journal of Political Philosophy* 190

Follett MP, *The New State* (Longmans, Green and Co., 1918)

Forbes HD, 'Trudeau as the First Theorist of Canadian Multiculturalism' in Stephen Tierney (ed.), *Multiculturalism and the Canadian Constitution* (University of British Columbia Press, 2007)

Franco P, *Hegel's Philosophy of Freedom* (Yale University Press, 1999)

French P, 'The Corporation as a Moral Person' (1979) 16(3) *American Philosophical Quarterly* 207

Friedman J, 'Pluralism or Relativism?'(1997) 11(4) *Critical Review* 469

Friedrich CJ, Introduction to Althusius' *Politica Methodice Digesta* (Harvard University Press, 1932)

Fuller LL, 'Two Principles of Human Association' in KI Winston (ed.), *Principles of Social Order* (Hart, 2002)

Galston WA, *Liberal Pluralism* (Cambridge University Press, 2002)

Galston WA, *The Practice of Liberal Pluralism* (Cambridge University Press, 2005)

Gardner J, *Law as a Leap of Faith* (Oxford University Press, 2012)

Garnett RW, ' "The Freedom of the Church": (Towards) an Exposition, Translation, and Defense' forthcoming (2013) *Journal of Contemporary Legal Issues*

Garnett RW, 'Religious Freedom, Church Autonomy, and Constitutionalism' (2009) 57 *Drake Law Review* 901

Garnett RW, 'The Freedom of the Church' (2007) 4 *Journal of Catholic Social Thought* 59

Gaus G, 'Public Justification and the Moral Right of Private Property' (Workshop on Capitalism and Morality, University of North Carolina-Chapel Hill, 9–10 April 2004) <http://www.unc.edu/~jabaker/gaus.pdf> accessed 16 September 2012

Geuss R, 'Kultur, Bilung, Geist' (1996) 35(2) *History and Theory* 151

Gierke O (FW Maitland (tr.)), *Political Theories of the Middle Age* (Cambridge University Press, 1900)

Gilbert M, *A Theory of Political Obligation* (Oxford University Press, 2006)

Gilbert M, *Sociality and Responsibility* (Rowman and Littlefield, 2000)

Gilbert M, *On Social Facts* (Princeton University Press, 1992)

Glenn HP, *Legal Traditions of the World* (4th edn) (Oxford University Press, 2010)

Gosseries A and Meyer L (eds), *Theories of Intergenerational Justice* (Oxford University Press, 2009)

Gosseries A and Vanderboght Y (eds), *Arguing about Justice* (Presses Universitaires de Louvain, 2011)

Grabill SJ, 'Introduction to "Selections from the Dicaeologicae"' (2006) 9(2) *Journal of Markets and Morality* 399

Grant TD, 'Defining Statehood: The Montevideo Convention and its Discontents' (1999) 37 *Columbia Journal of Transnational Law* 403

Gray J, *Isaiah Berlin* (Princeton University Press, 1996)

Green L, 'Legal Positivism' in Edward N Zalta (ed.), *The Stanford Encyclopedia of Philosophy (Fall 2009 Edition)* <http://plato.stanford.edu/archives/fall2009/entries/legal-positivism/> accessed 5 February 2013

Green L, 'Positivism and Conventionalism' (1999) 12 *Canadian Journal of Law and Jurisprudence* 50

Green L, 'The Concept of Law Revisited' (1996) 94 *Michigan Law Review* 1687

Green, L, *The Authority of the State* (Oxford University Press, 1988)

Griffiths J, 'What is Legal Pluralism?' (1996) 24 *Journal of Legal Pluralism* 1

Harris R, 'The Transplantation of the Legal Discourse on Corporate Personality Theories: From German Codification to British Political Pluralism and American Big Business' (2006) 63 *Washington and Lee Law Review* 1421

Hart HLA, 'Positivism and the Separation of Law and Morals' (1958) 71 *Harvard Law Review* 593

Hart HLA, 'Review of LL Fuller, *The Morality of Law*', 78 *Harvard Law Review* 1281

Hart HLA, *The Concept of Law* (2nd edn) (Oxford University Press, 1994)

Hegel GWH (A Wood (ed.) and HB Nisbet (tr.)), *Elements of the Philosophy of Right* (Cambridge University Press, 1991)

Heiman G, 'The Sources and Significance of Hegel's Corporate Doctrine' in ZA Pelczynski (ed.), *Hegel's Political Philosophy: Problems and Perspectives* (Cambridge University Press, 1971)

Himma KE, 'Do Philosophy and Sociology Mix? A Non-Essentialist Socio-Legal Positivist Analysis of the Concept of Law' (2004) 24(4) *Oxford Journal of Legal Studies* 717

Hirschl R and Shachar A, 'The New Wall Of Separation: Permitting Diversity, Restricting Competition' (2009) 30(6) *Cardozo Law Review* 2535

Hirst PQ (ed.), *The Pluralist Theory of the State* (Routledge, 1993)

Hirst PQ, 'JN Figgis, Churches and the State' (2002) 71 *The Political Quarterly* 104

Hirst PQ, 'Carl Schmitt's Decisionism' in Chantal Mouffe (ed.), *The Challenge of Carl Schmitt* (Verso, 1999)

Hirst PQ, *Associative Democracy: New Forms of Economic and Social Governance* (University of Massachusetts Press, 1994)

Hirst PQ, *From Statism to Pluralism: Democracy, Civil Society and Global Politics* (University College London Press, 1997)

Hobbes T (E Curley (ed.)), *Leviathan* (first published 1651) (Hackett, 1994)

Holmes S, *Passions and Constraint* (University of Chicago Press, 1995)

Holmes S, *The Anatomy of Antiliberalism* (Harvard University Press, 1993)

Holmes, OW and HJ Laski (MD Howe (ed.)), *Holmes-Laski letters* (Harvard University Press, 1953)

Horwitz P, 'Defending (Religious) Institutionalism' (2013) 99 *Virginia Law Review* 1049

Horwitz P, *First Amendment Institutions* (Harvard University Press, 2013)

Horwitz P, *The Agnostic Age: Law, Religion, and the Constitution* (Oxford University Press, 2011)

Hueglin TO, *Early Modern Concepts for a Late Modern World: Althusius on Community and Federalism* (Wilfrid Laurier University Press, 1999)

Humboldt W von, *The Limits of State Action* (Liberty Fund, 1993)

Hume D, *The History of England from the Invasion of Julius Caesar to the Revolution in 1688* (Liberty Fund, 1983)

Ilting KH, 'The Structure of Hegel's "Philosophy of Right"' in ZA Pelczynski (ed.), *Hegel's Political Philosophy: Problems and Perspectives* (Cambridge University Press, 1971)

Jackson F and Pettit P, 'Structural Explanation in Social Theory' in (D Charles and K Lennon (eds)), *Reduction, Explanation, and Realism* (Oxford University Press, 1992) 97

James VI and I, 'The Trew Law of Free Monarchies' in JP Sommerville (ed.), *Political Writings* (Cambridge University Press, 1994)

Kallen H, *Cultural Pluralism and the American Idea* (University of Pennsylvania Press, 1956)

Kant I, 'The Metaphysics of Morals' in MJ Gregor (ed.), *Practical Philosophy* (Cambridge University Press, 1996)

Kantorowicz EE, *The King's Two Bodies: A Study in Mediaeval Political Theology* (Princeton University Press, 1957)

Kelsen H, *Introduction to the problems of legal theory* (Oxford University Press, 1992)

King P, *The Ideology of Order: A Comparative Analysis of Jean Bodin and Thomas Hobbes* (2nd edn) (Frank Cass, 1999)

Knox TM, *Hegel's Philosophy of Rights* (Clarendon, 1952)

Kohn M, 'Empire's Law: Alexis de Tocqueville on Colonialism and the State of Exception' (2008) 41 *Canadian Journal of Political Science* 255

Kohn M and O'Neill D, 'A Tale of Two Indias: Burke and Mill on Empire and Slavery in the West Indies and America' (2006) 34 *Political Theory* 192

Kukathas C, *The Liberal Archipelago: A Theory of Diversity and Freedom* (Oxford University Press, 2003)

Kymlicka W, 'The New Debate over Minority Rights' in R Beiner and W Norman (eds), *Canadian Political Philosophy* (Oxford University Press, 2001) 159

Kymlicka W, *Liberalism, Community, and Culture* (Oxford University Press, 1989)

Kymlicka W, *Multicultural Citizenship* (Oxford University Press, 1995)

Laborde C, *Pluralist Thought and the State in Britain and France, 1900–25* (Macmillan, 2000)

Larmore CE, *Morals of Modernity* (Cambridge University Press, 1996)

Larmore CE, *Patterns of Moral Complexity* (Cambridge University Press, 1987)

Laski H, 'Morris Cohen's Approach to Legal Philosophy' (1947–48) 15 *University of Chicago Law Review* 575

Laski HJ, 'Law and the State' (1929) 9 (27) *Economica* 267

Laski HJ, *Authority in the Modern State* (Yale University Press, 1919)

Laski HJ, *Studies in Law and Politics* (first published 1932) (Archon Books, 1969)

Laski HJ, *Studies in the Problem of Sovereignty* (first published 1917) (Fertig, 1968)

Laski HJ, *The Foundations of Sovereignty and Other Essays* (Harcourt, Brace and Co., 1921)

Laski H, *A Grammar of Politics* (5th edn) (George Allen & Unwin, 1967)

Leiter B, 'Why Legal Positivism (Again)?' (9 September 2013), Australasian Society of Legal Philosophy <http://papers.ssrn.com/sol3/papers.cfm?abstract_id=2323013> accessed 11 September 2013

Leo XIII, *Rerum Novarum* (1891)

Levy J, 'From Pluralism to Constitutionalism' in M Bevir (ed.), *Modern Pluralism* (Cambridge University Press, 2012)

Levy JT, 'Federalism, Liberalism, and the Separation of Loyalties' (2007) 101(3) *American Political Science Review* 459

Levy JT, 'From Liberal Constitutionalism to Pluralism' in Mark Bevir (ed.), *Modern Pluralism: Anglo-American Debates Since 1800* (Cambridge University Press, forthcoming)

Levy JT, 'Self-Determination, Non-Domination, and Federalism' (2008) 23(3) *Hypatia* 60

Levy JT, *The Multiculturalism of Fear* (Oxford University Press, 2000)

Linklater, A, *The Transformation of Political Community* (Cambridge University Press, 1998)

List C and Pettit P, *Group Agency: The Possibility, Design, and Status of Corporate Agents* (Oxford University Press, 2011)

MacCormick N, *Questioning Sovereignty* (Oxford University Press, 2010)

Macdonald RA, 'Legal Bilingualism' (1997) 42 *McGill Law Journal* 119

Macdonald RA and MacLean J, 'No Toilets in Park' (2005) 50 *McGill Law Journal* 721

Macdonald RA, 'Unitary Law Re-Form, Pluralistic Law Re-Substance: Illuminating Legal Change' (2007) 67 *Louisiana Law Review* 1113

Macdonald RA, 'Custom Made—For a Non-chirographic Critical Legal Pluralism' (2011) 26 *Canadian Journal of Law and Society* 301

Maclure J, 'Multiculturalism and Political Morality' in D Ivison (ed.), *The Ashgate Research Companion to Multiculturalism* (Ashgate, 2010) 39

Magid HM, *English Political Pluralism: The Problem of Freedom and Organization* (Columbia University Press, 1941)

Maitland FW, 'Moral Personality and Legal Personality' in HAL Fisher (ed.), *Collected Papers*, Vol. III (Cambridge University Press, 1911)

Maitland FW, 'The Unincorporated Body' in HAL Fisher (ed.), *Collected Papers* Vol. III (Cambridge University Press, 1911)

Maitland FW (David Runciman and Magnus Ryan (eds)), *State, Trust and Corporation* (Cambridge University Press, 2003)

Marmor A, 'An Institutional Conception of Authority' (2011) 39 (3) *Philosophy and Public Affairs* 238

Marmor A, 'The Dilemma of Authority' (2011) 2 *Jurisprudence* 121

Marmor A, *Interpretation and Legal Theory* (2nd edn) (Hart, 2005)

Marmor A, *Law in the Age of Pluralism* (Oxford University Press, 2007)

Marmor A, *Philosophy of Law* (Princeton University Press, 2011)

Marmor A, *Positive Law and Objective Values* (Oxford University Press, 2001)

Marmor, *Social Conventions* (Princeton University Press, 2009)

McIlwain CH, *Constitutionalism, Ancient and Modern* (Cambridge University Press, 1947)

Mellone SH, 'The Scottish Church Case and Its Ethical Significance' (1905) 15(3) *International Journal of Ethics* 361

Merry SE, 'Legal Pluralism' (1988) 22 *Law and Society Review* 869

Michaels R, 'Global Legal Pluralism' (2009) 5 *Annual Review of Law and Social Science* 243

Michaels R, 'The Re-*State*-Ment of Non-State Law: The State, Choice of Law, and the Challenge From Global Legal Pluralism' (2005) 51 *Wayne Law Review* 1209

Millon-Delsol C, *L'état Subsidiaire* (Presses Universitaires de France, 1992)

Moltchanova A, 'Collective Agents and Group Moral Rights' 17(1) *The Journal of Political Philosophy* 23

Mullett CF, 'English Presbyterians and the Scottish Disruption: The Legal Phase' (1943) 12(4) *Church History* 255

Muñiz-Fraticelli VM, 'The Problem of a Perpetual Constitution' in A Gosseries & L Meyer (eds), *Theories of Intergenerational Justice* (Oxford University Press, 2009)

Murphy S, 'Principles of International Law' (Thompson, 2006)

Nelken D, 'Ehrlich's Legacies: Back to the Future in the Sociology of Law?' in M Hertog (ed.), *Living Law: Reconsidering Eugen Ehrlich* (Hart, 2009) 237

Newman D, *Community and Collective Rights* (Hart, 2011)

Nicholls D, *The Pluralist State: The Political Ideas of JN Figgis and His Contemporaries* (2nd edn) (St. Martin's, 1994)

Nicholls D, *Three Varieties of Pluralism* (Macmillan, 1974)

Oakeshott M, *On Human Conduct* (Oxford University Press, 1975)

Ortega y Gasset J, *Europa y la Idea de Nación* (Alianza Editorial, 1985)

Ossewarde MRR, 'Three Rival Versions of Political Enquiry: Althusius and the Concept of Sphere Sovereignty' (2007) 90:1 *The Monist* 106

Perry S, 'Associative Obligations and the Obligation to Obey the Law' in S. Hershowitz (ed.), *Exploring Law's Empire* (Oxford University Press, 2008), 183–205

Pettit P, *A Theory of Freedom* (Oxford University Press, 2001)

Pettit P, *The Common Mind* (Oxford University Press, 1993)

Phillips, M (1994) 'Reappraising the real entity theory of the corporation' 21 *Florida State University Law Review* 1061

Pippin RB, 'Mine and Thine? The Kantian State' in P Guyer (ed.), *The Cambridge Companion to Kant and Modern Philosophy* (Cambridge University Press, 2006)

Pitts J, 'Legislator of the World? A Rereading of Bentham on Colonies' (2003) 31(2) *Political Theory* 200

Pitts J, *A Turn to Empire: The Rise of Imperial Liberalism in Britain and France* (Princeton University Press, 2006)

Pius XI, *Quaddragessimo Anno* (1931)

Pontifical Council for Justice and Peace, *Compendium of the Social Doctrine of the Church* (Libreria Editrice Vaticana, 2004)

Postema G, *Bentham and the Common Law Tradition* (Clarendon Press, 1986)

Preda A, 'Group rights and shared agency' *Journal of Moral Philosophy* 9 (2012): 229

Preda A, 'Group rights and shared interests' (2012) 61(2) *Political Studies* 250

Radin MJ, *Reinterpreting Property* (University of Chicago Press, 1993)

Rawls J, 'Two Concepts of Rules' in S Freeman (ed), *Collected Papers* (Harvard University Press, 1999)

Rawls J, *A Theory of Justice* (Belknap, 1971)

Rawls J, *A Theory of Justice: Revised Edition* (Harvard University Press, 1999)

Rawls J, *Justice as Fairness: A Restatement* (Harvard University Press, 2001)

Rawls J, *Political Liberalism* (Columbia University Press, 1993)

Raz J, *Between Authority and Interpretation* (Oxford University Press, 2010)

Raz J, *Ethics in the Public Domain: Essays in the Morality of Law and Politics* (Oxford University Press, 2001)

Raz J, *Practical Reason and Norms* (Oxford University Press, 1999)

Raz J, *The Authority of Law* (Oxford University Press, 1983)

Raz J, *The Morality of Freedom* (Oxford University Press, 1986)

Rochefoucauld F de la (EH Blackmore (ed.) and AM Blackmore and Francine Giguère (trs)), *Collected Maxims and Other Reflections* (Oxford University Press, 2007)

Rosenblum NL, *Membership and Morals: The Personal Uses of Pluralism in America* (Princeton University Press, 1998)

Rosenblum NL, *On the Side of Angels* (Princeton University Press, 2008)

Ross D, 'Group Doxastic Rationality Need Not Supervene on Individual Rationality' (2006) 44 *The Southern Journal of Philosophy* 106

Rousseau J-J (V Gourevitch (ed.)), *The Social Contract* (first published 1762) (Cambridge University Press, 1997)

Rudolph SH, 'Presidential Address: State Formation in Asia—Prolegomenon to a Comparative Study' (1987) 46(4) Journal of Asian Studies 731

Runciman D, *Pluralism and the Personality of the State* (Cambridge University Press, 1997)

Rundle K, *Forms Liberate: Reclaiming the Jurisprudence of Lon L Fuller* (Hart, 2012)

Saunders HD, 'Civil Death: A New Look at an Ancient Doctrine' (1970) 11 *William and Mary Law Review* 988

Schahar A, *Multicultural Jurisdictions* (Cambridge University Press, 2001)

Schauer F, 'Positivism before Hart' (2011) 24 *Canadian Journal of Law and Jurisprudence* 455

Schmitt C, 'Ethic of State and Pluralistic State' in Chantal Mouffe (ed.), *The Challenge of Carl Schmitt* (Verso, 1999)

Schmitt C, *The Concept of the Political* (first published 1932) (University of Chicago Press, 2007)

Schneiderman D, 'Harold Laski,Viscount Haldane, and the Law of the Canadian Constitution in the EarlyTwentieth Century' (1998) 48 (4) *University of Toronto Law Journal* 521

Schragger R and Schwartzman M, 'Against Religious Institutionalism' 99 *Virginia Law Review* 917 (2013)

Searle J, *The Construction of Social Reality* (Free Press, 1995)

Sebok AJ, *Legal Positivism in American Jurisprudence* (Cambridge University Press, 1998)

Shapiro S, *Legality* (Harvard University Press, 2011)

Sheppard S, (ed.), *The Selected Writings of Sir Edward Coke* (Liberty Fund, 2003)

Smith A, *An Inquiry into the Nature and Causes of the Wealth of Nations* (Liberty Fund, 1976)

Smith R, *Stories of Peoplehood* (Cambridge University Press, 2003)

Sommerville JP, (ed.), *Political Writings* (Cambridge University Press, 1994)

Song S, 'Multiculturalism' in EN Zalta (ed.), *The Stanford Encyclopedia of Philosophy* (Winter edn, 2010) <http://plato.stanford.edu/archives/win2010/entries/multiculturalism/> accessed 22 August 2012

Song S, *Justice, Gender, and the Politics of Multiculturalism* (Cambridge University Press, 2007)

Sorkin D, 'Wilhelm Von Humboldt: The Theory and Practice of Self-Formation (Bildung), 1791-1810' (1983) 44(1) *Journal of the History of Ideas* 55–73

Stoljar N, 'Interpretation, Indeterminacy and Authority: Some Recent Controversies in the Philosophy of Law' (2003) 11(4) *The Journal of Political Philosophy* 470

Stoljar N, 'Is Positivism Committed to Intentionalism?' in T Campbell and J Goldsworthy (eds), *Judicial Power, Democracy and Legal Positivism* (Ashgate, 2000) 169–83

Strauss L, 'Relativism' in TL Pangle (ed.), *The Rebirth of Classical Political Rationalism* (University of Chicago Press, 1989)

Swaine L, *The Liberal Conscience* (Cambridge University Press, 2006)

Tamanaha BZ, 'The Contemporary Relevance of Legal Positivism' (2007) 32 *Australian Journal of Legal Philosophy* 1

Tamanaha BZ, 'The Folly of the "Social Scientific" Concept of Legal Pluralism' (1993) 20(2) *Journal of Law in Society* 192

Tamanaha BZ, 'Understanding Legal Pluralism' (2007) 29 *Sydney Law Review* 375

Tamanaha BZ, *A General Jurisprudence of Law and Society* (Oxford University Press, 2001)

Tamanaha BZ, *Beyond the Formalist-Realist Divide: The Role of Politics in Judging* (Princeton University Press, 2010)

Tamanaha BZ, *Law as a Means to an End* (Cambridge University Press, 2006)

Tamanaha BZ, *On the Rule of Law* (Cambridge University Press, 2004)

Taylor C and Guttmann A, *Multiculturalism: Examining the Politics of Recognition* (Princeton University Press, 1994)

Tocqueville A de (J Pitts (ed.)), *Writings on Empire and Slavery* (John Hopkins Press, 2000)

Tuomela R, 'Group Beliefs' (1992) 91 *Synthese* 285

Twinning W, 'Normative and Legal Pluralism: A Global Perspective' (2010) 20 *Duke Journal of Comparative and International Law* 473

Waldron J, 'Legal Pluralism and the Contrast Between Hart's Jurisprudence and Fuller's' in (P Cane (ed.)), *The Hart-Fuller Debate in the Twenty-First Century* (Hart, 2010) 135–55

Waldron J, 'Normative (or Ethical) Positivism' in (J Coleman (ed.)), *Hart's Postscript: Essays on the Postscript to the Concept of Law* (Oxford University Press, 2001) 410

Waldron J, 'Positivism and Legality: Hart's Equivocal Response to Fuller' (2008) 83(4) *New York University Law Review* 1135

Waldron J, *Law and Disagreement* (Oxford University Press, 1999)

Waldron J, *The Right to Private Property* (Clarendon Press, 1988)

Walker E, 'Don't Throw out My Baby—Why Dalton McGuinty Was Wrong to Reject Religious Arbitration' (2006) 11 *Appeal: Rev. Current L. & L. Reform* 94

Walzer M, *Spheres of Justice* (Basic Books, 1983)

Walzer M, *The Jewish Political Tradition* (Yale University Press, 2000)

Webb LC (Leicester C Webb (ed.)), 'Corporate Personality and Political Pluralism' in *Legal Personality and Political Pluralism* (Melbourne University Press, 1958)

Weber M, 'Politics as a Vocation' in HH Gerth and C Wright Mills (eds), *From Max Weber: Essays in Sociology* (Oxford University Press, 1946)

Weber M, 'Religious Rejections of the World and their Directions' in HH Gerth and C Wright Mills (eds), *From Max Weber: Essays in Sociology* (Oxford University Press, 1946)

Weinstock D, 'Self-Determination for (Some) Cities?' in A Gosseries and Y Vanderboght (eds), *Arguing about Justice* (Presses Universitaires de Louvain, 2011)

Wellman C, *Real Rights* (Oxford University Press, 1995)

Wendt A, 'The State as a Person in International Theory' (2004) 30(2) *Review of International Studies* 289

Whitbeck JV, 'The State of Palestine Exists' (2011) 18 *Middle East Policy* 62

Williams B, *Moral Luck* (Cambridge University Press, 1981)

Williams R, 'Civil and Religious Law in England: A Religious Perspective' (2008) 10(3) *Ecclesiastical Law Journal* 262

Williams R, 'Law, Power and Peace: Christian Perspectives on Sovereignty' (David Nicholls Memorial Lecture, The University Church of St. Mary the Virgin, Oxford, 29 September 2005) <http://www.dnmt.org.uk/dnmt/images/docs/dnmlecture_2005.pdf> accessed 22 August 2012

Witte J, 'The Archbishop and Marital Pluralism' (2008) 10(3) *Ecclesiastical Law Journal* 337

Wolff, RP, *In Defense of Anarchism* (University of California Press, 1998)

Wood AW, *Hegel's Ethical Thought* (Cambridge University Press, 1990)

Woodman GR, 'Legal Pluralism and the Search for Justice' (1998) 40(2) *Journal of African Law* 152

Young IM, *Global Challenges* (Polity, 2007)

Index

Note: all legal cases cited are indexed under 'legal cases'.

The manufacturer's authorised representative in the EU for product safety is Oxford University Press España S.A. of el Parque Empresarial San Fernando de Henares, Avenida de Castilla, 2 – 28830 Madrid (www.oup.es/en or product.safety@oup.com). OUP España S.A. also acts as importer into Spain of products made by the manufacturer.

www.ingramcontent.com/pod-product-compliance
Lightning Source LLC
LaVergne TN
LVHW011752200926
848484LV00003B/682

9780199673889